Music Research

Music Research

A Handbook

Laurie J. Sampsel
The University of Colorado at Boulder

New York   Oxford
OXFORD UNIVERSITY PRESS
2009

Oxford University Press, Inc., publishes works that further Oxford University's
objective of excellence in research, scholarship, and education.

Oxford New York
Auckland Cape Town Dar es Salaam Hong Kong Karachi
Kuala Lumpur Madrid Melbourne Mexico City Nairobi
New Delhi Shanghai Taipei Toronto

With offices in
Argentina Austria Brazil Chile Czech Republic France Greece
Guatemala Hungary Italy Japan Poland Portugal Singapore
South Korea Switzerland Thailand Turkey Ukraine Vietnam

Published by Oxford University Press, Inc.
198 Madison Avenue, New York, New York 10016
http://www.oup.com

Oxford is a registered trademark of Oxford University Press.

ISBN: 978-0-19-517119-8

Library of Congress Cataloging-in-Publication Data

Sampsel, Laurie J.
   Music research : a handbook / Laurie J. Sampsel.
      p. cm.
   Includes bibliographical references and index.
   ISBN-13: 978-0-19-517119-8 (hardcover : acid-free paper)   1. Music—Bibliography.
2. Music—History and criticism—Bibliography.   3. Music—Bibliography of
bibliographies.   4. Musicology.   I. Title.
   ML113.S28 2009
   780.72—dc22   2007048927

Printing number: 9 8 7 6 5 4 3 2

Printed in the United States of America
on acid-free paper

This book is dedicated to my dad,

Elvern Sampsel

(8/21/1926–2/3/2006)

Contents

Figures

Preface

At the beginning of each semester I ask the students in my bibliography classes to complete the following sentence with the first thing that comes to mind. "I do not like doing research because it is…." The resulting list usually includes "time-consuming," "frustrating," "hard to know how to start," and so on. Almost always one or two students say, "But research can be so rewarding." Or one says, "I love it when I find something really helpful." We also talk about the negative list as being very similar to the way they feel about time spent in the practice room. They understand the pay-off for tedious hours of practice, but many have not felt the benefits from painstaking care in their research. Several weeks later we have a similar discussion about writing.

By the end of each semester, most students have gotten a taste of the rewards of research and writing. Many have said that the homegrown text I use is part of the reason they were able to succeed in the class. That is why when I was approached about revising that text for publication, I was eager to do so. Throughout my work on this book, which was indeed tedious at times, I have been reminded again and again about the rewards of careful research and writing. These tasks are indeed like learning to play an instrument, in that we can spend a lifetime improving our skills.

Audience

Music Research is designed for graduate-level music bibliography and research classes and may also work for some upper-level undergraduate classes. The primary target audience is master's students, though doctoral students and undergraduates will also find it a helpful supplement.

Approach

The overriding goal for *Music Research* is to be as useful as possible for music bibliography classes. With that in mind, this textbook focuses on teaching the research process and points students toward the most important music research tools. Pedagogical aids are included to enhance teaching and learning. This book is informed by the information literacy movement, which is broader than traditional bibliography classes or bibliographic instruction. *Music Research* emphasizes learning research skills, critically evaluating information, writing effectively, and citing sources properly. It is based on over ten years of experience teaching graduate music bibliography at the University of Colorado at Boulder.

Other books strive to list music research tools comprehensively. In comparison, *Music Research* is a handbook rather than a bibliography and emphasizes major research, writing, and citation tools that graduate music students need to know. Some of the titles included are most appropriate for master's-level students, while others are included specifically with the doctoral student in mind.

Contents

The book is divided into two main parts. The first (Chapters 1 through 14) is devoted to research process and tools. The second (Chapters 15 and 16) is devoted to resources on writing about music, style manuals, plagiarism, and citation of sources. In addition, a number of appendixes, a glossary, and an index are given.

Part One is arranged by the type of research tool, for example, music encyclopedias, periodical indexes, and discographies. The arrangement is from general to specific, following the typical research process. Each chapter includes a discussion about the general uses of the tools and an annotated bibliography pointing out the purpose, scope, strengths, and weaknesses of each individual research tool. Both print and electronic resources are included.

The most important general music research tools in English, French, German, Italian, and Spanish are covered. Examples were selected, in part, to apply to as many music libraries as possible. Additional common topics have been included throughout, such as resources in the broad disciplines of musicology, ethnomusicology/world music, theory, and music education. Narrower topics include specific groups of musicians (e.g., women and African Americans), individual significant composers (see Appendix C), common performance media and instruments/voice (e.g., chamber music and piano), and genres and styles (e.g., jazz and opera). Further, topics likely to be of interest to the target audience—those devoted to the music of the United States, Great Britain, and Canada—are also covered.

Following the format established with research tools, Part Two presents major guides in writing and citation. Rather than offering writing instruction in Chapter 15, tips on finding writing books are provided as well as recommendations of existing resources. All three major style guides are included in Chapter 16.

Features

- *Music Research* is a handbook designed for classroom use, rather than a bibliography intended for use by librarians and scholars.
- Although selective, the most important music research tools are included. Emphasis is on titles in English, but the major French, German, Italian, and Spanish resources are included as well.
- Most entries are annotated and include review citations.
- Stays current through updates on the companion website maintained by the author and hosted by Oxford University Press, http://www.oup.com/us/musresearch.
- Provides evaluation checklists for each type of research tool to help students develop critical evaluation skills.
- Suggested readings are given in each chapter.

- Offers advice for students researching and writing theses or other formal scholarly projects.
- Includes a section on avoiding plagiarism, with examples.
- Includes appendixes with music citation examples for Chicago, APA, and MLA Style in a variety of formats.
- Includes a glossary and combined author, title, and subject index.

Ancillaries

One of the major challenges with a text on research is keeping it current. The companion website hosted by Oxford University Press assists with this goal in addition to providing supplemental information. The website will be updated regularly, at least once a year before the beginning of each fall semester. The website also provides additional information, including a list of major music associations and journals. Visit this text's website at http://www.oup.com/us/musresearch.

For Students

Several features of *Music Research* are intended to help as you develop your research and writing skills in music. In each chapter you will find a discussion of the uses of the particular type of research tool. In addition, you will learn how to find them using Library of Congress subject headings and classification numbers. The annotated bibliographies evaluate and describe the research tools. Look for the asterisks indicating the major music research tools that you should be familiar with. The Evaluation Checklists will assist you in thinking critically about the research tools as well as the materials you find researching topics of interest. The appendixes, especially the citation format guides, will help you document your research. Use the Glossary to look up terms and concepts that are unfamiliar. Finally, check the companion website for updated information.

For Faculty

One of the overriding goals for this text was to be as useful as possible for instructors, both music librarians and music faculty, teaching a bibliography class. For that reason, it includes pedagogical aids that I hope you find useful, especially if you have not taught music bibliography before.

Because you may wish to customize your instruction of research process, writing, and documentation style, the chapters on those topics (1, 15, and 16) present the major existing resources. This will allow you to personalize your instruction while exposing students to alternative approaches. As throughout the book, these chapters include tips on finding resources on these topics and include recommendations in the bibliographies. Plagiarism is discussed, and examples of proper and improper usage of sources are provided.

To get the most from this text, terms included in the Glossary appear in **boldface** type when they are first discussed in the text. The figures and illustrations give an introduction to major resources before students try them out for the first time. Titles marked with asterisks (*) are major research tools that you might emphasize in class.

The Suggested Readings are useful as assignments before a class session on the relevant tools and can serve as a touchstone for in-class discussion. The reading introductions may help you in selecting among those included. The companion website updates the Suggested Readings lists to include recent writings.

The Evaluation Checklists included in each chapter could be used in class as exercises or perhaps as assignments. For instance, students (individually or in groups) could be asked to fill out a checklist for a particular title, or the lists could be used as worksheets for comparing resources.

If you are a music faculty member teaching the class, you will probably find that, in addition to the information in this book, meeting with your music librarian is very helpful. Although the research tools selected for inclusion are widely held, your library may not have them all. This is especially true for expensive online subscription resources. Even if your library subscribes to a title (e.g., *RILM Abstracts*), you will need to determine which vendor (and which search interface) your students have access to. You may also need to help your students find local call numbers (especially if your library does not use Library of Congress classification numbers), set up remote access to online resources, and so on.

The sixteen chapters correspond to a typical sixteen-week semester. This text was designed to proceed in the order reference tools are often used by students in the research process. For instance, encyclopedias and dictionaries appear before periodical indexes. However, there are many ways to approach research. You may want to begin with searching online catalogs (Chapter 4) instead. Or you may wish to introduce Internet resources (Chapter 14) sooner. Another approach would be to use Part Two (on writing, citation formats, etc.) earlier. The chapters can be used in any order you choose, but you may wish to begin with Chapter 1, because it discusses research process, types of sources, and other basic information. Appendix B presents basic search tips useful for many research tools. Yet another approach might be to organize your course topically. For example, the focus on representative composers is included throughout and could serve as an orientation for a composer-specific approach to research.

The following suggestions might help when teaching groups other than master's and DMA students. For undergraduates, you might focus on the major sources in each chapter. The most important research tools are marked with an asterisk. For more advanced students, the reviews could be assigned as additional readings, and sources mentioned in the text could also be explored.

A few words about my methodology are in order. I have personally examined the vast majority of sources included in the bibliographies or mentioned in the text. I have tried to include the most useful sources available and those that are most widely held by libraries. In most cases, the two goals are complementary. One exception is iconographies; the high cost of many of the best titles makes their purchase prohibitive for many libraries. In some chapters (for example, Chapter 14 on Internet resources), representative examples were included. In this case, additional resources are included on the companion website.

The categories of topics, such as music of the United States, Great Britain, and Canada, were selected in hopes that they would be most relevant for the students using the book. The major composers selected for inclusion throughout were chosen with the same goal (see Appendix C). Additional topics on broad disciplines (e.g., musicology,

ethnomusicology/world music, theory, and music education) as well as narrower subjects (e.g., opera, jazz) were chosen on the basis of my experience of common topics
selected for research by graduate students.

Whenever possible, review citations were included in the annotations. These are
not exhaustive; the reviews cited were the most detailed and informative. When more
than one is listed, it is because they either express a different evaluation of the title at
hand or, alternatively, more than one review was considered outstanding. The selection
was subjective. Whenever possible, reviews in English were chosen rather than those in
another language.

Acknowledgments

Over the ten years I have been teaching graduate-level music bibliography, I have
watched many students develop their research skills by using the sources and methods included in this text. While not all of those students were excited about taking the
course, by the end of the semester most were much more comfortable finding information and evaluating it. I have learned something from each and every student, and they
have all contributed to the creation of this book.

I need to thank Executive Editor Jan Beatty from Oxford University Press, who
suggested this book to me. Jan's patience and kindness during difficult periods kept me
writing. She and the staff at OUP have made this book possible. Thanks to them all:
Marianne Paul, Production Editor; Lauren Mine, Assistant Editor; and Cory Schneider,
Assistant Editor.

I would also like to acknowledge the reviewers of the manuscript, whose sugges-
tions and thoughtful insights served as a guide: Steve Gerber, George Mason University;
Alan Green, Music/Dance Library, Ohio State University; Rebecca Littman, Golda Meir
Library, University of Wisconsin-Milwaukee; Erin Mayhood, University of Virginia;
Bruce MacIntyre, Brooklyn College; Scott McBride, Morehead State University;
Ruthann McTyre, Rita Benton Music Library, University of Iowa; Jane Penner, Music
Library, University of Virginia; Carl Rahkonen, Indiana University of Pennsylvania;
Jennifer Thomas, University of Florida; Pantelis Vassilakis, DePaul University; Liza
Vick, Loeb Music Library, Harvard University; Daniel Zager, Sibley Music Library,
Eastman School of Music, University of Rochester.

So many other people assisted me with this book in large and small ways. There are
too many publishers, authors, editors, and colleagues to list individually. Special thanks
are due to two colleagues who were especially helpful: Zdravko Blažeković and Paul
Cary. Blažeković's knowledge of music iconography was indispensable to Chapter 12.
Cary read drafts, served as a sounding board, and lent his eagle eye to the Glossary.

Much of this text is based on models provided by Karl Kroeger and Deane Root.
Kroeger was my predecessor at the music library at the University of Colorado at
Boulder, and he left me his course materials—including the beginnings of this text—
when he retired in 1994. I took music bibliography from Deane Root at the University of
Pittsburgh at the beginning of my graduate work in musicology there. Many ideas and
approaches included here were inspired by Kroeger and Root.

A number of graduate student research assistants aided enormously with this project. Thanks go first and foremost to Mark Charles Smith and Trudi Wright. Ben Riggs,

Margaret Higginson, and Ross Hagen helped as well. Also at the University of Colorado at Boulder, I would like to thank the following current and former staff members of the Waltz Music Library: Marcelyn H. D'Avis, Joe Grobelny, Anita Ortman, and Leah Riddick. The University Libraries were supportive of this book throughout, as were my colleagues in the Musicology Department of the College of Music.

Special thanks go to my family and friends, especially my husband, Don Puscher. Not only did he pull extra shifts as chief cook and bottle washer, but he formatted, proofed, and edited the entire manuscript. His writing and editing skills improved this book enormously. Thanks to my sons, Harrison and Blake, for repeatedly saying "You can do it, Mommy!"

Even with the assistance of everyone already mentioned, I am sure this book has mistakes and omissions. I alone take the blame for these. However, I will gladly accept corrections and suggestions from faculty, students, and other readers.

Abbreviations

AMC	American Music Center
AMICO	*Art Museum Image Consortium*
AMS	American Musicological Society
APA	American Psychological Association
ARBA	*American Reference Books Annual*
ARSC	Association of Recorded Sound Collections
BC	*Bach Compendium*
BMIC	British Music Information Centre
BPL	Boston Public Library
BWV	*Bach-Werke-Verzeichnis*
CAIRSS	Computer-Assisted Information Retrieval Service System
CAML	Canadian Association of Music Libraries, Archives, and Documentation Centres
CATNYP	New York Public Library Online Catalog
CGOS	*Columbia Guide to Online Style*
CIMCIM	International Committee of Musical Instrument Museums and Collections
CINAHL	*Cumulative Index of Nursing and Allied Health Literature*
CIRCME	Callaway International Resource Centre for Music and Education
CMM	*Corpus mensurabilis musicae*
CMS	College Music Society
CPM	*Catalogue of Printed Music*
CRL	Center for Research Libraries
CSA	Cambridge Scientific Abstracts
CSIC	Consejo Superior de Investigaciones Científicas
CUNY	City University of New York
CURL	Consortium of Research Libraries in the British Isles
D	Deutsch (Schubert thematic catalog)
DDM	*Doctoral Dissertations in Musicology*
DDT	*Denkmäler deutscher Tonkunst*

DEUMM	*Dizionario enciclopedico universale della musica e dei musicisti*
DIP	*International Directory of Dissertations in Progress*
DKL	*Das Deutsche Kirchenlied*
DMEH	*Diccionario de la música española e hispanoamericana*
DMS	*Dissertationsmeldestelle*
DOAJ	*Directory of Open Access Journals*
DRAM	*Database of Recorded American Music*
DTB	*Denkmäler der Tonkunst in Bayern*
DTÖ	*Denkmäler der Tonkunst in Österreich*
EEBO	*Early English Books Online*
EMC	*Encyclopedia of Music in Canada*
ERIC	*Education Resources Information Center*
ETD	Electronic Theses and Dissertations
GMO	*Grove Music Online*
H	Hoboken (Haydn thematic catalog)
HAM	*Historical Anthology of Music*
HRAF	Human Relations Area Files
HTI	*Hymn Tune Index*
HWV	Händel Werke Verzeichnis
IAML	International Association of Music Libraries, Archives, and Documentation Centres
IBTD	*International Bibliography of Theatre and Dance*
ICM	International Council of Museums
IFLA	International Federation of Library Associations and Institutions
IIMP	*International Index to Music Periodicals*
IIPA	*International Index to the Performing Arts*
ILL	Inter-Library Loan
IMS	International Musicological Society
IPM	*Index to Printed Music*
ISAM	Institute for Studies of American Music
ISMIR	International Symposium on Music Information Retrieval
IUCAT	Indiana University Library Catalog
JAMS	*Journal of the American Musicological Society*
JSTOR	Journal Storage Project

K	Köchel (Mozart thematic catalog)
KVNM	De Koninklijke Vereniging voor Nederlandse Muziekgeschiedenis
LC	Library of Congress
LCSH	Library of Congress Subject Headings
MENC	Music Educators National Conference
MGG	*Die Musik in Geschichte und Gegenwart*
MIR	Music Information Retrieval
MLA	Modern Language Association
	Music Library Association
MOD	*Music, Opera, Dance and Drama in Asia, the Pacific and North America*
MTO	*Music Theory Online*
MUSA	*Music of the United States of America*
MUSE	*MUsic SEarch*
NAMM	International Music Products Association (originally National Association of Music Merchandisers)
NASM	National Association of Schools of Music
NAWM	*Norton Anthology of Western Music*
NDLTD	Networked Digital Library of Theses and Dissertations
NG2	*New Grove Dictionary of Music and Musicians*, 2nd ed.
NISC	National Information Services Corporation
NUCMC	*National Union Catalog of Manuscript Collections*
NYPL	New York Public Library
OCLC	Online Computer Library Center
OMO	*Oxford Music Online*
PAYE	*Performing Arts Yearbook for Europe*
POMPI	*Popular Music Periodicals Index*
PQDT	*ProQuest Dissertations and Theses*
RAMH	*Resources of American Music History*
RCMI	Research Center for Music Iconography
RIdIM	Répertoire international d'iconographie musicale or International Repertory of Musical Iconography
RILM	Répertoire international de littérature musicale or International Repertory of Music Literature
RIPM	Répertoire international de la presse musicale or Retrospective Index to Music Periodicals

RISM	Répertoire international des sources musicales or International Inventory of Musical Sources
RLG	Research Libraries Group
RLIN	Research Libraries Information Network
RQ	*Reference Quarterly*
SEM	Society for Ethnomusicology
SGAE	Sociedad General de Autores y Editores
SGS	*Smithsonian Global Sound*
SMT	Society for Music Theory
SONIC	Sound Online Inventory and Catalog (LC)
TCE	*The Canadian Encyclopedia*
UMI	University Microfilms, Inc.
UNESCO	United Nations Educational, Scientific and Cultural Organization
UTET	Unione Tipografico-Editrice Torinese
WERM	*World's Encyclopædia of Recorded Music*
WWV	*Wagner Werk-Verzeichnis*

PART ONE

Research Process and Research Tools

CHAPTER 1

Guides to the Research Process
and Research Tools

Sometimes one of the most difficult hurdles of research is simply getting started. Where do I begin? What techniques should I use? What methodology is appropriate? Are there reference tools on my specific topic to jump-start my research? Has someone else already done what I am interested in? Is there a broader interest in my topic? Is inspiration available? Are there models of excellence to turn to for motivation?

The tools and readings listed here were created to help answer these and other questions. From the role of research to specific techniques and the most complete bibliography of music reference tools in print, they are intended to help the researcher. These guides fall into two broad categories: research process and research tools. Of course, the two are related, and some of the books deal with both to varying degrees. What are not included here, however, are guides devoted exclusively to writing. Those are covered in Chapter 15.

Consideration of the types of sources in existence for your research is important. Are primary sources available, or only secondary and tertiary sources? Also, for music this classification of source materials can vary from that for other disciplines. Two main definitions for primary sources are expressed in the literature. One is that the "raw materials," or original documents/performances, are **primary sources**.[1] Another is that the primary sources are those as close as possible to the creator of the materials being studied, for instance, a **manuscript** in the composer's hand and documents contemporaneous with the composition or performance. **Secondary sources** are writings and studies based on primary sources, such as books and journal articles. **Tertiary sources** are based on secondary sources, including articles and books, but also indexes, directories, and so on.

---

[1]For example, see Kate L. Turabian, *A Manual for Writers of Research Papers, Theses, and Dissertations*, 7th ed. (Chicago: University of Chicago Press, 2007), 25.

One way to visualize the difference between primary, secondary, and tertiary sources is to imagine the musical event of interest as a pebble being dropped into a pond of water. The pebble's impact is the primary source. The ripples closest to the splash are similar to secondary sources in that they are closest to the primary sources. The larger ripples further away from the pebble are similar to tertiary sources by being more removed in space and time.

What is considered a primary source for music can vary from one topic to another. Earlier I used a manuscript in the composer's hand as an example of a primary source for art music. In jazz, a primary source could be a sound recording, since jazz lives more in performance as an improvisational art than in Western classical music.

Another consideration throughout your research involves the types of musical scores you use in your study and performance. Examples range from heavily edited scores to facsimiles of manuscripts or prints. For most scholarly endeavors you will want to use a **critical**, or **scholarly edition**. For performance, though, a **performing edition** may better fill your needs. Some musicians prefer playing or singing from **Urtext editions**, which are presented without editorial changes. Regardless of the type of edition, it should be clearly indicated what changes were made by an editor and what was original to the sources of the edition (often a primary source or the best possible secondary sources). These topics are explored in more detail in Chapter 7 in relation to composers' complete works editions, historical sets, and musical monuments.

Both general and music-specific research process books are included here. The general books are valuable because, to a certain extent, research is research. The authors of *The Craft of Research*, for example, have done an excellent job of distilling elements common to many disciplines. The broader approach of books like this one helps you focus on the big issues of research, such as whom your research is for and why it matters.

On the other hand, subject and subdiscipline guides are also useful, especially in areas like music education. Guides to music research as well as guides for subdisciplines have been included. However, bibliographies or "guides to research" for the narrower areas of music research are included in Chapter 10, which is devoted to music bibliographies.

The other titles listed here are guides to research and reference tools or guides to the guides. Again, both general and music-specific works have been included; they are arranged from general to specific. The former are useful for interdisciplinary topics. Some of the music guides strive for comprehensiveness, for example, the "Duckles" (*Music Reference and Research Materials: An Annotated Bibliography*). Others, like this text, are selective. With the selective bibliographies, the selection criteria are important. Still others focus on a subdiscipline. For all of these tools, currency is significant, as are the inclusion of annotations and a useful index.

The titles listed in the following bibliography are best referred to as needed throughout your work, rather than being read from cover to cover before beginning. They include both general and specific advice in varying degrees. Some of these books are "thinking" books; others are "doing" books. Both types have value, but you want to go to them at the "right" time in your research; see the annotations for suggestions. The asterisks indicate the most highly recommended titles in each category.

RESEARCH PROCESS

Music Research Process

1.1 Colwell, Richard. *MENC Handbook of Research Methodologies*. New York: Oxford University Press, 2006.
Sponsored by the Music Educators National Conference (MENC). Includes 9 chapters by various authors on research philosophy as well as qualitative, quantitative, and historical research processes in music education. Reviewed by John Schuster-Craig in *Fontes artis musicae* 54, no. 1 (Jan.–Mar. 2007): 142–44.

1.2 Druesedow, John E., Jr. *Library Research Guide to Music: Illustrated Search Strategy and Sources*. Library Research Guides Series, no. 6. Ann Arbor, MI: Pierian, 1982.
Uses a case study (the relationship between Debussy and Stravinsky) to illustrate the research paper process up to the point of writing. Especially valuable for its discussion of narrowing a research topic. Although the specific tools mentioned are now out-of-date, the process outlined remains helpful. And although written primarily for the undergraduate, the book includes topics that are relevant for many graduate students as well, such as using foreign-language sources for the first time. Reviewed by Ann P. Basart in *Notes* 39, no. 2 (Dec. 1982): 353–54.

1.3 Foreman, Lewis, ed. *Information Sources in Music*. Munich: K. G. Saur, 2003.
Each chapter of this book covers a different music research topic or a different type of information source, written by a variety of authors. The goal is to include both print and nonprint sources. The result is a mix of approaches, including some formats and professions not commonly discussed, such as concert programs and secondhand music dealers, respectively. Reviewed by Christopher Cipkin in *British Journal of Music Education* 20, no. 3 (Nov. 2003): 335–36.

1.4 Phelps, Roger, Lawrence Ferrara, Ronald Sadoff, and Edward Warburton. *A Guide to Research in Music Education*. 5th ed. Lanham, MD: Scarecrow, 2005.
Like Colwell, the authors focus on the research process in music education. Topics include qualitative research, data analysis, experimental research, and nonexperimental research as well as a chapter on music and technology. Reviewed by Michael Burnett in *Music Teacher* 84, no. 10 (Oct. 2005): 63.

1.5 Pruett, James, and Thomas Slavens. *Research Guide to Musicology*. Sources of Information in the Humanities, no. 4. Chicago: American Library Association, 1985.
The first and longest part of this book, "Introduction to Research in Music," provides an overview of types of musicological research and a history of the discipline. Also included is a historiographical survey of musicological research arranged by style period. The second part of the book is a listing of reference tools that is now too out-of-date to be useful. Reviewed by Lenore Coral in *Notes* 43, no. 1 (Sept. 1986): 42–44.

1.6 Watanabe, Ruth. *Introduction to Music Research*. Englewood Cliffs, NJ: Prentice Hall, 1967.
This is another research classic that is still valid today for the sections that are not time sensitive. For example, "Approaches to Music Research" and "Selection

of a Research Topic" remain helpful, while "Library Catalog Cards" and the bibliography chapters are not. Watanabe wrote for "the young graduate student" (v), and her book was intended for a bibliography course. Reviewed by D. W. Krummel in *Notes* 24, no. 3 (Mar. 1968): 481–82.

*1.7   Wingell, Richard, J., and Silvia Herzog. *Introduction to Research in Music.* Upper Saddle River, NJ: Prentice Hall, 2001.

Another book intended as a music bibliography text. The first part includes a mix of research procedure and unannotated lists of resources as well as a detailed chapter on the history of music notation, printing, and publishing. The second part focuses on writing and includes a sample musicological paper with commentary. Perhaps most useful for musicology students.

General Research Process

1.8   Barzun, Jacques, and Henry F. Graff. *The Modern Researcher.* 6th ed. Belmont, CA: Thomson Learning/Wadsworth, 2004.

The first edition of *The Modern Researcher* was published in 1957, and since then it has been viewed as a classic guide. Both Barzun and Graff are historians; this book originated from a course in historical methodology at Columbia University. Includes practical advice on giving presentations and using time wisely, topics not found in the other guides listed here. The preface states, "This is a *reading book*, not a collection of rules of thumb for solving isolated 'problems'" (v). This difference is an important one to keep in mind when using this versus *The Craft of Research*, which employs the other approach. Reviewed in *Reference and Research Book News* 19, no. 1 (Feb. 2004): 259.

*1.9   Booth, Wayne C., Gregory G. Colomb, and Joseph M. Williams. *The Craft of Research.* 2nd ed. Chicago: University of Chicago Press, 2003.

From the first thoughts on a topic to the last revision of your writing, *The Craft of Research* has advice for the beginner as well as the more experienced researcher and writer. The authors have done an admirable job of breaking their topics into short sections that are quick to read and have aided usability via bullets, numbered lists, flowcharts, and "Quick Tips." All three authors are or have been professors of English as well as writers, and their advice is practical. They approach research and writing as learnable crafts and stress logic in the process and clarity in the final product. Reviewed by George M. Eberhart in *College and Research Libraries News* 64, no. 5 (May 2003): 344.

1.10   Mann, Thomas. *The Oxford Guide to Library Research.* 3rd ed. New York: Oxford University Press, 2005.

Mann, a reference librarian at the Library of Congress, focuses on library-centered research using both print and electronic resources. He clearly explains the need to understand which of the latter are available free of charge and which are subscription based. Arranged by search methods (using controlled vocabulary, browsing books by subject, using bibliographies, etc.), Mann discusses in detail such topics as Library of Congress cataloging, use of materials not available locally, experts as sources, and other topics not covered by the other texts included here. Reviewed by J. P. Burton in *Choice* 43, no. 8 (Apr. 2006): 1366.

RESEARCH TOOLS

Music Research Tools

1.11   Brockman, William. *Music: A Guide to the Reference Literature*. Littleton, CO: Libraries Unlimited, 1987.
Brockman was selective in his *Guide*, with the goal of listing the "important current and retrospective sources of information on music" (xii). Concentrating on English-language publications, he included around 850 titles. Brockman's model annotations are detailed and thoughtful. They not only describe and evaluate the sources but also compare them. Furthermore, they are well written and enjoyable to read. Includes author/title and subject indexes. Reviewed by John Wagstaff in *Music and Letters* 70, no. 3 (1989): 394–95.

*1.12   Crabtree, Phillip, and Donald Foster. *Sourcebook for Research in Music*. Rev. and expanded by Allen Scott. 2nd ed. Bloomington, IN: Indiana University Press, 2005.
Also selective, Crabtree, Foster, and Scott have done an admirable job of including sources for the various subdisciplines of music: performance, education, ethnomusicology, musicology, and so on. This book includes very few annotations, focusing instead on lists of citations with explanatory introductions and advice on research techniques. Sometimes the organization is puzzling. Includes author and title indexes but no subject index. Reviewed by D. W. Krummel in *Choice* 43, no. 10 (June 2006): 1794.

*1.13   Duckles, Vincent, and Ida Reed. *Music Reference and Research Materials: An Annotated Bibliography*. 5th ed. New York: Schirmer Books, 1997.
Widely acknowledged as the most complete, scholarly, and best-indexed annotated bibliography of music reference titles. A team of compilers included over 3,800 entries. This is the first edition compiled without Duckles. Michael Keller was advisory editor, and Linda Solow Blotner created the combined author, title, and subject index. See also "Electronic Resources in Duckles 5," a website compiled by Brad Short with links to the citations from Chapter 12 at http://www.lib.ku.edu/musiclib/duckles.shtml. Reviewed by John Wagstaff in *Notes* 54, no. 4 (June 1998): 911–13.

1.14   Marco, Guy A. *Information on Music: A Handbook of Reference Sources in European Languages*. 3 vols. Littleton, CO: Libraries Unlimited, 1975–1984.
Contents: Volume I: *Basic and Universal Sources*, 1975; Volume II: *The Americas* (with Ann Garfield and Sharon Paugh Ferris), 1977; and Volume III: *Europe* (with Sharon Paugh Ferris and Ann Olszewski), 1984.
More comprehensive in selection (like Duckles) and more inclusive of general sources (like Mixter). Additional volumes of this annotated bibliography

were initially planned. Unlike the other major tools mentioned, Marco's has not
enjoyed updates through new editions. The Canadian music section, however, was
supplemented by Marlene Wehrle in *Fontes artis musicae* 41, no. 1 (1994): 40–52.
Indexes include authors, titles, and subjects (using Library of Congress subject
headings). Vol. 1 reviewed by Peter Ward Jones in *Music and Letters* 58, no. 3
(July 1977): 454–55. Vol. 2 reviewed by Gordon Rowley in *Fontes artis musicae*
26, no. 1 (1979): 62–63. Vol. 3 reviewed by Ann P. Basart in *Reference Quarterly
(RQ)* 24 (Winter 1984): 231–32.

General Research Tools

1.15 Balay, Robert. *Guide to Reference Books*. 11th ed. Chicago: American Library
      Association, 1996.
      This standard general reference bibliography is useful not so much for its music
      section, which cannot compete with the other guides listed here, but rather for
      the rest of the volume. It is helpful for identifying nonmusic tools for those with
      interdisciplinary topics. Includes around 16,000 annotated entries. A new edition,
      titled *Guide to Reference*, to be published online, is anticipated. Reviewed by
      Robert Ridinger in *Choice* 33 (June 1996): 1591–92.

1.16 Mixter, Keith E. *General Bibliography for Music Research*. 3rd ed. Warren, MI:
      Harmonie Park Press, 1996.
      Mixter's approach is unique in that he provides references useful for music
      research in nonmusic sources. Includes over 1,200 sources, predominantly pub-
      lications from North America and Europe. Titles are discussed in bibliographic
      essays, with the full citations presented at the end of each chapter. Concentrates
      on bibliographies that can lead the researcher to sources. Includes name and title
      indexes but no subject index. Reviewed by John Wagstaff in *Fontes artis musicae*
      45, no. 2 (Apr.–June 1998): 195–96.

EVALUATION CHECKLIST

The following evaluation checklist is general enough to be useful for most writings about music and research tools. More specific checklists are included in
each chapter in the rest of Part One of this text. Cost is only included for materials that may not be subscribed to by your library. In addition, see the article by
David Hunter and others.[2]

• What is the purpose of this text? Are the author's goals defined?
• Is the scope of the subject defined?

[2]David Hunter and others, "Music Library Association Guidelines for the Preparation of
Music Reference Works," *Notes* 50, no. 4 (June 1994): 1329–38.

- Does the title have a long history with multiple editions?
  - What is the author's or editor's authority?
  - Is the publisher well respected?
  - What is the publication date? Is the source kept current?
  - Is the title peer reviewed or refereed? Has it been positively reviewed?
  - What are the work's strengths and weaknesses?
  - Is any bias acknowledged?
  - Is the content accurate?
  - Is the title widely cited as reputable?
  - Is the content unique, or is it available elsewhere?
  - Is the content presented thoughtfully?
- Is it well written?
- Is the database or website well designed?
- Is it easy to read, use, or search?
  - Is the indexing adequate?
  - What language is it in?

SUGGESTED READINGS

The suggested readings deal with questions such as the role of research in scholarship as well as with research technique and process. All were written by scholars with not only information but also knowledge, experience, and wisdom to share.

Barzun, Jacques, and Henry F. Graff. "Finding the Facts." Chap. 3 in *The Modern Researcher*. 6th ed. Belmont, CA: Thomson Learning/Wadsworth, 2004.

Booth, Wayne C., Gregory G. Colomb, and Joseph M. Williams. "Thinking in Print," Chap. 1 in *The Craft of Research*. 2nd ed. Chicago: University of Chicago Press, 2003.

Duckles, Vincent. "The Library of the Mind: Observations on the Relationship Between Musical Scholarship and Bibliography." In *Current Thought in Musicology*, edited by John W. Grubbs, 277–96. Austin: University of Texas Press, 1976.

Krummel, D. W. "Introduction." Chap. 1 in *Bibliographies: Their Aims and Methods*. London: Mansell, 1984.

Sadie, Stanley, ed. *The New Grove Dictionary of Music and Musicians*. 2nd ed. New York: Grove, 2001. S.v. "Bibliography of Music," by Stanley Boorman. Also available from *Grove Music Online*. http://www.oxfordmusiconline.com.

CHAPTER 2

General Music Encyclopedias
and Dictionaries

An encyclopedia or dictionary is a good place to begin with most music research questions.[1] The purpose of **lexicography**, or the making of dictionaries, is to provide accurate factual information and authoritative summaries of topics. Examples of facts are birth and/or death dates for musicians, the number of strings on a particular instrument, and the date a work was composed. If this is the type of information you need, you may be able to find your answers by consulting an encyclopedia, perhaps even by consulting a one-volume work.

Summaries of musical topics are helpful when beginning a research project. For example, if you are interested in the music of Brahms, especially the symphonies, scanning the Brahms article in *The New Grove Dictionary of Music and Musicians*, 2nd ed. (*NG2*), might help you decide whether you want to continue with the topic and, if so, give you further ideas about how you might do so. Reading the section on the orchestral works would give you an overview of contexts and issues related to the symphonies; the works list would provide details about their dates of composition, publication, and premiere; and the bibliography would give you an idea about the amount, currency, and languages of writings available on the symphonies.

The encyclopedias and dictionaries discussed in this chapter range in size from one to twenty-nine volumes in length. The differences stem from their purpose and audience. One-volume encyclopedias, such as *The Oxford Companion to Music*, have a broader group of readers (including musical amateurs), are relatively inexpensive, provide brief factual information, and are more readily updated. They offer these benefits in a format that you can carry around and read from cover to cover if you wish.

The multi-volume dictionaries not only provide more detailed information (sometimes as long as a book on certain subjects) but can also be more inclusive, i.e., more

---

[1]The two terms are used interchangeably in this text, since that is how they are used in the titles of published reference tools.

encyclopedic, in the number of topics covered. In addition to covering musicians, genres, and instruments, for example, articles on individual cities, musical organizations, and performance practice can also be included. Musical examples and illustrations may be more lavish.

Although very different in size and scope, both encyclopedias just mentioned are authoritative. How can you judge the quality of the scholarship of an encyclopedia? The checklist provided later in this chapter, just before the Suggested Readings, can help. Currency matters because, in most instances, you want to use the most up-to-date information available. This is particularly the case with the articles' bibliographies, works lists, and dates (e.g., death dates and performance dates). One-tried-and true method for evaluating currency is to check the dates of the works cited in an encyclopedia's bibliographies. However, make sure that the articles—and not just the bibliographies—contain new information as well. The method of publication also affects an encyclopedia's currency. Is the publication print or online? If it includes multiple volumes, was it published serially (one volume at a time) or all at once when completed?

The latest edition of *Die Musik in Geschichte und Gegenwart* (commonly called *MGG*) is an example of the serial approach. The first volume was published in 1994 and was completed in 2007. All twenty-nine volumes of the *NG2*, on the other hand, were published in 2001. Because the publication of *MGG* spanned more than a decade, the research reflects that date range; the later volumes are more recent than the earlier ones. Of course, not all the articles in *NG2* were completed just before publication. One can only imagine the *NG2* editorial staff's push to finish the final edits of so many volumes. Both publication approaches are valid.

New Grove (2nd ed.), however, was the first comprehensive music encyclopedia to become available electronically via subscription on the Internet as part of *Grove Music Online* (*GMO*). Launched at the same time the second edition of the print encyclopedia was published, it has already been improved significantly and has been updated more than once. See the later discussion of *GMO*.

There are advantages as well as disadvantages to having encyclopedias available online. Around-the-clock access, full text searching, audio examples, and frequent updates are major advantages. The use of an online encyclopedia such as *Wikipedia* should be considered carefully. While much of the content is excellent, it is all user contributed, and information should be verified before use in research. Other concerns with online encyclopedias include the inability to browse in the traditional sense, and, more significantly, the differences in preserving an "edition" as an historical document.

Why would the survival of earlier versions of an encyclopedia article be desirable? Although the importance of currency has already been mentioned, researchers often need to turn to older editions of encyclopedias and dictionaries. For example, composers and (especially) performers popular in the 1920s would very likely be covered more extensively in the fifth edition of Grove's *Dictionary* (1954) than in the current edition. The changing perspective over time on a given subject can be studied this way as well. Sometimes, information contemporaneous with your topic can be invaluable. Performance practice is one such example.

Another consideration is editorial bias. The word *bias* has a negative connotation, which is not always appropriate to the current discussion. The suggested reading by

Hans Lenneberg refers to this as "chauvinism" or, more positively, as "national pride." An American encyclopedia is likely to include more American topics and composers and to devote more space to those topics. In a 2001 letter to the editor of the *New York Times* in response to a review stating that the *NG2* was still too British, editor Stanley Sadie wrote, "I have always recognized that even in an international dictionary some bias in favor of English, American, Canadian and Australian music and that of other English-speaking nations is not only unavoidable but perfectly proper."[2] Proper or not, intentional or not, every editor is human, and humans do have biases.

As a researcher, your goal is to be aware of an editor's bias and to use it to your advantage. If you are interested in a French topic, by all means go to a French encyclopedia. When possible, use a special encyclopedia or dictionary for a topic that has been traditionally underrepresented in the general tools. That is why special music dictionaries devoted to women, blacks, and certain genres of music are necessary. These and other special encyclopedias and dictionaries are the subject of the next chapter. Editors certainly strive to be more inclusive and international today than in the past.

Another consideration with encyclopedias is readability or usability. No one ever questioned the authority of the "old" *MGG*. However, the small typeface and high number of abbreviations (especially in the works lists) was described in one article as "sheer torture" to read.[3] Thankfully, the new edition is much easier on the eyes and nerves. Typeface aside, are the articles easy to read? Are they clear and understandable? Do you learn something from them? How are disputed topics handled? How well edited are the articles? Of course a multi-volume encyclopedia will contain errors, but they should not be pervasive or egregious. With *GMO* the question of usability joined the list of considerations for encyclopedias, as it has with other electronic reference tools.

Finally, this may be the first time you have consulted a foreign-language encyclopedia. If so, keep in mind the following strategies for dealing with those in German, French, Italian, or other Western European languages. As a musician you are used to working with titles of musical works and writings about music in a variety of languages. Those skills enable you to use the works lists and bibliographies of the articles regardless of the language of the text. You will be able to find birth and death dates and read common words that are English cognates. For example, the German word for composer is Komponist. Illustrations and musical examples speak for themselves.

New Grove (2nd ed.) does not have the answer to every question; we need more than one encyclopedia and are lucky to have so many good ones to consult. The following list is highly selective. Only those that attempt comprehensive, or general, coverage by including persons, terms, places, instruments, etc., have been included here. Most of the tools described attempt international coverage of Western and/or non-Western musics. Others focus on smaller geographical areas but cover them in the same way, for example, *The New Grove Dictionary of American Music*. Encyclopedias devoted to specific geographical regions have been included here as long as their coverage is

---

[2]Stanley Sadie, letter to the editor, *New York Times*, 4 Feb. 2001.
[3]Mark Germer, "The New *Musik in Geschichte und Gegenwart*: First Impressions," *Notes* 52, no. 1 (Sept. 1995): 42.

comprehensive. German-, French-, Italian-, and Spanish-language encyclopedias have each been represented in addition to English-language volumes.

To find these or other encyclopedias in your local library use the appropriate subject headings and call numbers. In the Library of Congress (LC) cataloging system, the subject heading assigned to comprehensive dictionaries is normally "Music—Dictionaries" or "Music—Encyclopedias." For those not in English, the language is added, for example, "Music—Dictionaries—German." The Library of Congress call numbers are ML100 for the international encyclopedias and ML101 for those devoted to a country or region.[4]

The asterisks indicate the most highly recommended title(s) in each category. Researchers needing a comprehensive listing should consult the article "Dictionaries and Encyclopedias of Music" by James Coover in the *NG2* or *GMO*. Coover lists over 1,650 titles in chronological order.

MULTI-VOLUME GENERAL MUSIC ENCYCLOPEDIAS AND DICTIONARIES

English

2.1 Hitchcock, H. Wiley, and Stanley Sadie. *The New Grove Dictionary of American Music.* 4 vols. London: Macmillan, 1986.

Based in part on the 1980 *New Grove* (1st ed.), this dictionary, nicknamed *AmeriGrove,* is much more detailed and covers a much broader area of American music than the larger encyclopedia. Many of the approximately 5,000 articles were new, and many entries from *New Grove* (1st ed.) were thoroughly revised and updated. The interpretation of "American" music is broad, although popular music is not covered extensively. A majority of the entries are biographical. Signed articles by approximately 900 prominent scholars in American music. Lavishly illustrated. Includes many cross-references, but no index. A second edition is in progress under editor Charles Garrett. Six volumes are proposed, and it will be published by Oxford University Press and added to *Grove Music Online* beginning in 2008. Reviewed by Allen P. Britton in *American Music* 5, no. 2 (Summer 1987): 194–203; Richard Crawford in *College Music Symposium* 27 (1987): 172–86; and Mary Wallace Davidson et al. in *Notes* 44, no. 1 (Sept. 1987): 43–47.

*2.2 Macy, Laura. *Grove Music Online.* Oxford: Oxford University Press, 2001–. Part of *Oxford Music Online,* at http://www.oxfordmusiconline.com.

Grove Music Online includes over 47,000 articles from *NG2, The New Grove Dictionary of Opera, The Norton/Grove Dictionary of Women Composers,* and *The New Grove Dictionary of Jazz* (2nd ed.). For a discussion of the content of *GMO,* please see the entry for the print encyclopedia. The online publication offers advantages over the print for subscribers: around-the-clock access, full text searching, and updatability. Online extras include links to audio streaming services (such as *Classical Music Online*) and indexes (such as *RILM*). The *GMO*

---

[4]For more on LC call numbers, see Appendix A.

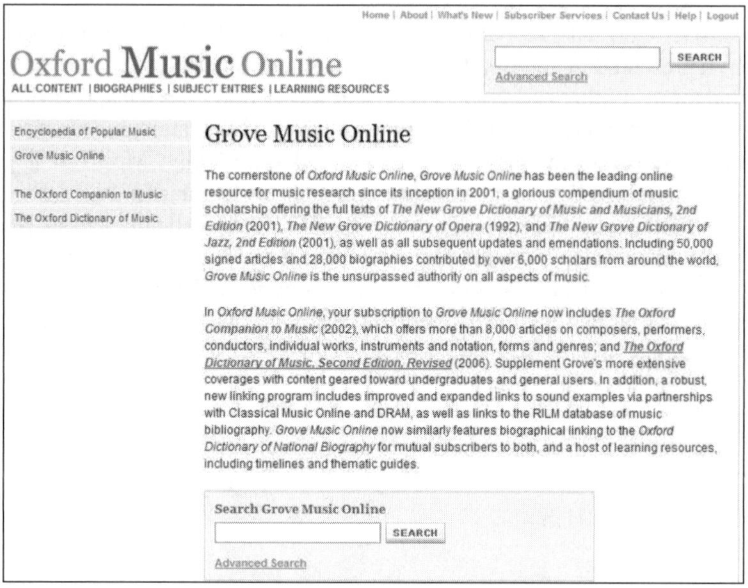

Figure 2-1 *Grove Music Online (GMO)* Homepage. *(Oxford Music Online c. Oxford University Press 2007)*

homepage, shown in Figure 2-1, includes a basic search box. The basic search is designed to lead you to the individual articles quickly. It retrieves articles with the search term(s) present in the article titles and implicitly combines search terms with a Boolean "or."[5] Despite the implicit "or," the relevancy ranking usually places the article you are looking for at the top of the results list. For example, the search for "John Doe" will find all the "Johns" as well as all the "Does," but "John Doe" appears first. The advanced search option, shown in Figure 2-2, is preferable to the basic search box. The "Advanced Search" allows you to search the full text of the encyclopedia using the full range of Boolean operators. Specialized searches of the articles' works lists and bibliographies, among others, are possible and are very useful. Articles updated since the initial publication in 2001 have a date stamp on the left side of the screen; see Figure 2-3. Areas for usability improvement in *GMO* include the following. Printing entire articles is cumbersome. The search options are not intuitive. See the "Grove Music Online Help Guide" and the context-specific help. Articles from the different titles included on Oxford Music Online are identified below each entry; see Figure 2-4. Reviewed by Lenore Coral in *Notes* 58, no. 2 (Dec. 2001): 406–8; Linda Fairtile in *Journal of the American Musicological Society (JAMS)* 56, no. 3 (Fall 2003): 748–54; Allan Kozinn in *New York Times* 15 Feb. 2001; and Peter Phillips in *Musical Times* 143, no. 1879 (Summer 2002): 74–77.

---

[5]See Appendix B for an explanation of Boolean search terms.

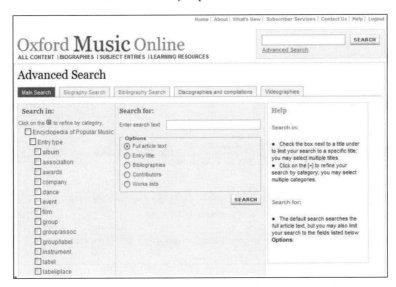

Figure 2-2 *OMO* Advanced Search Screen *(Oxford Music Online c. Oxford University Press 2007)*

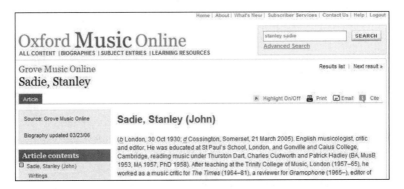

Figure 2-3 *OMO* Updated, Date-Stamped Article *(Oxford Music Online c. Oxford University Press 2007)*

2.3   Marsh, James. *The Encyclopedia of Music in Canada/Encyclopédie de la musique au Canada*. Historica ed. Toronto: Historica Foundation of Canada, 2003–. http://www. thecanadianencyclopedia.com/index.cfm?PgNm=EMCSubjects&Params=U1.
Similar to *AmeriGrove* in its goals, *The Encyclopedia of Music in Canada* (*EMC*) is available free of charge. The "Historica edition" is now part of *The Canadian Encyclopedia* (*TCE*) and contains around 4,000 articles. Revision is ongoing. Articles are available in English and French; they are signed and include bibliographies, selective works lists, discographies, and filmographies. Similar to the second edition, in that contributors (about 500) are Canadian. Search and browse options are less powerful than those of *GMO*, and at present there are no illustrations. Second edition (print) reviewed by Ken DeLong in *Notes* 50,

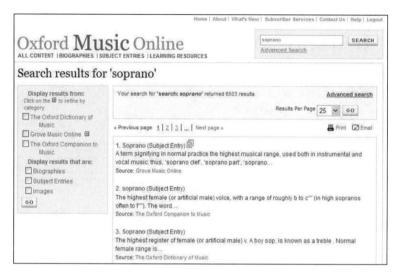

Figure 2-4 *OMO* Search Results with Dictionary Titles *(Oxford Music Online c. Oxford University Press 2007)*

no. 4 (June 1994): 1449–50 and Charlotte Leonard in *Fontes artis musicae* 40, no. 3 (July–Sept. 1993): 268–69. Online version reviewed by John E. Druesedow, Jr., in *Choice* 40, Special Issue Web 7 (Aug. 2003): 93.

*2.4   Nettl, Bruno, Ruth Stone, James Porter, and Timothy Rice. *The Garland Encyclopedia of World Music.* 10 vols. New York: Garland, 1998–2002. Also available online from Alexander Street Press at http://www.alexanderstreet.com. Contents: Volume 1: *Africa*, edited by Ruth Stone, 1998; Volume 2: *South America, Mexico, Central America, and the Caribbean*, edited by Dale Olsen and Daniel Sheehy, 1998; Volume 3: *The United States and Canada*, edited by Ellen Koskoff, 2001; Volume 4: *Southeast Asia*, edited by Terry E. Miller and Sean Williams, 1998; Volume 5: *South Asia: The Indian Subcontinent*, edited by Alison Arnold, 2000; Volume 6: *The Middle East*, edited by Virginia Danielson, Scott Marcus, and Dwight Reynolds, 2002; Volume 7: *East Asia: China, Japan, and Korea*, edited by Robert Provine, Yosihiko Tokumaru, and J. Lawrence Witzleben, 2002; Volume 8: *Europe*, edited by Timothy Rice, James Porter, and Chris Goertzen, 2000; Volume 9: *Australia and the Pacific Islands*, edited by Adrienne Kaeppler and J. W. Love, 1998; Volume 10: *The World's Music: General Perspectives and Reference Tools*, edited by Ruth Stone, 2002. The only multi-volume encyclopedia to date devoted to world music. Rather than an A–Z listing, each volume is arranged more like a textbook than an encyclopedia. Use of the indexes is essential. Each volume is devoted to a specific geographic area or areas. Most volumes are divided into three parts: an introduction to the musical culture(s), issues and processes in the music of the area(s), and regional or country case studies. Signed chapters are by leading ethnomusicologists, and bibliographical references are included. Each volume, except the last, is accompanied by a compact disc. Includes musical examples and other illustrations. Vols. 1–2, 4, and 9 reviewed by Helen Myers in *Ethnomusicology* 47, no. 2 (Spring–Summer 2003): 263–67. Vol. 1 also reviewed by Veit Erlmann in *JAMS* 51, no. 2 (Summer 1998): 407–9. Vol. 3 reviewed by Charles Hamm in *JAMS* 57, no. 1 (Spring 2004): 193–201. Vol. 5 reviewed by Kathryn Hansen in *Asian Music* 34, no. 1 (Fall–Winter 2002–03): 155–58 and by Richard J. Wolfe in *Ethnomusicology* 48, no. 2 (Spring/Summer 2004): 278–83. Vol. 6 reviewed by Benjamin Brinner in *Notes* 59, no. 3 (Mar. 2003): 654–57. Vol. 7 reviewed by Henry Johnson in *Notes* 59, no. 3 (Mar. 2003): 657–59. Vol. 8 reviewed by Martin Stokes in *JAMS* 56, no. 1 (Spring 2003): 214–20. Vol. 10 reviewed by Christopher Schiff in *Notes* 60, no. 2 (Dec. 2003): 446–68.

*2.5   Sadie, Stanley, and John Tyrrell. *The New Grove Dictionary of Music and Musicians*. 2nd ed. 29 vols. New York: Grove, 2001.

The leading scholarly English-language encyclopedia of music, with entries by over 6,000 recognized international scholars. Edited by an international board. Attempts to deal objectively and comprehensively with all fields of music, covers all countries and all time periods, yet a British bias persists. Includes increased coverage of twentieth-century composers, women, world music, and recent approaches to musicology. Includes around 29,000 articles, some very lengthy. About two-thirds of the entries are biographies, and most of these are of composers. Includes complete works lists for major composers and detailed bibliographies. Important manuscripts and early music prints are covered to about 1700. Well illustrated. Includes index. See also *Grove Music Online*. Reviewed by Mark Germer in *Notes* 58, no. 2 (Dec. 2001): 320–25; James Oestreich in *New York Times* 21 Jan. 2001; Andrew Porter in *Times Literary Supplement* (London) 23 Nov. 2001; Charles Rosen in *New York Review of Books* 48, no. 10 (21 June 2001): 29–32; Alex Ross in *New Yorker* 77, no. 18 (9 July 2001): 82–86; and Judy Tsou in *Fontes artis musicae* 48, no. 2 (Apr.–June 2001): 190–94. Stanley Sadie responded to Oestreich in a letter to the editor of *New York Times* 4 Feb. 2001.

French

2.6   Honegger, Marc. *Dictionnaire de la musique*. 4 vols. Paris: Bordas, 1970–76.

Contents: *Les hommes et leurs œuvres* (biographies), 2 vols., 1970; *Science de la musique: Technique, formes, instruments* (subjects), 2 vols., 1976.

French encyclopedia in two parts: vols. 1–2 are a biographical dictionary; vols. 3–4 include articles on form, technique, and musical instruments. Long articles on important musicians and subjects are signed. Brief bibliographies appended to most articles. Good illustrations (some in color). Contributors comprise a group of international scholars. Useful now primarily for the subject volumes, since the biography has been updated; see later. *Science de la musique* (vols. 3–4) reviewed by Jean-Jacques Eigeldinger in *Revue musicale de Suisse romande* 30, nos. 2–3 (Autumn 1977): 75–76.

*2.7   ———. *Dictionnaire de la musique*. [New ed.] 2 vols. Paris: Bordas, 1993.

New edition of the biography section only, *Les hommes et leurs œuvres*. Includes primarily, but not exclusively, composers. Contributions from over 200 international authors. Longer articles are signed. Includes works lists and bibliographies. French bias. Includes color illustrations, like the first edition. Needs updating. The 1986 edition reviewed by Roger Nichols in *Music and Letters* 71, no. 4 (Nov. 1990): 524–26.

German

2.8   Blume, Friedrich. *Die Musik in Geschichte und Gegenwart: Allgemeine Enzyklopädie der Musik.* 17 vols. Kassel, Ger. Bärenreiter, 1949–1986.
      The "old" *MGG* is still needed for its coverage of topics not carried over in the second edition. This first edition was not divided into parts, but published with topics and biographies integrated into one alphabetical listing. It was published serially between 1949 and 1986, with two supplements: A–D (1973) and E–Z (1979). Articles written by scholars eminent in their fields. Coverage similar to *New Grove* (1st ed.). Difficult to use because of typography, layout, and frequent abbreviations. Articles are well illustrated with black-and-white pictures. The supplements correct and update earlier articles and occasionally add new ones. Vol. 17 (1986) is a comprehensive index to the entire set. Early volumes reviewed by Willi Apel in *JAMS* 8, no. 1 (Spring 1955): 43–45; Charles Warren Fox in *Notes* 12, no. 1 (Dec. 1954): 92–93; and Paul Henry Lang in *Musical Quarterly* 38, no. 3 (July 1952): 477–79. After the supplementary volumes came out, Lang wrote an "Epilogue" in *Notes* 36, no. 2 (Dec. 1979): 271–81.

*2.9 Finscher, Ludwig. *Die Musik in Geschichte und Gegenwart*: *Allgemeine Enzyklopädie der Musik.* 2nd ed. 27 vols. Kassel, Ger. Bärenreiter, 1994–2007. Contents: *Sachteil* [Subjects], 10 vols., 1994–1999; *Personenteil* [Biographies], 17 vols., 1999–2007.
      New edition of the leading scholarly German encyclopedia. Published serially, the *Sachteil* (subjects) includes over 1,500 entries in 10 vols., and the *Personenteil* (biographies) has over 18,000 entries written by over 2,000 scholars from 55 countries. International editorial board and authors. Much easier to use than the first edition, with larger fonts and works lists modeled after those in *New Grove* (1st ed.). Expanded in size from first edition, with articles newly written or extensively revised. Includes color illustrations. Bias toward German topics. For example, the article on Wolfgang Amadeus Mozart is over twice as long as the one in *NG2*. *Sachteil* vol. 1 reviewed by Mark Germer in *Notes* 52, no. 1 (Sept. 1995): 39–44; David Fallows in *Early Music* 23, no. 1 (Feb. 1995): 151–52; and Bruno Nettl in *World of Music* 37, no. 2 (1995): 103–5.

Italian

*2.10 Basso, Alberto. *Dizionario enciclopedico universale della musica e dei musicisti.* 16 vols. Turin, It.: Unione Tipografico-Editrice Torinese (UTET), 1983–1999. Contents: *Il lessico*, 4 vols., 1983–84; *Le biografie*, 8 vols., 1985–88; *Appendice*, 1 vol., 1990; *I titoli e i personaggi*, 3 vols., 1999.

Substantial, scholarly Italian encyclopedia published serially in three parts. *Il lessico* includes articles on musical subjects, terms, and concepts. *Le biografie* covers composers, singers, conductors, instrumentalists, writers on music, etc. The titles and characters series (*I titoli e i personaggi*) is the most recent. Sometimes called *DEUMM*. Some signed articles (except for *I titoli e i personaggi*) by an international group of scholars. Good works lists, good bibliography, excellent illustrations (many in color). Part three, with its focus on characters (historical, mythological, Biblical, etc.) and titles of staged music, is unique among the encyclopedias listed here. The coverage of characters and their treatment in staged music is not available in *Grove Opera*. Particularly good coverage of Italian music and musicians. *Il lessico* reviewed by Hans Lenneberg in *Notes* 42, no. 3 (Mar. 1986): 538–40. *Le biografie* reviewed by Lenneberg in *Notes* 45, no. 1 (Sept. 1988): 72–74 and *Notes* 46, no. 1 (Sept. 1989): 83–84. *I titoli e i personaggi* reviewed by Martina Rommel in *Reference Reviews Europe Annual* 6 (2000): 161.

Spanish

*2.11   Casares Rodicio, Emilio, José López-Calo, and Ismael Fernández de la Cuesta. *Diccionario de la música española e hispanoamericana*. 10 vols. Madrid: Sociedad General de Autores y Editores (SGAE), 1999–2002.

Published by the Spanish Society of Authors, Composers and Publishers, this ten-volume set (sometimes called *DMEH*) includes about 24,000 entries in Spanish on Spanish and Latin American music. Over 700 contributors from Spanish-speaking countries. Includes all genres of music from the geographic areas covered. Asserts that 80 percent of the entries are unique. Articles are signed and include bibliographies (some excellent), works lists and editions, and musical writings by the subjects. Each volume includes a guide to use in English. Includes black-and-white illustrations, many of them small and of poor quality. Reviewed by Martina Rommel in *Reference Reviews Europe Annual* 7 (2001): 146.

SINGLE-VOLUME GENERAL MUSIC ENCYCLOPEDIAS AND DICTIONARIES

The two single-volume tools included here were both written by a group of scholars. Others are available that were written entirely or primarily by one person. The advantage of the latter approach is a consistency of value judgments and style difficult to achieve otherwise. What is lacking, however, are the opinions of subject experts. "One-person" dictionaries to consider include Michael Kennedy's *Oxford Dictionary of Music*, 2nd ed. (2006) and Don Randel's *The Harvard Concise Dictionary of Music and Musicians* (1999).

*2.12   Latham, Alison. *The Oxford Companion to Music*. Oxford: Oxford University Press, 2002. Also available online from *Oxford Music Online*. http://www.oxfordmusiconline.com.

This title succeeds Percy Scholes's one-volume *The Oxford Companion to Music* from 1938 and Denis Arnold's two-volume *The New Oxford Companion to Music* from 1983. Focus is on Western classical music. Popular and non-Western music coverage is greatly reduced from the earlier two-volume *Companion*. It is one of the best places to find named compositions and their composers. No works lists. Bibliographies are brief and selective; many articles lack them completely. More current than the *Norton/Grove Concise*. Reviewed by David Schulenberg in *Music and Letters* 84, no. 4 (Nov. 2003): 644–46.

2.13   Sadie, Stanley, and Alison Latham. *The Norton/Grove Concise Encyclopedia of Music*. Rev. ed. New York: W. W. Norton, 1994.

A one-volume work written for a broad audience. Has a British bias, like *The Oxford Companion*. Also published in London under the title *The Grove Concise Dictionary of Music*. There are no bibliographies, and the entries are brief and unsigned. Selective, classified works lists are included for major composers. Includes performers, terms, conductors, titles (including nicknames), etc. Non-Western music is also included. Biographies comprise about 60 percent of the entries. Some illustrations. First edition reviewed by Michael Kennedy in *Music and Letters* 70, no. 4 (Nov. 1989): 517–18 and Geraldine Ostrove in *Notes* 47, no. 3 (Mar. 1991): 796–97.

EVALUATION CHECKLIST

The following checklist has been adapted in part from Hunter and others.[6]

- Are the articles/entries signed?
- Are bibliographies and/or discographies included?
  - Are they extensive?
  - Are they current?
  - What additional content is present?
  - Are there illustrations?
  - Are musical examples provided?
- Are the authors experts on their topics, large in number, international, etc.?
- Who edited the work: a single editor, a small group of editors, an international editorial board with a chief editor?
- Is the format print and/or online?
- What is the source of information: new research or a previous edition?
- Does the title have a long history with multiple editions?

---

[6]David Hunter and others, "Music Library Association Guidelines for the Preparation of Music Reference Works," *Notes* 50, no. 4 (June 1994): 1329–38.

- What is the work's scope?
- Regarding the works lists:
  - Are they complete or selective?
  - Do they include dates (composition, premiere, publication)?
  - Do they include opus numbers, thematic catalog numbers, keys, etc.?
  - Do they list location of works in major published editions?
- Are cross-references and index present?

SUGGESTED READINGS

The goals and processes of music lexicography are discussed by the editors of *NG2* and *MGG*. The three decades between these writings point out differences between the two generations of dictionaries. The chapter by Lenneberg discusses issues related to bias in music encyclopedias. The *NG2* article by Coover and Franklin includes the listing of music encyclopedias and dictionaries mentioned previously.

Blume, Friedrich. *"Die Musik in Geschichte und Gegenwart*: A Postlude." *Notes* 24, no. 2 (Dec. 1967): 217–44.

Lenneberg, Hans. "Collective Biography and National Pride." Chap. 5 in *Witnesses and Scholars: Studies in Musical Biography.* New York: Gordon and Breach, 1988.

Sadie, Stanley, ed. *The New Grove Dictionary of Music and Musicians.* 2nd ed. New York: Grove, 2001. S.v. "Dictionaries and Encyclopedias of Music," by James Coover and John Franklin. Also available from *Grove Music Online.* http://www.grovemusiconline.com.

———. *"The New Grove*, Second Edition." *Notes* 57, no. 1 (Sept. 2000): 11–20.

CHAPTER 3

Special Music Encyclopedias
and Dictionaries

Special encyclopedias and dictionaries limit their content to a particular musical topic rather than attempting comprehensive coverage. They range in length from a single volume to several. Because of their narrow focus coverage is usually more detailed than the comprehensive titles discussed in Chapter 2, and they often include information not available in the general dictionaries. For example, you should look up an opera in *Grove Opera*, rather than in *NG2*, for more detailed information. The range of topics to which special encyclopedias may be devoted is very broad, and publication of these tools is much more frequent than with the comprehensive dictionaries. Likewise, updated editions appear more frequently.

The general criteria for critical evaluation discussed in the previous chapter apply to special encyclopedias as well. And there are also a few additional considerations. Special dictionaries are more likely to be compiled hurriedly to meet current interest and market appeal, especially for popular music topics. Haste breeds error. Be sure to continue looking for the normal critical apparatus and objectivity (bibliographies, discographies, etc.). Special encyclopedias are more likely to be one-person projects. In these cases, consider the editor's qualifications for writing on the subject. Is he or she a scholar or a journalist, for example? What is the source of the information? Is it based on research, or was it obtained from questionnaires sent to musicians? Is the topic covered completely, or are some aspects excluded? Are the editor's criteria for inclusion clearly presented in the introduction?

The Library of Congress call number for topical dictionaries is ML102, with the first **cutter** for the topic. For example, opera dictionaries have the call number ML102 .O6. Look for most biographical dictionaries under ML105–107. Dictionaries of terms are given the call numbers ML108–109. The Library of Congress subject headings also vary by subtopic. The subject headings include "Dictionaries" for those tools with short entries and "Encyclopedias" for those with longer articles. Biographical dictionaries are cataloged with the subject heading "Music—Bio-bibliography—Dictionaries." Other examples include "Musical Instruments—Dictionaries," "Jazz—Encyclopedias," and simply "Music—Dictionaries."

The following types of special encyclopedias are included: biographical, jazz and popular music, instruments, musical terms and works, opera and musical theater, and miscellaneous. The following listing is highly selective; to find others, use the appropriate subject headings and call numbers for your library. The asterisks indicate the most highly recommended title(s) in each category.

BIOGRAPHICAL ENCYCLOPEDIAS AND DICTIONARIES

The following are *general* biographical dictionaries. Some include only composers or only certain groups of people, for example, women. Those limited by a subject are listed later with the relevant topical dictionaries and encyclopedias. Of course, the comprehensive encyclopedias are also excellent sources of biographical information. Keep in mind with biographical dictionaries that some are compiled from questionnaires sent to living musicians. These have the advantage of being from the musician while simultaneously possibly compromising objectivity and accuracy.

General Biographical Encyclopedias and Dictionaries

3.1   Eitner, Robert. *Biographisch-Bibliographisches Quellen-Lexikon der Musiker und Musikgelehrten der christlichen Zeitrechnung bis zur Mitte des neunzehnten Jahrhunderts.* 10 vols. Leipzig, Ger.: Breitkopf and Härtel, 1898–1904. Reprint, New York: Musurgia, 1947.

A monument of music lexicography. As a bibliography of source materials, this work by Eitner has been largely superceded by RISM. Despite its age, it is still useful as a biographical tool, especially for composers born before 1771. Also valuable for its lists of works. Reviewed by Michel Brenet in *La Revue musicale* (1905): 480–89.

*3.2   Elster, Robert. *International Who's Who in Classical Music.* London: Europa Publications, 2002–.

This annual publication includes only living musicians. It is international in scope but has a British bias. No criteria for inclusion are stated. With over 8,000 entries, it includes many musicians not found elsewhere. Older editions (some under different titles and issued by different publishers) useful for names dropped from recent ones. Information is obtained via questionnaires from the individuals included. As a result, the information is only as complete and accurate as the respondent wants it to be. Entries include: education, career highlights, publications, awards, dates, and contact information (including e-mail addresses for some). See also the companion *International Who's Who in Popular Music.* The 20th ed. (2004) was reviewed by Denby Richards in *Musical Opinion* 127, no. 1441 (July–Aug. 2004): 69.

3.3   Gurlitt, Wilibald. *Riemann Musik Lexikon. Personenteil.* 12th ed. 4 vols. Mainz, Ger.: Schott, 1959–1975.

The first two volumes were published in 1959 and 1961. The third volume is the *Sachteil*, edited by Hans Eggebrecht; it is not discussed here. The two *Ergänzungsbänden* were published in 1972 and 1975, edited by Carl Dahlhaus. The supplement volumes add new information as well as corrections and updates. Very good for German and European names, including many not found elsewhere. Reviewed by Denis Arnold in *Music and Letters* 58, no. 3 (July 1977): 345–46.

3.4   Jacques Cattell Press. *ASCAP Biographical Dictionary.* 4th ed. New York: R. R. Bowker, 1980.
       Compiled for the American Society of Composers, Authors, and Publishers. No more editions have appeared. Includes over 8,000 entries for the membership of the time as well as all the publisher members (7,000). Brief biographies and major published works are included. Useful for names not included elsewhere. Reviewed by Alan Hoffman in *Notes* 39, no. 1 (Sept. 1982): 103–4.

3.5   Kutsch, Karl-Josef, Leo Riemens, and Hansjörg Rost. *Grosses Sängerlexikon.* 4th ed. 7 vols. Munich: K. G. Saur, 2003.
       Standard biographical source for singers. About 18,750 singers are included, from the end of the sixteenth century forward. Unsigned entries include dates, voice type, career summary, and repertoire. Some include bibliographies and discographies. Third ed. reviewed by Vivian Liff in *Opera* 50, no. 11 (Nov. 1999): 1373–74.

3.6   Morton, Brian, and Pamela Collins. *Contemporary Composers.* Chicago: St. James Press, 1992.
       Provides complete works lists and brief biographical information for 500 composers active in the early 1990s. Intended to be a guide for listeners, the signed articles include information obtained from the composers, their publishers, or agents. Short bibliographies and discographies are included. Indicates the composers' publishers. Includes many obscure composers. Reviewed by Arnold Whittall in *Music and Letters* 74, no. 2 (May 1993): 312–14.

3.7   Randel, Don Michael. *The Harvard Biographical Dictionary of Music.* Cambridge, MA: Belknap Press of Harvard University Press, 1996. Available online from CredoReference at http://corp.credoreference.com.
       Companion to the *Harvard Dictionary of Music.* Includes around 5,500 musicians, with an American bias. Focuses on the twentieth century. Emphasis is on classical music; includes mostly composers and some performers of historical importance. Covers some jazz and popular musicians. Most entries are short, and all are unsigned, with selected works lists and bibliographies. Written by 20 or so authors, many former or current students at Cornell. No criteria for inclusion is given. There are problems with editing and currency. Some photos are included. Reviewed by Christopher Hatch in *Opera Quarterly* 14, no. 1 (Autumn 1997): 137–41; Wilfrid Mellers in *Times Literary Supplement (London)* 1 Nov. 1996; and Robert Stevenson in *Inter-American Music Review* 16, no. 2 (Spring–Summer 2000): 114–16.

*3.8   Slonimsky, Nicolas, and Laura Kuhn. *Baker's Biographical Dictionary of Musicians.* Centennial ed. [9th ed.]. 6 vols. New York: Schirmer Books, 2001. Available online from Alexander Street Press at http://www.alexanderstreet.com or from Gale at http://gale.cengage.com.

With over 15,000 names, *Baker's* is the best English-language biographical dictionary of musicians. Though it focuses on composers and performers, musicologists, theorists, critics, impresarios, etc., are also included. International coverage for not only classical musicians, but also major pop and jazz musicians. Expanded greatly since previous edition (1992). In addition to new entries (2,000 new pop and jazz and 1,000 new classical), some articles have been revised. All of the entries are signed. Created by over 60 contributors and 4 editors. Complete classified works lists included for major composers. Not all entries have works lists. Bibliographies are included, but most are very short. Works lists and bibliographies are in paragraph format. A selective discography is given for jazz and pop musicians. Includes many names not found elsewhere. Has three indexes: by genre, by nationality, and by name of women included (without volume and page number references). Edited for many years by Nicolas Slonimsky; now edited by Laura Kuhn. Additional editors are Dennis McIntire (classical), Lewis Porter (jazz), and William Ruhlmann (pop). Reviewed by Bonna Boettcher in *Notes* 58, no. 3 (Mar. 2002): 544–47 and Paula Elliot in *Music Reference Services Quarterly* 8, no. 2 (2002): 89–91.

3.9 Slonimsky, Nicolas, Laura Kuhn, and Dennis McIntire. *Baker's Biographical Dictionary of Twentieth-Century Classical Musicians.* New York: Schirmer Books, 1997.
Includes 500 new entries from the 8th edition of *Baker's*; some of these musicians are not in the Centennial Edition of *Baker's*. Some of the articles carried over from *Baker's* 8th edition were significantly expanded. Entries are brief and unsigned. A few nonclassical musicians are included, for example, Frank Zappa. Complete works lists are included in most cases (classified by genre), bibliographies, and writings by the musician. Reviewed by Richard Burbank in *Notes* 54, no. 3 (Mar. 1998): 705–7.

Encyclopedias and Dictionaries of Women Musicians

3.10 Burns, Kristine. *Women and Music in America Since 1900: An Encyclopedia.* 2 vols. Westport, CT: Greenwood, 2002.
One of the few women's encyclopedias that includes musicians other than composers, for example, music educators. For that reason it is worth consulting. Around 260 biographies are included. Articles are signed by 200 or so contributors; not all are specialists on their topics. Some photos. All include brief bibliographies (usually 1–2 sources), but many are just citations to other encyclopedia articles. There are no works lists for composers (even major ones). Not strictly a biographical dictionary; topical entries are also included. Includes indexes. Reviewed by Margaret D. Ericson in *Notes* 60, no. 3 (Mar. 2004): 703–6.

3.11 Cohen, Aaron I. *International Encyclopedia of Women Composers.* 2nd ed. 2 vols. New York: Books and Music, 1987.
This one-person work includes brief biographical sketches and detailed works lists for over 6,000 women composers from all countries and eras. Many more women included than in *The Norton/Grove Dictionary of Women Composers*; it

remains useful because of its broad scope. Includes a lengthy numbered bibliography in volume 2; individual entries refer to these numerical sources. Fourteen appendices and an extended discography at the end give access to special aspects of the composers. Has problems with editing and accuracy. Reviewed by Judy Tsou in *Notes* 46, no. 3 (Mar. 1990): 633–35.

*3.12 Sadie, Julie Anne, and Rhian Samuel. *The Norton/Grove Dictionary of Women Composers*. New York: W. W. Norton, 1995.
The most recent and smallest special-subject spin-off from *Grove*, The many new entries not found in previous *Grove* dictionaries have been added to *GMO*. Signed articles give brief biographical sketches, works lists (often complete), and bibliographies for about 900 women composers from the Western tradition, covering those born up to around 1955. All entries are relatively short. Includes some illustrations, mostly photos. Written by over 300 international scholars, but an Anglo/British bias is noticeable. Cross-referenced for problems of maiden name versus married name. Includes a chronology of women composers (from Sappho in the seventh century B.C.E. to the premiere of Judith Weir's opera, *Blond Eckbert*, in 1994), and a name/term index. Reviewed by Liane Curtis in *Journal of Musicological Research* 20, no. 3 (2001): 254–60 and Catherine Parsons Smith in *Women and Music* 1 (1997): 79–84.

Encyclopedias and Dictionaries of Black Musicians

*3.13 Floyd, Samuel A., Jr. *International Dictionary of Black Composers*. 2 vols. Chicago: Fitzroy Dearborn, 1999. Available online from Alexander Street Press at http://alexanderstreet.com.
Floyd is Director Emeritus of the Center for Black Music Research at Columbia College. Compiled with an editorial board and advisory committee. Written by around 100 scholars. Living composers and relatives of deceased ones were contacted for information. Includes black composers from North and South America, Europe, and Africa, but entries are primarily for Americans. Both art and popular music composers are included, although 87 of the 185 entries are for art music composers. Signed articles, works lists, bibliographies and discographies, location of archives, many photos. Major entries are fairly long. No index. Reviewed by Gerard Béhague in *Latin American Music Review/Revista de Música Latinoamericana* 21, no. 2 (Fall–Winter 2000): 250–53.

Encyclopedias and Dictionaries of American Musicians

3.14 Jacques Cattell Press. *Who's Who in American Music: Classical*. 2nd ed. New York: R. R. Bowker, 1985.
Includes nearly 7,000 musicians and music educators working in America at the time it was compiled. Includes many names not found elsewhere. Data for most entries came from questionnaires. Dates and places of birth and study are often omitted. Career information, teaching posts, publications, awards, and the entree's address at the time are included. Geographical and professional indexes at the end.

Problems with editing are evident. Intended to be biennial, but no new editions appeared. Reviewed by George R. Hill in *Notes* 41, no. 3 (Mar. 1985): 518–19.

Encyclopedias and Dictionaries of Canadian Musicians

3.15 MacMillan, Keith, and John Beckwith. *Contemporary Canadian Composers.* Toronto: Oxford University Press, 1975.
Includes about 150 composers active from 1920 until the period of compilation. Almost exclusively art music composers. Most of the articles are unsigned. They include works lists, recordings, and bibliographies. Some have photos. Sponsored by the Canadian Music Centre. Contributors include Canadian composers and musicologists. Reviewed by Carl Morey in *University of Toronto Quarterly* 45, no. 4 (Summer 1976): 429–32. French edition, *Compositeurs canadiens contemporains,* edited by Louise Laplante (Montreal: Université du Québec, 1977), reviewed by Kathleen Toomey in *Notes* 35, no. 1 (Sept. 1978): 86.

DICTIONARIES OF MUSICAL TERMS

3.16 Boccagna, David. *Musical Terminology: A Practical Compendium in Four Languages.* Stuyvesant, NY: Pendragon, 1999.
Provides around 575 equivalent terms in English, French, Italian, and German. Arranged in four sections, one for each language. Includes no definitions. Intended primarily to aid the performer and conductor with terms found in scores. Reviewed by Larry Lobel in *ARBA* 31 (2000): 505–6.

3.17 Eggebrecht, Hans. *Handwörterbuch der musikalischen Terminologie.* Stuttgart, Ger.: F. Steiner, 1972–.
An ongoing project published in loose-leaf serial format. Very thorough, including history and etymology for terms and term families. Provides examples of the words as used in music literature. Each addition updates the index. Now edited by Albrecht Riethmüller. Reviewed by John Caldwell in *Music and Letters* 71, no. 4 (Nov. 1990): 524.

3.18 Ely, Mark, and Amy Rashkin. *Dictionary of Music Education: A Handbook of Terminology.* Chicago: GIA, 2005.
Primarily terms, although some persons (music educators, psychologists, etc.) are included as well. The unsigned entries are short and without bibliographies. Includes terms from psychology, general education, and music, which may not be necessary (for example, "depression," "kindergarten," and "timbre"). This is the first of its kind, and it does bring together a great deal of information potentially useful for the music educator. Includes cross-references but no index. Reviewed by Martin D. Jenkins in *Music Reference Service Quarterly* 9, no. 3 (2005): 43–45.

3.19 Holmes, Thom. *The Routledge Guide to Music Technology.* New York: Routledge, 2006.
Most up-to-date technology dictionary available. Includes digital audio production and distribution. Entries are brief, and some biographies are included. Has a timeline, bibliography, and indexes.

3.20 Kaufmann, Walter. *Selected Musical Terms of Non-Western Cultures: A Notebook-Glossary*. Warren, MI: Harmonie Park Press, 1990.

Includes terms about music and dance from Asia, Africa, and Oceania. Mostly terms used by performers are defined, as are musical instruments. Definitions are short, but many refer to a lengthy bibliography in the back that includes over 320 sources. Best for terms dealing with the art music cultures of India and China, Kaufmann's areas of expertise. Reviewed by Carl Rahkonen in *Notes* 48, no. 1 (Sept. 1991): 127–28 and R. Anderson Sutton in *Ethnomusicology* 35, no. 3 (Fall 1991): 426–28.

3.21 Latham, Alison. *Oxford Dictionary of Musical Terms*. Oxford: Oxford University Press, 2004.

The most recent pocket-sized dictionary of around 2,500 musical terms for a broad audience. Many entries were drawn from *The Oxford Companion to Music* (entry 2.12), edited by Latham. Includes some musical examples. Easy to read. Reviewed by Christopher Wintle in *Music and Letters* 87, no. 2 (May 2006): 298–300.

3.22 Leuchtmann, Horst. *Terminorum Musicae Index Septem Linguis Redactus*. Budapest, Hungary: Akadémiai Kiadó, 1978.

Like Boccagna, earlier, but includes approximately 7,000 term equivalents in seven languages (German, English, French, Italian, Spanish, Hungarian, and Russian) in one alphabetical list. Includes definitions when no equivalent exists. Sponsored in part by the International Musicological Society. Introductory material is in German. Reviewed by Michael Ochs in *Notes* 35, no. 3 (Mar. 1979): 619–20.

*3.23 Randel, Don Michael. *The Harvard Dictionary of Music*. 4th ed. Cambridge, MA: Belknap Press of Harvard University Press, 2003. Available online from Credo Reference at http://corp.credoreference.com.

Standard, well-respected English-language dictionary for musical terms. Previous editions published in 1944, 1969 (both edited by Willi Apel), and 1986. The last, titled *The New Harvard Dictionary of Music*, was also edited by Randel. Previous editions remain useful for terms not carried over. Some articles are unchanged from 1986. Expanded coverage of non-Western music, popular styles, and musical instruments, although the focus remains Western art music. Randel was assisted by a 9-member editorial board and over 110 contributors, primarily American. Longer articles are signed and include bibliographies (many detailed). Unfortunately, some of the detailed articles related to research, for example, "Dictionaries and Encyclopedias" and "Periodicals," no longer include the lists of titles present in the previous edition. Reviewed by Joseph Szydlowski in *Notes* 61, no. 3 (Mar. 2005): 741–43 and Hugh Wood in *Times Higher Education Supplement (London)* 14 May 2004.

3.24 White, Glenn, and Gary J. Louie. *The Audio Dictionary*, 3rd ed. Seattle: University of Washington Press, 2005.

Includes terminology for recording, sound reinforcement, and musical acoustics as well as some longer entries. Provides brief definitions, and illustrated with line drawings. Includes several appendixes and a bibliography. Reviewed by J. M. King in *Choice* 43, no. 4 (Dec. 2005): 636.

ENCYCLOPEDIAS AND DICTIONARIES
OF MUSICAL INSTRUMENTS

The titles listed next are limited to encyclopedias and dictionaries. Purely pictorial works, exhibition catalogs, and the like have been omitted here. Although they are not reference works, per se, they are often good sources for high-quality images of musical instruments. One example is Anthony Baines's *European and American Musical Instruments* (London: Viking, 1966). For pictorial works on musical instruments, see Chapter 12 (entries 12.10–12.17).

General Instrument Encyclopedias and Dictionaries

3.25 Baines, Anthony. *The Oxford Companion to Musical Instruments*. Oxford: Oxford University Press, 1992.
    Newer than *Grove Instruments*, but a spin-off of the *New Oxford Companion to Music* (1983). Many articles have been recycled, but some have been newly written or revised by Baines and 14 contributors. Includes both Western and non-Western instruments. Most entries are brief, all are unsigned. Some have short bibliographies. Good illustrations. Scholarly, but intended for nonprofessionals. Includes an appendix of instrument makers and a bibliography of works cited. Reviewed by Laurence Libin in *Music and Letters* 74, no. 4 (Nov. 1993): 565–66.

3.26 Marcuse, Sibyl. *Musical Instruments: A Comprehensive Dictionary*. Corrected ed. New York: W. W. Norton, 1975.
    Truly a dictionary, useful for finding definitions for instrument names in various languages and so on. Indebted to Sachs, next, but updates his work as well as translating it. Includes a bibliography of sources cited. No illustrations. Reviewed by Anthony Baines in *Musical Times* 118, no. 1610 (Apr. 1977): 302.

3.27 Sachs, Curt. *Real-lexikon der Musikinstrumente*. Hildesheim, Ger.: G. Olms, 1913. Reprint, Hildesheim, Ger.: G. Olms, 1962 and New York: Dover, 1964.
    A standard, although dated, dictionary of instruments. In fact, it was the first devoted exclusively to the topic. Sachs was a path-breaking scholar of musical instruments; he and Erich von Hornbostel created a classification system for instruments. Includes non-Western instruments as well as those from the earliest times. Includes line drawings and musical examples as well as a general bibliography and index of names. Reviewed by Guy Oldham in *Musical Times* 107, no. 1486 (Dec. 1966): 1064–65 and J. A. Westrup in *Music and Letters* 47, no. 3 (July 1966): 277–78.

*3.28 Sadie, Stanley. *The New Grove Dictionary of Musical Instruments*. 3 vols. London: Macmillan, 1984.
    The first of the *New Grove* (1980) spin-off dictionaries, this is the most scholarly and comprehensive encyclopedia of Western and non-Western instruments. Also includes articles on performance practice and instrument makers. The

Western-instrument articles are taken from the *New Grove* (1980), mostly with only updates of the bibliographies. About 10,000 entries on non-Western and folk instruments were newly written by around 400 contributors. Entries place instruments in the Hornbostel-Sachs instrument classification system. Quality of the illustrations is uneven. Reviewed by André Larson in *Journal of the American Musicological Society* 41, no. 2 (Summer 1988): 375–82 and William P. Malm in *Ethnomusicology* 30, no. 2 (Spring–Summer 1986): 337–39.

Encyclopedias and Dictionaries of Specific Instruments

3.29 *Encyclopedia of Keyboard Instruments*. 3 vols. New York: Routledge, 2003–2006. Contents: Vol. 1: *The Piano: An Encyclopedia*, 2nd ed. edited by Robert and Margaret Palmieri, 2003; Vol. 2: *The Harpsichord and Clavichord: An Encyclopedia*, edited by Igor Kipnis, 2007; Vol. 3: *The Organ: An Encyclopedia*, edited by Douglas Bush and Richard Kassel, 2006.
Scholarly, signed articles written by expert contributors. Includes entries for instrument makers, performers, and composers. Longer entries include bibliographies. Includes illustrations and an index. Vol. 1 reviewed by Holling Smith-Borne in *Music Reference Services Quarterly* 8, no. 2 (2002): 103–5. Vol. 3 reviewed by Timothy J. McGee in *Library Journal* 131, no. 2 (July 1, 2006): 111.

ENCYCLOPEDIAS AND DICTIONARIES OF OPERA AND MUSICAL THEATER

Opera and musical theater are areas of great popularity among musical amateurs. Here, too, be on the lookout for dictionaries intended for the opera lover rather than for the music researcher. One tool of this type with a long history is *The New Kobbé's Opera Book* by the Earl of Harewood and Anthony Peattie, 11th ed. (New York: Putnam's Sons, 1997). It is not truly a dictionary of opera, and it covers fewer operas than many titles listed next (around 500). Nevertheless, it provides more detailed plot synopses than can be found elsewhere.

Encyclopedias and Dictionaries of Opera

3.30 Bourne, Joyce, and Michael Kennedy. *Who's Who in Opera: A Guide to Opera Characters*. Oxford: Oxford University Press, 1998. Also available online from the *Oxford Reference Online Premium Collection* at http://www.oxfordreference.com. Includes over 2,500 characters from around 280 operas, operettas, and musicals. Includes 27 longer "special articles" by singers or scholars on specific roles they know well. (e.g., Martin Isepp, Janet Baker, Bryn Terfel, and Thomas Hampson). Not nearly as comprehensive or detailed as the *I titoli e i personaggi* section of *DEUMM* (entry 2.10). Reviewed by Christopher Hatch in *Opera Quarterly* 16, no. 3 (Summer 2000): 461–63.

3.31 Dahlhaus, Carl, and Sieghart Döhring. *Pipers Enzyklopädie des Musiktheaters: Oper, Operette, Musical, Ballett*. 7 vols. Munich: Piper, 1986–1997.

Not limited to Western art music, but biased toward German, French, Italian, and English operas. Signed articles include bibliographies and information on musical sources. About 100 authors contributed to each volume. Does not include discographies, but recordings are mentioned in some articles. Does not include entries on performers or librettists. Well-illustrated with many color plates. Last volume is an index. Vol. 1 reviewed by Ulrich Weisstein in *Cambridge Opera Journal* 1, no. 2 (July 1989): 195–201.

3.32 Holden, Amanda. *The New Penguin Opera Guide*. London: Penguin Books, 2001.

This is the successor to *The Viking Opera Guide* from 1993, and it is the most comprehensive book of its class. Has only entries on composers and operas (including musicals and other genres), about 2,500 of them. Written by over 120 contributors, with signed articles. Composer entries (around 850) include bibliographies, and those for operas suggest recordings. Very comprehensive coverage of composers who have written operas. Includes illustrations and indexes for librettists and titles. Reviewed by Rupert Christiansen in *Opera* 53, no. 3 (Mar. 2002): 359–60. Previous edition reviewed by David Littlejohn in *Notes* 51, no. 3 (Mar. 1995): 843–64.

3.33 LaRue, C. Steven. *International Dictionary of Opera*. 2 vols. Detroit, MI: St. James Press, 1993. Available online from Gale at http://gale.cengage.com.

Between *Grove Opera* and the one-volume dictionaries in scope, this title includes primarily persons connected with opera (200 composers, 300 singers, 60 conductors, directors, etc.) and 400 titles. About 1,100 signed entries by around 200 contributors (primarily North Americans). Includes plot summaries of major operas, but excludes operatic terms and concepts. Articles have bibliographies. Uneven in quality, but includes longer bios of singers, and entries include critical evaluation, often lacking in *Grove Opera*. Well illustrated, with many full-page black-and-white plates. Includes indexes. Reviewed by William Albright in *Opera Quarterly* 10, no. 4 (1994): 95–98, David Littlejohn in *Notes* 51, no. 3 (Mar. 1995): 843–64, and Leslie Troutman in *RQ* 33, no. 2 (Winter 1993): 288–89.

*3.34 Sadie, Stanley. *The New Grove Dictionary of Opera*. 4 vols. New York: Macmillan, 1992. Available online from *Oxford Music Online* at http://www.oxfordmusiconline.com.

The most comprehensive and scholarly English-language dictionary of opera. Some of the approximately 10,000 articles are based on entries in *The New Grove Dictionary* (1980), but they are predominantly new. Entries include biographical sketches of composers (around 2,900), librettists (about 500), singers (around 2,500), conductors, directors, and others concerned with opera; histories and descriptions of opera houses, companies, and organizations; plot summaries for important operas; terms and concepts related to opera; and significant characters. The articles on individual operas (around 2,000) are especially useful. Includes bibliographies but no discographies. Excludes non-Western opera. Includes black-and-white illustrations. The appendixes include: (A) role names in various operas and (B) incipits of arias, ensembles, etc., in various operas. Full text is available and searchable on *Grove Music Online*. See Figure 2-4 for an example of the icon used to identify articles from *Grove Opera*. Some articles have been updated on *Grove Music Online*. Sadie's one-volume work based on *Grove Opera*, *The Grove Book of Operas*, 2nd ed., includes only opera entries (Oxford: Oxford University Press, 2006). Reviewed by Robert Craft in *Times Literary Supplement (London)* 23 Apr. 1993; Paul Griffiths in *New Yorker* 69, no. 3 (8 Mar. 1993): 108–10; David Littlejohn in *Notes* 51, no. 3 (Mar. 1995): 843–64; and Charles Rosen in *New York Review of Books* 40, no. 8 (22 Apr. 1993): 10–15.

3.35 Warrack, John, and Ewan West. *The Oxford Dictionary of Opera*. Oxford: Oxford University Press, 1992.

One of the most scholarly one-volume opera dictionaries. The approximately 4,500 entries are unsigned, but some include bibliographies and selected works lists. British bias. Good for concise definitions of opera-related terms. Includes around 750 composers, 900 singers, 600 operas, and 85 characters. No illustrations or index. Needs updating. *The Concise Oxford Dictionary of Opera* is available online from the *Oxford Reference Online Premium Collection* at http://www.oxfordreference.com. Reviewed by Julian Budden in *Music and Letters* 74, no. 4 (Nov. 1993): 579–81; Christopher Hatch in *Opera Quarterly* 10, no. 3 (1994): 157–60; and David Littlejohn in *Notes* 51, no. 3 (Mar. 1995): 843–64.

Encyclopedias and Dictionaries of Musical Theater

*3.36 Gänzl, Kurt. *The Encyclopedia of the Musical Theatre*. 2nd ed. 3 vols. New York: Schirmer Books, 2001.

Gänzl's intent was to include articles on around 3,000 important international musicals. Entries for shows include a list of important performances and recordings. Those for performers include a list of musicals. Those for composers, lyricists, and librettists include a list of shows and a brief bibliography. Includes some color illustrations. Coverage expanded from first edition to include more musicals outside of London and New York City. Includes about 4,500 entries. Reviewed by Samantha Gust in *Reference and User Services Quarterly* 41, no. 3 (Spring 2002): 292 and D. Aviva Rothschild in *ARBA* 33 (2002): 562–63.

ENCYCLOPEDIAS AND DICTIONARIES OF PERFORMANCE PRACTICE

3.37 Jackson, Roland. *Performance Practice: A Dictionary-Guide for Musicians*. New York: Routledge, 2005.

This unique dictionary includes entries for musical terms, composers, genres, and instruments from all style periods. Jackson is an expert in performance practice. Most entries include brief bibliographies. Generous musical examples. Includes black-and-white illustrations of varying quality. Includes a listing of "theorists and early writers" at the beginning, with a bibliography of their writings as well as an index. Reviewed by K. D. Underwood in *Choice* 43, no. 4 (Dec. 2005): 631.

ENCYCLOPEDIAS AND DICTIONARIES OF JAZZ, ROCK, AND POPULAR MUSIC

If you are researching a popular music or jazz topic, do not forget to consult the general encyclopedias and dictionaries discussed in Chapter 2. *The Garland Encyclopedia of World Music* (entry 2.4), in particular, includes popular music. Many popular music dictionaries are intended for general readers; keep that in mind as you consult these and other titles.

Encyclopedias and Dictionaries of Jazz

3.38 Feather, Leonard, and Ira Gitler. *The Biographical Encyclopedia of Jazz.* Oxford: Oxford University Press, 1999.
Updated, revised, and expanded edition of Feather's earlier jazz encyclopedias. Entries are brief, but include discographies, film appearances, videos, etc. Feather died during the work on this volume and it was finished by Gitler. Includes around 3,300 international jazz biographies for those active from the 1920s on. Includes discographies of recordings on CD. Reviewed by Jack Sohmer in *JazzTimes* 30, no. 3 (Apr. 2000): 70, 157.

*3.39 Kernfeld, Barry. *The New Grove Dictionary of Jazz*, 2nd ed. 3 vols. New York: Grove, 2002. Available online from *Oxford Music Online* at http://www.oxford musiconline.com.
Most scholarly and comprehensive encyclopedia on jazz. Revision and expansion of the first edition from 1988; includes around 7,750 entries by over 300 contributors. Includes over 2,000 additional biographies and other new topics, such as hip-hop, reggae, and acid jazz. Articles are signed, except for the very short ones. Includes bibliographies, discographies, and filmographies. New resources include the incorporation of web sources in the bibliographies and a comprehensive calendar of jazz births and deaths (in Appendix 2). Full text is available and searchable on *Grove Music Online*. See Figure 2-4 for an example of the icon used to identify articles from *Grove Jazz*. Some articles have been updated on *Grove Music Online*. Reviewed by Gordon Theil in *Notes* 59, no. 1 (Sept. 2002): 45–48.

Encyclopedias and Dictionaries of Rock and Popular Music

3.40 Clarke, Donald. *MusicWeb Encyclopaedia of Popular Music.* London: MusicWeb-International, 2001–. http://www.musicweb-international.com/encyclopaedia.
The print editions (1989 and 1998) of this dictionary were titled *The Penguin Encyclopedia of Popular Music.* This online version includes the articles from both print editions as well as some additions and updates. Clarke includes some topical entries, but the approximately 4,000 entries are primarily biographies of persons and groups. Clarke and his contributors sometimes include excerpts from reviews in the unsigned entries. Very broad coverage. Available free of charge to individuals. First print edition reviewed by Stephen Barnard in *Popular Music* 11, no. 1 (Jan. 1992): 111–15 and Amanda Maple in *Fontes artis musicae* 40, no. 1 (Jan.–Mar. 1993): 64–65.

3.41 *Contemporary Musicians: Profiles of the People in Music.* Detroit, MI: Gale
     Research, 1989–. Also available online from Gale at http://gale.cengage.com.
     Published serially; editors vary. So far around 60 volumes have been issued,
     containing a total of about 3,500 biographies. Eclectic in choice of subjects (vol-
     ume 48 includes both Frederica von Stade and "Weird" Al Yankovic), but recent
     volumes have included more popular musicians than classical. Signed articles,
     usually two to three pages long. Some include photos. Includes bibliographies,
     discographies, and contact information. Each includes a "For the Record" box
     with a brief biographical and career summary. Each volume includes a cumula-
     tive index. Vols. 21–24 reviewed by B. Lee Cooper in *Popular Music and Society*
     24 (Spring 2000): 122–24.

3.42 Elster, Robert. *International Who's Who in Popular Music.* London: Europa
     Publications, 2002–.
     Similar to its classical counterpart. Includes around 5,000 entries for pop, rock,
     folk, jazz, world, and country musicians. In addition to the bios and career sum-
     maries, includes information on artists' representatives and other contact infor-
     mation. The 6th ed. (2004) reviewed by Denby Richards in *Musical Opinion* 127,
     no. 1441 (July–Aug. 2004): 69.

3.43 Gammond, Peter. *The Oxford Companion to Popular Music.* Oxford: Oxford
     University Press, 1991.
     An alphabetical listing covering a wide range of "popular" musics, from operetta
     and popular song to jazz and rock. Covers both performers and terms. British
     bias, and best on the first half of the twentieth century. Includes song titles, for
     example, "Home Sweet Home." Indexes of "People and Groups," "Shows and
     Films," and "Songs and Albums" at the end provide detailed access. Entries are
     generally short and limited to basic facts. Short bibliographies, works lists, and
     so on are included with some entries. Reviewed by Stephen Barnard in *Popular
     Music* 11, no. 1 (Jan. 1992): 111–15 and Amanda Maple in *Fontes artis musicae*
     41, no. 1 (Jan.–Mar. 1993): 64–65.

3.44 Hardy, Phil. *The Faber Companion to 20th-century Popular Music.* Rev. ed.
     London: Faber and Faber, 2001. Available online from Credo Reference at
     http://corp.credoreference.com.
     Hardy's one-volume guide has been titled both *Da Capo* and *Faber*, since it was
     first published in 1990. Unlike the MusicWeb and Oxford volumes, Hardy's is
     limited strictly to people and groups, over 2,500 of them. Especially good for
     rock and the later half of the century. The 1990 edition reviewed by Stephen
     Barnard in *Popular Music* 11, no. 1 (Jan. 1992): 111–15 and Harry Shapiro in
     Times Literary Supplement (London) 18 Jan. 1991.

*3.45 Larkin, Colin. *The Encyclopedia of Popular Music.* 4th ed. 10 vols. New York:
     Muze; Oxford: Oxford University Press, 2006. Available online from Oxford
     Music Online at http://www.oxfordmusiconline.com.
     The most comprehensive and scholarly encyclopedia devoted to popular music.
     Includes approximately 18,500 entries. Larkin defines popular music broadly,
     focusing on the period since 1900. International scope, with U.S. and U.K.
     bias. The articles are fairly detailed, although unsigned. No bibliographies,

but discographies are included. Albums are rated using a five-star system. Includes a general index and a song title index. Former editions titled: *Guinness Encyclopedia of Popular Music.* Spin-off volumes have been published, for example, *The Virgin Encyclopedia of Jazz.* Reviewed by Brian Doherty in *Choice* 44, no. 10 (June 2007): 1722.

3.46 Shepherd, John, David Horn, Dave Laing, and Paul Oliver. *The Continuum Encyclopedia of Popular Music of the World.* London: Continuum, 2003–. Contents: Part 1, 2 vols., 2003; Part 2, 5 vols., 2005; Part 3, 6 vols., 2008?; Part 4, 5 vols., 2009?; Part 5, 5 vols., 2011?

Projected to be a five-part set. International editorial board. Volumes 1–2 (Part 1) were published in 2003; they are titled "Media, Industry and Society" and "Performance and Production," respectively, Volumes 3–7 (Part 2) were published in 2005 and are devoted to popular music in various locations. Parts 3, pop genres, and 4–5, biographies, are being planned. Scholarly. Articles are signed. Devoted to twentieth-century recorded pop music. Detailed bibliographies and discographies are included. Each volume has an index. Minimal illustrations. Vols. 1–2 reviewed by Elizabeth Wells in the *ARSC Journal* 35, no. 2 (Fall 2004): 269–71. Vol. 2 reviewed by Helmi Järviluoma in *Popular Music* 23, no. 3 (Oct. 2004): 378–80. Vols. 3–7 reviewed by James E. Perone in *Library Journal* 130, no. 12 (July 2005): 118.

3.47 Wasserstein, Stephen. *Baker's Biographical Dictionary of Popular Musicians Since 1990.* 2 vols. New York: Schirmer Reference, 2004. Also available online from Gale at http://gale.cengage.com.

Devoted to the last decade of the twentieth century in the U.S. Includes around 575 original entries—about half are on pop and rock. Also included are country, R & B, hip-hop, and other styles. Includes some classical surprises (about 30 of them). Pierre Boulez is included, as are Philip Glass and James Galway. Only 24 contributors; many are writers for newspapers and magazines. Accurate but not scholarly. Intended for students and the general public. Articles are signed. Most include selective discographies; some include brief bibliographies. Some photos. Includes an index. Reviewed by Grove Koger in *Reference and User Services Quarterly* 43, no. 4 (Summer 2004): 340–41.

MISCELLANEOUS MUSIC ENCYCLOPEDIAS AND DICTIONARIES

Special encyclopedias have been written on a great many musical topics beyond those already listed. Here are a few more examples of what is available. Use the appropriate subject headings and call numbers to search for more on topics of interest to you.

3.48 Hoffmann, Frank, and Howard Ferstler. *Encyclopedia of Recorded Sound*, 2nd ed. 2 vols. New York: Routledge, 2005.

New edition of the work originally edited by Guy A. Marco and published by Garland Publishing in 1993. Has 3,000 entries on a wide variety of topics, including record labels, recording techniques, equipment, genres, terms, and formats. Biographical entries on inventors, sound engineers, and some performers are also included (selection criteria for performers are unclear). Six-member advisory board and over 60 international contributors. Some articles are signed. The article on related journals is outstanding. Includes illustrations, cross-references, and an index. Reviewed by Timothy C. Fabrizio in *ARSC Journal* 36, no. 1 (Spring 2005): 102–4.

3.49   Room, Adrian. *A Dictionary of Music Titles: The Origins of the Names and Titles of 3,500 Musical Compositions.* Jefferson, NC: McFarland, 2000.
Includes around 3,500 vocal and instrumental pieces with distinctive titles. Entries provide a translation for non-English titles and the composer, date, and so on. A description of the work and its background is provided; brief plots are given for operas. Includes a bibliography. Reviewed in *Booklist* 96, no. 21 (July 2000): 2056, 2058.

EVALUATION CHECKLIST

Evaluation of special encyclopedias and dictionaries is similar to general encyclopedias and dictionaries; see the checklist for Chapter 2.
Additional considerations:

- Is the scope clearly defined?
- Who is the intended audience?
- Is the work scholarly?

SUGGESTED READINGS

Two types of readings are suggested: general comments on music lexicography (Duckles and Randel) and accounts of specific dictionaries and their creation (Gänzl, Gitler, and Slonimsky).

Duckles, Vincent. "Some Observations on Music Lexicography." *College Music Symposium* 11 (1971): 115–22.
Gänzl, Kurt. Preface to the Second Edition of *The Encyclopedia of the Musical Theatre.* 2nd ed. 3 vols. New York: Schirmer Books, 2001.
Gitler, Ira. "The Making of a Jazz Encyclopedia." *JazzTimes* 29, no. 9 (Nov. 1999): 48–52.
Randel, Don Michael. "Defining Music." *Notes* 43, no. 4 (June 1987): 751–66.
Slonimsky, Nicolas. "Introduction: Lexicographis Secundus Post Herculem Labor." Introduction to *Baker's Dictionary of Music.* New York: Schirmer Books, 1997.

CHAPTER 4

Library Catalogs

You search your local college, university, or conservatory library catalog to find musical scores, sound recordings, books, and journals in that library's collection. Your local catalog will give you your library's call number for a title, show whether it is on course reserve, and indicate its availability. It may also provide information about the special or archival collections held by your institution, including finding aids and collection descriptions. Digitized copies of rare materials may be available through your library's homepage or **online catalog**.

In addition to providing bibliographic information about materials physically owned by your campus library, catalogs are gateways to a wealth of electronic information, including online reference tools, e-books, digital audio libraries, and online scores. You will need to search other library catalogs and databases as well when your local library does not have the item you need. This chapter provides tips on searching and gives examples of common types of library catalogs. The focus here is on published materials rather than on archival or manuscript materials.

Finding music materials in libraries is often more difficult than finding materials in many other subject areas. One of the most common ways to search a catalog is by title. Consider the lack of unique titles for much instrumental music. How many composers do you think have written a Symphony No. 1? Why isn't Beethoven's Third Symphony cataloged under the title *Eroica*? What about foreign-language titles in general? Do you need to search for Mozart's *The Magic Flute* by using the German title, *Zauberflöte*? In searching *Zauberflöte*, do you need to enter the umlaut?

Author searches are often not much better. Large music collections may include thousands of items in a wide variety of formats by a single major composer and high numbers of records for individual works. For example, even if you searched for Mozart's *The Magic Flute* using the title *Zauberflöte* (without the umlaut or the initial article), your local library catalog may include about a hundred entries with that title.

The next step may be to consider the format or type of item you are looking for. This, too, is not as simple as you might think at first. Scores of *Die Zauberflöte* include full scores and piano-vocal scores; recordings include CDs and LPs; and videos might be on DVD or VHS. Books on the opera may include analyses, historical context, or the libretto. Maybe you just want a score for an art song but need it in a particular key. What if your teacher wants you to find a certain edition? How would you find that aria arranged for woodwind quintet (with the parts)? If your library does not have what you need, how can you find another library that does own it?

These are a few of the challenges involved with searching for music. Do you know where to find all this information in the catalog records? How do you structure your search to find exactly what you want from the beginning? What is the next step if your library does not have the item you need? This chapter helps you master the basic skills needed to search for music materials effectively and efficiently in any catalog as well as identifying ways to find and search in other libraries' catalogs, consortium catalogs, or bibliographic utilities.

So far, you have probably been imagining a web-based online catalog, but not all libraries have online catalogs, or the online catalog may not include all of the library's holdings. The Library of Congress is a good example. Their holdings are listed in a combination of print and online catalogs that is so confusing to explain to researchers that the staff recommends you ask for help if you cannot find what you are looking for. Older libraries are more likely to have this type of situation. Sometimes a card catalog is only available onsite at a particular library. Others have been reproduced in book, microform, or CD-ROM format for distribution. Card catalogs offer an ease of use with only author, title, and subject access, but they offer much less in overall search capability.

Even within the world of online catalogs, not all are the same. A basic level of functionality can be expected from any library catalog software, called **integrated library software** by librarians. In terms of bells and whistles, however, there are differences that can significantly impact a music searcher.

To reiterate, there are a number of challenges related to searching music:

- The number of common/genre titles (symphony, sonata, quartet, etc.)
- The number of foreign-language titles
- The number of pieces known primarily by nicknames or programmatic titles (for example, *Moonlight Sonata*)
- The number of formats: books, scores, recordings, videos (various types of each)

An understanding of the following concepts will assist you in overcoming these challenges:

- Knowledge of **authority headings** for names, titles, and subjects (**controlled vocabulary** rather than **uncontrolled vocabulary**)
- Knowledge of the "limit" and "sort" functions in your catalog
- Knowledge of the different types of searches (word, subject, title, author) and when to use each
- Knowledge of what is included in the bibliographic records and what is included in each search index

These concepts are explored next using common search types for illustration.

AUTHOR SEARCHES

Use an "author" search for composers, performers (soloists and ensembles), arrangers, editors, transcribers, conductors, and so on as well as for book authors. If you can, it is often useful to search by the name of a conductor, performer, arranger, etc., rather than by the name of a prolific composer (for example, search for Hogwood, Christopher rather than for Bach, Beethoven, Mozart, etc.).

- Make sure you type in last name first.
- Spell the name correctly. Most library software is not sophisticated enough to forgive minor spelling errors, unlike Amazon.com, for example.
- Know the dates or approximate dates of your "author." This can help with common names like Richard Wagner.
- Search under the form of the name used in the catalog. Do you enter "Tchaikovsky" or "Chaikovski"? What about Josquin? Is his name indexed under "Josquin" or "Des Prez" or "Prez"?
- Use authority headings for names. These can be found via your catalog's cross-references, if present. Look for the arrows and the message asking to redirect your searches.

Examples:

Heseltine, Philip → Warlock, Peter

Chaikovsky → Tchaikovsky

TITLE SEARCHES

Library catalogs do not include citations for articles in journals and other serials. To find those you will need to use periodical indexes, which are covered in Chapter 5. The listing of the contents of many score and recording sets and anthologies may be absent entirely or may be inconsistently available in your catalog. The contents of music sets and series, for example, are found using the indexes described in Chapter 7.

- In title searches, word order matters, punctuation and diacritics generally do not. Enter searches *without* initial articles (for example, "a," "an," and "the").
- The titles present in cataloging or bibliographic records include not only the title on the item itself, but also the work's **uniform title**. Unless you know the exact title of the specific item for which you are searching, use the uniform title when searching musical works.
- The uniform title **collocates** all of the various manifestations of the piece(s), regardless of what is on the title page, CD notes, etc. Once I was helping a student who was looking for the Henle edition of the Bach *English Suites*. Her search on the title

"English Suites" had found fewer than ten hits, including only a couple of scores by American publishers. She was frustrated that we did not have the Henle. When we searched under the uniform title "Englische Suiten," more than double the entries were found, including the Henle edition, which, coincidentally, had the German title on the title page as well as being the uniform title in the catalog record. That is why the search using the English words did not retrieve the score.

- There are two types of uniform titles: distinctive and nondistinctive.
    - *Distinctive uniform titles*: Basically these are the original titles in the original languages. They are called distinctive because the titles are generally unique.

Examples:

> *Fidelio*
> *Die Zauberflöte*
> *Fanfare for the Common Man*

While this sounds simple enough, sometimes there are surprises. For example, most musicians would think the uniform title for Stravinsky's *The Rite of Spring* would be the French *Le Sacre du printemps*, although it is actually the Russian *Vesna sv'i'ashchenna'i'a* (without the diacritics).

- *Nondistinctive uniform titles:* Sometimes called "form" uniform titles, these begin with the form/genre title, with additional identifying elements in a structured format. These titles have less meaning unless associated with a composer's name.

Examples:

> Symphonies, no. 9, op. 125, D minor (Beethoven)
> Sonatas, flute, harpsichord, BWV 1032, A major (Bach)
> Concertos, violin, orchestra, K 219, D major (Mozart)

Nondistinctive uniform titles may be singular (if the composer wrote only one piece in the form) or plural (if she or he wrote more than one). Plural titles without a qualifier are used for all of the compositions in the genre.

- **Collective uniform titles:** A subset of nondistinctive uniform titles is the collective title. This type of uniform title is used for a collection of pieces published in one score or recording. Collections range in scope; examples include a recording with four string quartets by Mozart to his complete works. These uniform titles may include a form or instrumentation as well as the qualifier "Selections." Those for a composer's complete works are just "Works."

Examples:

> Mozart, Wolfgang Amadeus, 1756–1791. Quartets, strings. Selections (for four string quartets)
> Mozart, Wolfgang Amadeus, 1756–1791. Violin, piano music (for all the violin and piano music in any form)

Mozart, Wolfgang Amadeus, 1756–1791. Symphonies (refers to all 50 or so of them)

Mozart, Wolfgang Amadeus, 1756–1791. Works (for Mozart's complete works)

Your online catalog may have cross-references that will help you determine uniform titles.

Examples:

Moonlight sonata → Beethoven, Ludwig Van, 1770–1827. Sonatas, piano, no. 14, op. 27, no. 2, C# minor

Four Seasons → Vivaldi, Antonio, 1678–1741. Cimento dell'armoniae dell'inventione

If your local catalog does not provide cross-references, you can search the Library of Congress Authorities online for free at http://authorities.loc.gov. Subjects, names, titles, and name/title headings are all available; browsing the titles under a composer's name is the easiest way to get started.

Once you have identified the uniform title for a work, use it in your search. Uniform titles include the composer's name and sometimes dates as well as the title of the work. The way catalog software handles uniform titles varies. If present in your catalog, the cross references shown earlier will redirect your search to the author search at the point where the title falls alphabetically. Not all catalogs handle this the same way. Another way to search is to enter the title portion of the uniform title in the catalog's title search.

Your library's catalog may label both the title on the piece and the uniform title simply as "title," whereas others use "uniform title" to distinguish between the two. Additional uniform titles for additional works included on a recording or in a score anthology are labeled less consistently from one catalog to the next. The following are possibilities: "added entry," "other author(s)," "includes," or "other names." These additional titles include the composer's name and typically appear toward the end of the bibliographic record.

Another use for uniform titles for musical works is as subject headings. The uniform title, including the composer's name, will also be a valid subject heading to assist you in finding writings about the work.

Author/Title Searches

Some online catalogs allow the very useful combination of the author and title in one search. In other catalogs it is possible through limiting or an advanced keyword search. To use the author/title search most effectively, follow the earlier hints for entering the "author." Use as much of the name as you know to speed up the search and increase accuracy. Usually, the title portion of the search is a keyword search on the title. In some catalogs, this portion of the search is the same as "Limiting by Other Words in Title." In other words, you may type in title keywords. Some catalogs do not allow limiting (by format, date, etc.) after an author/title search.

Example:

> author: Copland, Aaron
> title: common man
> (finds all entries for Copland's *Fanfare for the Common Man*)

KEYWORD SEARCHES AND SUBJECT HEADING SEARCHES

Each of these types of searches has benefits and definite advantages in certain situations. Many times you'll want to use both types in your research.

Keyword Searches

Keyword searches, sometimes called *word searches*, are enticing because they are an easy way to get started searching and almost always yield a result. Unfortunately, they are also slow and "messy." They tend to yield a large number of **false drops** (records that meet your search criteria but are not what you are looking for). For example, a word search on "perfect pitch" may find books on baseball as well as those on absolute pitch.

Some library catalogs offer a *labeled* keyword search, which allows you to specify where each word is found in the records. This is a very useful way to combine author and title in a single search while still having the option to limit the search results further. An example would be the search for "a:Beethoven and t:92" to find the Beethoven Seventh Symphony, which is op. 92.

Doing a good job with word searches requires careful thought about your search terms (synonyms, for example) and the use of Boolean operators, truncation, phrase searches, proximity, and so on. See Appendix B for definitions and examples of these search aids. Refer to your library catalog's online help to see which are available for your use. You will also need to know which parts of the catalog records are searchable in the keyword index; asking a librarian may be the easiest way to find out.

Using word searches to lead you to the Library of Congress (LC) subject heading for the topic at hand is a technique called **triangulation**. If you do not know the subject heading for a particular topic, use a word search to find an example of what you are looking for. Then look at the subject heading(s) assigned to that item and use that in a subject search. For example, a word search for "black and music and history and united and states" could help you find the LC subject heading "African-Americans—Music—History and criticism."

Library of Congress (LC) Subject Headings

Library of Congress subject headings are similar to uniform titles, in that they represent a controlled vocabulary approach to the catalog. They are used widely by many English-speaking countries in their library catalogs. Using subject headings (rather than keywords) ensures that you will find everything in the catalog on your topic, and the search will yield results faster and with far greater precision.

You may be able to find subject headings online if your catalog includes subject cross references. The technique called *triangulation*, just described, is another way to determine the subject headings appropriate for your topic. Subject headings are usually labeled "subject(s)" and their location in the bibliographic record varies from catalog to catalog.

There are two principles guiding the assignment of subject headings: be as specific as possible, and use as many as necessary (with limits). At least 20 percent of a book, score, or recording must be devoted to a topic before a subject heading is assigned to it.

Keep in mind that older terminology is often involved. For example, "Afro-American" was used for many years in subject headings before it was switched to "African-American."

Format Issues

Like uniform titles, some subject headings are form or genre headings. Use singular and plural forms appropriately:

- Use singular headings for books about the genre (e.g., Sonata).
- Use plural headings for the actual music (e.g., Sonatas).

Enter the form followed by the medium. "And" is for when one instrument is accompanied by another; "with" is used before an accompanying ensemble and with vocal music.

- Trumpet and piano music
- Concertos (Flute with jazz ensemble)
- Songs (Medium voice) with orchestra
- Songs (High voice) with piano

Use topical headings:

- Christmas music
- Sea songs
- Psalms

Enter "arranged" to find arrangements (not originally for that medium):

- Orchestra music, Arranged

Use names as subject headings:

- Biographies—use the same authority headings as the subject's name.
- Be sure also to use a musician's last name in a word search to find chapters, essays, etc., devoted to the person.

Use subdivisions, including:

- Scores and parts
- Scores

- Parts
- Vocal scores
- United States (or other place names)
- Librettos
- Excerpts
- History and criticism
- Methods
- Studies and exercises

Pattern headings are useful as models for similar headings. Look in the print *Library of Congress Subject Headings* volumes or in the book *Music Subject Headings* to study these examples.[1]

Compositions:	Operas
Composers:	Wagner
Instruments:	Piano

Keyword Searches and Title Searches

Keyword searches can also be used to find titles that are only listed in a contents note in records for scores and sound recordings. This is often true for shorter works (songs or piano pieces) published in collections. Searching the contents notes via a word search may be the only way to determine if the library has the piece you are looking for. If you do not find a piece by title, always try a word search next. For example, if your title search for the Elvis song "Blue Suede Shoes" finds nothing, try a word search on the phrase "Blue Suede Shoes" to find the song in a collection.

LIMITING SEARCH RESULTS

The ability of your catalog to limit results is very powerful for music searches. Some catalogs allow you to apply limits before you search, others require you to limit after a search has been completed. Here are some commonly available ways to limit your search results:

- Year of publication
- Language
- Format of material
- Publisher
- Location in library

---

[1]Library of Congress, *Library of Congress Subject Headings*, 28th ed. Washington, DC: Library of Congress, 2005, and Harriette Hemmasi, *Music Subject Headings: Compiled from the Library of Congress Subject Headings*, 2nd ed. Lake Crystal, MN: Soldier Creek Press, 1998.

- Other words in Author
- Other words in Title
- Other words in Subject Headings

Limiting by format is also very helpful. The following options are the ones you will probably use most:

- Recordings
- Scores
- Audiovisual
- Books

Limiting by year of publication is also useful. So is location in library, if you can limit just to your music library's location.

Limiting by other words in author, title, and subject heading is also useful. For example, if you want to find a musical by Rodgers and Hammerstein, without also pulling up those by Rodgers and Hart, start with an author search on "Rodgers, Richard," and limit by "Hammerstein." You will get only the records with both authors. A similar example is to find Mozart's *Marriage of Figaro* with a title limit. Begin with an author search, "Mozart, Wolfgang" and limit to other words in title "*Marriage*" (or, even better, use the uniform title "*Nozze*").

There are many ways to formulate most any search. Experiment with the various ways of performing the same searches until you feel comfortable with the capabilities of your library's catalog software.

CONTENTS OF BIBLIOGRAPHIC RECORDS

So far the discussion has focused on access points in the records. But bibliographic information included in the physical description, publication information, and notes fields is also important.

The physical description of the item will indicate the item's format in many cases, for example, "1 vocal score," "4 parts," "2 videodiscs." In the case of sound recordings, you need to look at the size as well, because "1 sound disc" could be either an LP record or a CD; the size will clarify the format. For books, the number of pages or volumes is indicated. The physical description may be labeled "description," "descript," or "physical description" in your local catalog. No physical description is present in the bibliographic records for electronic resources.

A material's physical format may be reflected several places in the bibliographic record. Remember to look at the title(s), subject heading(s), and notes for format information in addition to the physical description. Some call numbers also indicate format; for example, in the **Library of Congress call number** system, M numbers are assigned to musical scores; many libraries use their own local call number system for musical recordings.

The publication information includes place of publication, publisher, and date. This area of the bibliographic record might be labeled "**imprint**," "publisher," "published/produced," or something similar.

The notes fields include information of interest, especially for scores and sound recordings. Examples include the listing of contents, performers, language, and edition. The notes may all be labeled simply "notes," or more specific labels may be enployed to identify "contents" or "table of contents" in your catalog. Many libraries make some of their notes fields searchable in a word or title search.

Other parts of the bibliographic record to consult include the edition, series, and publisher's number. You will also want to pay attention to the local information indicating an item's call number, specific location, and circulation status. Many catalogs display the local information in a box to highlight it.

EXAMPLES OF LIBRARY CATALOGS

Local Libraries

Throughout this text, asterisked items indicate the major tools within categories. In this chapter, your local college, conservatory, or university library catalog is the most important for you to learn to use well. The following library catalogs were chosen as examples, in part because of the fine music collections they represent and in part to demonstrate various integrated library software packages. Your library may very well have one of the catalog software packages illustrated here. Regardless of the software used in your library, choose the advanced search option if one exists, become familiar with its capabilities through online help or user guides, and do not forget to ask for assistance from library staff when you need it.

Indiana University Libraries use the Sirsi Corporation's software for their catalog called IUCAT (http://www.iucat.iu.edu); see Figure 4-1. Use the "Advanced Keyword" search to apply limits before you search.

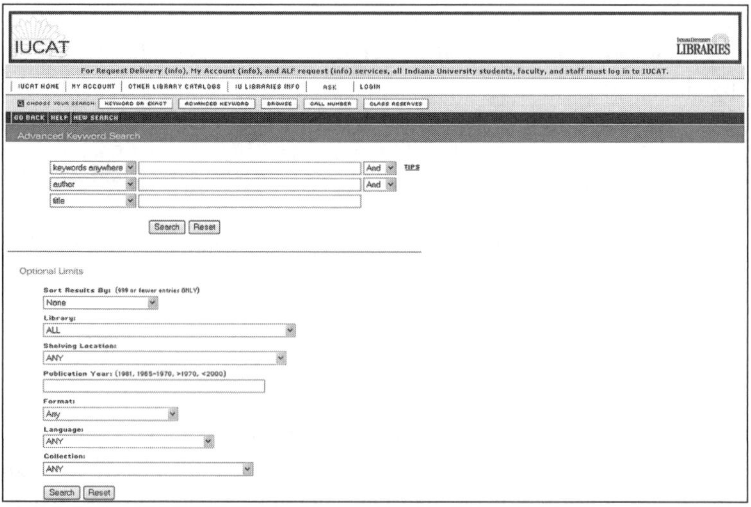

Figure 4-1 Indiana University's Catalog, IUCAT: Advanced Keyword Search *(Courtesy of Indiana University Libraries)*

The combined catalog of the University of California Libraries (including the holdings of the Jean Gray Hargrove Music Library at UC Berkeley) is called MELVYL (http://melvyl.cdlib.org). It uses the Aleph software from the Ex Libris company; see Figure 4-2. This catalog allows limiting from both the basic and advanced search screens. The results screens provide more information than most.

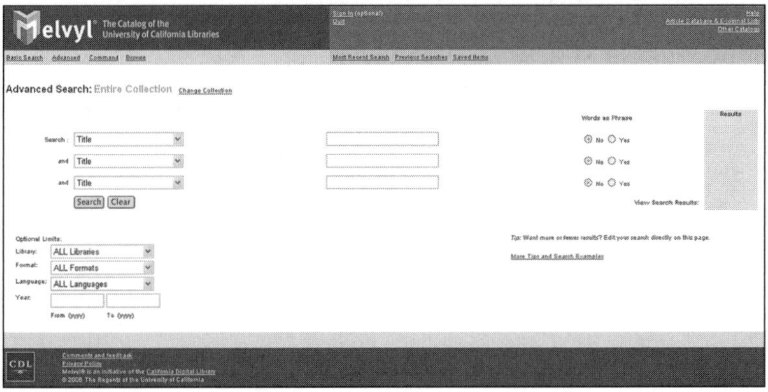

Figure 4-2 University of California Libraries' Catalog, MELVYL: Advanced Search *(Copyright © 2007, The Regents of the University of California)*

The University of North Texas uses Innovative Interfaces for its library catalog (http://iii.library.unt.edu). See Figure 4-3 for an example of its advanced search screen. This catalog not only provides cross references for names but also allows the searcher to limit to specific types of sound recordings.

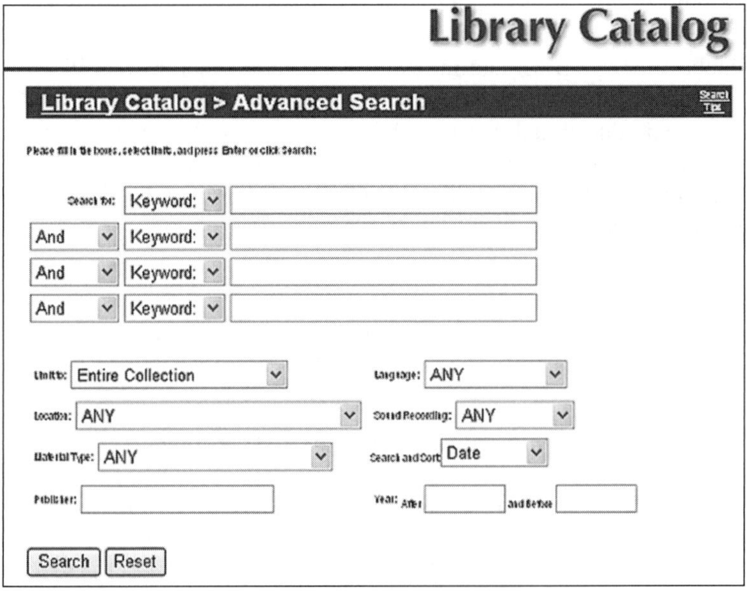

Figure 4-3 University of North Texas's Library Catalog: Advanced Search *(Courtesy of the University of North Texas Libraries)*

The Sibley Music Library at the University of Rochester's Eastman School of Music uses Endeavor Information System's *Voyager Catalog* (http://sibley.lib.rochester.edu). Try the "Advanced Search" option. See Figure 4-4.

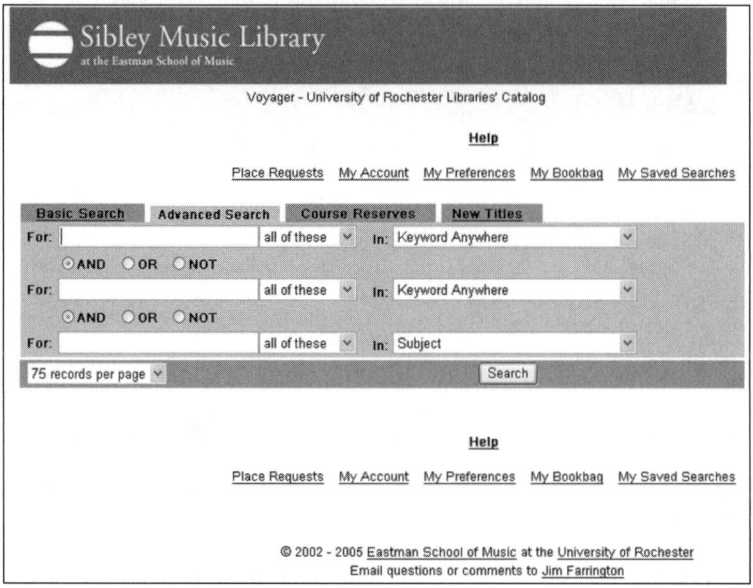

Figure 4-4 Sibley Music Library's Catalog, *Voyager*: Advanced Search *(Courtesy of the Sibley Music Library of the Eastman School of Music, University of Rochester)*

The examples just presented are all academic libraries. But there are many fine public library music collections in the United States as well. Examples include the Boston Public Library (BPL) and the New York Public Library (NYPL). Both have a combination of card and online catalogs representing their holdings. Both had their card catalogs reproduced and distributed by the G. K. Hall Company under the title *Dictionary Catalog of the Music Collection*. The BPL online catalog is at http://www.bpl.org catalogs; the NYPL research collection catalog, *CATNYP*, is at http://catnyp.nypl.org. The print catalogs for these libraries are listed next.

4.1 Boston Public Library. *Dictionary Catalog of the Music Collection.* 20 vols. Boston: G. K. Hall, 1972.
Reproduced catalog cards for around 80,000 items. Includes the Allen A. Brown Collection. A supplement was issued in 1977. Reviewed by Dennis North in *ARBA* 1973: 391–92.

4.2 *G. K. Hall Bibliographic Guide to Music. Boston*: G. K. Hall, 1975–2003.
Annual publication that updated the New York Public Library *Dictionary Catalog.* Title was *Bibliographic Guide to Music* from 1975 to 1998. Includes items cataloged by the NYPL as well as the Library of Congress. Reviewed by Alan Asher (2002 volume) in *ARBA* 2004: 509–10.

4.3 New York Public Library. *Dictionary Catalog of the Music Collection*, 2nd ed. 45 vols. Boston: G. K. Hall, 1982.
First published in 33 vols. in 1965. Supplements were issued in 1973 and 1976.

Library Consortia

A **consortium** is an association of libraries formed to share resources in order to pro-vide better services and broader collections for researchers. If your college or university is a member of a consortium, materials from the participating libraries may be available for you to borrow. You can probably receive materials from a statewide consortium, for example, more quickly than via interlibrary loan. If your college, conservatory, or uni-versity belongs to a consortium, you should become familiar with its online catalog.

One such consortium is the Ohio Library and Information Network (OhioLINK). The *OhioLINK Catalog* represents the holdings of about 85 Ohio colleges and univer-sities at http://olc1.ohiolink.edu/search. See Figure 4-5. Like the University of North Texas, it uses software from Innovative Interfaces Incorporated.

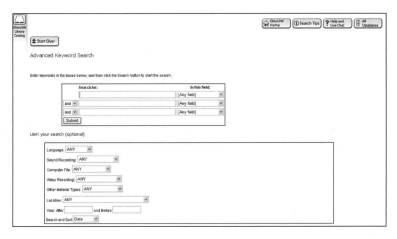

Figure 4-5 Ohio Library and Information Network, *OhioLINK Catalog*: Advanced Keyword Search *(Courtesy of Ohio Library and Information Network)*

One of the largest library consortia in North America is the Center for Research Libraries (CRL), with over 200 libraries participating. The Center's website at http://www.crl.edu includes a link to its online catalogs, including special and digital collections. The main CRL catalog is available at http://www.crl.edu/catalog; materials are available to researchers from member libraries via interlibrary loan or electronic document delivery.

National Libraries

Most every **national library** has an excellent research collection, especially for items published in the respective country. Such "libraries of deposit" are responsible for col-lecting and cataloging materials copyrighted or published in the country. Remember that the primary function of national libraries is not to serve the general public. For example, the Library of Congress's primary mission is to serve the U.S. Congress. However, serious researchers are usually accommodated. The major national libraries have online catalogs, but they may have additional catalogs in other formats as well. Begin your searching of these collections with the online catalogs.

The Library of Congress (LC) represents itself as the largest library in the world, with over 130 million items. The LC homepage, http://www.loc.gov, provides links to a number of catalogs (including the *SONIC* catalog of sound recordings) and online collections called *American Memory*. The Library of Congress has a fine music collection of over eight million items that, as already noted, is described through a number of catalogs, including the various versions of the *National Union Catalog* and its online catalog (using Endeavor software) at http://catalog.loc.gov. See Figure 4-6.

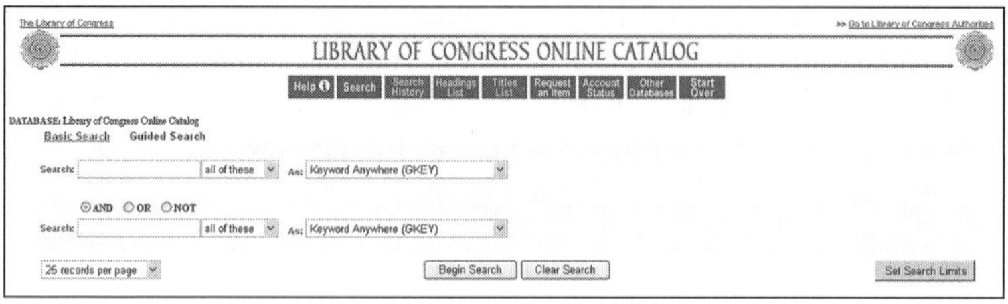

Figure 4-6 Library of Congress Online Catalog: Guided Search *(Courtesy of the Library of Congress)*

In addition to the LC online catalogs, the following major print catalogs, which also include records contributed by many other major libraries, may be consulted. The records in the print catalogs published after 1980 are available in the online catalog. You may also want to search the print LC Copyright Office *Catalog of Copyright Entries* or the *National Union Catalog of Manuscript Collections* (*NUCMC*), which is available in both print and online formats. The online version of the *NUCMC* is searchable for free at http://www.loc.gov/coll/nucmc; it is also available through the fee-based database *ArchivesUSA* (see http://archives.chadwyck.com) from ProQuest/UMI.

4.4   Library of Congress. *Library of Congress Catalog: Music and Phonorecords.* 11 vols. Washington, DC: Library of Congress, 1953–72.
      Music catalog records were previously included in the 5-year cumulations of the *National Union Catalog*. Volume 27 of the 1953–57 cumulation included the music records. Volumes 51–52 of the 1958–62 cumulation included music. The three volumes from 1963 to 1967 and the five volumes from 1968 to 1972 were published under the title *National Union Catalog: Music and Phonorecords*. A reprint edition of all 11 vols. was titled *National Union Catalog: Music and Phonorecords*. Continued by *Music, Books on Music, and Sound Recordings*.

4.5   ———. *Music, Books on Music, and Sound Recordings.* 25 vols. Washington, DC: Library of Congress, 1973–89.
      Continues the *Library of Congress Catalog: Music and Phonorecords*. Cumulated for 1973–77 (8 vols.), 1978–82 (7 vols.), and 1983–89 (10 vols.). Also published in microfiche. Continued by the *Music Catalog*.

4.6   ———. *Music Catalog.* Washington, DC: Library of Congress, 1990–2002. Microfiche.
      Continues *Music, Books on Music, and Sound Recordings*. Nothing currently continues the *Music Catalog*, although LC still makes its catalog records available to libraries. The NISC publication of the same title includes later LC music records.

4.7 ———. *The National Union Catalog: Pre-1956 Imprints: A Cumulative Author List Representing Library of Congress Printed Cards and Titles Reported by Other American Libraries.* 754 vols. London: Mansell, 1968–81.

Not limited to music, the Pre-1956 Imprints includes the original 685 volumes published 1968–81 and a 68-volume supplement published 1980–81. Only includes author entries. Does not include sound recordings. Discussed by William Welsh in "Last of the Monumental Book Catalogs." *American Libraries* 12, no. 8 (Sept. 1981): 464–68.

Both of the following catalogs include LC records (as well as records from other libraries) that were not included in the foregoing catalogs.

4.8 *Music Catalog.* Baltimore, MD: National Information Services Corporation (NISC), 2001–.

Includes LC records from 1960 to the present, including some that were previously unpublished. Also includes cataloging contributed from other libraries. Covers the contents of *Music, Books on Music and Sound Recordings* and *Music Catalog.* Updated annually. Published as a subscription-based online database called *BiblioLine*, as a CD-ROM with the same title, and as part of the *MUSE (MUsic SEarch)* CD-ROM. The LC catalog portion of *MUSE* was reviewed by Péter Jacsó in *Computers in Libraries* 16, no. 2 (Feb. 1996): 78–81.

4.9 Olmsted, Elizabeth. *Music Library Association Catalog of Cards for Printed Music, 1953–1972.* 2 vols. Totowa, NJ: Rowman and Littlefield, 1974.

Includes around 30,000 reproduced cataloging records that were contributed by libraries between the late 1950s and the early 1970s but not included in the *National Union Catalog.* The cataloging varies in quality and legibility. Does not indicate which libraries own each title. Reviewed by James R. Heintze in *Library Quarterly* 45, no. 1 (Jan. 1975): 109.

The national library of the United Kingdom is the British Library (http://www.bl.uk). Its *Integrated Catalogue* is available online at http://catalogue.bl.uk. See Figure 4-7. The British Library uses the Aleph catalog software. Additional catalogs (manuscripts, sound archive, etc.) as well as digitized titles from the collection, titled the *Online Gallery*, are also available from the Library's homepage.

Although now incorporated into the *Integrated Catalogue*, the following are two earlier catalogs of the printed music in the British Library.

4.10 British Library. *Catalogue of Printed Music in the British Library to 1980 (CPM).* 62 vols. London: K. G. Saur, 1981–87.

Known as *CPM*, this catalog in book format includes published music held by the British Library that was published before 1980 and cataloged in time to be included. The records in *CPM* are now incorporated into the *Integrated Catalogue.* Reviewed by O. W. Neighbour in *Brio* 17, no. 2 (Autumn–Winter 1980): 54–56.

4.11 *CPM Plus.* 2nd ed. London: Bowker-Saur, 1997.

Published as a CD-ROM and including updates to 1996, this version of the *Catalog of Printed Music* is no longer available. Search options are more sophisticated than the *Integrated Catalogue.* Updated and largely superceded by the *Integrated Catalogue.* Reviewed by Paul Andrews in *Brio* 36, no. 1 (Spring–Summer 1999): 78–79.

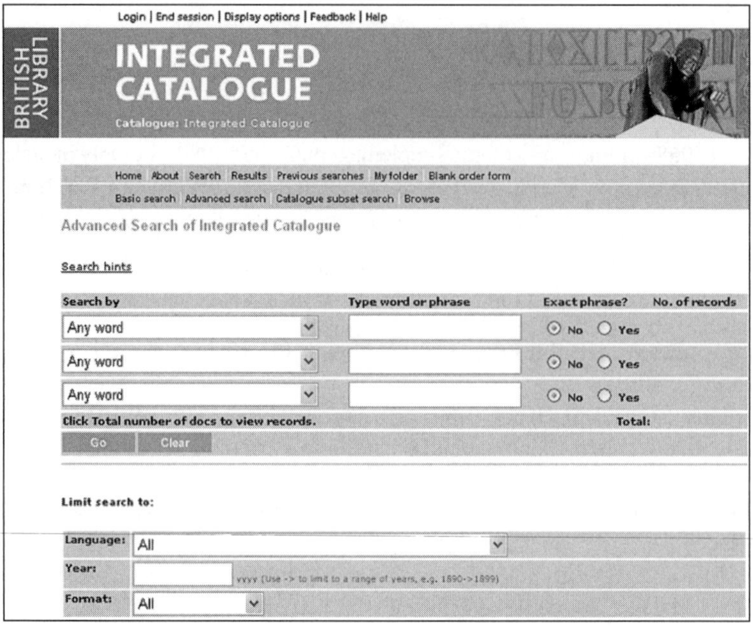

Figure 4-7 The British Library's *Integrated Catalogue*: Advanced Search *(Courtesy of the British Library)*

The holdings of the British Library are also searchable via *Copac* (http://copac.ac.uk), the union catalog of the UK's Consortium of Research Libraries (CURL), which includes around thirty libraries. In addition to the British Library, the National Library of Scotland, and the National Library of Wales, major university libraries, including Cambridge and Oxford, are members. The list of members is available at the CURL website at http://www.curl.ac.uk.

Library and Archives Canada, the national library of Canada (http://www.collectionscanada.ca) provides access to over 30 million records from its own collections as well as other Canadian libraries via its national catalog, *Amicus*. See http://www.collectionscanada.ca/amicus.

Another national library with a major music collection is the Bibliotèque Nationale de France. See http://www.bnf.fr/pages/catalogues.htm for its catalogs in French. Scores, manuscripts, books, and recordings are in *Catalogue BN-OPALE PLUS*.

The European Library website includes a catalog to the combined collections of the forty-three national libraries of Europe. Selected items from the collections (called "Treasures") have been digitized and are available online as well. See http://www.theeuropeanlibrary.org.

Bibliographic Utilities

A **bibliographic utility** is a large cooperative database created by librarians for use by themselves as well as by researchers. Searching these databases, which include the titles and holding libraries of thousands of international collections, broadens your research pool considerably, extending it far beyond your local library. Many of the items can be borrowed through interlibrary loan; copies, scans, or microfilm may be available for others.

*4.12   Online Computer Library Center (OCLC). *WorldCat.* Dublin: OH: OCLC, 1992–. http://www.oclc.org/worldcat.

WorldCat is the largest bibliographic database. Currently it has over 58 million titles contributed by its over 9,000 member libraries since 1971. *WorldCat* is the name for the search engine developed for the OCLC Online Union Catalog. It is offered as the cornerstone of its suite of databases, called *FirstSearch. WorldCat* is easy to search, fast, and flexible. See the advanced search screen in Figure 4-8. Many OCLC member libraries have the capability of allowing patrons to request titles through interlibrary loan directly in *WorldCat.* Searching *WorldCat* is second in importance only to developing your skills with your local library catalog.

Unlike the other catalogs discussed so far, utilities are not free. However, *WorldCat* has a free version for individuals called WorldCat.org at http://WorldCat.org. It is an attempt to reach the nonlibrary community who research using Internet search engines.

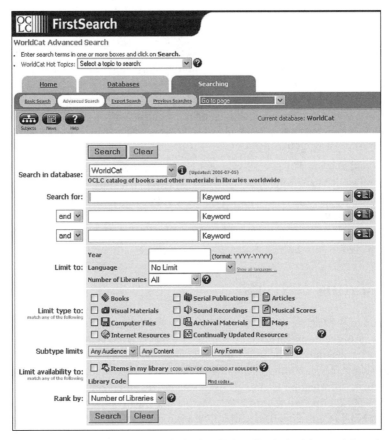

Figure 4-8 *WorldCat* (the OCLC Online Union Catalog): Advanced Search *(Image published with permission of OCLC. WorldCat© is a registered trademark and/or service mark of OCLC Online Computer Library Center, Inc.)*

FINDING LIBRARY CATALOGS

You may need to find and use both online and print catalogs for a particular library. Both LibDex at http://libdex.com and LibWeb at http://lists.webjunction.org/libweb provide links to libraries and their catalogs available online. The International Federation of Library Associations and Institutions (IFLA) website provides links to national libraries at http://www.ifla.org/VI/2/p2/national-libraries.htm. Links specifically for music collections are available from Music Web Hunter at http://www.kendavies.net/musicwebhunter/musiclibraries.html and at the Indiana University Music Library's Worldwide Internet Music Resources at http://www.music.indiana.edu/music_resources/musiclib.html.

You can consult your local library catalog to find other libraries' catalogs in print, microform, etc. They are given LC call numbers in the ML136–139 range. LC subject headings include the library's name, with the subdivision "Catalogs," for example, "British Library—Catalogs." Union catalogs are given the subject heading "Catalogs, Union." The best listing of print catalogs for music libraries and collections is "Catalogs of Music Libraries and Collections," Chapter 7 of the Duckles bibliography (entry 1.13).

In addition, for private music collections or musical instrument collections, see the following listings of collections and their catalogs as well as the articles on these types of collections in *Grove Music Online* (entry 2.2).

4.13 Coover, James. *Musical Instrument Collections: Catalogues and Cognate Literature*. Detroit Studies in Music Bibliography, no. 47. Detroit, MI: Information Coordinators, 1981.
Includes instrument collections in institutions, those exhibited, and those owned privately. Bibliography includes catalogs as well as writings about the collections. Includes two appendixes and an index. Reviewed by Paula Morgan in *Notes* 39, no. 2 (Dec. 1982): 360–61.

4.14 ———. *Private Music Collections: Catalogues and Cognate Literature*. Detroit Studies in Music Bibliography, no. 81. Warren, MI: Harmonie Park Press, 2001. This bibliography covers published and unpublished writings and catalogs of named and unnamed private collections. Holding locations are included for most sources. Has an index. Reviewed by John Wagstaff in *Music and Letters* 84, no. 1 (Feb. 2003): 110–12.

INFORMATION CENTERS

In addition to the various types of libraries already described, music information centers are a resource to explore. Many countries have national centers for the promotion of their countries' music. The following three examples all have collections with online catalogs. The American Music Center (AMC) has a website at http://www.amc.net. The British Music Information Centre (BMIC) specializes in contemporary British music; see its website at http://www.bmic.co.uk. With a website in both English and French, the Canadian Music Centre is online at http://www.musiccentre.ca. Additional centers can be identified through the website of the International Association of Music Information Centres at http://www.iamic.net.

EVALUATION CHECKLIST

Perhaps for the first time you will be using more than one online library catalog, and you will develop preferences. Also keep in mind that your local librarians might welcome feedback on their catalog's usability for students.

- How good is the search engine and database design?
- Are uniform titles easy to search?
- Does the catalog provide cross-references for titles, subjects, and names?
- Are search limits available, including those for specific types of recordings?
- Are the holdings clear for serials, multi-volume works, etc., as well as for materials not held locally?
- Is it easy to distinguish online from print, especially for periodicals?
- Are help screens or handouts available and useful?
- How easy is it to request materials from other branches or libraries?
- Is a federated (multi-database) search available?
- How does the catalog function as a portal to web resources?
- Is everything in the collection cataloged online?
- How are special and archival collections included?
- Is it easy to contact a librarian by e-mail or phone?

SUGGESTED READINGS

The readings by Fenske et al. and Young provide additional information on searching using uniform titles and LC subject headings, respectively. The Coffman article compares traditional library catalogs to Amazon.com and calls for improvements. King's piece discusses research on search strategies of musicians.

Coffman, Steve. "Building Earth's Largest Library: Driving into the Future." *Searcher* 7, no. 3 (Mar. 1999): 34–37, 40–47.

Fenske, David, Michael Fling, Brenda Nelson-Strauss, and Shirlene Ward. "Making the Most of the Music Library: Using Uniform Titles." William and Gayle Cook Music Library, Indiana University. Online at http://library.music.indiana.edu/collections/uniform/uniform.html (Accessed Jan. 2006).

King, David M. "Catalog User Search Strategies in Finding Music Materials." *Music Reference Services Quarterly* 9, no. 4 (2005): 1–24.

Young, J. Bradford. "Introduction to the Structure and Use of Library of Congress Subject Headings for Music and Materials about Music." In *Music Subject Headings: Compiled from Library of Congress Subject Headings*, compiled by Harriette Hemmasi, 1–28. Lake Crystal, MN: Soldier Creek Press, 1998.

CHAPTER 5

Periodical Indexes for Music

Articles published in music **journals** and **magazines** are an important part of the body of research on most topics. Periodical articles are often the most current sources of information on a subject. In a journal article, an author can delve into a narrow topic in more detail than in a dictionary or encyclopedia and often more comprehensively than in books. Articles tend to focus on one small aspect of a broader topic. **Periodicals** are published more quickly than books and can present current research more rapidly. In addition to scholarly articles, periodicals include other types of writings, such as interviews, bibliographies, reviews, and letters.

The number of music periodicals being published around the world is higher than you might think. *Music Index* alone claims to index 400 current periodicals annually. If you consider how many individual articles are published in all the issues of those journals in a single year, you begin to see the problem of indexing them. When you further consider the number of years some music journals have been published, the challenge grows very quickly. *Music Index Online* includes more than one million article citations dating mostly from 1975. Clearly, **periodical indexes** are an important research tool for finding a wealth of writings about music.

Finding articles in music journals and magazines requires the use of periodical indexes. While the journals themselves are cataloged in your local library's catalog, the contents of the journals are not included. For example, your library's online catalog will tell you that the library subscribes to the *Journal of the American Musicological Society* (*JAMS*), but it will not tell you the titles and authors of the articles included in the latest issue. Likewise, the union catalog (*WorldCat*) does not index the contents of **serial** publications such as journals, magazines, and newspapers.

Some journals publish their own indexes on a regular or irregular basis. Your online catalog will help you find these, which are shelved with the bound issues of the journal in many libraries as a supplement to the journal. One example is Karen Little's *Notes: An Index to Volumes 1–50* (Canton, MA: Music Library Association, 1995). This type of index is very useful if one exists for a key journal or journals in your areas of interest. Music periodicals are given a call number in the range ML1 to ML27, although some devoted to a specific topic are given LC classification numbers for that topic. For example, *Music Theory Spectrum* has the call number MT6 for music theory.

Music periodicals range in purpose, level of scholarship, and audience. Some are **refereed**, or **peer-reviewed**, meaning that the articles were accepted for publication by an editor in consultation with various readers. For example, *JAMS* is one of the most respected refereed journals in musicology. Some periodical indexes, such as *International Index to Music Periodicals* (*IIMP*), allow you to limit your search to articles published in refereed journals.

Getting journal articles has traditionally been at least a two-step process. First a periodical index was used to find the citation for the article. The **citation** typically includes the author and title of the article, title of the journal, volume, issue number (or month/season), pages, and subjects. An **abstract** summarizing the contents of the article might be included. Abstracts can help you decide, before you go any further, whether the article will be useful. With citation in hand, the next step was finding the journal itself via your library's online catalog to see if the particular volume needed is held and available. For journals not owned by your library, a third step was requesting them through interlibrary loan.

While this process is still sometimes necessary, today the number of **full text databases** (like *International Index to Music Periodicals Full Text*), repositories of online journals (such as *JSTOR* and *Project Muse*), journals published online (including *Eighteenth-Century Music*), and open-access titles (for example *Music Theory Online*) often makes this a one-step process. Publishers are also increasingly moving their titles to online versions. Often your library will have recent volumes of a journal available online while older volumes are still only available in print. Older journals may be housed in an **offsite storage facility**.

You will need to become familiar, by database title, format (paper, CD-ROM, or online), and vendor, with what your library subscribes to. To do this, consult your local online catalog and any listings of online databases/indexes or subject guides provided by your library. Some periodical indexes are still available in print; these will have an LC call number in the ML113–119 range and usually have the LC subject heading "Music—Periodicals—Indexes." Online periodical indexes do not usually have a call number, but are assigned the same LC subject heading or "Music—Periodicals—Indexes—Databases."

Some periodical indexes are available from more than one vendor, perhaps with slightly different titles. For example, *Répertoire internationale de literature musical/ International Repertory of Music Literature* (*RILM*) *Abstracts* is available from multiple vendors (Cambridge Scientific Abstracts [CSA] Illumina, EBSCO, NISC, OCLC, and Ovid), each with a different search interface to the database.

Keep in mind that the developer of an index is sometimes the same as the publisher and sometimes not. For example, EBSCO licenses (but does not publish) *RILM Abstracts*, but it does publish others, such as *Academic Search Premier* and *Business Source Premier.* Among the general periodical indexes, company mergers and partnerships are sometimes reflected in databases changing names. The landscape of periodical indexes changes frequently. This can result in surprises for you as a researcher if your favorite index is switched to a new vendor or changes name. When in doubt, ask your librarian for explanations.

Your searching will be expedited if you can search more than one database at a time. For example, in OCLC's *FirstSearch* you could search *WorldCat*, *RILM Abstracts*, *ERIC*, and *ArticleFirst* simultaneously. If your library subscribes to the EBSCO versions of *Music Index*, *RILM Abstracts*, and *Répertoire international de la presse musicale/Retrospective Index to Music Periodicals* (*RIPM*), you can search all three as well as *Academic Search Premier* with one search. In other words, you need to know if your library subscribes to *RILM Abstracts* and so on, but you also need to know which version(s) you have access to and what other databases of interest are offered by that same vendor. Unfortunately, there is still no single mega-index for music periodicals (or general periodicals for that matter, although the situation is rapidly improving). Researchers need to search several databases to conduct a comprehensive search for periodical articles on a given topic. If searching on an interdisciplinary topic (e.g., stage fright) or one with a body of general literature (e.g., music education) you should also consult additional indexes (*PsycINFO* and *ERIC*, respectively).

The indexes listed in this chapter vary in coverage, although they do have some overlap. You should also be aware that each periodical index will have its own subject headings, and none of them use the Library of Congress subject headings (although *Music Index*'s were initially based on LCSH). The form of names used for authors and composers varies as well. You will need to determine the most appropriate subject headings in each for your topic. Often combining the subject heading(s) with carefully chosen keywords using Boolean operators is the most effective search strategy. The use of advanced or expert search options is recommended. See Appendix B for an explanation of Boolean search terms.

The time lag between when an article is published and when citations for it appear varies from one index to the next. The indexes' update or publication schedules affect their timeliness, too. For example, two of the indexes described here (*LexisNexis Academic* and *ProQuest Newsstand*) are updated several times a day, while *Retrospective Index to Music Periodicals* (*RIPM*) is updated every six months.

This discussion of periodical indexes is divided into the following sections: major music periodical indexes, retrospective periodical indexes, other music periodical indexes, ceased music periodical indexes, periodical indexes for related disciplines, major general periodical indexes, and major newspaper indexes. A section on finding online journals is also included. As throughout this text, an asterisk indicates that a particular index is a major research tool.

MAJOR MUSIC PERIODICAL INDEXES

The three major international periodical indexes for music are *IIMP*, *Music Index*, and *RILM Abstracts*. As mentioned earlier, you need to search all three for most topics. However, each has its particular strengths and weaknesses that you should be aware of. Keep in mind the dates of coverage and what is offered by each, along with the article citations (i.e., abstracts or full text of articles). See the articles by Alan Green ("Keeping Up with the Times"), Leslie Troutman, and Martin D. Jenkins listed in the Suggested Readings for detailed comparisons of the three. Green's study indicates that only about 26 percent of the total number of music periodicals are indexed by all three. See this text's companion website for updated coverage information on each index.

*5.1 *International Index to Music Periodicals* (*IIMP*). Ann Arbor, MI: Chadwyck-Healey/ProQuest, 1996–. http://iimp.chadwyck.com; *International Index to Music Periodicals Full Text* (*IIMPFT*). Ann Arbor, MI: Chadwyck-Healey/ProQuest, 1998–. http://iimpft.chadwyck.com.

IIMP is the newest of the major music periodical indexes, and it is the only one that was born in electronic format. With over 530,000 citations, it indexes over 430 periodicals from 25 countries in 17 languages, but the coverage is mostly English. Good for popular music and performance, like *Music Index*. Includes abstracts. Full text version has over 120 titles available. Some retrospective indexing for certain core titles. Those indexed retrospectively are covered back to their first volume. That is why some articles date back to 1874, although most are from 1996 or later. *IIMP* is the easiest to search of the three indexes listed here. See Figure 5-1 for the *IIMPFT* search screen.

Figure 5-1 *International Index to Music Periodicals Full Text Search Screen (Image published with permission of ProQuest CSA. Further reproduction is prohibited without permission)*

Use "select from a list," especially for subject terms. Subject terms used with keywords works very effectively. Subject terms are short and use intuitive language. Check "exclude all reviews" or "peer-reviewed articles only" as appropriate. Includes links to *JSTOR* and *Project MUSE*. The online version is updated monthly, and the indexing lag is usually about two months. Can be searched in combination with *IIPA*. Includes links to *Naxos Music Library* audio and reference files. Available on CD-ROM (*IIMP* only) and online from ProQuest. Reviewed by Christine Oka in *Library Journal* 129, no. 5 (Mar. 2004): 115.

*5.2   *Music Index: A Subject-Author Guide to Music Periodical Literature*. Sterling Heights, MI: Harmonie Park Press, 1949–; *Music Index Online*. Sterling Heights, MI: Harmonie Park Press, 1999–. http://www.harmonieparkpress.com/ MusicIndex.asp.

Music Index is the oldest of the three major music periodical indexes. It started in 1949 on paper, and the indexing through the mid-1970s is only available in the paper version. Be sure to search the cumulated paper volumes as appropriate for your research needs. The online version, which began in 1999, is slowly adding the earlier indexing. Figure 5-2 shows the *Music Index* search screen from Harmonie Park Press. Includes citations from a total of about 800 journals, more than either *IIPM* or *RILM Abstracts*, from 40 countries in 22 languages. Includes over 1 million records online. Currently indexes about 400 periodicals each year. Includes citations only, no abstracts or full text. Good coverage for music education, jazz, and performance. Second-best international coverage after *RILM Abstracts*. Subject headings are broad, especially for music education topics, so use them in conjunction with keywords. Includes links to *JSTOR*. Indexing lag is typically six months. Updated quarterly. Available in print and online from Harmonie Park Press and online from

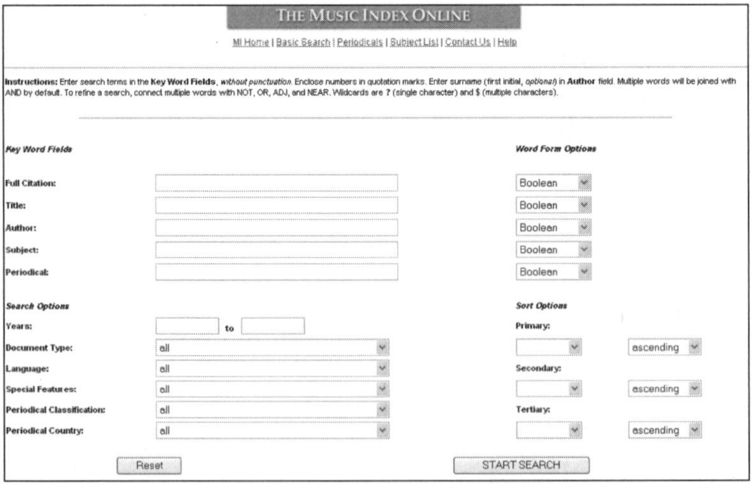

Figure 5-2 *Music Index* Expert Search Screen from Harmonie Park Press
(Courtesy of Harmonie Park Press, Sterling Heights, Michigan)

EBSCO. Reviewed by Lois Kuyper-Rushing in *Charleston Advisor* 5, no. 1 (July 2003): 38–41.

*5.3   Répertoire international de littérature musicale/International Repertory of Music Literature/Internationales Repertorium der Musikliteratur (RILM). *RILM Abstracts of Music Literature.* New York: RILM, 1967–. http://www.rilm.org. *RILM Abstracts* has the broadest coverage, including books, conference proceedings, articles in Festschriften, etc. (See Chapter 6.) A result of the international cooperative, nonprofit project called Répertoire international de littérature musicale/International Repertory of Music Literature. *RILM Abstracts* began in 1967, and the coverage from then until the present is available online. Has about half a million citations from over 740 core and primary journals, with an extensive list of titles indexed selectively. Citations include detailed abstracts written by authors or volunteers. Has the best international and foreign-language coverage, with nearly 300 languages represented. Has the shortest indexing time lag of the three in this category, with some citations typically dating from the previous month. Most scholarly, especially for musicology, ethnomusicology, and music theory. Subject headings are phrase based and often lengthy. See Figure 5-3 for the Advanced Search Screen for *RILM Music Abstracts* on OCLC's *FirstSearch.*

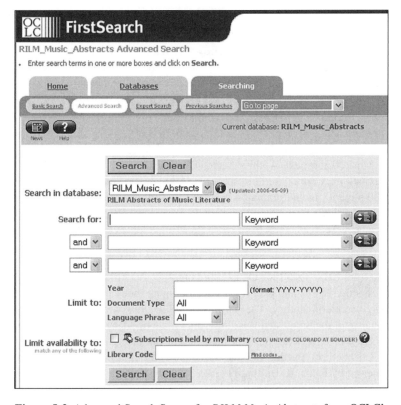

Figure 5-3 Advanced Search Screen for *RILM Music Abstracts* from OCLC's *FirstSearch (Image published with permission of OCLC* and Copyright © *Répertoire International de Littérature Musicale)*

Some vendors offer full text or full text links. Available in print from RILM, on CD-ROM (*MUSE: MUsic SEarch*) from NISC, and online (updated monthly) from several vendors (CSA Illumina, EBSCO, NISC, OCLC, and Ovid). MUSE CD-ROM reviewed by Robert Skinner in *Notes* 48, no. 3 (Mar. 1992): 945–53. Online version reviewed by Donna Arnold, et al. in *Notes* 61, no. 1 (Sept. 2004): 197–205 and Guy Leach in *Charleston Advisor* 4, no. 1 (July 2002): 10–15.

RETROSPECTIVE PERIODICAL INDEXES

The oldest of the three major music periodical indexes is *Music Index*, which began in 1949. Needless to say, articles for many music topics were being published in the nineteenth and early twentieth centuries, but the indexing for these has been spotty at best. The following research tools attempt to fill in this gap. In addition, *IIMP* is retrospectively indexing some periodicals on a title-by-title basis. Once a title is selected, it is indexed back to its first volume. See also *Periodicals Index Online*, which includes three centuries of indexing from 1665 to 1995. Other retrospective citations can be found in the New York Public Library *Dictionary Catalog of the Music Collection* (entry 4.3), which includes reproduced handwritten cards indexing articles by subject.

5.4   Blom, Eric. *A General Index to Modern Musical Literature in the English Language: Including Periodicals for the Years 1915–1926*. New York: Da Capo, 1970. First published 1927 by Curwen & Sons.
      A single-volume attempt to index periodicals before *Music Index* began in 1949. Citations (all English-language) are listed in a single alphabetical listing. British bias. No index. Reviewed by Lillian M. Ruff in *Consort*, no. 28 (1972): 121.

*5.5 Cohen, Robert H. *Répertoire international de la press musicale/Retrospective Index to Music Periodicals (RIPM)*. Baltimore, MD: RIPM, 1988–. http://www.ripm.org. Sponsored by the International Musicological Society; International Association of Music Libraries, Archives and Documentation Centres; and UNESCO's International Council for Philosophy and Humanistic Studies. Coverage dates from 1800 to 1950. Includes about a half million citations, with annotations from over 100 periodicals from 15 countries in 13 languages. See Figure 5-4 for the *RIPM* Advanced Search screen from EBSCO. Print volumes (over 210) are dedicated to particular periodical titles; each journal has to be searched separately. Available in print and CD-ROM (from NISC) and online (since 2000). Online version (available from EBSCO, NISC, OCLC, and Ovid) is recommended; it is updated every six months. RIPM and RILM are cooperating to index music periodicals from the early twentieth century. The *RIPM Online Archive* with full text is anticipated. See also, in the Suggested Readings, the article by Mary Wallace Davidson on the selection of American music periodicals for the index. Print version reviewed by M. Elizabeth C. Bartlet in *JAMS* 43, no. 3 (Fall 1990): 498–504. Online version reviewed by Diana R. Hallman in *Notes* 58, no. 2 (Dec. 2001): 408–11.

5.6   Krohn, Ernst C. *The History of Music: An Index to the Literature Available in a Selected Group of Musicological Publications*. St. Louis, Washington University, 1952.

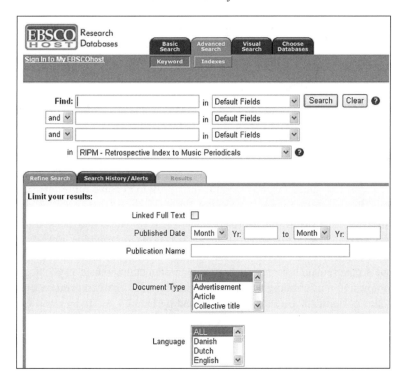

Figure 5-4 *RIPM* Advanced Search Screen from EBSCO *(Courtesy of EBSCO and RIPM)*

Similar in purpose to Blom but broader in scope. Indexes 39 periodicals, mainly in English and German. Citations are arranged by style period. Includes a name index. Reviewed by Scott Goldthwaite in *JAMS* 6, no. 3 (Fall 1953): 250–51.

5.7   *Readers' Guide Retrospective: 1890–1982.* New York: H. W. Wilson, 2002–. http://www.hwwilson.com.
A general online database with nearly a century of coverage dating from the late nineteenth century. Includes more than 3 million articles from about 375 periodicals. Includes only citations, no abstracts or full text. Can be searched with *Readers' Guide Full Text.* Reviewed by B. L. Robinson-Jones in *Choice* 41, no. 2 (Oct. 2003): 307.

OTHER MUSIC PERIODICAL INDEXES

The indexes listed here are not as large or as comprehensive as *IIMP*, *Music Index*, or *RILM Abstracts*; however, they are more specialized, and all are free. No asterisks have been assigned in this category, because these tools are narrower in scope. Search them if they are appropriate for your research needs.

5.8   Asmus, Edward P. *Music Education Search System.* Miami: University of Miami, 1998–. http://www.music.miami.edu/mess.

Includes citations in three separate indexes: 17,000 citations from 12 music education periodicals (most are indexed from their first issue), 4,500 abstracts for pre-
1965 publications (compiled by music educators William Poland and Henry Cady
at Ohio State University), and citations from the journal *Boletín de investigacio
educativo musical.*

5.9   Library and Archives Canada. *Canadian Music Periodical Index.* Ottawa,
       ON: Library and Archives Canada, 1996–. http://www.collectionscanada.ca/
       cmpi-ipmc/index-e.html.
       Offers about 30,000 citations from 500 Canadian music periodicals. Date cover-
       age is from the late nineteenth century onward. Focus was initially on Canadian
       music and musicians but was expanded in 1999 to become more international in
       scope. Reviewed by Lisa R. Philpott in *Notes* 64, no. 2 (Dec. 2007): 344–51.

5.10   University of Texas at San Antonio Department of Music and Institute for Music
       Research. *CAIRSS for Music (Computer-Assisted Information Retrieval Service
       System).* San Antonio: University of Texas, 1994–. http://imr.utsa.edu/CAIRSS.htm.
       Topics covered include research in music education, music psychology, music
       therapy, and music medicine. Includes citations only. Sixteen primary and 11 sec-
       ondary periodicals are indexed. Discussed by Donald A. Hodges and Charles T.
       Eagle in *Texas Music Education Research* (1994): 23–27.

5.11   University of Victoria Faculty of Education. *Music Education Resource Base.*
       Victoria, BC: University of Victoria, 1995–. http://www.merb.org.
       Citation index that includes the *Canadian Music Index.* Coverage is 1956 to the
       present. Indexes about 35 periodicals, mostly Canadian. Reviewed by Lisa R.
       Philpott in *Notes* 64, no. 2 (Dec. 2007): 344–51.

CEASED MUSIC PERIODICAL INDEXES

The indexes listed next are no longer active; their publication or updating has ceased.
Although not useful for finding recent articles, they can still be helpful when doing
comprehensive or historical research. As with the preceding section, no asterisks have
been assigned here.

5.12   Clark, Chris, Andy Linehan, and Paul Wilson. *POMPI: Popular Music Periodicals
       Index.* 5 vols. London: British Library National Sound Archive, 1988–91.
       Covers about 60 jazz and popular music periodicals. Has a British bias. Arranged
       by subject. Reviewed by Linda M. Fidler in *Notes* 47, no. 2 (Dec. 1990): 390–91.

5.13   Institute for Therapeutics Research. *Music Psychology Index/Music Therapy
       Index.* 3 vols. Denton, TX: Institute for Therapeutics Research, 1976–84.
       First volume is titled *Music Therapy Index.* International in scope, it focuses on the
       psychological and medical aspects of music. Coverage is back to 1960. Reviewed by
       Michael A. Keller and Carol A. Lawrence in *Notes* 36, no. 3 (Mar. 1980): 575–600.

5.14   *Music Article Guide.* 31 vols. Philadelphia: Information Services, 1966–96.
       Was very good for music education and the music industry, especially in America.
       Indexes about 150 periodicals. Includes brief abstracts. Was issued quarterly with

no cumulations, except for a 3-year cumulative index for 1986–88. Reviewed by Bennet Ludden in *Notes* 24, no. 4 (June 1968): 719–20.

5.15 Ruecker, Norbert. *Jazz Index: Bibliography of Jazz Literature in Periodicals and Collections.* 7 vols. Frankfurt: N. Ruecker, 1977–87.

Still useful for the jazz researcher interested in the period covered, 1977–1983. Indexes about 50 periodicals, including foreign ones not indexed elsewhere. Reviewed by Eddie S. Meadows in *American Music* 3, no. 3 (Fall 1985): 356–57.

5.16 Staatliches Institut für Musikforschung Preußischer Kulturbesitz. *Bibliographie des Musikschrifttums.* 34 vols. Leipzig, Ger.: F. Hofmeister; Mainz, Ger.: Schott, 1936–2001.

Similar to *RILM Abstracts* in focus and scope, includes both books and articles in European languages. Indexes about 500 periodicals, including nonmusic journals. Citations grouped by subject. Coverage began in 1936. Last volume published was Vol. 34, covering 1988 (published in 2001). The last few volumes include between 8,000 and 10,000 citations. An online version is being planned. Reviewed by Richard Andrewes in *Musical Times* 121, no. 1650 (Aug. 1980): 503.

5.17 Weinberger, Norman M. *MuSICA Research Database: The Music & Science Information Computer Archive.* Carlsbad, CA: International Music Products Association (NAMM), 1994–. http://www.music-research.org/ResearchTools/musicadb.html.

Database of over 50,000 abstracts back to 1965, created from 1992 to 2001 at the University of California, Irvine. Focus is on research related to music psychology and medicine. Not being updated. Reviewed by Yale Fineman in *Notes* 58, no. 2 (Dec. 2001): 411–14.

PERIODICAL INDEXES FOR RELATED DISCIPLINES

The indexes listed here are useful for topics that cross over into a related or broader body of literature. This list is selective; many more are available. Additional titles include *Philosophers' Index* and *Cumulative Index of Nursing and Allied Health Literature (CINAHL)*. Search your local library catalog, look for subject listings of indexes or research databases, and ask a librarian to identify others available for your use. Your library may also have a different version of these indexes, CD-ROM rather than online, for example. None of these titles have been given an asterisk, because they are specialized and should be searched when appropriate for a particular topic.

American History

5.18 *America: History and Life.* Santa Barbara, CA: ABC-CLIO, 1964–. http://www.abc-clio.com.

Excellent for U.S. and Canadian history. This abstract database indexes over 1,700 journals (also includes dissertations). Includes over a half million entries for articles in 40 languages (the majority are in English). Online coverage is from 1964; it is updated monthly. *Historical Abstracts*, also published by ABC-CLIO, may also be helpful for historical music studies. Recently purchased by EBSCO. Reviewed by Tom Gilson in *Charleston Advisor* 1, no. 1 (July 1999): 11–12.

Business

5.19 *Business Source Premier.* Ipswich, MA: EBSCO, 1999–. http://www.epnet.com.
    Excellent database for music business information. Includes full text for over 8,800
    business publications (over 1,000 are peer-reviewed journals). Full text dates as far
    back as 1965, with more planned. Updated daily. Reviewed by Burton Callicott in
    Charleston Advisor 7, no. 1 (July 2005): 19–22.

Education

5.20 Institute of Education Sciences. *Education Resources Information Center (ERIC).*
    Washington, DC: U.S. Dept. of Education, 1966–. http://www.eric.ed.gov.
    Leading education database, valuable for music education researchers. Includes
    1.2 million citations, with abstracts for over 1,000 education journals dating back
    to 1966. Also includes nonjournal documents. Has been available in print, micro-
    form, and CD-ROM, and now available online. Access is free from U.S. Dept. of
    Education (see URL just given) and via subscription from a wide group of vendors
    (including CSA Illumina, EBSCO, OCLC, and ProQuest). ERIC updates the data-
    base weekly. Some full text is available from ERIC; other full text access varies
    by vendor. Reviewed by Christina Cicchetti in *Charleston Advisor* 2, no. 4 (Apr.
    2001): 5–8 and *Charleston Advisor* 3, no. 2 (Oct. 2001): 12–15.

Humanities

5.21 *Arts & Humanities Citation Index.* Philadelphia: Thomson Scientific, 1976–.
    http://scientific.thomson.com.
    In addition to indexing over 1,000 arts and humanities journals and 7,000 science
    and social science titles, this index allows you to search the cited references within
    the articles. In other words, you can determine which sources have been used
    by other authors. Coverage back to 1975. Includes abstracts from 1999 forward.
    Available from Thomson Scientific through *Web of Science* and also from OCLC,
    Dialog, and DataStar. Updated weekly. *Web of Science* version reviewed by David
    Stern and Chuck Hamaker in *Charleston Advisor* 1, no. 2 (Oct. 1999): 5–10, 13.

5.22 *Humanities Full Text.* New York: H. W. Wilson, 1997–. http://www.hwwilson.com.
    Good for music topics related to other areas in the humanities. Includes over
    640,000 citations (from 1984) and abstracts (from 1994) of about 600 English-
    language periodicals (over 400 peer-reviewed journals). Full text is available for
    over 200 journals back to 1995. Updated daily. Indexing is available in other
    versions (*Humanities Index* and *Humanities Abstracts*) and is complemented by
    Humanities Index Retrospective: 1907–1984. Reviewed by Helene Williams in
    Library Journal 128, no. 5 (Mar. 2003): 124.

Language and Literature

5.23 *Linguistics and Language Behavior Abstracts.* Bethesda, MD: CSA, 1985–.
    http://www.csa.com.

Good for topics such as vocal production. Includes over 360,000 records with abstracts from 1,500 serials. Coverage is back to 1973. Also includes book chapters and dissertations. For earlier articles, search the print *Language and Language Behavior Abstracts,* with coverage back to 1967. Updated monthly. Also available on CD-ROM and online from Ovid.

5.24 Modern Language Association. *MLA International Bibliography.* New York: MLA, 1926–. http://www.mla.org.

Covers literature, language, linguistics, folklore (including music), dramatic arts, etc. Regularly indexes about 3,300 journals. Includes 1.8 million citations. No abstracts or full text. Also indexes books and dissertations. Online coverage back to 1926; updated ten times a year. Includes *JSTOR* links. Published in print, CD-ROM, and online (since 1979). Available from a number of vendors (CSA, EBSCO, Gale, OCLC, and ProQuest); some make full text available. Reviewed by Jody Condit Fagan in *Charleston Advisor* 5, no. 1 (July 2003): 12–18.

Performing Arts

5.25 American Society for Theatre Research. *International Bibliography of Theatre and Dance (IBTD); International Bibliography of Theatre and Dance with Full Text (IBTD with Full Text).* Ipswich, MA: EBSCO, 2005–. http://www.epnet.com.

Helpful for musical theater and dance topics. Includes about 60,000 entries (citations and abstracts) for journal articles, books, and dissertations. Full-text version includes 120 online journal titles and over 50 books and encyclopedias. Updated twice a month. Earlier title (in paper) was *International Bibliography of Theatre.*

5.26 *International Index to the Performing Arts (IIPA).* Ann Arbor, MI: Chadwyck-Healey/ProQuest, 1998–. http://iipa.chadwyck.com/home; *International Index to the Performing Arts Full Text (IIPAFT).* Ann Arbor, MI: Chadwyck-Healey/ProQuest, 1999–. http://iipaft.chadwyck.com.

Has some overlap with Chadwyck-Healey's *IIMP*, but includes broader coverage of performing arts; especially good for theater, film, and dance music. Includes over 400,000 citations with brief abstracts from over 240 journals dating back to 1864 (most are from 1998 on). Eighty journals are full text. Search options are the same as for *IIMP*, including the options to exclude reviews and to limit results to peer-reviewed journals. Can be searched with *IIMP*. Online version updated monthly. Available on CD-ROM (*IIPA* only) and online from ProQuest. Reviewed by Christine Oka in *Library Journal* 129, no. 5 (Mar. 2004): 115.

Science and Medicine

5.27 National Library of Medicine. *Medline.* Bethesda, MD: National Library of Medicine, 1966–. http://www.nlm.nih.gov.

Relevant for music and health topics. Includes citations and abstracts for over 4,800 international biomedical journals, mostly in English, indexed by the National Library of Medicine. Coverage is back to 1965. *Medline* is available free (like *ERIC*) as part of PubMed at http://www.pubmed.gov or from vendors, including OCLC, CSA, and EBSCO. Partial full text is available from some vendors, and update schedule also varies by vendor. Reviewed by Sandi Parker in *Charleston Advisor* 1, no. 3 (Jan. 2000): 5–10.

5.28 *Web of Science*. Philadelphia: Thomson Scientific, 1997–. http://scientific.thomson.com. Includes the *Social Sciences Citation Index* and *Arts & Humanities Citation Index* along with *Science Citation Index Expanded*. Updated weekly. Reviewed by David Stern and Chuck Hamaker in *Charleston Advisor* 1, no. 2 (Oct. 1999): 5–10, 13.

Social Sciences and Psychology

5.29 American Psychological Association (APA). *PsycARTICLES*. Washington, DC: APA, 2001–. http://www.apa.org.
      Includes full text for over 60 peer-reviewed journals published by the APA, the Canadian Psychological Association, and Hogrefe Publishing Group. Includes over 116,000 articles. Coverage from 1985, with historical content dating back to 1894. Updated daily. Available from several vendors in addition to the APA, including CSA, EBSCO, OCLC, and ProQuest. *PsycARTICLES* reviewed by Rick Anderson in *Charleston Advisor* 3, no. 3 (Jan. 2002): 41–43.

5.30 ———. *PsycINFO*. Washington, DC: APA, 1975–. http://www.apa.org.
      Indexes over 2,000 journals (almost all are peer-reviewed) from 50 countries in 25 languages. Includes about 2.25 million records. Also includes English books and dissertations. Includes abstracts. Coverage dates back to the 1890s and includes data from the paper *Psychological Abstracts* and the CD-ROM *Psych Lit*. Available from the APA as well as multiple vendors (including CSA, OCLC, ProQuest, EBSCO, and Thomson). Updated weekly. *PsycINFO* reviewed by Michael Lackey in *Charleston Advisor* 1, no. 3 (Jan. 2000): 11–17, 21.

5.31 *Social Sciences Citation Index*. Philadelphia: Thomson Scientific, 1956–. http://scientific.thomson.com.
      Useful for topics related to music psychology, music therapy, music behavior, etc. Includes citations and abstracts for 1,700 scholarly journals. Another 3,300 are selectively indexed. Online coverage is complete back to the beginning of the index in paper format in 1956. Updated weekly. Also available from Dialog. *Web of Science* version reviewed by David Stern and Chuck Hamaker in *Charleston Advisor* 1, no. 2 (Oct. 1999): 5–10, 13.

MAJOR GENERAL PERIODICAL INDEXES

The large indexes listed next are examples of what is available from some of the major indexing companies. Your library may subscribe to one, some, or all of them. All include music periodicals, all are updated frequently, and many include full text. Some free general periodical indexes are available. *IngentaConnect*, mentioned as part of Gale's *General OneFile*, is one example. At http://www.ingentaconnect.com you can search for free but must pay for access to the articles. Another is *Google Scholar* at http://scholar.google.com. *Google Scholar* generated a lot of interest when it was launched, and it is worth watching to see if it develops into a useful tool for scholarly music research. Generally speaking, the indexes listed here should be your first choices if they are available.

*5.32 *Academic Search Premier.* Ipswich, MA: EBSCO, 2000–. http://www.epnet.com.
One of the largest sources of full-text peer reviewed journals. Includes citations
and abstracts for over 8,000 periodicals, with full text for about 4,500 of them.
Also indexes major newspapers. Backfiles to 1975 are available for over 100 jour-
nals. Easy to search. Updated daily. Reviewed by Cheryl LaGuardia in *Library
Journal* 127, no. 8 (May 2002): 142.

5.33 *ArticleFirst.* Dublin, OH: OCLC, 1992–. http://firstsearch.oclc.org.
The largest database in terms of number of titles, with over 16,000 jour-
nals indexed. Does not include abstracts or full text, however. Coverage
begins in 1990. Has over 19.5 million citations. Part of OCLC's *FirstSearch.*
Updated daily. Reviewed by Mick O'Leary in *Information Today* 11, no. 4
(Apr. 1994): 1–2.

*5.34 *General OneFile.* Farmington Hills, MI: Cengage Learning/Gale, 2000–.
http://gale.cengage.com.
Gale's largest database indexes over 11,000 titles, with over 6,000 of them
full text periodicals. Indexes newspapers. Includes over 63 million records.
Abstracts are included for some citations. Coverage dates back to 1980. *General
OneFile* includes *IngentaConnect* database as well. Updated daily. Reviewed by
Christopher Holly in *Library Journal* 125, no. 19 (Nov. 2000): 107.

5.35 *Internationale Bibliographie der Zeitschriftenliteratur/International Bibliography of Periodical Literature in the Humanities and Social Sciences (IBZ).*
Munich: K. G. Saur, 1993–. http://www.saur.de.
This index (known as "The Dietrich" in Europe, after its founder) began in 1899
and is well respected for scholarly research. Indexes 6,000 periodicals from 40
countries in as many languages, although about half are in English. European
bias. Can be searched in English or German. Updated monthly. Online coverage goes back to 1983; see print for earlier indexing. Reviewed by Elizabeth
McKeigue in *Library Journal* 129, no. 6 (Apr. 2004): 130–31.

5.36 *Periodicals Index Online.* Ann Arbor, MI: Chadwyck-Healey/ProQuest, 2005–.
http://pio.chadwyck.com.
Previously titled *Periodical Contents Index.* Citation database of about 16 million
articles from around 5,000 periodicals in 44 languages. Some citations include
abstracts. Coverage dates from 1665 to 1995. Focus is on the humanities and
social sciences. Full text is available via the companion database, *Periodicals
Archive Online,* with about 475 full text titles. Includes *JSTOR* links. Updated
two or three times a year. Reviewed by Gail Golderman and Bruce Connolly in
Library Journal netConnect (Winter 2006): 24–25.

5.37 *Readers' Guide Full Text, Mega Edition.* New York: H. W. Wilson, 1996–.
http://www.hwwilson.com.
Readers' Guide has been around with various formats and titles since
1900. Provides full text of over 200 general periodicals back to 1994 and
indexing with abstracts for 400 titles back to 1983. Updated daily. Can be
searched with *Readers' Guide Retrospective: 1890–1982.* Also available
on CD-ROM. Reviewed by B. L. Robinson-Jones in *Choice* 41, no. 2 (Oct.
2003): 307.

MAJOR NEWSPAPER INDEXES

Newspaper indexes are useful for finding information on topics of current interest, concert reviews, obituaries, and so on. A number of indexes are available for major newspapers, such as the *New York Times* and the London *Times*. Both LexisNexis and ProQuest have a number of indexes available with varying degrees of coverage. Newspaper indexes have the most frequent update schedules. Some of the general periodical indexes, for example, *Academic Search Premier* and Gale's *General OneFile*, also index some major newspapers.

> 5.38 *LexisNexis Academic*. Dayton, OH: LexisNexis, 1998–. http://www.lexisnexis.com. Provides full text of over 350 newspapers, mostly from the U.S. and Europe. Some are available the same day they are published. Includes the *New York Times* back to 1980 and the London *Times* back to 1985. Also indexes 400 news-related magazines and journals. The "Quick News Search" is recommended. Updated several times a day. Reviewed by Tom Kmetz in *Charleston Advisor* 3, no. 3 (Jan. 2002): 38–41.

> *5.39 *ProQuest Newsstand*. Ann Arbor, MI: ProQuest, 1994–. http://www.proquest.com. Libraries can subscribe to a package of major newspapers or customize the list of titles included for their institution. Includes citations with abstracts for over 500 papers and full text for 350. Some are available the same day they are published. Like *LexisNexis*, it includes the *New York Times* back to 1980, but the London *Times* only back to 1992. Easy to search and to determine the titles indexes as well as their coverage dates. Updated several times a day. Reviewed by Cheryl LaGuardia in *Library Journal* 129, no. 5 (Mar. 2004): 116.

> 5.40 *Times Digital Archive*. Farmington Hills, MI: Gale, 2003–. http://gale.cengage.com. The *Times* (London) from 1785 to 1985 is digitized and searchable in its entirety, including even advertisements. Covers over 7.6 million articles. Easy to search and navigate. Reviewed by Jody Condit Fagan in *Charleston Advisor* 6, no. 4 (Apr. 2005): 54–58.

FINDING ONLINE JOURNALS

Your local library catalog may include a separate listing of electronic journals (e-journals), or you may need to search for them in the regular online catalog under a title or periodical title search. The two collections of online journals, *JSTOR* and *Project MUSE,* are excellent archives of online articles, and periodical indexes are increasingly providing links from their citations to the articles in these digital repositories. *JSTOR* and *Project MUSE* are complementary, with *JSTOR* providing back volumes and *Project MUSE* offering current issues. Another growing source of online articles is via publication in an **open-access journal**. Open-access journals are available for free as an alternative to subscription-based journals. The *Directory of Open Access Journals* (*DOAJ*) provides a listing of scholarly journals in music and other subjects at http://www.doaj.org.

> *5.41 Johns Hopkins University Press, and Milton S. Eisenhower Library. *Project MUSE: Scholarly Journals Online*. Baltimore: Johns Hopkins University Press, 1995–. http://muse.jhu.edu.

Online repository of current volumes of over 300 peer-reviewed journals from nonprofit publishers or associations in the humanities, arts, and social sciences. Includes 11 music journals dating from 2000 and later. Updated as journals become available. Reviewed by Chuck Hamaker in *Charleston Advisor* 1, no. 4 (Apr. 2000): 40–42.

*5.42 *JSTOR*. Music Collection (also part of Arts & Sciences III Collection). New York: JSTOR, 2003–. http://www.jstor.org.

JSTOR stands for *Journal Storage Project*, which began in 1995. Includes back-files of over 600 scholarly journals. Has an embargo on current full-text content ranging from three to five years per title. The Music Collection includes 32 titles. Updated with new journal content annually. Reviewed by Gail Golderman and Bruce Connolly in *Library Journal netConnect* (Winter 2006): 22–24.

EVALUATION CHECKLIST

See also readings by Green, Jenkins, and Troutman in the Suggested Readings.

- What is the index's format: print, CD-ROM, or online?
- How long is the indexing time lag?
- How frequently is the index updated?
- How comprehensive is the coverage of titles?
- How many citations are included?
- How accurate are the citations?
- How many titles are indexed?
    - Are the titles international?
    - How many languages are represented?
    - Are the titles scholarly or popular?
    - What is indexed in addition to periodicals (e.g., dissertations or Festschriften)?
- What is the publication date range indexed?
- Is full text provided?
    - Is full text in PDF or HTML?
    - Are links to full text provided (e.g., in *JSTOR*)?
- Are abstracts included?
- How good is the search interface?
    - Is it easy to use?
    - Is the subject heading schema intuitive?
    - Are the indexes browsable (for names, subjects, etc.)?
    - Can multiple indexes be searched simultaneously?
    - Are newer types of search available (such as visual)?
- Are links provided to other content (for e.g., audio or reference)?

SUGGESTED READINGS

Four of the readings compare the three major music periodical indexes: Gillie, Green ("Keeping Up with the Times"), Jenkins, and Troutman. In "The *RILM* Project," Green discusses *RILM* in detail. Davidson offers insight into the selection of titles for inclusion in the *RIPM* project. Finally, Clarence et al. discuss general reference tools, especially periodical indexes, useful for musicians.

Clarence, Judy, Paula Elliot, Stephen Landstreet, and Howard Rodriguez. "'Look That Up in Your *Funk and Wagnall's*!': Music Reference Using Alternative Sources." *Music Reference Services Quarterly* 8, no. 3 (2004): 25–36.

Davidson, Mary Wallace. "The Riddle of RIPM's Americas Initiative." *Bulletin of the Society for American Music* 32, no. 1 (Winter 2006): 5, 9.

Gillie, Esther. "Fauré at Your Fingertips: Can You Find All You Need Online?" *Choral Journal* 44, no. 2 (Sept. 2003): 9–15.

Green, Alan. "Keeping Up with the Times: Evaluating Currency of Indexing, Language Coverage and Subject Area Coverage in the Three Music Periodical Index Databases." *Music Reference Services Quarterly* 8, no. 1 (2001): 53–68.

———. "The *RILM* Project: Charting the Seas of Modern Musicological Literature." *College Music Symposium* 40 (2000): 42–54.

Jenkins, Martin D. "A Descriptive Study of Subject Indexing and Abstracting in *International Index to Music Periodicals*, *RILM Abstracts of Music Literature*, and *The Music Index Online*." *Notes* 57, no. 4 (June 2001): 834–63.

Troutman, Leslie. "Comprehensiveness of Indexing in Three Music Periodical Index Databases." *Music Reference Services Quarterly* 8, no. 1 (2001): 39–51.

CHAPTER 6

Indexes to Music Dissertations, Theses, Conference Papers, and Festschriften

Finding music dissertations and theses, conference papers, articles in Festschriften, and other articles published in collections requires a mix of tools already discussed and some new ones as well. The catalogs described in Chapter 4 and periodical indexes covered in Chapter 5 are helpful for these types of documents. For example, *RILM Abstracts* (entry 5.3) indexes everything discussed in this chapter as well as journal articles, while others do not. Following are introductions to each category and a bibliography of research tools helpful for finding them.

DISSERTATIONS AND THESES

Doctoral dissertations and master's theses are important to researchers for a number of reasons. They represent original research; often they are "cutting edge" in some way. Like periodical articles, they focus on a narrow topic yet cover it in a detailed, comprehensive manner. Good dissertations and theses will have an exhaustive literature search that can be helpful for your own research. Excellent ones can serve as models for your own thesis if you will be writing one for your degree. Often a fine dissertation or thesis will be revised and published as a book or articles.

There are several challenges with dissertations and theses. Traditionally, they have been available in paper or microform. The copy available in these formats may be of poor quality, especially any reproduced illustrations or musical examples. They may have local call numbers at your institution's library. The quality can vary significantly. While some are outstanding, others are surprisingly bad. Accessibility can be difficult. Often only the author's institution's library will own a thesis, particularly if at the master's level. Interlibrary loan is often unpredictable with dissertations and theses, and it is sometimes impossible. Purchasing them from University Microfilms, Inc. (UMI), via *ProQuest Dissertations and Theses* (*PQDT*), is one option. Contacting the author directly should be a last resort.

One relatively recent initiative intended to help increase access is the submission of electronic theses and dissertations (**ETDs**). Some colleges and universities require electronic submission; at other schools, electronic submission is optional. In time, ETDs will likely be the norm.

ETDs raise questions about submission, access, storage, and preservation. Some colleges and universities are making ETDs available through institutional repositories or shared repositories. The *OhioLINK* consortium mentioned in Chapter 4 provides access to ETDs from member institutions, for example. The Networked Digital Library of Theses and Dissertations (NDLTD) is an international group of around 175 institutions that hosts a union catalog of ETDs. Furthermore, the Library of Congress named UMI as the official repository for ETDs from the U.S. Other concerns revolve around copyright and fair use and whether or not ETDs will be viewed as "published" by conventional publishers. These issues and others are discussed in the article by Yale Fineman in the Suggested Readings. See also the extensive *Guide for Electronic Theses and Dissertations,* published by UNESCO on the web at http://www.etdguide.org.

Dissertations and theses may or may not have LC subject headings describing the topic of the document. Your local online catalog might have a format limit for them. If not, use the note in the record, which includes the degree, institution, and date, to devise keyword searches. A doctoral dissertation from the University of Colorado at Boulder from 2005 would have the following note: "Thesis (Ph.D.)—University of Colorado, 2005."

Dissertations and theses are included in several of the tools already covered in earlier chapters. For example, *WorldCat* (entry 4.12) includes dissertations and many master's theses not indexed elsewhere. In *WorldCat* you can limit your search results to "thesis/dissertation" using the subtype limit under "any content" in the Advanced Search option. Some periodical indexes include citations and/or abstracts for dissertations, while others do not. Of the major music periodical indexes, *RILM Abstracts* (entry 5.3) and *Music Index* (entry 5.2) include dissertations, but *IIMP* (entry 5.1) does not. Examples of other periodical indexes that do include dissertations are *America: History and Life* (entry 5.18), *ERIC* (entry 5.20), and *MLA International Bibliography* (entry 5.24).

Some music periodicals include listings of completed dissertations and/or those in progress. These may be published regularly or irregularly. For example, *Die Musikforschung* includes an annual listing, titled "Im Jahre XXXX angenommene musikwissenschaftliche Dissertationen," which always appears in Heft 2 (issue number 2) of each volume. See also the web database of the Gesellschaft für Musikforschung, at http://musikwiss.uni-muenster.de, which includes theses in progress. *Ethnomusicology* has published an annual list of dissertations and theses for the past several years, but it is not always in the same issue. *Music Theory Online* (*MTO*) announces dissertations and has a cumulative index of them available online at http://www.societymusictheory. org/mto/mto-dissertations.php. *Nuova rivista musicale italiana* included bibliographies in volumes 21 (1987), 22 (1988), and 28 (1994), titled "Le tesi in storia della musica discusse nelle università italiane." Similarly, the *Research Chronicle of the Royal Musical Association* includes listings in various volumes, most notably in volumes 3 (1963), 25 (1992), and 27 (1994). None have appeared recently in either *Nuova rivista musicale italinana* or *Research Chronicle.*

Also be aware that there are published bibliographies of doctoral dissertations and theses on specific topics. These can be very helpful if one is available for the subject you are researching. Examples include two titles by James R. Heintze, *American Music Studies: A Classified Bibliography of Master's Theses.* (Detroit, MI: Information Coordinators, 1984) and *Igor Stravinsky: An International Bibliography of Theses and Dissertations, 1925–2000*, 2nd ed. (Warren, MI: Harmonie Park Press, 2001). Another example is *Canadian Music and Education: An Annotated Bibliography of Theses and Dissertations* by Diane E. Peters (Lanham, MD: Scarecrow, 1997). These all include the subject heading "Dissertations, Academic—Bibliography" and may have a place name as well, e.g., "Dissertations, Academic—Canada—Bibliography." In addition they include a topical heading, e.g., "Stravinsky, Igor, 1882–1971—Bibliography." The LC call numbers will vary, as these do, although all are in the bibliographies range. ML120 is for bibliographies by place; ML128 is for bibliographies by topic; and ML134 for those about composers.

Research tools specifically dedicated to dissertations and theses are listed next. Be sure also to search *WorldCat*, *RILM Abstracts*, and *Music Index*, as mentioned earlier. Music-specific guides are listed first followed by general sources. Additional web-based indexes of dissertations are provided at this text's companion website. Asterisks indicate major tools in each category.

INDEXES OF DISSERTATIONS AND THESES

Music-Specific Indexes of Dissertations and Theses

6.1   Adkins, Cecil, and Alis Dickinson. *Doctoral Dissertations in Musicology.* Philadelphia: American Musicological Society (AMS), 1952–1996.
A project of the AMS in conjunction with first the Music Teachers National Association and later the International Musicological Society. Editors and title varied. Included only North American titles (U.S. and Canadian) through the 1972 edition; became more international with the 1977 edition. The two important cumulative editions were published in 1984 (7th North American and 2nd International editions) and 1996 (2nd series, 2nd Cumulative edition). Arranged by style period (Baroque, Classical, etc.). Citations lack abstracts. Includes indexes for subject and author. All entries from the print editions are present in *DDM-Online* along with corrections and updates. Reviewed by Dennis North in *ARBA* (1972): 400.

6.2   Council for Research in Music Education. *International Directory of Dissertations in Progress (DIP).* Urbana-Champaign: University of Illinois, 1969–. Dissertations are arranged by category (topic). Does not include abstracts. Indexes include author, advisor, institution, and category. In print from 1969 to 1997 with various titles, including *Institutional Directory of Approved Music Education Dissertations in Progress* and *Approved Doctoral Dissertations in Progress in Music Education.* Expected to be continued online at http://www.crme.uiuc.edu.

*6.3   Mathiesen, Thomas J. *Doctoral Dissertations in Musicology-Online (DDM-Online).* Center for the History of Music Theory and Literature: Indiana University, 1996–. http://www.music.indiana.edu/ddm.

Free website that includes all the records from the print editions of *Doctoral Dissertations in Musicology* with corrections as well as updates from 1995 on. Database is searchable and browsable; see Figure 6-1. Does not include abstracts, but records do have keywords. Includes completed dissertations as well as those in progress. Information is entered by the authors. Reviewed in the *Scout Report* at http://scout.wisc.edu/Archives/SPT--FullRecord.php?ResourceId=2031 and by Andrew Toulas in *Notes* 63, no. 1 (Sept. 2006): 159–63.

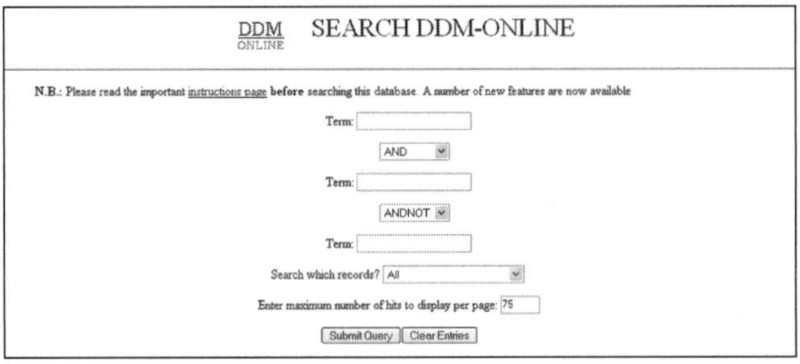

Figure 6-1 *Doctoral Dissertations in Musicology-Online* Search Screen *(With permission of the Center for the History of Music Theory and Literature, Jacobs School of Music, Indiana University)*

General Indexes of Dissertations and Theses

6.4   Center for Research Libraries. *Foreign Doctoral Dissertations.* Chicago: CRL, 2000–. http://www.crl.edu/content.asp?l1=5&l2=23&l3=44&l4=25.
Free, searchable database of 20,000 dissertations. Loans are possible for member institutions. No abstracts are included. CRL holds 750,000 uncataloged foreign dissertations, so searching the CRL catalog or contacting CRL may be necessary. Fewer than 100 include the subject "music."

6.5   *Index to Theses.* London: Expert Information, 1996–. http://www.theses.com.
Fee-based database of over 500,000 British and Irish theses dating back to 1716. Abstracts are included for about half, dating from 1970 on. A search on music (code A4a) pulls up over 2,000 hits. Nicely designed and easy to search. The online database includes all the records from the print versions, titled *Index to Theses Accepted for Higher Degrees by the Universities of Great Britain and Ireland* and *Index to Theses with Abstracts Accepted for Higher Degrees by the Universities of Great Britain and Ireland.* Also available in paper. Reviewed briefly in *Online* 28, no. 2 (Mar.–Apr. 2004): 10.

6.6   Networked Digital Library of Theses and Dissertations (NDLTD). *ETD Union Catalog.* Blacksburg, VA: NDLTD, 2001–. http://www.ndltd.org/browse.en.html.
Free union catalog of ETDs from the approximately 175 members of the NDLTD. Various search engines are offered; the OCLC Collection Search and Clustering and the Scirus ETD Search are recommended. The database contains over 250,000 dissertations and will continue to grow as ETDs become the norm in higher education. Reviewed by B. M. Lopez-Fitzsimmons in *Choice* 44, no. 2 (Oct. 2006): 262.

6.7 ProQuest Dissertations & Theses (PQDT). Ann Arbor, MI: UMI, 2005–. http://proquest.com.

The best source for dissertations and master's theses. International but primarily North American. Coverage goes back to 1861 and includes about 2.3 million dissertations and theses. Subscription-based database includes basic and advanced search options, abstracts (for dissertations from 1980 and theses since 1988), and a free 24-page preview (from 1997). Dissertations and theses from your own institution can be downloaded for free. ProQuest is a leader in the move to electronic theses and dissertations. In 1998, the Library of Congress designated UMI as the official U.S. repository for ETDs. ProQuest has committed to digitize all dissertations submitted from 1997 on regardless of the format submitted. The only subject headings for music are "Music" (over 27,000 records) and "Music Education" (ca. 6,000 records), so use keyword searching in combination with them. See the Advanced Search Screen in Figure 6-2. You may purchase dissertations or theses from ProQuest, but you may want to try getting them via ILL first. Your purchase options may be a PDF file, hard copy, and/or microform. This database was previously titled *ProQuest Digital Dissertations.* Also available in print and CD-ROM from ProQuest and online (without full text or 24-page previews) from other vendors (OCLC, Dialog, and Ovid). Reviewed by Doris Small Helfer in *Searcher* 11, no. 7 (July–Aug. 2003): 46–48 and Andrew Toulas in *Notes* 63, no. 1 (Sept. 2006): 159-63.

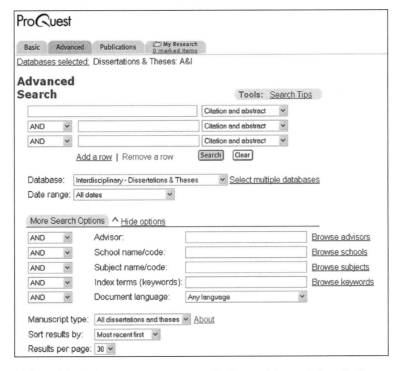

Figure 6-2 *ProQuest Dissertations and Theses* Advanced Search Screen *(Image published with permission of ProQuest CSA. Further reproduction is prohibited without permission)*

6.8   *Theses Canada Portal/Portail de Thèses Canada.* Ottawa, ON: Library and
       Archives Canada, 2004–. http://www.collectionscanada.ca/thesescanada.
       Free database that includes citations for about 250,000 Canadian theses from
       1965 on included in *AMICUS.* Records include abstracts and subject headings.
       Full text available for those completed in 1998 and later. Others are available on
       microform for lending. Reviewed by Lisa R. Philpott in *Notes* 64, no. 2 (Dec.
       2007): 344–51.

French

6.9   Gribenski, Jean. *French Language Dissertations in Music: An Annotated
       Bibliography.* RILM Retrospectives, no. 2. New York: Pendragon, 1979.
       Includes abstracts for around 450 dissertations from 45 universities (mostly from
       France) dating from 1883 to 1976. Arranged by subject, with indexes for authors,
       subjects, date, and university. Reviewed by Geraldine Ostrove in *Notes* 36, no. 2
       (Dec. 1979): 377–78.

German

6.10 *Dissertationsmeldestelle (DMS).* Kassel, Ger.: Gesellschaft für Musikforschung,
       1998–. http://musikwiss.uni-muenster.de.
       Free website that includes German-language dissertations from Austria,
       Switzerland, and Germany from 1998. No abstracts are included. Pay atten-
       tion to the search instructions; for example, you need to search Mozart as
       "%moza%". Once completed, the projects are published in the society's journal,
       Die Musikforschung.

6.11 Schaal, Richard. *Verzeichnis deutschsprachiger musikwissenschaftlicher Dis-
       sertationen: 1861–1960.* Kassel, Ger.: Bärenreiter, 1963.
       Includes about 3,000 entries without abstracts. Arranged alphabetically by author.
       A supplement was published in 1974 updating through 1970. Includes one index
       of topics and authors. Reviewed by Erich Schenk in *Die Musikforschung* 17, no. 4
       (Oct.–Dec. 1964): 421–23.

CONFERENCE PAPERS AND CONGRESS REPORTS

Scholars often present work in progress at conferences to get feedback. As a result,
these **conference papers** may or may not be published except as part of a **conference
report** or **proceeding**. Published conference proceedings can be hard to find in online
catalogs. The details of a conference—its name, place, and date—can be difficult to
remember. The titles of the papers and names of the presenters may not all be included
in the catalog records. Sometimes there is a long time lag between the date of the conference and the publication of the papers.

     Yet conference reports can be valuable for research. Conferences devoted to a par-
ticular topic, for example, a single composer, can result in a significant contribution to
the scholarship on that musician. Tracking the topics, frequency, and so on of conferences is also valuable for those conducting historiographical studies in music.

When searching for conference proceedings in your online catalog or union catalog, you can locate **congress reports** by entering the LC subject heading subdivision "Congresses" with the topical subject heading. Congresses on one topic are assigned the LC call number for that subject. Others on multiple topics are given call numbers in the ML35–38 range.

The following research tools, along with *WorldCat*, *RILM Abstracts*, *ERIC*, etc., provide access to published conference papers. Also, the *NGO* article "Congress Reports" (see the Suggested Readings) includes a chronological listing of conference reports.

INDEXES OF CONFERENCE PAPERS AND CONGRESS REPORTS

Music-Specific Indexes of Conference Papers and Congress Reports

6.12 Briquet, Marie. *La musique dans les congrès internationaux (1835–1939).* Publications de la Société française de musicologie, sér. 2, no. 10. Paris: Heugel, 1961.
Includes a listing of 164 congress reports, arranged by subject. Includes indexes by place, date, author, and subject. Reviewed by Richard Schaal in *Die Musikforschung* 17, no. 2 (Apr.–June 1964): 183.

*6.13 Cowdery, James R., Zdravko Blažeković, and Barry S. Brook. *Speaking of Music: Music Conferences, 1835–1966.* RILM Retrospective Series, no. 4. New York: RILM, 2004.
Largely supersedes earlier bibliographies of conference proceedings. Papers are arranged using the *RILM Abstracts* numerical subject codes. Each is assigned an accession number that includes the subject code and an abbreviation indicating the type of paper. Includes abstracts. Has three indexes: conference location; sponsor; and authors and subjects. Reviewed by Manuel Erviti in *Notes* 62, no. 1 (Sept. 2005): 106–7.

6.14 Tyrrell, John, and Rosemary Wise. *A Guide to International Congress Reports in Musicology: 1900–1975.* New York: Garland, 1979.
Listing is chronological and then alphabetical by place. All the papers from a conference are listed together. Includes indexes by place; titles, series, and sponsor; author and editor; and subject. Reviewed by Walter Gerboth in *Notes* 36, no. 4 (June 1980): 902–3.

General Indexes of Conference Papers and Congress Reports

*6.15 *PapersFirst.* Dublin, OH: OCLC, 1995–. http://www.oclc.org.
This is the more useful of the two OCLC databases devoted to international conference proceedings, because you can search by author and title and get more specific information about the papers given at a particular conference. No abstracts are included. OCLC states that coverage begins in 1993, but some earlier papers are included.

6.16 *ProceedingsFirst*. Dublin, OH: OCLC, 1995–. http://www.oclc.org.
      This companion database to *PapersFirst* is useful primarily for finding informa-
      tion about the conferences rather than for the specific papers presented. The papers
      and authors are listed but are not searchable. Sometimes just called *Proceedings*.

FESTSCHRIFTEN

A **Festschrift** is a collection of essays published in a book to honor an individual (for
an important birthday or anniversary or as a memorial) or an institution. The German
word has been adopted for all collections of this type in any language.

Because of their nature, the articles or chapters included in a Festschrift are often
written by scholars working in the same area as the honoree. Just as with congress
reports, the individual titles and authors of papers may not be included in the catalog
records for Festschriften in your local or union catalog. The papers are often very
good; scholars tend to do good work when writing to honor a colleague they respect.

Festschriften on a single topic are assigned LC subject headings and LC call
numbers for that subject. Those on a variety of topics are given the call number ML55.
An LC subject heading is included for the name of the person or institution being hon-
ored if more than 20 percent of the book is about that person or institution. Festschriften
and the individual papers contained within them are not easy to find.

In addition to the research title given next, *RILM Abstracts* is the best database to
search for those Festschriften published after 1967 when RILM began. Papers included
are identified as "Article in a Festschrift" in the document type field. RILM was recently
awarded a grant from the National Endowment for the Humanities to create an index to
music Festschriften published before 1967.

INDEXES OF FESTSCHRIFTEN

Music-Specific Indexes of Festschriften

*6.17 Gerboth, Walter. *An Index to Musical Festschriften and Similar Publications*.
       New York: W. W. Norton, 1969.
       Ironically, this was first published in a Festschrift dedicated to Gustave Reese
       (LaRue, Jan, ed. *Aspects of Medieval and Renaissance Music: A Birthday
       Offering to Gustave Reese*. New York: W. W. Norton, 1966). The 1969 publica-
       tion is an update and revision of the original. In three parts: a list of Festschriften
       by honoree, a listing of articles by subject, and an author–subject index. Most
       Festschriften listed date from the late nineteenth century up to 1967. Reviewed
       by Donald Seibert in *Notes* 26, no. 4 (June 1970): 760–61.

General Indexes of Essays

6.18 *Essay and General Literature Index*. New York: H. W. Wilson, 1900–.
      http://www.hwwilson.com.

Online version coverage begins in 1984 and includes around 65,000 papers from over 5,000 books. Search the paper volumes for earlier indexing from 1900. Includes articles published in Festschriften. Citations do not include abstracts. A search on "music" as a keyword brought up about 2,500 hits. Updated daily. Also available in print and CD-ROM. Reviewed by Susan Gilroy in *Library Journal* 125, no. 20 (Dec. 2000): 200, 202.

EVALUATION CHECKLIST

Evaluation of these research tools is similar to periodical indexes; see also the checklist for Chapter 5.

Here are some special considerations for theses and dissertations, adapted in part from Toulas.[1]

- Are theses listed completed or registered or in progress?
- How good is the search engine and browsing functionality?
- Which and how many nationalities are included?
- What is the date range of indexing?
- Are abstracts or full text available?

SUGGESTED READINGS

The readings listed describe the writings on music covered in this chapter and discuss their uses and issues related to them. Fineman's article discusses the advantages and disadvantages of ETDs for music. The two *New Grove* articles explain congress reports and Festschriften, respectively. In addition, "Congress Reports" includes a list of published reports dating from 1860 to 2002. Tyrell's article describes the value of congress reports to historiographical studies.

Fineman, Yale. "Electronic Theses and Dissertations in Music." *Notes* 60, no. 4 (June 2004): 893–907.

Sadie, Stanley, ed. *The New Grove Dictionary of Music and Musicians*. 2nd ed. New York: Grove, 2001. S.v. "Congress Reports," by Nigel Simeone and David A. Threasher. Also available from *Grove Music Online*. http://www.oxfordmusiconline.com.

Sadie, Stanley, ed. *The New Grove Dictionary of Music and Musicians*. 2nd ed. New York: Grove, 2001. S.v. "Festschriften," by Nigel Simeone. Also available from *Grove Music Online*. http://www.oxfordmusiconline.com.

Toulas, Andrew. "Dissertation Databases on the Web." *Notes* 63, no. 1 (Sept. 2006): 159–63.

Tyrrell, John. "Congress Reports as History." *Musical Times* 121, no. 1646 (Apr. 1980): 238–41.

---

[1]Andrew Toulas, "Dissertation Databases on the Web," *Notes* 63, no. 1 (Sept. 2006): 159–63.

CHAPTER 7

Indexes to Music in Complete Works Editions, Musical Monuments, Historical Sets, and Anthologies

As a researcher and performer, there are times when the music you need is not available in an edition other than a composer's complete works edition, a historical set or musical monument, or an anthology. Other times, perhaps for study purposes, you may want to see a group of similar pieces in one collection, for example, in a historical anthology. Historical sets and musical monuments include examples of music of a particular type, genre, period, or geographical area. Because these editions, especially those published since World War II, are typically critical and scholarly, they are useful sources of information about the music as well. For example, you can turn to a composer's complete works edition for the source of a text for vocal music and to get information about the original sources (manuscript and early editions) for a particular work.

Finding music in large multi-volume sets can be a little more complicated than finding music published either individually or in smaller collections. I have seen students daunted by rows of volumes of these scores sitting on the library shelves and not having a good idea of how to find the piece(s) they need. Most libraries do not catalog the contents of each volume of these sets, so searching your local library catalog will often only tell you if your library has a particular set, give you the call number, and list the volumes held. These are usually serial publications and are typically cataloged like journals, without a listing of the contents. The next logical question is whether the sets themselves provide access to the individual pieces, either through a detailed index to the entire set or through the tables of contents of each volume. Unfortunately, the answer to this question is often "no," because the sets are typically published over a span of years and not necessarily in volume-number order. Also, many of these sets are published in European languages (often German), so the use of separate English-language indexes is often easier for many English-speaking graduate students. Before describing the specific indexes that list the contents of these multi-volume scores, different types of sets and series will be explained along with the potential uses of the music they contain.

Music scholars do not always employ the same terminology for these large sets and series of music scores. For example, the articles in *Grove Music Online* (*GMO*) and the *Harvard Dictionary of Music* (listed in the Suggested Readings) differ in their choice of terminology. In this discussion three distinctions will be made. First, a composer's complete works edition will refer to the entire output of a particular composer. Next, historical sets and musical monuments will be grouped together because they are indexed in the same tools, have the same base call number, and are often used in the same ways by students. These include large multi-volume publications of music from a particular country or region and style period and in a certain genre or medium. Also in this category, though not including edited music, are series of music published in facsimile. Broude Brothers and Garland are two publishers of **facsimile editions**. Third are smaller anthologies, those consisting of just one or a few volumes. Those anthologies are published as companions to music history texts and are discussed in Chapter 9, which is devoted to histories. However, the indexes described here can be used to find music included in those anthologies as well.

COMPLETE WORKS EDITIONS

Complete works editions (sometimes called **collected editions**) attempt to present editions of all of the musical works by an individual composer. The titles of composers complete works include (in German) Werke, Sämtliche Werke, Neue Ausgabe sämtlicher Werke, and Gesamtausgabe; (in French) Œuvres or Œuvres complètes; (in Latin) Opera omnia; (in Italian) Opere, Opere complete, and Tutte; and (in Spanish) Obras or Obras completas.

In the LC classification system, these are given the call number M3, subarranged alphabetically by the composer's last name. The LC subject headings for composers complete works editions are often not particularly helpful; for example, the subject heading is often simply "Music," although sometimes the composer's name followed by "Works" is used. The best way to search for them in online catalogs is to do an author search for the composer and simply the title "works." Citations for complete works editions are also included in *GMO* composer articles, just before the works lists.

Be aware that although an edition may be called "complete" it may not include every single piece by a composer. For example, recently discovered works and arrangements may be omitted, or perhaps the edition was never finished. Sometimes editions are published for a subset of a composer's compositions, for example, *Collected Works for Solo Keyboard* by C. P. E. Bach. These are given the LC call number M3.1. Furthermore, a complete works edition for a composer with a relatively small output may be included as one or more volumes of a historical set or musical monument. For example, the series *Corpus mensurabilis musicae* (*CMM*), which focuses on polyphonic music from the fourteenth through the sixteenth centuries, includes complete works editions for many composers of the period, including Dufay (listed later), Isaac, and Rore.

Sorting out the publication details of these editions can be challenging. As already mentioned, they are often published over a wide span of years, one volume at a time, and often not in volume-number order. They are often cooperative ventures involving multiple editors or publishers. Many of these editions have been reprinted by publishers such as J. W. Edwards, Da Capo, Dover, Broude Brothers, and Gregg Press. These reprints may or may not keep the same volume numbering as the original publication.

Some have been reissued on microform. The Keith E. Mixter article in the Suggested Readings discusses these issues further.

Some composers, like Bach, have had their complete works editions revisited in order to provide more accurate editions reflecting contemporary editing practices and to incorporate the most current research. Generally speaking, you should use a "new" complete works edition when one is available and if it includes the piece you need. Other composers with both old and new editions include Beethoven, Brahms, Mozart, Schubert, and Schumann. Additional composers with more than one collected works edition include Handel, Haydn, and Mendelssohn.

The new Bach and Mozart editions were each in progress for over fifty years. The J. S. Bach *New Edition of the Complete Works/Neue Ausgabe sämtlicher Werke* started in 1954. It was completed in 2007 with over 100 volumes in nine series. The main nine series of the Mozart *New Edition of the Complete Works/Neue Ausgabe sämtlicher Werke* were published from 1955 to 1991. Since then work continued on a supplement of around twenty-five volumes. Completion is anticipated soon.

On the other hand, some major composers have not yet had a complete works edition of their music published. Examples include Charles Ives and Igor Stravinsky. See the reading related to C. P. E. Bach, later, for a discussion of some of the issues surrounding funding and publication of composers complete works editions. The most comprehensive listing of these editions accompanies the *GMO* article "Editions, Historical," in the Suggested Readings.

Because complete works editions for composers with a large output include many volumes, they are often further divided into series. Often the series are by genre. For example, the nine series of the new Bach edition mentioned earlier use this model: Series I is for cantatas; Series II is for the masses, passions, and oratorios; and so on. Other possibilities for complete or collected works include arranging the works chronologically or even alphabetically by title. Further division of the volumes within a series can include parts.

Finally, you will need a page number to get to the individual work you are looking for. In other words, you will need several numbers (at least series, volume, and page) and will need to know what each number represents. There is also the possibility that your library may not have the original publication for some complete works editions. **Reprint editions** by publishers like Dover are usually published with a variant of the series and volume arrangement of the original.

Examples of Composers Complete Works Editions

Appendix C lists the composers that have been chosen to serve as examples throughout the remainder of this text. Composers from that list who have complete editions of their works published are listed next. This list is selective; other editions do exist for some of these composers. The ones listed here are generally the best respected or the most widely held by libraries. If more than one is available, the recommended edition has an asterisk.

Bach, Johann Sebastian

7.1   *Johann Sebastian Bach's Werke.* Edited by the Bach-Gesellschaft. 47 vols. Leipzig, Ger.: Breitkopf and Härtel, 1851–99.

*7.2   *Neue Ausgabe sämtlicher Werke.* Edited by the Johann-Sebastian-Bach-Institute Göttingen and the Bach-Archiv, Leipzig. 103 vols. Kassel, Ger.: Bärenreiter, 1954–2007.

Beethoven, Ludwig van

7.3   *Ludwig van Beethoven's Werke: Vollständige kritisch durchgesehene überall berechtigte Ausgabe.* Edited by Eusebius Mandyczewski and others. 25 series. Leipzig, Ger.: Breitkopf and Härtel, 1862–88.

7.4   *Supplemente zur Gesamtausgabe.* Edited by Willy Hess. 14 vols. Wiesbaden, Ger.: Breitkopf and Härtel, 1959–71.

*7.5   *Werke.* [New ed.] Edited by the Beethoven-Archiv, Bonn, Munich: G. Henle, 1961–. Ongoing, with 35 vols. published and 56 planned.

Brahms, Johannes

*7.6   *Neue Ausgabe sämtlicher Werke.* Edited by the Johannes Brahms Gesamtausgabe eingetragener Verein and the Gesellschaft der Musikfreunde, Wien. Munich: G. Henle, 1996–. Ongoing, with 7 vols. published and 65 planned.

7.7   *Sämtliche Werke.* Edited by Gesellschaft der Musikfreunde, Wien. 26 vols. Leipzig, Ger.: Breitkopf and Härtel, 1926–27.

Chopin, Frédéric

7.8   *Complete Works: According to the Autographs and Original Editions with Critical Commentary.* Edited by Ignace J. Paderewski and others. 21 vols. Warsaw: Fryderyk Chopin Institute; Kraków: Polish Music Publications, 1949–62.

Debussy, Claude

7.9   *Œuvres complètes de Claude Debussy.* Edited by François Lesure and others. Paris: Durand, 1985–2018? Ongoing, with 14 vols. published and 34 planned.

Dufay, Guillaume

7.10   *Opera Omnia.* Edited by Heinrich Besseler. 6 vols. *Corpus mensurabilis musicae*, 1. Rome: American Institute of Musicology, 1951–66. Vol. 6 was revised by David Fallows in 1995.

Handel, George Frideric

7.11   *George* Frederic *Händels Werke.* Edited by the Deutschen Händel-Gesellschaft. 102 vols. Leipzig, Ger.: Breitkopf and Härtel, 1858–1902.

*7.12   Hallische *Händel-Ausgabe/Halle Handel Edition.* Edited by the Georg Friedrich Händel-Gesellschaft. Kassel, Ger.: Bärenreiter, 1955–. Ongoing, with 69 vols. published and around 130 planned.

Haydn, Franz Joseph

7.13   *Werke.* Edited by Haydn-Institute, Cologne. Munich: G. Henle, 1958–. Ongoing, with 93 vols. published and 111 planned.

Josquin des Prez

*7.14 *New Josquin Edition.* Edited by Willem Elders and others. Utrecht, Neth.: Koninklijke Vereniging voor Nederlandse Muziekgeschiedenis (KVNM), 1987–. Ongoing, with 32 vols. published and 60 planned.

7.15 *Werken van Josquin des Prez.* Edited by Albert Smijers and others. 55 vols. Amsterdam: G. Alsbach, 1921–69.

Landini, Francesco

*7.16 *The Works of Francesco Landini.* Edited by Leonard Ellinwood. Mediaeval Academy of America Publication, no. 36. Cambridge, MA: Mediaeval Academy of America, 1939.

7.17 *The Works of Francesco Landini.* Edited by Leo Schrade. Polyphonic Music of the Fourteenth Century, vol. 4. Monaco: Editions de l'Oiseau-Lyre, 1958.

Liszt, Franz

7.18 *Franz Liszts Musikalische Werke.* Edited by Franz Liszt-Stiftung. 33 vols. Leipzig, Ger.: Breitkopf and Härtel, 1907–36.

*7.19 *Neue Ausgabe sämtlicher Werke/New Edition of the Complete Works.* Edited by Zoltan Gárdonyi and others. Budapest: Editio Musica, 1970–. Ongoing, with 42 vols. published and 53 planned.

Machaut, Guillaume de

*7.20 *Musikalische Werke.* Edited by Friedrich Ludwig and Heinrich Besseler. 4 vols. Leipzig, Ger.: Breitkopf and Härtel, 1926–54.

7.21 *The Works of Guillaume de Machaut.* Edited by Leo Schrade. 2 vols. Polyphonic Music of the Fourteenth Century, vols. 2–3. Monaco: Editions de l'Oiseau-Lyre, 1956.

Monteverdi, Claudio

*7.22 *Opera omnia.* Edited by the Fondazione Claudio Monteverdi. Instituta et monumenta. Ser. 1. Monumenta, vol. 5. Cremona, It.: Fondazione Claudio Monteverdi, 1970–. Ongoing, with 13 vols. published and 20 planned.

7.23 *Tutte le opere di Claudio Monteverdi.* Edited by G. Francesco Malipiero. 17 vols. Asolo, It.: Malipiero; Vienna: Universal Edition, 1926–68.

Mozart, Wolfgang Amadeus

*7.24 *Neue Ausgabe sämtlicher Werke.* Edited by the Internationale Stiftung Mozarteum, Salzburg. 99 vols. Kassel, Ger.: Bärenreiter, 1955–91. Publication of supplement (ca. 25 vols.) is ongoing and is expected to be completed soon. Also available online free of charge at *NMA Online* at http://dme.mozarteum.at.

7.25 *Wolfgang Amadeus Mozart's Werke.* Edited by Johannes Brahms and others. 24 series. Leipzig, Ger.: Breitkopf and Härtel, 1877–1905.

Palestrina, Giovanni Pierluigi da

7.26 *Le opere complete di Giovanni Pierluigi da Palestrina.* Edited by Raffaele Casimiri. 34 vols. Rome: Fratelli Scalera, 1939–87.

Pérotin

7.27 *The Works of Perotin.* Edited by Ethel Thurston. New York: Kalmus, 1970.

Schoenberg, Arnold

7.28 *Sämtliche Werke.* Edited by the Akademie der Künste, Berlin. Mainz, Ger.: Schott; Vienna: Universal Edition, 1966–2010? Ongoing, with 61 vols. published and around 80 planned.

Schubert, Franz

7.29 *Franz Schubert's Werke.* Edited by Eusebius Mandyczewski, Johannes Brahms, and others. 39 vols. Leipzig, Ger.: Breitkopf and Härtel, 1884–97.

*7.30 *Neue Ausgabe sämtlicher Werke.* Edited by the Internationale Schubert-Gesellschaft. Kassel, Ger.: Bärenreiter, 1964–. Ongoing, with 55 vols. published and about 80 planned.

Schumann, Robert

7.31 *Robert Schumann's Werke.* Edited by Clara Schumann, Johannes Brahms, and others. 35 vols. Leipzig, Ger.: Breitkopf and Härtel, 1881–93.

*7.32 *Sämtliche Werke/Complete Works.* Edited by the Robert Schumann-Gesellschaft, Düsseldorf. [New ed.] Mainz, Ger.: Schott, 1991–. Ongoing, with 15 vols. published and 45 planned.

Verdi, Giuseppe

7.33 *The Works of Giuseppe Verdi/Le opere di Giuseppe Verdi.* Edited by Philip Gossett and others. Milan: G. Ricordi; Chicago: University of Chicago Press, 1983–2025? Ongoing, with 12 vols. published and 37 planned.

Wagner, Richard

7.34 *Sämtliche Werke.* Edited by the Gesellschaft zur Förderung der Richard Wagner-Gesamtausgabe and the Bayerische Akademie der Schönen Künste, München. Mainz, Ger.: Schott, 1970–2010? Ongoing, with 51 vols. published and 69 planned.

MUSICAL MONUMENTS AND HISTORICAL SETS

As mentioned earlier, several types of historical sets and musical monuments exist. Sometimes these are called *collected editions* as well. Both include music by multiple composers. **Historical sets** might include music selected to illustrate the overall history of music or the development of a particular musical genre. Sometimes they are devoted to a type of music, for example, choral music. **Musical monuments** present the music of a certain country or region. Other names include **Denkmäler** in German; Monuments in French; Monumenti in Italian; Monumenta in Latin; and Monumentos in Spanish. Many of these editions were inspired by nineteenth-century nationalism and were government funded.

In the LC classification system, these are given the call number M2, subarranged alphabetically by the title. The LC subject headings are assigned appropriate to the contents. For example, *Recent Researches in the Music of the Baroque Era* has the subject headings "Music—17th century" and "Music—18th century."

The easiest to use and most complete listings of these titles appears in Hill and Stevens *Collected Editions, Historical Series & Sets, & Monuments of Music: A Bibliography* available online as *Index to Printed Music (IPM)*. A more up-to-date listing can be found in the *GMO* article "Editions, Historical," but it is arranged chronologically and is not as comprehensive.

A few examples of each of the various types of historical sets and musical monuments will help illustrate their differences.

Examples of Musical Monuments by Place

7.35 *Denkmäler der Tonkunst in Bayern (DTB)*. Old series. Edited by the Gesellschaft zur Herausgabe von Denkmälern der Tonkunst in Bayern. 38 vols. Leipzig, Ger.: Breitkopf and Härtel, 1900–38. Also known as *Denkmäler deutscher Tonkunst,* 2nd series. New series. Edited by the Gesellschaft für Bayerische Musikgeschichte. Wiesbaden, Ger.: Breitkopf and Härtel, 1967–. Ongoing, with 16 vols. published and 21 planned.

7.36 *Denkmäler der Tonkunst in Österreich (DTÖ)*. Edited by Guido Adler and others. Vienna: Artaria; Universal Edition; Österreichischer Bundesverlag; Graz, Aus.: Akademische Druck- und Verlagsanstalt, 1894–. Ongoing, with 154 vols. published.

7.37 *Denkmäler deutscher Tonkunst (DDT)*. 1st series. Edited by Rochus Freiherr von Liliencron and others. 65 vols. Leipzig, Ger.: Breitkopf and Härtel, 1892–1931. New ed. Edited by Hans Joachim Moser and others. 65 vols. Wiesbaden, Ger.: Breitkopf and Härtel, 1957–61. 2nd series of *DDT* is also known as *Denkmäler der Tonkunst in Bayern.*

7.38 *Monumentos de la música española*. Edited by the Instituto Español de Musicología. Barcelona, Spain: Consejo Superior de Investigaciones Científicas (CSIC), 1941–. Ongoing, with 71 vols. published.

7.39 *Music of the United States of America (MUSA)*. Edited by Richard Crawford. Madison, WI: A-R Editions, 1993–. Part of *Recent Researches in American Music*. Ongoing, with 16 vols. published and 40 planned.

7.40 *Musica Britannica: A National Collection of Music*. Edited by Anthony Lewis and others. London: Stainer and Bell, 1951–. Ongoing, with 84 vols. published.

7.41 *Recent Researches in American Music*. Edited by John Graziano. Madison, WI: A-R Editions, 1976–. Ongoing, with 59 vols. published.

Examples of Historical Sets by Style Period

Middle Ages

7.42 *Recent Researches in the Music of the Middle Ages and Early Renaissance.* Edited by Charles M. Atkinson and others. Middleton, WI: A-R Editions, 1975–. Ongoing, with 35 vols. published.

Renaissance

7.43 *Corpus mensurabilis musicae (CMM).* Edited by Armen Carapetyan and others. Middleton, WI: American Institute of Musicology, 1947–. Ongoing, with 413 vols. published.
Polyphonic music of the fourteenth–sixteenth centuries. Includes many complete works editions for composers from that period.

7.44 *Recent Researches in the Music of the Renaissance.* Edited by James Haar and others. Middleton, WI: A-R Editions, 1964–. Ongoing, with 150 vols. published.

Baroque

7.45 *Recent Researches in the Music of the Baroque Era.* Edited by Christoph Wolff and others. Middleton, WI: A-R Editions, 1964–. Ongoing, with 146 vols. published.

Classical

7.46 *Recent Researches in the Music of the Classical Era.* Edited by Neal Zaslaw and others. Middleton, WI: A-R Editions, 1975–. Ongoing, with 75 vols. published.

Romantic

7.47 *Recent Researches in the Music of the Nineteenth and Early Twentieth Centuries.* Edited by Rufus Hallmark and others. Middleton, WI: A-R Editions, 1979–. Ongoing, with 43 vols. published.

Additional Examples of Sets and Series

The titles listed here are devoted to the music of a genre or medium. Some are limited by a place as well as a time period, or other criteria.

7.48 *Das Chorwerk.* Edited by Friedrich Blume and Kurt Gudewill. Wolfenbüttel, Ger.: Kallmeyer; Möseler, 1929–. Ongoing, with 144 vols. published.
Includes choral music, primarily from the Renaissance.

7.49 *Corpus of Early Keyboard Music.* Edited by Willi Apel. Middleton, WI: American Institute of Musicology, 1963–. Ongoing, with 74 vols. published.
Keyboard music from the fourteenth to seventeenth centuries, mostly from Italy, Spain, Germany, and Poland.

7.50 *Diletto musicale: Doblingers Reihe alter Musik.* Vienna: Doblinger, 1955–. Ongoing, with approximately 1220 vols. published.
Instrumental music (mostly Viennese chamber music) from the eighteenth to nineteenth centuries.

7.51 *Earlier American Music.* Edited by H. Wiley Hitchcock. 28 vols. New York: Da
      Capo, 1972–91.
      Facsimiles of eighteenth to nineteenth-century American music.

7.52 *Hortus Musicus.* Kassel, Ger.: Bärenreiter, 1950–. Ongoing, with 281 vols.
      published.
      Primarily Baroque and Classical chamber music.

7.53 *Monuments of Music and Music Literature in Facsimile.* Series 1. Music, 26
      vols. New York: Broude Bros., 1965–78; Series II. Music Literature, 89 vols.
      New York: Broude Bros., 1965–79.
      Facsimiles of music and writings about music mostly from the sixteenth to eigh-
      teenth centuries.

7.54 *Nagels Musik-Archiv.* Edited by Alfred Grensser and others. 256 vols. Hannover,
      Ger.: Nagel; Kassel, Ger.: Bärenreiter, 1927–83.
      Performing editions consisting of primarily chamber music from the eighteenth
      century.

7.55 *Le pupitre: Collection de musique ancienne.* Edited by François Lesure and others.
      84 vols. Paris: Heugel, 1967–2007.
      Performing editions of early music through the Baroque.

7.56 *Recent Researches in the Oral Traditions of Music.* Edited by Philip V. Bohlman.
      Madison, WI: A-R Editions, 1993–. Ongoing, with 7 vols. published.
      Music outside the Western classical tradition.

7.57 *The Symphony 1720–1840.* 60 vols. Edited by Barry S. Brook and Barbara B.
      Heyman. New York: Garland, 1979–85.

ANTHOLOGIES

Anthologies are usually only one or a few volumes in length. They are often intended
for use in the classroom, although they are useful for independent study and sometimes
performance as well. Some include sound recording examples or have recordings available for purchase separately. Those anthologies published to accompany textbooks are
listed in Chapter 9. The LC call numbers for anthologies are MT6.5 and MT91. The
appropriate LC subject headings are "Music analysis—Music collections" and "Music
appreciation—Music collections."

Examples of Anthologies

7.58 Benjamin, Thomas, Michael Horvit, and Robert Nelson. *Music for Analysis:
      Examples from the Common Practice Period and the Twentieth Century.* 6th ed.
      New York: Oxford University Press, 2006. Published with a CD.

7.59 Briscoe, James R. *Contemporary Anthology of Music by Women.* Bloomington:
      Indiana University Press, 1997. Has accompanying CDs.

7.60 ———. *New Historical Anthology of Music by Women.* Bloomington: Indiana
      University Press, 2004. Has accompanying CDs.

7.61 Burkhart, Charles. *Anthology for Musical Analysis*. 6th ed. Belmont, CA: Thomson/Schirmer, 2004.

7.62 Davison, Archibald T., and Willi Apel. *Historical Anthology of Music (HAM)*. Rev. ed. 2 vols. Cambridge, MA: Harvard University Press, 1949–50. Has accompanying LPs.

7.63 Parrish, Carl. *A Treasury of Early Music*. New York: W. W. Norton, 1958. Reprint, Mineola, NY: Dover, 2000. Has accompanying LPs.

7.64 Parrish, Carl, and John Ohl. *Masterpieces of Music before 1750: An Anthology of Musical Examples from Gregorian Chant to J. S. Bach*. New York: W. W. Norton, 1951. Reprint, Mineola, NY: Dover, 2001. Has accompanying LPs.

7.65 Turek, Ralph. *Analytical Anthology of Music*, 2nd ed. New York: McGraw-Hill, 1992.

7.66 Wennerstrom, Mary H. *Anthology of Twentieth-Century Music*, 2nd ed. Englewood Cliffs, NJ: Prentice Hall, 1988.

INDEXES OF COMPLETE WORKS EDITIONS, MUSICAL MONUMENTS, HISTORICAL SETS, AND ANTHOLOGIES

The indexes listed here vary in their arrangement. Before going to one of them, it is helpful to know the identification numbers associated with the music you are looking for. You may need to look up the piece by date of composition, opus number, thematic catalog number (see Chapter 8), or number in the title (e.g., String Quartet No. 2). This information can typically be found in the works list for the composer in any major encyclopedia or dictionary, such as *GMO*. As throughout this text, the asterisks indicate that a particular index is a major research tool. See this text's companion website for updated information.

7.67 Charles, Sydney Robinson. *A Handbook of Music and Music Literature in Sets and Series*. New York: Schirmer Books, 1972.
Superseded by later tools, except for the 85 entries in section C, which indexes music literature (writings about music) included in historical sets and musical monuments. Includes a composer/author/title index. Reviewed by Dale Good in *Notes* 30, no. 4 (June 1974): 789–90.

7.68 Heyer, Anna H. *Historical Sets, Collected Editions, and Monuments of Music: A Guide to Their Contents*. 3rd ed. 2 vols. Chicago: American Library Association, 1980.
Heyer was long considered the standard reference tool for finding music published in composers' complete works editions (M3s) as well as musical monuments and historical sets (M2s). Now largely superseded by Hill for monuments and sets and *GMO* for composers' complete works editions. Heyer does include some older publications not included by Hill and Stephens. Reviewed by George R. Hill in *Notes* 38, no. 3 (Mar. 1982): 593–94.

*7.69 Hill, George R. *Index to Printed Music: Collections & Series (IPM)*. Baltimore, MD: NISC, 2004–. http://www.nisc.com.

IPM is the online, subscription-based version of Hill and Stephen's bibliography. The advanced search option is recommended; see Figure 7-1. Currently, *IPM* includes primarily the material published in 1997, although the enhanced search options make the online version preferable. Recently the Music Library Association was awarded a 3-year grant from the Mellon Foundation to support the completion and updating of the database. The number of entries is planned to double as a result. Updated quarterly. Also available on CD-ROM.

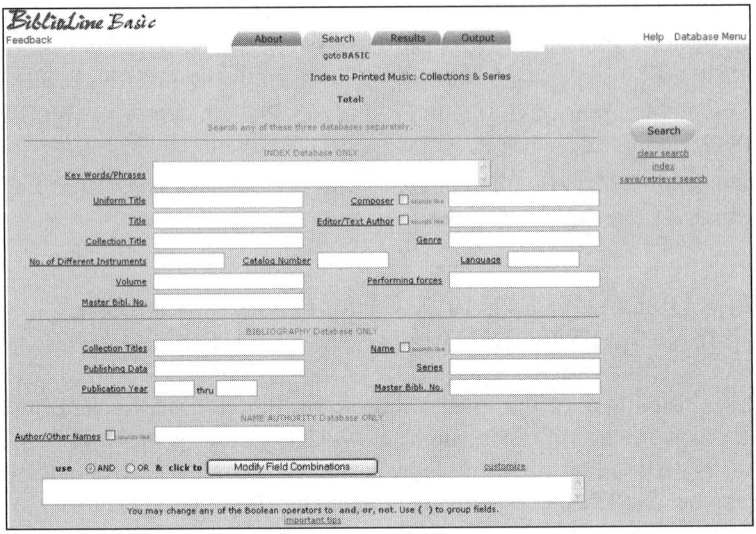

Figure 7-1 *Index to Printed Music (IPM)* Advanced Search Screen *(2007 © BiblioLine, Service of NISC)*

7.70   Hill, George R., and Norris L. Stephens. *Collected Editions, Historical Series & Sets & Monuments of Music: A Bibliography.* Fallen Leaf Reference Books in Music, 14. Berkeley, CA: Fallen Leaf, 1997.
The best available source for finding music in musical monuments and historical sets (M2s), although the online version is recommended. Coverage through 1995, with a few 1996 imprints added. Lists composers' complete works editions, but only citations are given. Includes author, title, and series entries as well as cross-references. Total citations number around 9,300 and include individual titles of compositions. Sometimes the cross-references are confusing, and there is no index. See the online version. Reviewed by John Wagstaff in *Brio* 34, no. 2 (Autumn–Winter 1997): 95–99.

7.71   Hilton, Ruth B. *An Index to Early Music in Selected Anthologies.* Music Indexes and Bibliographies, no. 13. Clifton, NJ: European American Music Corp., 1978.
Indexes the contents of 19 anthologies. Largely superceded by Murray, but includes six anthologies, most devoted to early music, not indexed by Murray. Includes indexes for composers/titles and subjects. Reviewed by Susan T. Sommer in *Notes* 35, no. 3 (Mar. 1979): 641–42.

*7.72 Macy, Laura. *Grove Music Online* (*GMO*). Oxford: Oxford University Press, 2001–. http://www.oxfordmusiconline.com.

The works lists included in *GMO* are often the most up-to-date index to composers' complete works editions. A column or two at the far right will be devoted to the major editions. See the key to the abbreviations and explanation of the information presented at the beginning of the works list and, in some cases, at the beginning of the appropriate section of the list. For example, if you are looking for the Schubert song "Gretchen am Spinnrade," start at the beginning of the works list; see Figure 7-2. Here you will find the citations and abbreviations for the old (SW) and new (NSA) Schubert editions. Next, look at the beginning of the songs section. The note indicates that the songs are in series 20 of the SW and series 4 of the NSA; see Figure 7-3. It also explains that the two numbers in the column for each indicate the volume and page numbers. Finally, see the entry for the specific song in the works list; see Figure 7-4. The last column on the

Figure 7-2 *GMO*, Beginning of Schubert Article Works List *(Oxford Music Online c. Oxford University Press 2007)*

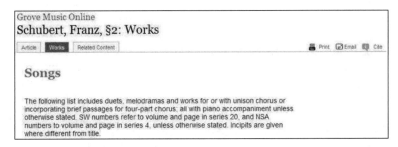

Figure 7-3 *GMO*, Beginning of Songs Section of Schubert Works List *(Oxford Music Online c. Oxford University Press 2007)*

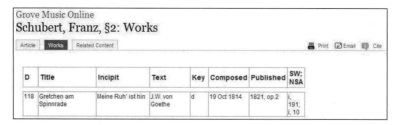

Figure 7-4 *GMO*, Excerpt of Schubert Works List Including "Gretchen am Spinnrade" *(Oxford Music Online c. Oxford University Press 2007)*

right gives the volume and page for each edition. Now you have all the information to find "Gretchen am Spinnrade" in both Schubert editions. In the SW, the song is in series 20, volume 1, page 191; in the NSA it is in series 4, volume 1, page 10. The old SW is not owned by many libraries in its original Breitkopf and Härtel edition. The Dover reprint edition (titled *Complete Works*) is much more widely held. Although the Dover reprint kept the music in the same order and with the same page numbers, the volumes were combined. The table of contents in the reprint edition will direct you to the first half of volume 13 for the first volume of series 20 of the SW. Finding that your library has a reprint edition is one challenge in the process of using collected works editions. Another is that the organization can vary in the presentation of the music from one edition to the next, even for the same composer. The SW numbered the songs by date of composition ("Gretchen am Spinnrade" is number 31), while the NSA arranged them by opus number ("Gretchen am Spinnrade" is opus 2). The works lists are also searchable through *GMO*'s advanced search works list option or your browser's "find in page" function.

*7.73 Murray, Sterling E. *Anthologies of Music: An Annotated Index*. 2nd ed. Detroit Studies in Music Bibliography, no. 68. Warren, MI: Harmonie Park Press, 1992.

Murray indexes the contents of 44 shorter anthologies, including those devoted to nineteenth- and twentieth-century music, some that accompany texts, and multiple editions of some titles. About 4,670 musical examples are indexed. More current and comprehensive than Hilton. Includes a subject/genre index. The key to symbols and abbreviations is given on the inside of the front and back covers and in the Introduction. Reviewed by Holly E. Mockovak in *Notes* 51, no. 2 (Dec. 1994): 573–74.

7.74 Perone, James E. *Musical Anthologies for Analytical Study: A Bibliography*. Music Reference Collection, no. 48. Westport, CT: Greenwood, 1995.

Indexes 14 anthologies used widely in colleges and universities as an aid to music theory professors. Anthologies of music for analysis were chosen rather than historical anthologies. Also useful for independent study and analysis purposes. Every excerpt and piece included in the anthologies is indexed. Perone provides indexes of composers and sources, titles, and theoretical topics. Reviewed by Jane Magrath in *Clavier* 36, no. 1 (Jan. 1997): 44.

EVALUATION CHECKLIST

The following checklist was adapted in part from Root and Cassaro.[1]

- Is an editorial policy statement included?
  - Is the purpose of the edition explained?
  - Is the edition's scope defined (is it logical, consistently followed, etc.)?
- What type of edition is it (critical, performance, facsimile, etc.)?
- Is it well-edited? Are editorial changes clearly indicated? Are sources well-selected?
- Is critical commentary included?
- Are the sources listed?
- Does the edition include an introduction providing historical or cultural context?
- Are bibliography and notes provided?
- What is the editorial structure/oversight (board composition, review process)?
- Is the edition arranged logically?
  - Are the table of contents, indexes, and classified lists adequate?
  - Are dubious attributions included separately?
- Who is the publisher (commercial, noncommercial, collaborative)?
- Does the edition have financial sponsorship (and by whom)?
- What is the date or date range of the edition?
  - Were modern editorial standards followed?
  - Was the edition completed, abandoned, or in progress?
- Is the edition appropriate for performance?
  - Are parts provided?
  - Are performance practice suggestions included?
- Are illustrations included (photos, facsimiles of chief sources, etc.)?
- What are the languages of the edition (are translations of notes, texts, etc. given)?

SUGGESTED READINGS

The readings by Brett, Eisen, and Gossett discuss the editing process. Brett, general editor of *The Byrd Edition* (1970–2005), gives an overview of the issues surrounding editions of early music. Eisen compares the old and new Mozart editions, including the choice of sources and editorial decisions. Those by Corneilson (managing editor) and Crawford (editor-in-chief) explain the decisions behind and funding for two editions

---

[1]Deane L. Root and James P. Cassaro, "Syllabus for Principles of Research and Bibliography," Course materials, Music 2111, University of Pittsburgh, 2001.

they are involved with, the ongoing *C. P. E. Bach Edition* and *Music of the United States of America*, respectively. The articles in *New Grove* and *Harvard* dictionaries provide an overview of historical editions. Finally, Mixter offers a discussion of the bibliographical complexities of these large sets and series.

Brett, Philip. "Text, Context, and the Early Music Editor." In *Authenticity and Early Music: A Symposium*, edited by Nicholas Kenyon, 83–114. Oxford: Oxford University Press, 1988.

Corneilson, Paul. "The C. P. E. Bach Edition and the Future of Scholarly Editions." *Music Reference Services Quarterly* 8, no. 1 (2001): 27–37.

Crawford, Richard. "*MUSA's* Early Years: The Life and Times of a National Editing Project." *American Music* 23, no. 1 (Spring 2005): 1–38.

Eisen, Cliff. "The Old and New Mozart Editions." *Early Music* 19, no. 4 (Nov. 1991): 513–32.

Gossett, Philip. "Toward a Critical Edition of *Macbeth*." In *Verdi's Macbeth: A Sourcebook*, edited by David Rosen and Andrew Porter, 199–209. New York: W. W. Norton, 1984.

Mixter, Keith E. "Scholarly Editions: Their Character and Bibliographic Description." In *Foundations in Music Bibliography*, edited by Richard D. Green, 47–58. New York: Haworth, 1993. Simultaneously published in *Music Reference Services Quarterly* 2, nos. 1–2 (1993): 47–58.

Randel, Don Michael. *The Harvard Dictionary of Music*. 4th ed. Cambridge, MA: Belknap Press of Harvard University Press, 2003. S.v. "Editions, Historical" by Harold E. Samuel and Lenore Coral.

Sadie, Stanley, ed. *The New Grove Dictionary of Music and Musicians*. 2nd ed. New York: Grove, 2001. S.v. "Editions, Historical," by Sydney Robinson Charles et al. Also available from *Grove Music Online*. http://www.oxfordmusiconline.com.

CHAPTER 8

Thematic Catalogs

Thematic catalogs have a number of uses in music research. They are a good place to start if you need information about a piece of music you are studying or performing. Some will help you positively identify a piece. Others will help you study a composer's output or a specific repertory. Thematic catalogs include the information helpful for searching for a composition using the uniform title (see Chapter 4) and for finding the music in composers complete works editions (see Chapter 7). Additional uses, including "name that tune," are described in this chapter.

Thematic catalogs include musical **incipits** for the compositions cataloged, along with other information about the works. These excerpts may be the major themes in a movement or piece, or they may be the opening measures. The inclusion of the musical excerpt distinguishes thematic catalogs from other catalogs or works lists and makes the exact identification of the work possible. Some thematic catalogs allow you to search by themes; others simply include them. These are sometimes called **thematic locators**. Some catalogs include both.

Thematic catalogs exist for individual composers, multiple composers, particular repertories, library or archive collections, and publishers. The most common, however, are those devoted to a single composer. Compilers of thematic catalogs assign a sequential numeric or alphanumeric identifier to each piece. Works become known by these identifiers, which are often included on published editions and on performance programs, like opus numbers. They are also used in uniform titles, as described in Chapter 4.

Thematic catalogs have a number of uses. The most common include the following:

- Exact identification of a work
- Guide to a composer's output, a particular repertory, archive, etc.
- Information about the piece, including information on the location of manuscripts and early editions and bibliographic citations for writings about it

- Documentation of works that once existed but are no longer extant
- Aid to memory (i.e., name that tune)

For a survey of historical uses, see the article by Barry Brook in *Grove Music Online* (*GMO*), per the Suggested Readings, later.

As with all reference tools, some cautions for thematic catalogs are in order. Like composers complete works editions, thematic catalogs may not be entirely complete. Also like complete works editions, older thematic catalogs may not have been compiled with today's scholarly rigor. Many of the earliest were compiled by musical amateurs. Older thematic catalogs will not be up-to-date with the literature, recently discovered works, revised chronology of composition, etc. Accuracy may also be a problem, especially with those compiled by a music publisher or others compiled by nonscholars.

Sometimes thematic catalogs are published as part of a composer's complete works edition or a historical set/musical monument. The Handel thematic catalog is part of the *Hallische Händel-Ausgabe*; Schubert's is part of the *Neue Ausgabe sämtlicher Werke*. Barry Brook and Barbara B. Heyman compiled a thematic catalog as part of the multi-volume set *The Symphony, 1720–1840*. Stand-alone thematic catalogs are frequently published by Pendragon Press and Harmonie Park Press.

Keep in mind the challenges of representing musical themes without using musical notation in the thematic locators. The indexes or guides for many thematic catalogs rely on a variety of methods for doing this, some of which date back to the characters available on the typewriter. Some of these techniques include using letter names for pitches (Barlow and Morgenstern, Bryant and Chapman), using solfège syllables (Diehl and Wasson), using numbers to indicate pitches in a scale (Temperley), and indications of whether the melody goes up or down or repeats (McAll and Parsons). These all require you to manipulate the melody you are looking for before you begin. For example, you may need to transpose it to the key of C major or C minor. Or you might need to jot down the contour of the melody. Most of us need to use paper and pencil to do this step first, before consulting an index. Those who like puzzles tend to enjoy these indexes more than those who do not. With these indexes, it is very helpful to take the time to read the instructions on how to use them.

Thematic catalogs on the web are under development. The potential for creating a mega-catalog of musical themes with a variety of search options is exciting. Perhaps it will even be possible to play a tune on a MIDI keyboard or sing into a microphone to "name that tune." *Themefinder*, one of the best available currently, is described later. The annual International Symposium on Music Information Retrieval (ISMIR) and its proceedings are a good way to keep abreast of developments in this direction. A listing of music information retrieval (MIR) projects is available at http://mirsystems.info/index.php?id=mirsystems.

BIBLIOGRAPHIES OF THEMATIC CATALOGS

The Brook and Viano bibliography is unique as a research tool for thematic catalogs. As throughout this text, the asterisk indicates that it is a major research tool. See this text's companion website for updated information on thematic catalogs.

*8.1 Brook, Barry S., and Richard Viano. *Thematic Catalogues in Music: An Annotated Bibliography.* 2nd ed. Annotated Reference Tools in Music, no. 5. Stuyvesant, NY: Pendragon, 1997.

Brook and Viano list thematic catalogs (including those in preparation) as well as writings about them. Entries are under composer, library, or compiler. Most entries are annotated. See the guide to use on pages xliv–xlv. Includes appendixes and an index. Reviewed by Heikki Poroila in *Fontes artis musicae* 46, no. 1–2 (Jan.–June 1999): 175–77.

SINGLE-COMPOSER THEMATIC CATALOGS

While many major composers have thematic catalogs, others do not. Some have proved problematic to compile because of the existence of variant versions of pieces. Some composers who you might expect to have thematic catalogs do not. For example, none currently exists for Debussy, Monteverdi, Palestrina, Schoenberg, or Stravinsky. On the other hand, some fairly minor composers (e.g., Philipp Dulichius, Georg Gebels, and Eduard Tubin) do have thematic catalogs, because a scholar took an interest in compiling one and found a willing publisher. Thematic catalogs for Rameau, Sibelius, and Scriabin are relatively new. Other composers, like Liszt, have one or more thematic catalogs, but none have been widely accepted. A new thematic catalog is being prepared for Liszt by Mária Eckhardt and Rena Charnin Mueller.

For composers lacking a thematic catalog, other research tools may be available. Some composers have a catalog of works that does not include themes. These can be in the form of a published book. Examples include François Lesure's *Catalogue de l'œuvre de Claude Debussy* (Geneva: Éditions Minkoff, 1977), Josef Rufer's *The Works of Arnold Schoenberg: A Catalogue of His Compositions, Writings, and Paintings* (London: Faber and Faber, 1962), and Clifford Cæsar's *Igor Stravinsky: A Complete Catalogue* (San Francisco: San Francisco Press, 1982). The composer bio-bibliographies and guides to research included in Chapter 10 include works lists, as do major encyclopedia articles (for instance, those in *GMO*), and some biographies do as well. Finally, see Jerzy Chwiałkowski's *The Da Capo Catalog of Classical Music Compositions* (New York: Da Capo, 1996), which includes works lists for 132 composers.

Some composers have well-respected thematic catalogs that are in need of a new edition. As Otto Erich Deutsch, compiler of the Schubert thematic catalog quipped, "A thematic catalog should be published for the first time in its second edition!"[1] Currently a new edition (the 7th) is in progress for Mozart (neue/new Köchel) by Neal Zaslaw. See the article by Paul van Reijen (Suggested Readings) for a discussion about why a new edition of Köchel is needed.

The information typically included in a composer thematic catalog includes:

- Title(s) of work
- Date and place of composition and premiere
- Author of text (if applicable)

---

[1]Otto Erich Deutsch, *Franz Schubert Thematisches Verzeichnis seiner Werke in chronologischer Folge* (Kassel, Ger.: Bärenreiter, 1978), xvi.

- Medium of performance
- Dedication
- Location in the complete works edition
- Musical incipit(s) for each movement and a measure count or duration
- Location of important manuscripts
- Information about first and other important editions
- Bibliography of writings about the piece and possibly discography

Figure 8-1 is an example of the entry in a composer thematic catalog, James Sinclair's *A Descriptive Catalogue of the Music of Charles Ives*. While this example is in English,

235. Disclosure

Medium: Med voice (e^1–g^2), pf
Duration: 1 min., 15 mm. (Andante moderato)

114 Songs, Peer (1954)

First line(s): Thoughts, which deeply rest at evening | at sunrise gayly thrilled the mind

Text: One 7-line stanza, unattributed in *114 Songs*; author identified as Charles Ives in *Twelve Songs* and KirkC.

Source: No holographs or MS copies; emendations in Ives's Copy E of *114 Songs* (f6159).

John Kirkpatrick (pf), Aug 1954 (issued in 1954 by Overtone Records, Over. 7).

Date: Composed in 1921. Dated 1921 in *114 Songs*. AG: 1921.

Derivation: Included, in a planned orchestration, as mvt ii of the unrealized *Set of Proposed Movements [II]* [#x655].

Publication:
1. *114 Songs* (Redding, CT: C. E. Ives, 1922), no. 7; repr. 1923 in *Fifty Songs*. Copyright assigned 1954 to Peer International; repr. 1954 in *Twelve Songs*, p. 26; repr. 1961 in *Sacred Songs*, p. 31 (in later printings p. 15).
2. Ives Society critical edn, *129 Songs*: no. 123, by H. Wiley Hitchcock, in prep.

Borrowing: Possible borrowing: OLIVET.

Literature: KirkC: 6B67b; AG: z142. *Memos*, 168. BlockB: W138, B291. Feder 1992, 312, 316; Burkholder 1995, 288–91.

Discography: Hall 1964/3, 96; Cohn 1981, 917; Oja 1982: 5307.

First recording: Helen Boatwright (S) and

Figure 8-1 Excerpt from James B. Sinclair, *A Descriptive Catalogue of the Music of Charles Ives* (New Haven, CT: Yale University Press, 1999), 235 *(Courtesy of Yale University Press)*

be aware that many catalogs are in Western European languages, especially German. This entry, for the Ives song "Disclosure," includes information about recordings of the piece. Writings about the pieces are also included by Sinclair when they exist.

Some alphanumeric "catalog" numbers for composer thematic catalogs are probably already familiar to you. Usually the alpha portion is the first initial of the compiler's last name. Examples include Köchel (K) numbers for Mozart's works, Deutsch (D) numbers for Schubert, and so on. BWV (*Bach Werke Verzeichnis*) numbers for Bach are an exception, but sometimes they are referred to as Schmieder (S) numbers, despite the compiler's humble wishes that he not be given credit.

The arrangement of thematic catalogs varies. Typical methods include chronological, based on date of composition (Mozart and Schubert); some are by medium/genre (Bach and Haydn); and others are by opus number (Beethoven). As a result, the catalog numbers mean different things. A low Köchel number indicates that the work is early in Mozart's output, but a low BWV number simply indicates a vocal work by Bach.

The thematic catalogs for Bach, Haydn, and Mozart are complicated enough to use that searchable guides to them have been created by McAll, Bryant and Chapman, and Hill and Gould, respectively. Each represents a different method of indexing the works of these prolific composers to make it easier to use the relevant thematic catalog. They are, in effect, guides to the guides.

There are three main ways to find out if a thematic catalog exists for a particular composer. The first is to use the Brook and Viano bibliography, *Thematic Catalogues in Music*, listed earlier. Published in 1997, it includes thematic catalogs published as monographs or as articles and even those included in dissertations.

The second way is to search for them in your library's online catalog or union catalog (*WorldCat*). Thematic catalogs are assigned a Library of Congress (LC) subject heading for the composer's name, with the subdivision "Thematic catalogs." For example, Mozart's thematic catalog has the subject "Mozart, Wolfgang Amadeus, 1756–1791—Thematic catalogs." The LC call number for single-composer thematic catalogs is ML134, with the first cutter for the composer's last name. So the Mozart catalog is probably under the call number ML134 .M9, if your library uses LC call numbers.

The third way to find them is to consult the bibliography of a current encyclopedia, for example, *Grove Music Online* (entry 2.2). Thematic catalogs are listed in composer articles either with the editions of music (before the works list) or early in the bibliography.

Following is a listing of thematic catalogs (and guides to them) available for the composers used throughout this text as examples; see Appendix C. Those included are typically widely accepted as the standard for that composer, selected by LC for use in its cataloging, or chosen by Brook and Viano as the best available. If more than one is listed for a composer, the asterisk indicates the recommended catalog. See this text's companion website for updates.

Examples of Single-Composer Thematic Catalogs

Bach, Johann Sebastian

*8.2   Schmieder, Wolfgang. *Thematisch-systematisches Verzeichnis der musikalichen Werke von Johann Sebastian Bach: Bach-Werke-Verzeichnis (BWV)*. 2nd ed. Wiesbaden, Ger.: Brietkopf and Härtel, 1990.

Arranged by genre, beginning with vocal music and followed by instrumental works. Works are assigned a BWV number. Reviewed by Christoph Wolff in *Notes* 49, no. 2 (Dec. 1992): 543–44.

8.3   Schulze, Hans-Joachim, and Christoph Wolff. *Bach Compendium: Analytisch-bibliographisches Repertorium der Werke Johann Sebastian Bachs (BC)*. 4 vols. Frankfurt: C. F. Peters, 1985–89.

Four volumes devoted to the vocal music were published. Pieces are arranged into work groups that loosely follow Schmieder and are given numbers A-H. The BWV numbers are also provided. Three additional volumes were planned but have not been completed. Reviewed by John Butt in *Notes* 47, no. 2 (Dec. 1990): 361–68.

Beethoven, Ludwig van

8.4   Kinsky, Georg, and Hans Halm. *Das Werk Beethovens: Thematischbibliographisches Verzeichnis seiner sämtlichen vollendeten Kompositionen*. Munich: G. Henle 1955.

Works are presented in opus-number order. Reviewed by Otto Kinkeldey in *JAMS* 10, no. 2 (Summer 1957): 119–24.

Brahms, Johannes

8.5   McCorkle, Margit L., and Donald M. McCorkle. *Johannes Brahms: Thematisch-bibliographisches Werkverzeichnis*. Munich: G. Henle, 1984.

Arranged by opus number. Reviewed by David Brodbeck in *JAMS* 42, no. 2 (Summer 1989): 418–31.

Chopin, Frédéric

8.6   Chominski, Józef M., and Teresa D. Turło. *Katalog dzieł Fryderyka Chopina/A Catalogue of the Works of Frederick Chopin*. Documenta Chopiniana, 4. Warsaw: Polskie Wydawnictwo Muzyczne (PWM), 1990.

Works are arranged alphabetically by title. Reviewed by Henri Musielak in *Revue de musicologie* 80, no. 1 (1994): 143–44.

*8.7   Kobylanska, Krystyna. *Frédéric Chopin: Thematisch-bibliographisches Werkverzeichnis*. Edited by Ernst Herttrich. Translated by Helmut Stolze. Munich: G. Henle, 1979.

Works are listed by opus number. Reviewed by Jeffrey Kallberg in *JAMS* 34, no. 2 (Summer 1981): 357–65.

Handel, George Frideric

8.8   Baselt, Bernd. *Thematisch-systematisches Verzeichnis*. Händel-Handbuch, vols. 1–3. Kassel, Ger.: Bärenreiter, 1978–1986.

Thematic catalog is in volumes 1–3 of the 5-volume Händel-Handbuch, which is a supplement to the *Hallische Händel-Ausgabe*. Arranged by genre, beginning with stage works. Pieces are assigned an HWV number (Händel Werke Verzeichnis). Vol. 1 reviewed by Winton Dean in *Music and Letters* 64, nos. 3–4 (July–Oct. 1983): 232–34.

Vol. 2 reviewed by Mary Ann Parker-Hale in *JAMS* 39, no. 3 (Fall 1986): 655–63. Vol. 3 reviewed by Terence Best in *Music and Letters* 69, no. 1 (Jan. 1988): 66–67.

Haydn, Franz Joseph

8.9   Hoboken, Anthony van. *Joseph Haydn: Thematisch-bibliographisches Werkverzeichnis*. 3 vols. Mainz, Ger.: Schott, 1957–78.
Volume 1 includes instrumental works; volume 2 includes vocal music; volume 3 is an index. Arrangement is by genre. Works are assigned H numbers. Vol. 1 reviewed by Otto Erich Deutsch in *Music Review* 18, no. 4 (Nov. 1957): 330–36. Vol. 2 reviewed by Karl Geiringer in *JAMS* 25, no. 3 (Fall 1972): 471–73. Vol. 3 reviewed by George R. Hill in *Notes* 36, no. 1 (Sept. 1979): 102–103.

Ives, Charles

8.10   Sinclair, James B. *A Descriptive Catalogue of the Music of Charles Ives*. New Haven, CT: Yale University Press, 1999.
Arranged by genre, beginning with symphonies. Songs are listed alphabetically by title. See Figure 8-1. Reviewed by David Nicholls in *Notes* 57, no. 1 (Sept. 2000): 114–15.

Mozart, Wolfgang Amadeus

8.11   Köchel, Ludwig Ritter von, et al. *Chronologisch-thematisches Verzeichnis sämtlicher Tonwerke Wolfgang Amadé Mozarts*, 6th ed. Wiesbaden, Ger.: Breitkopf and Härtel, 1964.
Works are listed chronologically by date of composition. Pieces are assigned a K number. K^6 numbers refer to the 6th edition of the catalog. Reviewed by Jan LaRue in *JAMS* 20, no. 3 (Fall 1967): 495–501 and Bernard E. Wilson in *Notes* 21, no. 4 (Fall 1964): 531–40.

Schubert, Franz

8.12   Deutsch, Otto Erich, and Werner Aderhold. *Franz Schubert: Thematisches Verzeichnis seiner Werke in chronologischer Folge*. New ed. Kassel, Ger.: Bärenreiter, 1978.
Arranged chronologically, this thematic catalog was published as part of the new Schubert complete works edition (Serie VIII: Supplement Band 4). Pieces are assigned D numbers. Reviewed by Robert Winter in *19th Century Music* 3, no. 2 (Nov. 1979): 154–62.

Schumann, Robert

8.13   McCorkle, Margit L. *Thematisch-Bibliographisches Werkverzeichnis*. Mainz, Ger.: Schott, 2003.
Arranged by opus number. Part of the new complete Schumann edition (Series VIII: Supplemente Band 6). Reviewed by Nicholas Marston in *Fontes artis musicae* 51, nos. 3–4 (July–Dec. 2004): 414–17 and Linda C. Roesner in *Journal of the American Liszt Society* 52-53 (Fall-Spring 2002–2003): 166–73.

Verdi, Giuseppe

8.14 Hopkinson, Cecil. *A Bibliography of the Works of Giuseppe Verdi, 1813–1901.* 2
      vols. New York: Broude Bros., 1973–78.
      Arranged by genre with vocal music first. Only volume 1 includes incipits. Vol.
      1 reviewed by Julian Budden in *Music and Letters* 55, no. 3 (July 1974): 345–47.
      Vol. 2 reviewed by Andrew Porter in *Fontes artis musicae* 27, no. 1 (Jan.–Mar.
      1980): 55–56.

Wagner, Richard

8.15 Deathridge, John, Martin Geck, and Egon Voss. *Wagner Werk-Verzeichnis
      (WWV): Verzeichnis der musikalischen Werke Richard Wagners und ihrer
      Quellen.* Mainz, Ger.: Schott, 1986.
      Arrangement is chronological. Works are given WWV numbers. Reviewed by
      Barry Millington in *Music and Letters* 69, no. 3 (July 1988): 396–98.

Guides and Locators for Single-Composer Thematic Catalogs

Bach, Johann Sebastian

8.16 McAll, May deForest [Payne]. *Melodic Index to the Works of Johann Sebastian
      Bach.* Rev. ed. New York: C. F. Peters, 1962.
      Groups 3,872 themes into six alphabetical groups based on melodic contour. Use
      the finding charts at the beginning to identify the appropriate numerical group;
      then look that up in the melodic index to identify the specific piece. Reviewed by
      Elizabeth Trustam in *Brio* 2, no. 1 (Spring 1965): 22–23.

Haydn, Franz Joseph

8.17 Bryant, Stephen C., and Gary W. Chapman. *A Melodic Index to Haydn's
      Instrumental Music: A Thematic Locator for Anthony van Hoboken's Thematisch-
      bibliographisches Werkverzeichnis, Vols. I and III.* Thematic Catalogues, no. 8.
      New York: Pendragon, 1982.
      Includes 2 parts: incipits in original keys and transposed to C major/minor.
      Incipits are represented with letters and arranged alphabetically. Indicates
      Hoboken group and location. Reviewed by Karl Geiringer in *Notes* 41, no. 1
      (Sept. 1984): 70–71.

Mozart, Wolfgang Amadeus

8.18 Hill, George R., and Murray Gould. *A Thematic Locator for Mozart's Works: As
      Listed in Koechel's Chronologisch-Thematisches Verzeichnis—Sixth Edition.*
      Music Indexes and Bibliographies, no. 1. Hackensack, NJ: J. Boonin, 1970.
      Includes 2 sections: themes arranged by intervallic size and themes arranged
      alphabetically (the latter is recommended). Themes are transposed to begin on the
      pitch C. Read the preliminary material on notation of grace notes, etc. Reviewed
      by Neal Zaslaw in *Notes* 28, no. 3 (Mar. 1972): 445–46.

THEMATIC CATALOGS FOR PARTICULAR REPERTORIES

Thematic catalogs exist for instrumental and vocal concert repertories (Barlow and Morgenstern), early music (RISM A/II and B/IV), hymn tunes (Temperley and Wasson), and so on. Some are intended to help you identify a tune from memory or performance; others are designed to catalog a repertory. Some are searchable; others are not.

To find this type of thematic catalog, one can again turn to the Brook and Viano bibliography and your local library or union catalog. This type of thematic catalog has LC subject headings and call numbers reflecting the music included. Again, the subdivision "Thematic catalogs" is used. The Barlow and Morgenstern catalog of vocal music has the subject heading "Vocal music—Thematic catalogs." It has the LC call number ML128 .V7, the call number for bibliographies of vocal music.

Just as some major composers have no thematic catalogs, some repertories are underrepresented; jazz, popular music, and folk music are examples. The thematic catalogs listed are representative examples; this list is not exhaustive.

Please note that the thematic portions of RISM are listed here in the early music section. RISM stands for Répertoire international des sources musicales or International Inventory of Musical Sources in English. The remaining portions of RISM will be covered in later chapters, primarily Chapter 10. Briefly explained, RISM is the third of four international cooperative musicological "R" projects. (RILM and RIPM are the first two, RIdIM—the fourth—is covered in Chapter 12.) RISM's goal is to identify and locate all sources of musical scores and writings about music up to 1800. Some portions have extended past 1800. RISM publications are issued in three series: A (devoted to works by single composers), B (devoted to musical collections by multiple composers as well as bibliographies on various topics), and C (directories of music libraries). See Appendix D for a complete list of RISM. Of the thematic catalogs in RISM, the most commonly used are A/II for manuscripts by individual composers 1600–1850 and B/IV for manuscripts by more than one composer from the eleventh to sixteenth centuries.

Examples of Thematic Catalogs for Particular Repertories

Standard Concert Repertory

8.19 Barlow, Harold, and Sam Morgenstern. *A Dictionary of Musical Themes.* New York: Crown, 1948.

Includes around 10,000 themes arranged alphabetically by composer and title in "themes" section. To find a melody, transpose it to C major/minor before looking it up in the alphabetically arranged notation index in the back to find the alphanumeric code for the theme in the front. Also includes a title index. Reviewed by Charles Seeger and Richard S. Hill in *Notes* 5, no. 3 (June 1948): 375–76.

8.20 ———. *A Dictionary of Vocal Themes.* New York: Crown, 1950.

Similar to the instrumental volume with the addition of an index to the first line of text. Includes over 8,000 themes from various genres of vocal music. Reviewed by Harold Spivacke in *Notes* 8, no. 2 (Mar. 1951): 334–35.

*8.21 Huron, David. *Themefinder.* Stanford, CA: Center for Computer Assisted Research in the Humanities, 1996–. http://www.themefinder.org.

A project of the Center for Computer Assisted Research in the Humanities at Stanford University and the Cognitive and Systematic Musicology Laboratory at Ohio State University, *Themefinder* is one of the best web-based thematic catalogs. It includes about 35,000 incipits in three sets: classical, folk, and Renaissance. The last set is taken primarily from Harry Lincoln's *The Latin Motet: Indexes to Printed Collections, 1500–1600* (Ottawa, ON: Institute of Mediaeval Music, 1993). Searches can be entered several ways (pitch name, interval, scale degree, contour, etc.) and can be found at the beginning or within the incipit. Figure 8-2 shows the search screen. Also includes browsable composer thematic incipits. Reviewed briefly in *Strad* 117, no. 1393 (May 2006): 17.

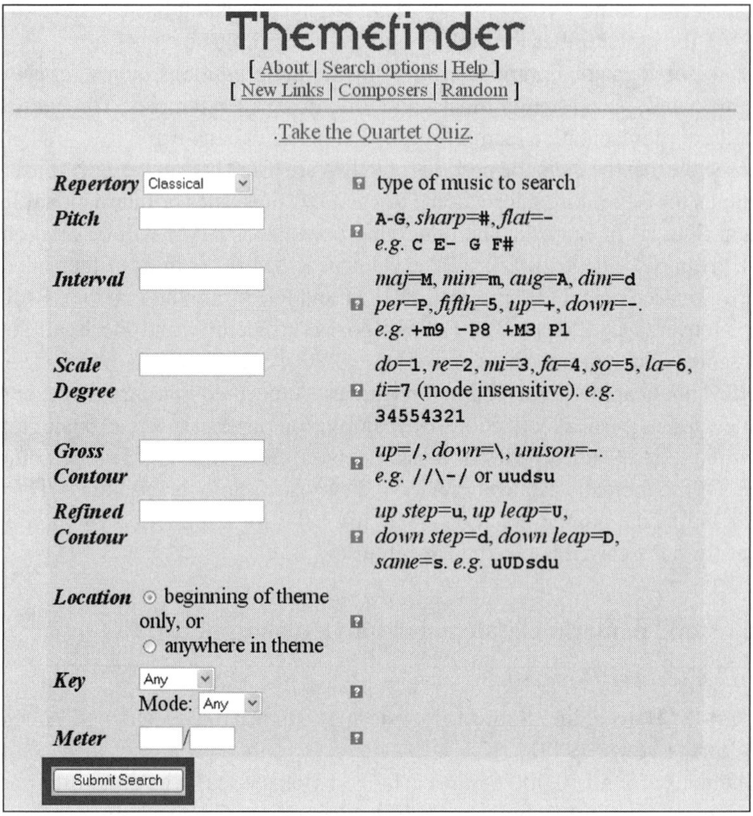

Figure 8-2 *Themefinder* Search Screen *(Used by permission of the Center for Computer Assisted Research in the Humanities)*

8.22 Parsons, Denys. *The Directory of Tunes and Musical Themes.* Cambridge, UK: Spencer-Brown, 1975.

Includes over 10,000 classical themes and around 4,000 popular ones. Parsons is the only catalog listed here that includes a section devoted to popular music. Based on melodic direction (notated with U, D, and R, for up, down, and repeat). Can be used by people who do not read music. Arrangement is alphabetical beginning with all Ds at the beginning, followed by Rs and Us. National anthems are also included. Reviewed by Marsha Berman in *Notes* 33, no. 3 (Mar. 1977): 601–2.

Early Music

8.23 Bryden, John R., and David G. Hughes. *An Index of Gregorian Chant*. 2 vols. Cambridge, MA: Harvard University Press, 1969.

Sources are mostly modern service books and a handful of medieval manuscripts available in facsimile. Volume 1 is an alphabetical listing of chant texts. Volume 2 is the thematic index that uses a code based on half-step melodic motion. For example, an ascending whole step is notated with a "2" and a descending perfect fifth with "–7." Begins with the largest descending intervals. Reviewed by Don Michael Randel in *Notes* 27, no. 3 (Mar. 1971): 477–78.

RISM: *Répertoire international des sources musicales/Internationales Quellenlexikon der Musik/International Inventory of Musical Sources (arranged by RISM number)*

Series A/II: *Manuscripts by Individual Composers after 1600*

*8.24 *RISM Online: Series A/II, Music Manuscripts after 1600*. Baltimore: NISC, 2002–. http://www.nisc.com.

The best way to find the location of manuscripts by individual composers during the period from 1600 to 1850. Includes over half a million entries representing works by nearly 20,000 composers from over 30 countries. Can be searched in a number of ways. See Figure 8-3. Use the Advanced Search Mode to enter musical themes using the "Plain & Easy Code." Updated every six months. Also available on CD-ROM Munich: K. G. Saur, 1995–. Was previously available on microform. The online version is recommended. Online version (previously offered for free by Harvard University) and CD-ROM version (published by K. G. Saur) reviewed by Calvin Elliker in *Notes* 55, no. 4 (June 1999): 980–84.

Series B/IV: *Manuscripts of Polyphonic Music, 11th–16th Centuries*

8.25 Reaney, Gilbert. *Manuscripts of Polyphonic Music: 11th–Early 14th Century*. RISM, B/IV/1. Munich: G. Henle, 1966.

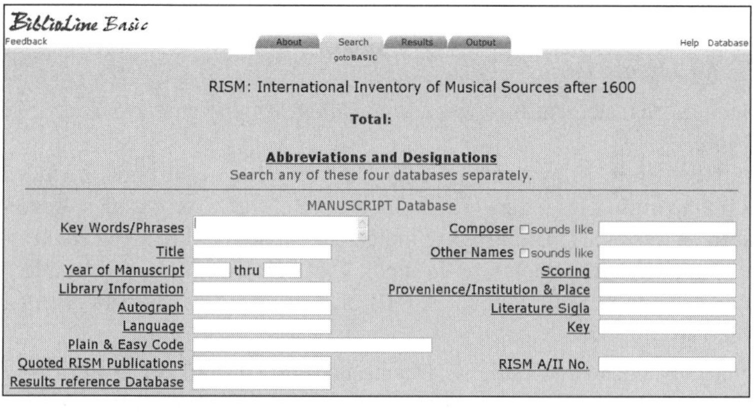

Figure 8-3 *RISM: International Inventory of Musical Sources after 1600* Advanced Search Screen from NISC (*2007 © BiblioLine, Service of NISC*)

Arranged geographically. Reviewed by Gemt Vellekoop in *Mens en melodie* 22, no. 12 (Dec. 1967): 381–82.

8.26 ———. *Manuscripts of Polyphonic Music: c. 1320–1400*. RISM, B/IV/2. Munich: G. Henle, 1969.

Arranged geographically. Reviewed by Ernest Sanders in *Music and Letters* 51, no. 4 (Oct. 1970): 458–59.

8.27 Wathey, Andrew. *Manuscripts of Polyphonic Music: The British Isles, 1100– 1400*. RISM, B/IV/1–2 Sup. Munich: G. Henle, 1993.

Arranged geographically. Reviewed by Martin Staehelin in *Die Musikforschung* 47, no. 4 (Oct.–Dec. 1994): 412–14.

8.28 Fischer, Kurt von, and Max Lütolf. *Handschriften mit mehrstimmiger Musik: Des 14.,15. und 16. Jahrhunderts*. 2 vols. RISM, B/IV/3–4. Munich: G. Henle, 1972.

Arranged geographically. Reviewed by Charles Hamm in *JAMS* 27, no. 3 (Fall 1974): 518–22.

8.29 Bridgman, Nanie. *Manuscrits de musique polyphonique: XVe et XVIe siècles: Italie*. RISM, B/IV/5. Munich: G. Henle, 1991.

Arranged geographically. Reviewed by Allan W. Atlas in *Notes* 49, no. 1 (Sept. 1992): 64–67 and Margaret Bent in *JAMS* 48, no. 2 (Summer 1995): 272–83.

Series B/IX: Hebrew Sources of Music and Music Theory

8.30 Adler, Israel. *Hebrew Notated Manuscript Sources up to circa 1840: A Descriptive and Thematic Catalogue with a Checklist of Printed Sources*. 2 vols. RISM, B/ IX/1. Munich: G. Henle, 1989.

Volume 2 contains the melodic incipits with a system similar to that of Bryden and Hughes. Reviewed by Macy Nulman in *Notes* 47, no. 4 (June 1991): 1176–77.

Series B/XII: Persian Sources of Music and Music Theory

8.31 Massoudieh, Mohammad Taghi. *Manucrits persans concernant la musique*. RISM, B/XII. Munich: G. Henle, 1996.

Organized alphabetically by manuscript title, with unattributed ones listed separately.

Hymns and Hymn Tunes

8.32 Diehl, Katharine Smith. *Hymns and Tunes: An Index*. New York: Scarecrow, 1966.

Compiled from 78 hymnals used by U.S. churches at the time. Includes around 12,000 hymns. Uses letters (D for Do, R for Re, etc.) to represent solfège syllables based on movable Do. Sharps are indicated, but no flats are given enharmonically. To identify a hymn, look it up in Index V of Part Two, arranged in solfège order, to find the numeric code for Index III of Part Two. Reviewed in *Hymn* 18, no. 1 (Jan. 1967): 27–28.

8.33 Temperley, Nicholas, Charles G. Manns, and Joseph Herl. *The Hymn Tune Index: A Census of English-Language Hymn Tunes in Printed Sources from 1535 to 1820*. 4 vols. Oxford, UK: Clarendon Press, 1998; Temperley, Nicholas, Charles G. Manns,

Joseph Herl, and David Zeiders. *The Hymn Tune Index [Online] (HTI)*. Urbana-Champaign: University of Illinois, 2001–. http://hymntune.library.uiuc.edu.
Scholarly catalog of over 17,500 hymn tunes from over 1,700 sources. Uses a numeric code based on scale degree that ignores accidentals, rests, grace notes, etc. The free online version is highly recommended over the print, because it includes additional sources and enhanced access to the content. In the print version, use the index in vol. 2 that provides the number for the tune census in vols. 3–4. Print version reviewed by Nym Cooke in *JAMS* 56, no. 3 (Fall 2003): 710–20 and online version reviewed by Laurie J. Sampsel in *Notes* 59, no. 3 (Mar. 2003): 713–15.

8.34 Wasson, D. DeWitt. *Hymntune Index and Related Hymn Materials*. 3 vols. Studies in Liturgical Musicology, no. 6. Lanham, MD: Scarecrow, 1998. Available on CD-ROM.
Similar to Diehl with letters representing solfège syllables. Intended for the church musician, indexes about 34,000 hymn tunes from over 400 hymnals dating from 1900 through the 1980s. The melodic index appears in vol. 1 and provides the numeric code for vol. 2–3. The CD-ROM version published by Scarecrow Press in 2001 is recommended over the print version. Print version reviewed by Daniel Zager in *Notes* 56, no. 1 (Sept. 1999): 126–28 and CD-ROM version reviewed by Laurie J. Sampsel in *Notes* 59, no. 3 (Mar. 2003): 713–15.

Collections, Archives, Libraries, and Publishers

A few examples of thematic catalogs for particular collections or publishers of music are given next. Those for libraries are often given call numbers consistent with library catalogs, ML136. Those for publishers are ML145. The subdivision "Thematic catalogs" is assigned to these as well. The following listing is again highly selective.

8.35 Brook, Barry S. *The Breitkopf Thematic Catalogue: The Six Parts and Sixteen Supplements, 1762–1787*. New York: Dover, 1966.
Reprint of the original catalogs. Arranged chronologically. Reviewed byO. W. Krummel in *Notes* 24, no. 4 (June 1968): 697–700.

8.36 Duckles, Vincent, and Minnie Elmer. *Thematic Catalog of a Manuscript Collection of Eighteenth-Century Italian Instrumental Music in the University of California, Berkeley Music Library*. Berkeley: University of California Press, 1963.
Arranged alphabetically by composer. Reviewed by O. W. Krummel in *Notes* 22, no. 3 (Mar. 1966): 1025–26.

8.37 Écorcheville, Jules. *Catalogue du fonds de musique ancienne de la Bibliothèque Nationale*. 8 vols. New York: Da Capo, 1972.
The Da Capo is a 4-volume reprint of the original 8 volumes (Paris: Société internationale de musique, 1910–14). Includes some early music manuscripts from the Bibliothèque nationale de France. Arranged alphabetically by composer or genre (for unattributed works).

8.38 Gombosi, Marilyn. *Catalog of the Johannes Herbst Collection*. Chapel Hill: University of North Carolina Press, 1970.
Arranged by type of work (congregation music, extended works, and miscellaneous). Reviewed by Susan T. Sommer in *Notes* 29, no. 2 (Dec. 1972): 258–59.

EVALUATION CHECKLIST

The following checklist was adapted from Hunter, which is reprinted in Brook and Viano.[2] Please note that not all of these will apply to every thematic catalog.

- Do the entries include:
    - Title, popular or alternative title, and opus or other identifying number?
    - Author or source of text for vocal music?
    - Full list of performing forces?
    - Duration of each movement?
    - Date and place of composition?
    - Premiere information (date, place, performers, reviews)?
    - Dedicatee(s)?
- What is the quality of the incipits?
    - Are they provided for each movement?
    - Is there more than one incipit per movement, if appropriate (main theme in addition to the opening measures)?
    - Do they include the number of measures in each movement?
    - Are differences between the **autograph** or other manuscript sources and standard printed texts indicated?
    - Are incipits multi-stave rather than a single line, if appropriate?
    - Are the original clefs, tempo, and expression markings included?
    - Is there a transcription of the original notation, if appropriate?
    - Are titles and sources cited together with incipits?
    - Are the performing forces indicated if short score is used?
- Are notes on textual accuracy included?
- Are references and/or a bibliography:
    - Provided?
    - Selective?
    - Current?
- Is a discography:
    - Provided?
    - Selective?
    - Current?
- How is the catalog organized?
    - By opus or other identifying number or by chronology (genre also possible)?
    - Are dubious attributions included separately?

[2]David Hunter and others, "Music Library Association Guidelines for the Preparation of Music Reference Works," *Notes* 50, no. 4 (June 1994): 1329–38.

- How is the catalog indexed?
  - By title?
  - Are the first lines of vocal texts included?
  - Is a classified list of all works provided?
  - Is there an index of themes?
- Is the coding of themes:
  - Accurate?
  - Intuitive?
  - Are there multiple options for entering themes (numerical, pitch name, solfège)?

SUGGESTED READINGS

The Brook and Viano introduction to *Thematic Catalogues in Music* presents the state of the thematic catalog in 1997. Deathridge and Gossett discuss more specifically the thematic catalogs they were or are compiling, respectively, for Wagner and Rossini. Winter offers a detailed review of the Schubert catalog. Reijen explains the need for a new Köchel, based on reviews of the sixth edition. The *New Grove* article, also by Brook, provides a brief introduction to thematic catalogs and their uses.

Brook, Barry S., and Richard Viano. "Further Reflections on the Past, Present, and Future of the Thematic Catalogue in Music." In *Thematic Catalogues in Music: An Annotated Bibliography*. 2nd ed., xxiii–xliii. Stuyvesant, NY: Pendragon, 1997. An earlier version with a similar title was published simultaneously in *Foundations in Music Bibliography*, edited by Richard D. Green, 27–46. New York: Haworth, 1993, and in *Music Reference Services Quarterly* 2, no. 1–2 (1993): 27–46.

Deathridge, John. "Cataloguing Wagner." *Musical Times* 124, no. 1680 (Feb. 1983): 92–96.

Gossett, Philip. "The Rossini Thematic Catalog: When Does Bibliographical Access Become Bibliographical Excess?" *Music Reference Services Quarterly* 2, no. 3 (1993): 271–80.

Reijen, Paul van. "Köchel 2000: Suggestions for a New Catalogue of Mozart's Works." *Fontes artis musicae* 42, no. 4 (Oct.–Dec.): 299–310.

Sadie, Stanley, ed. *The New Grove Dictionary of Music and Musicians*. 2nd ed. New York: Grove, 2001. S.v. "Thematic Catalogue," by Barry S. Brook. Also available from *Grove Music Online*. http://www.oxfordmusiconline.com.

Winter, Robert. "Cataloguing Schubert." *19th Century Music* 3, no. 2 (Nov. 1979): 154–62.

CHAPTER 9

Music Histories, Source Readings, and Chronologies

MUSIC HISTORIES

Music histories comprise a category of research tools with which you are already familiar. In fact, you likely own a few in your personal library from your undergraduate or graduate days. You may not think of them as reference tools; in fact, many of those listed here are primarily textbooks for use in college and university courses. However, they are valuable sources of information, are often written by experts on the topic (especially the style period histories), are frequently updated with new information, and most include bibliographic references and indexes. In these respects they demonstrate characteristics of quality reference tools and are useful for looking up information.

Some multi-volume histories, like Taruskin's *Oxford History of Western Music*, are more like reference tools than one-volume textbooks. They are too large to be used in most courses and too expensive for faculty to consider requiring their students to purchase them. See the Suggested Readings related to Taruskin, which has sparked a great deal of discussion. Multi-volume histories are something of a hybrid between textbook and reference tool. For example, they have the breadth of a reference tool but the narrative format and chronological arrangement of a history. The tool most like these discussed so far is the *Garland Encyclopedia of World Music* (entry 2.4).

Major publishers of music histories include W. W. Norton, Oxford University Press, and Prentice Hall. All three publish series devoted to music histories, which are described later. Norton and Oxford are already familiar to you as publishers of high-quality research tools. Other publishers represented include McGraw-Hill, Schirmer, and Bedford/St. Martin's.

Histories are generally not arranged like reference tools, with an alphabetical listing of topical articles. Rather, they usually present a chronological or concept-based narrative. Some have companion study guides. Newer titles are also being published with companion websites that enhance the text with supplementary materials, such as listening guides and sample quizzes. Also, unlike most reference tools, many histories intended for classroom use have accompanying score or recording anthologies.

One example of a score anthology with wider applications is the *Norton Scores: An Anthology for Listening*, published to accompany the music appreciation text *The Enjoyment of Music*. The contents of anthologies like this are indexed by the tools discussed in Chapter 7. In particular, use Murray's *Anthologies of Music: An Annotated Index* (entry 7.73) and Hilton's *An Index to Early Music in Selected Anthologies* (entry 7.71) for this purpose.

Many graduate music students teach music appreciation classes at some point in their career. The presence or absence of these accompanying materials is something you will want to consider when choosing a text for use in your own teaching. It is not too soon to begin developing preferences for history textbooks. In addition to their usefulness for looking up facts, histories are a good place to begin studying or reviewing your own knowledge of one or more music history topics. For example, many students review Burkholder, Grout, and Palisca's *A History of Western Music* extensively while studying for entrance, placement, or comprehensive exams for their graduate programs. The study guides, outline histories, and chronologies listed here are also very helpful for music history review.

Keep in mind that sometimes the best histories are not necessarily the best textbooks. This chapter includes both, with the annotations written to point out which are which. For example, in the area of American music studies, the books by Chase and Hamm are the better histories, but those by Kingman and Ferris are more useful as texts. Sometimes authors provide alternate versions. For example, Crawford created an abridged textbook version of his history, accompanied by a CD anthology of listening examples.

You can find histories by searching your library's catalog and databases such as *WorldCat*. In the LC classification system, most histories are given call numbers in the range ML159–ML360. The general histories (like Burkholder and Taruskin) published after 1800 have the call number ML160. The LC subject heading is "Music—History and criticism." Histories and texts for the different style periods are given call numbers from ML162 for ancient music to ML197 for twentieth-century music. The subject headings include the century, for example "Music—18th century—History and criticism." Call numbers in the ML198–ML360 range are assigned to histories of music of a specific place. Histories of music in the U.S. are ML200; those for Canada are ML205, and those for England are ML286. The subject headings include the place, "Music—United States—History and criticism." Some of these histories may be shelved in your library's reference collection (particularly the multi-volume ones); most are probably in the circulating **stacks**.

The other specialized histories have LC call numbers and subject headings specific to their topics. Histories of jazz are assigned the call number ML3506 and the subject heading "Jazz—History and criticism." Music appreciation texts are under MT6, with the subject heading "Music appreciation." Surveys of world music usually have the call number ML3545 and the subject heading "World music—History and criticism."

The asterisks in the following list indicate recommended titles. See this text's companion website for updated information on new titles or editions.

Multi-Volume Music Histories

9.1   *Neues Handbuch der Musikwissenschaft.* Edited by Carl Dahlhaus and Hermann
      Danuser. 13 vols. Laaber, Ger.: Laaber–Verlag, 1980–1995. Contents: Vol. 1:
      Die Musik des Altertums, edited by Albrecht Riethmüller and Frieder Zaminer,
      1989; Vol. 2: *Die Musik des Mittelalters*, edited by Hartmut Möller and Rudolf
      Stephan, 1991; Vol. 3, Part 1: *Die Musik des 15. und 16. Jahrhunderts (Teil
      1)*, edited by Ludwig Finscher, 1989; Vol. 3, Part 2: *Die Musik des 15. und
      16. Jahrhunderts (Teil 2)*, edited by Ludwig Finscher, 1990; Vol. 4: *Die Musik
      des 17. Jahrhunderts*, edited by Werner Braun, 1981; Vol. 5: *Die Musik des
      18. Jahrhunderts*, edited by Carl Dahlhaus, 1985; Vol. 6: *Die Musik des 19.
      Jahrhunderts*, edited by Carl Dahlhaus, 1980; Vol. 7: *Die Musik des 20.
      Jahrhunderts*, edited by Hermann Danuser, 1984; Vol. 8: *Aussereuropäische
      Musik (Teil 1)*, edited by Hans Oesch, 1984; Vol. 9: *Aussereuropäische Musik
      (Teil 2)*, edited by Hans Oesch, 1987; Vol. 10: *Systematische Musikwissenschaft*,
      edited by Carl Dahlhaus and Helga de la Motte-Haber, 1982; Vol. 11:
      Musikalische Interpretation, edited by Hermann Danuser, 1992; Vol. 12:
      Volks- und Popularmusik in Europa, edited by Doris Stockmann, 1992; Vol.
      13: *Register*, edited by Hans-Joachim Hinrichsen, 1995.

      The "Neues" refers to the 10-volume earlier title, *Handbuch der
      Musikwissenschaft,* edited by Ernst Bücken (Wildpark-Potsdam, Ger.:
      Akademische Verlagsgesellschaft Athenaion, 1928–32). The earlier title was
      more lavishly illustrated with color plates. In addition to volumes devoted to
      the style periods, the *Neues Handbuch* also includes coverage of non-Western
      music, musicology, interpretation, and folk and popular music in Europe. Vol. 1
      reviewed by David Wulstan in *Music and Letters* 73, no. 2 (May 1992): 268–69.
      Vol. 2 reviewed by Kurt von Fischer in *Die Musikforschung* 46, no. 2 (Apr.–June
      1993): 202–4. Vol. 3 reviewed by Christian Meyer in *Revue de musicologie* 77,
      no. 2 (1991): 339–41. Vol. 4 reviewed by George J. Buelow in *Music and Letters*
      67, no. 1 (Jan. 1986): 62–65. Vol. 5 reviewed by Eugene K. Wolf in *Journal of
      Musicological Research* 10, no. 3–4 (1991): 239–55. Vol. 6 reviewed by Douglas
      Johnson in *JAMS* 36, no. 3 (Fall 1983): 532–43. Vol. 7 reviewed by Douglas
      Jarman in *Music and Letters* 66, no. 2 (Apr. 1985): 172–73. Vol. 8 reviewed
      by René T.A. Lysloff in *Ethnomusicology* 30, no. 2 (Spring–Summer 1986):
      360–62. Vol. 9 reviewed by Bruno Nettl in *Ethnomusicology* 33, no. 1 (Winter
      1989): 147–49. Vol. 10 reviewed by Bojan Bujic in *Music and Letters* 66, no. 2
      (Apr. 1985): 135–37. Vol. 11 reviewed by Stephen Blum in *Notes* 51, no. 1 (Sept.
      1994): 173–75. Vol. 12 reviewed by Bruno Nettl in *Notes* 51, no. 1 (Sept. 1994):
      205–208.

9.2   *New Oxford History of Music.* Edited by J. A. Westrup and others. 10 vols.
      London: Oxford University Press, 1954–1990. Contents: Vol. 1: *Ancient and
      Oriental Music*, edited by Egon Wellesz, 1957; Vol. 2: *Early Medieval Music up
      to 1300*, edited by Dom A. Hughes, 1954; Vol. 3: *Ars Nova and the Renaissance:
      1300–1540*, edited by Dom A. Hughes and Gerald Abraham, 1960; Vol. 4: *The
      Age of Humanism: 1540–1630*, edited by Gerald Abraham, 1968; Vol. 5: *Opera
      and Church Music: 1630–1750*, edited by Anthony Lewis and Nigel Fortune,

1975; Vol. 6: *Concert Music: 1630–1750*, edited by Gerald Abraham, 1986; Vol. 7: *The Age of Enlightenment: 1745–1790*, edited by Egon Wellesz and F. W. Sternfeld, 1973; Vol. 8: *The Age of Beethoven: 1790–1830*, edited by Gerald Abraham, 1982; Vol. 9: *Romanticism: 1830–1890*, edited by Gerald Abraham, 1990; Vol. 10: *The Modern Age: 1890–1960*, edited by Martin Cooper, 1974.
A 10-volume history with a long life. The "new" in the title refers to the original *Oxford History of Music* of six volumes (1901–1905). Each volume of the *New Oxford History of Music* includes contributions from multiple authors published during a span of nearly four decades. Authoritative but uneven. Some articles are models. Overall, the set was viewed as out-of-date before it was completed. Read the detailed reviews before turning to these volumes. Each volume includes musical examples, facsimiles, bibliography, and index. A set of LP recordings, *The History of Music in Sound*, was issued, along with notes. Vol. 1 reviewed by Curt Sachs in *Notes* 15, no. 1 (Dec. 1957): 97–99. Vol. 2 reviewed by Charles Warren Fox in *Musical Quarterly* 41, no. 4 (Oct. 1955): 534–47. Vol. 3 reviewed by Richard H. Hoppin in *Musical Quarterly* 47, no. 1 (Jan. 1961): 116–25. Vol. 4 reviewed by Howard Mayer Brown in *Notes* 26, no. 2 (Dec. 1969): 254–56 and Claude V. Palisca in *JAMS* 23, no. 1 (Spring 1970): 133–36. Vol. 5 reviewed by Denis Arnold in *Music and Letters* 57, no. 3 (July 1976): 309–312. Vol. 6 reviewed by H. Diack Johnstone in *Music and Letters* 69, no. 1 (Jan. 1988): 70–74. Vol. 7 reviewed by Daniel Heartz in *Musical Times* 115, no. 1574 (Apr. 1974): 295–301. Vol. 8 reviewed by Leon Botstein in *Musical Quarterly* 70, no. 1 (Winter 1984): 146–52. Vol. 9 reviewed by Susan Youens in *College Music Symposium* 31 (1991): 136–40 and John Williamson in *Music and Letters* 73, no. 2 (May 1992): 291–96. Vol. 10 reviewed by Peter S. Odegard in *JAMS* 29, no. 1 (Spring 1976): 153–56.

9.3   *New Oxford History of Music*. 2nd ed. 2 vols. London: Oxford University Press, 1990–2001. Contents: Vol. 2, 2nd ed.: *The Early Middle Ages to 1300*, edited by Richard Crocker and David Hiley, 1990; Vol. 3., Part 1, 2nd ed.: *Music as Concept and Practice in the Late Middle Ages*, edited by Reinhard Strohm and Bonnie J. Blackburn, 2001.
This second edition was abandoned after the publication of two volumes. These volumes are similar to the first edition of the *New Oxford History of Music*, but they are more current. See the multi-volume Oxford history by Richard Taruskin for the succeeding title. Vol. 2 reviewed by Isobel W. Preece in *Notes* 48, no. 2 (Dec. 1991): 477–79. Vol. 3, Part 1 reviewed by Elizabeth E. Leach in *Music and Letters* 84, no. 2 (May 2003): 274–78.

*9.4   Taruskin, Richard. *The Oxford History of Western Music*. 6 vols. New York: Oxford University Press, 2005. Available online from *Oxford Music Online* at http://oxfordmusiconline.com. Contents: Vol. 1: *The Earliest Notations to the Sixteenth Century*; Vol. 2: *The Seventeenth and Eighteenth Centuries*; Vol. 3: *The Nineteenth Century*; Vol. 4: *The Early Twentieth Century*; Vol. 5: *The Late Twentieth Century*; Vol. 6: *Resources: Chronology, Bibliography, Master Index*.
The current edition varies greatly from the *New Oxford History*. The "new" is gone from the title and, in the nineteenth-century tradition, this set was written

by a single author, Berkeley musicologist Richard Taruskin. Loaded with musical examples, this well-written contextual history of Western art music does not attempt comprehensive coverage of major composers and works. Written for the graduate student and Taruskin's colleagues, it was initially intended to be a text for undergraduate music majors. Chronological, with two volumes devoted to the twentieth century. Volume 6 includes a chronology, bibliography of books in English, lists of the 1,800 musical examples, and an index. Reviewed by Leon Botstein in *Musical Quarterly* 87, no. 3 (Fall 2004): 359–69; Paul Griffiths in *Nation* 282, no. 9 (Mar. 6, 2006): 34–40; Charles Rosen in two parts: *New York Review of Books* 53, no. 3 (23 Feb. 2006): 41–45; 53, no. 4 (9 Mar. 2006): 44–48; Greg Sandow in *Wall Street Journal*, 27 Jan. 2005, eastern edition, sec. D; Hugh Wood and Christopher Wood in *Times Higher Education Supplement* (London) 20 May 2005.

Music History Series (W. W. Norton and Prentice Hall)

Norton History of Music Series

The Norton History of Music Series has been replaced by the publisher's newer titles released in the Norton Introduction to Music History Series. This listing is selective. The four volumes listed here are among those that are considered classics, are still useful as reference tools, and are still in print. The texts are listed chronologically by period.

9.5   Reese, Gustave. *Music in the Middle Ages: With an Introduction on the Music of Ancient Times*. New York: W. W. Norton, 1940.
      Reviewed by Willi Apel in *Speculum* 20, no. 1 (Jan. 1945): 119–22.

9.6   ———. *Music in the Renaissance*. Rev. ed. New York: W. W. Norton, 1959.
      Reviewed by E. H. Sparks in *Notes* 17, no. 4 (Sept. 1960): 569.

9.7   Bukofzer, Manfred F. *Music in the Baroque Era*. New York: W. W. Norton, 1947.
      Reviewed by Otto Kinkeldey in *Notes* 5, no. 2 (Mar. 1948): 224–25.

9.8   Einstein, Alfred. *Music in the Romantic Era*. New York: W. W. Norton, 1947.
      Reviewed by Richard S. Hill in *Notes* 4, no. 4 (Sept. 1947): 461–63.

**Norton Introduction to Music History Series*

This new series published by W. W. Norton, along with the Prentice Hall History of Music Series, is the best for histories and textbooks devoted to the individual style periods of music. Some of the older histories need updating. The Norton series includes companion anthologies of musical scores compiled by the authors to accompany each text. These are titled *Anthology of Medieval Music*, *Anthology of Renaissance Music*, etc. These titles are intended for upper-division music majors who have taken the standard music history survey and for graduate students. All are written by well-respected specialists in their areas.

9.9   Hoppin, Richard H. *Medieval Music*. New York: W. W. Norton, 1978.
      Reviewed by Charlotte Roederer in *Musical Quarterly* 65, no. 3 (July 1979): 447–51.

9.10 Atlas, Allan W. *Renaissance Music: Music in Western Europe, 1400–1600*. New York: W. W. Norton, 1998.

Reviewed by Noel O'Regan in *Music and Letters* 82, no. 2 (May 2001): 268–81.

9.11 Hill, John W. *Baroque Music: Music in Western Europe, 1580–1750.* New York: W. W. Norton, 2005.

Reviewed in *Reference and Research Book News* 20, no. 3 (Aug. 2005): 216.

9.12 Downs, Philip G. *Classical Music: The Era of Haydn, Mozart, and Beethoven.* New York: W. W. Norton, 1992.

Reviewed by David W. Jones in *Music and Letters* 75, no. 4 (Nov. 1994): 613–15.

9.13 Plantinga, Leon. *Romantic Music: A History of Musical Style in Nineteenth-Century Europe.* New York: W. W. Norton, 1984.

Reviewed by Carl Dahlhaus in *19th Century Music* 11, no. 2 (Fall 1987): 194–96 and Christopher Hatch in *Current Musicology* 37–38 (1984): 187–201.

9.14 Morgan, Robert P. *Twentieth-Century Music: A History of Musical Style in Modern Europe and America.* New York: W. W. Norton, 1991.

Reviewed by Arnold Whittall in *Music and Letters* 73, no. 3 (Aug. 1992): 468–71.

Prentice Hall History of Music Series

The Prentice Hall series presents an alternative to Norton. The volumes are shorter and are published without accompanying score anthologies, making them less expensive for students. Also, unlike Norton, some volumes are devoted to non-Western music. Those have been listed separately. Titles that have been taken over by other authors have been omitted. For example, Jeremy Yudkin's medieval history is cited rather than Albert Seay's *Music in the Medieval World*, 2nd ed. (1975). H. Wiley Hitchcock's *Music in the United States* is listed with the American histories rather than here. Some of the titles in this series, like Norton, need updating. Others are out of print.

Some good style period histories are not included in these series. For example, Jon Finson's *Nineteenth-Century Music: The Western Classical Tradition* (Upper Saddle River, NJ: Prentice Hall, 2002) is not part of the Prentice Hall History of Music Series. Another example by a different publisher is Bryan R. Simms' *Music of the Twentieth Century: Style and Structure*, 2nd ed. (New York: Schirmer, 1996). Use the subject heading searches described earlier to find others.

Style Period Histories

9.15 Yudkin, Jeremy. *Music in Medieval Europe.* Englewood Cliffs, NJ: Prentice Hall, 1989.

Reviewed by Julie Cumming in *Historical Performance* 2, no. 2 (Winter 1989): 93–95.

9.16 Brown, Howard Mayer, and Louise K. Stein. *Music in the Renaissance.* 2nd ed. Upper Saddle River, NJ: Prentice Hall, 1999.

Reviewed by Noel O'Regan in *Music and Letters* 82, no. 2 (May 2001): 268–81.

9.17 Palisca, Claude V. *Baroque Music.* 3rd ed. Englewood Cliffs, NJ: Prentice Hall, 1991.

Second edition reviewed by Denis Arnold in *Early Music* 10, no. 4 (Oct. 1982): 537–39.

9.18 Pauly, Reinhard G. *Music in the Classic Period*, 4th ed. Upper Saddle River, NJ: Prentice Hall, 2000.

First edition reviewed by E. Eugene Helm in *Notes* 25, no. 1 (Sept. 1968): 40–41.

9.19 Longyear, Rey M. *Nineteenth-Century Romanticism in Music*, 3rd ed. Englewood Cliffs, NJ: Prentice Hall, 1988.

Second edition reviewed by D. Kern Holoman in *Notes* 30, no. 4 (June 1974): 779–81.

9.20 Salzman, Eric. *Twentieth-Century Music: An Introduction*, 4th ed. Upper Saddle River, NJ: Prentice Hall, 2002.

Second edition reviewed by John Graziano in *Notes* 31, no. 3 (Mar. 1975): 574–75.

Area Histories

9.21 Béhague, Gerard. *Music in Latin America: An Introduction*. Englewood Cliffs, NJ: Prentice Hall, 1979.

Reviewed by Juan A. Orrego-Salas in *Latin American Music Review* 1, no. 1 (Spring–Summer 1980): 114–17.

9.22 Malm, William P. *Music Cultures of the Pacific, the Near East, and Asia*, 3rd ed. Upper Saddle River, NJ: Prentice Hall, 1996.

First edition reviewed by David Morton in *Ethnomusicology* 12, no. 1 (Jan. 1968): 140–44.

9.23 Nettl, Bruno, and Gerard Béhague. *Folk and Traditional Music of the Western Continents*, 3rd ed. Englewood Cliffs, NJ: Prentice Hall, 1990.

Second edition reviewed by William P. Malm in *Journal of Research in Music Education* 23, no. 3 (Fall 1975): 215–16.

9.24 Wade, Bonnie C. *Music in India: The Classical Traditions*. Englewood Cliffs, NJ: Prentice Hall, 1979.

Reviewed by Regula Burckhardt Qureshi in *Ethnomusicology* 27, no. 3 (Sept. 1983): 555–57.

General Music History Texts

Each of the texts listed next is intended for use with undergraduate music majors in music history survey classes. Each offers a complete package for professors and students, with score anthologies and sound recordings available. The standard text is *A History of Western Music* (known as "Grout," for its original author), which was first published in 1960.

9.25 Bonds, Mark E. *A History of Music in Western Culture*, 2nd ed. Upper Saddle River, NJ: Prentice Hall, 2006.

Bonds (University of North Carolina, Chapel Hill) has written his text to focus more broadly on music in culture. Includes composer profiles, source readings ("Primary Evidence"), "Focus Boxes" to elaborate on a topic without interrupting the narrative, and some discussion of performance practice. Good coverage of jazz, popular music, and women. Bonds's is the most beautifully illustrated text listed, with color reproductions of art, facsimiles of musical scores, photos of instruments, and examples of architecture. Includes appendixes and glossary, but has no bibliography or list of further readings. Accompanying scores and recordings in two volumes are published under the same title. Anthology is weaker than with Norton. An abridged version, *Brief History of Music in Western Culture*, is also available. First edition reviewed in *Reference and Research Book News* 18, no. 2 (May 2003): 197.

*9.26 Burkholder, J. Peter, Donald J. Grout, and Claude V. Palisca. *A History of Western Music*, 7th ed. New York: W. W. Norton, 2006.

An updated edition of Grout's classic music history text. Now in the hands of J. Peter Burkholder (Indiana University), the level of scholarship remains high, and this text is still the most widely used. Seventh edition includes more information on the twentieth century and music in America (from colonial times through jazz and modernism). Also has more source readings and more illustrations. The bibliography, titled "Further Reading," is over 60 pages. This is one of the features that make this text the best reference tool and study aid. Accompanied by the *Norton Anthology of Western Music* (5th ed.) and *The Norton Recorded Anthology of Western Music* (5th ed.), both in two volumes. The scores have been updated to include full orchestral scores, compared to piano reduction in previous volumes. Supplementary materials available for both instructors and students, including a teacher's manual, a study guide, and a website that incorporates listening quizzes, sample questions, flash cards, and the Norton Online Listening Lab. Reviewed in *Reference and Research Book News* 20, no. 4 (Nov. 2005): 246–51.

9.27 Stolba, K. Marie. *The Development of Western Music: A History*, 3rd ed. Boston: McGraw-Hill, 1998.

The oldest of the group, the late K. Marie Stolba's text is in need of a new edition. This history's strengths include Stolba's inclusion of women and the full-page color facsimiles of early music sources and artworks. Includes a glossary, a bibliography (out-of-date), and an index. Companion scores and recordings in two volumes were published under the same title. First edition reviewed by Warren Bourne in *Australian Journal of Music Education* 1 (1992): 93–95.

9.28 Wright, Craig, and Bryan R. Simms. *Music in Western Civilization*. Belmont, CA: Thomson/Schirmer, 2006.

Wright (Yale University) and Simms (University of Southern California) have written their text in over 80 short chapters. Similar to Bonds in coverage of jazz and popular music. Includes only a 2-page bibliography, along with a glossary and an index. The accompanying score and recording anthologies (compiled with Timothy Roden) are available in either two or three volumes, making them useful for those courses taught in either semesters or quarters. Reviewed in *Reference and Research Book News* 20, no. 4 (Nov. 2005): 247.

Music Appreciation Texts

In addition to the three well-respected music appreciation texts listed next, others may be of interest. Consider the following: Jean Ferris's *The Art of Listening*, 7th ed. (Boston:

McGraw-Hill, 2008); David Willoughby's *World of Music*, 6th ed. (Boston: McGraw-Hill, 2007); Craig M. Wright's *Listening to Music*, 5th ed. (Belmont, CA: Thomson/Schirmer, 2008); and Jeremy Yudkin's *Understanding Music*, 5th ed. (Upper Saddle River, NJ: Prentice Hall, 2008).

9.29 Kamien, Roger. *Music: An Appreciation*. Brief 6th ed. Boston: McGraw-Hill, 2008.

Chronological approach to music history for the nonmajor that includes jazz, rock, musicals, film music, and non-Western music in addition to Western art music. Highlights seven performers. Includes musical examples and illustrations. Has appendixes and an index. Comes with a CD-ROM. Has an accompanying CD set (5 CDs). No score anthology is offered. Companion website includes listening guides, study guides, etc. A longer edition is also published (9th edition, 2008). Standard edition reviewed in *Music Educators Journal* 88, no. 3 (Nov. 2001): 69.

*9.30 Kerman, Joseph, Gary Tomlinson, and Vivian Kerman. *Listen*. 6th ed. Boston: Bedford/St. Martin's, 2008.

Focuses on Western art music, with only a minimal nod toward non-Western music. Includes 29 listening charts. Has accompanying recordings (3 or 6 CDs), but no score anthology. Companion website features quizzes, flashcards, links, etc. Includes musical examples and many color illustrations. Includes an appendix with further listening, reading, and website suggestions. Has a glossary and an index. Third edition reviewed by Larry Worster in *College Music Symposium* 37 (1997): 142–47.

*9.31 Machlis, Joseph, and Kristine Forney. *The Enjoyment of Music: An Introduction to Perceptive Listening*. Shorter 10th ed. New York: W. W. Norton, 2007.

Distinguished by the accompanying *Norton Scores: An Anthology for Listening* (2 vols.) and *Norton Recordings* (4- or 8-CD sets), both also in their 9th edition, published in 2003. Similar to Kamien in inclusion of jazz, musical theater, rock, film music, and some world music. Has 55 listening guides. Companion CD-ROM, website (quizzes, glossary, etc.), and Norton Online Listening Lab enhance text. Includes musical examples and color illustrations. No additional bibliography or suggested listening. Has appendixes and an index. Seventh edition reviewed by Larry Worster in *College Music Symposium* 37 (1997): 142–47.

Study Guides and Outlines of Music History

Both titles listed here are excellent for review of music history, especially when studying for entrance, placement, or comprehensive exams. They differ slightly in focus and purpose, but they complement each other well. The bibliographies of texts such as *A History of Western Music* are another good source for review.

*9.32 Poultney, David. *Studying Music History: Learning, Reasoning, and Writing about Music History and Literature*, 2nd ed. Upper Saddle River, NJ: Prentice Hall, 1996.

This book is primarily about how to study music history and includes a chapter titled "Writing about Music." Devotes 1 chapter to each major era, from the

Middle Ages through the twentieth century. Chapters include era description, composer bios featuring one important work per composer, genre definitions, and a glossary of terms. The comparative style tables are especially helpful. Excludes jazz and popular music. Includes three sections of mystery source readings and scores to test the reader on concepts learned throughout the text. Reviewed by David Demsey in *Saxophone Journal* 24, no. 6 (July–Aug. 2000): 16.

*9.33 Wold, Milo, Gary Martin, James Miller, and Edmund Cykler. *An Outline History of Western Music*, 9th ed. Boston: McGraw-Hill, 1998.

Also arranged chronologically, but begins earlier than Poultney (with ancient times) and continues through the late twentieth century. Includes timelines, historical context, general period characteristics (melody, harmony, texture, etc.), important composers, and main musical genres for each era. This study guide is unique in that it also cites important theorists, scholars, treatises, and manuscripts for each period. Also includes a chapter on jazz and popular music of the twentieth century. Though no anthology or recordings accompany this book, an appendix of musical examples for examination and listening, which includes citations from popular anthologies such as *HAM* and *NAWM*, is included. Reviewed in *Music Educators Journal* 85, no. 1 (July 1998): 54.

Important Earlier Music Histories

9.34 Burney, Charles. *A General History of Music: From the Earliest Ages to the Present Period*. 4 vols. London, 1776–1789. Reprinted in 2 vols. with notes by Frank Mercer. New York: Dover, 1957.

An early attempt to record the whole history of Western music based on historical documentation. These volumes are particularly valuable because they include Burney's impression of music of his own day, especially regarding opera, and are an important source of information on eighteenth-century performance practice. Burney frequently shows a lack of understanding and objectivity about early music. However, not only is this a good source of musical information, but the literary style is very good. It set the precedent for the next several generations of historians. Discussed by Howard Brofsky in *Musical Quarterly* 65, no. 3 (July 1979): 313–45.

9.35 Hawkins, John. *A General History of the Science and Practice of Music*. 5 vols. London: Payne and Son, 1776. Reprinted in 2 vols, with an introduction by Charles Cudworth. New York: Dover, 1963.

Like Burney, another early attempt to record the whole history of Western music based on historical documentation. Hawkins attempts greater objectivity in presenting his data, rarely expressing a personal opinion, but the writing style is generally dense and ponderous. He gives extensive quotes from early treatises and numerous musical examples. Reviewed by Bernard E. Wilson in *Notes* 22, no. 3 (Spring 1966): 1026–27.

*9.36 Lang, Paul Henry. *Music in Western Civilization*. New York: W. W. Norton, 1941. Reprinted with a foreword by Leon Botstein. New York: W. W. Norton, 1997.

A classic general music history that was one of the first to consider music in cultural context. Although not intended to be a textbook, Lang's work helped establish musicology in America and is still influential today. Reviewed by Walter Piston in *Modern Music* 19, no. 1 (Nov.–Dec. 1941): 63–65.

Historiography

*9.37   Allen, Warren D. *Philosophies of Music History.* New York: American, 1939. Reprint, New York: Dover, 1962.

A classic of music historiography. In Part I Allen presents a history of music histories, and in Part II he covers philosophies of music history. The bibliography includes over 300 music histories, arranged chronologically, dating from 1600 to 1939. Includes a name index and a general index. Reviewed by Margaret Russell in *Music Journal* 21, no. 8 (Nov. 1963): 64–65.

9.38   Dahlhaus, Carl. *Foundations of Music History.* Translated by J. B. Robinson. Cambridge, UK: Cambridge University Press, 1983.

Dahlhaus, a major German musicologist, provides an overview of the methods, theories, and philosophies of music history. Similar in purpose to Allen. Dahlhaus suggests that music history should focus on works, composers, and ideas. Includes a bibliography and an index. Reviewed by Henry Raynor in *Music Review* 45, no. 2 (May 1984): 147–49 and F. W. Sternfeld in *Times Literary Supplement* (London) 7 Oct. 1983.

Special Topic Histories

World Music Surveys

9.39   Nettl, Bruno, Charles Capwell, Isabel K. F. Wong, Thomas Turino, Philip V. Bohlman, and Timothy Rommen. *Excursions in World Music.* 5th ed. Upper Saddle River, NJ: Prentice Hall, 2008.

A widely used text by 6 authors taking a regional approach to the survey of world music for the nonmajor, in 12 chapters. Written by fewer authors than the Titon, allowing for more consistency. Has an accompanying 3-CD anthology. Does not include musical examples or a bibliography. Many of the black-and-white illustrations are of poor quality. Includes a glossary and an index. First edition reviewed by Deborah Wong in *Ethnomusicology* 45, no. 3 (Fall 2001): 542–48.

9.40   Shelemay, Kay Kaufman. *Soundscapes: Exploring Music in a Changing World.* 2nd ed. New York: W. W. Norton, 2006.

Differs from the other texts described here by using a concept-based approach. Appropriate for nonmajors in a survey course. Nine of the chapters present case studies based on a theme, for example, "Music and Migration." Very easy for professors to pick and choose which chapters best suit their classroom needs. Includes only a few musical examples. Beautiful color illustrations. Has 79 listening guides for the 3-CD anthology. The student website includes 200 audio examples. Includes an appendix on classifying musical instruments, a glossary, bibliography, and an index. First edition reviewed by Vic Gammon in *World of Music* 46, no. 1 (2004): 135–39.

*9.41 Titon, Jeff Todd, ed. *Worlds of Music: An Introduction to the Music of the World's People*, 4th ed. Belmont, CA: Thomson/Schirmer, 2002.
Similar to Nettl. Widely used, regional-based text written by multiple authors. Unlike Nettl, Titon includes musical examples, although the Preface suggests it can be used by nonmajors. Covers 8 cultures in 10 chapters. Each chapter includes further reading and listening suggestions. Has an accompanying 4-CD set. Includes black-and-white illustrations. Companion website includes exercises, a glossary, sample text questions, etc. A shorter version is also available. Reviewed by Chris Goertzen in *Journal of American Folklore* 115, no. 455 (Winter 2002): 107–8.

Jazz Histories

9.42 Gioia, Ted. *The History of Jazz*. New York: Oxford University Press, 1997.
Not a textbook, but a good, well-researched introductory history of jazz. Discusses major figures and styles. Does not include musical examples or accompanying CDs. Includes a bibliography, recommended listening, and indexes. Reviewed by Peter Keepnews in *New York Times Book Review* 28 Dec. 1997.

*9.43 Gridley, Mark C. *Jazz Styles: History and Analysis*, 9th ed. Upper Saddle River, NJ: Prentice Hall, 2006.
The most popular text intended for jazz appreciation or history classes for nonmajors. Used for music majors as well. Comes with a demo CD and is accompanied by a 2-CD set and the Prentice Hall *Jazz Classics* CDs. Written without musical notation in the body, the listening guides use timing cues, as do the texts by Tanner and Martin. Includes illustrations. Appendixes include "Elements of Music"; a glossary; supplemental reading; and "For Musicians," with chord progressions, rhythm patterns, etc. Includes index. Seventh edition reviewed by Larry Appelbaum in *JazzTimes* 31 (Education Guide 2001–2002): 76–78.

9.44 Martin, Henry, and Keith Waters. *Jazz: The First 100 Years*, 2nd ed. Belmont, CA: Thomson/Schirmer, 2006.
The newest of the jazz textbooks, Martin and Waters focus on jazz after 1970. Intended for use with majors or nonmajors in either one or two semesters. Well researched and up-to-date. Includes a "primer" CD. Has an accompanying 2-CD set. Includes 44 listening guides. Accompanying website includes listening guides, audio clips, and web links. Additional listening downloads are suggested in each chapter. Unlike the others discussed here, this one includes musical examples in the body of the book. Beautifully illustrated, with many photos in color. Includes a "Jazz Basics" appendix, glossary, selected readings, a discography, DVDs and videos, and an index. First edition reviewed in *Reference and Research Book News* 20, no. 2 (May 2005): 233.

*9.45 Tanner, Paul O. W., David W. Megill, and Maurice Gerow. *Jazz*, 10th ed. Boston: McGraw-Hill, 2005.
Popular text for college classes (majors and nonmajors) in jazz history. Has an online learning center with listening software, quizzes, etc. Comes with a CD-ROM. Has 2 accompanying CDs with an optional third CD sold separately. Chapters organized primarily by style, but some are devoted to specific musicians.

Listening guides use timing cues. No musical examples in the text proper, but they appear in an appendix called "Notational Examples." Includes good photos of performers. Includes listening suggestions, a glossary, a bibliography, and an index. Eighth edition reviewed by John Kuzmich Jr. in *Jazz Education Journal* 29, no. 6 (May 1997): 60.

9.46 Tirro, Frank. *Jazz: A History.* 2nd ed. New York: W. W. Norton, 1993.
Chronological textbook with accompanying CD and videos. In need of a new edition. Includes 20 listening guides; 12 complete transcriptions and excerpts, and many musical examples and other illustrations (black-and-white). Includes a timeline, an annotated bibliography, a discography, a glossary, and an index. Respected for its coverage of music in the nineteenth century and the period before the term *jazz* was introduced. Reviewed by Larry Appelbaum in *JazzTimes* 31 (Education Guide 2001–2002): 76–78.

Rock and Popular Music Histories

Many histories of rock and popular music are available. Most focus exclusively on American rock. In addition to the titles listed next, the following are also worth consideration: Michael Campbell's *Popular Music in America: The Beat Goes On*, 2nd ed. (Belmont, CA: Wadsworth/Thomson, 2006); Katherine Charlton's *Rock Music Styles: A History,* 5th ed. Boston: McGraw-Hill, 2008; and Joe Stuessy and Scott Lipscomb's *Rock and Roll: Its History and Stylistic Development*, 5th ed. (Upper Saddle River, NJ: Prentice Hall, 2006).

*9.47 Covach, John. *What's That Sound?: An Introduction to Rock and Its History.* New York: W. W. Norton, 2006.
Well-indexed, chronological text covering the 1920s through ca. 2000 for majors and nonmajors, covering a broad range of topics in rock, pop, and related musical styles by a well-respected rock scholar. Most recent text included here. Thoroughly researched and fairly comprehensive. Includes 77 listening guides with detailed descriptions. No musical examples. Best on rock in the 1960s and 1970s. Has specific sections on female rock/pop musicians and black rock music subgenres. Has online website with chapter outlines for study as well as customizable music anthologies powered by iTunes and MSN. Using a digital anthology allowed Covach more freedom in choosing listening examples than the CD compilation approach. No bibliography, but each chapter ends with suggestions for further reading. Reviewed in *Reference and Research Book News* 21, no. 3 (Aug. 2006): 254.

9.48 Garofalo, Reebee. *Rockin' Out: Popular Music in the USA*, 4th ed. Upper Saddle River, NJ: Prentice Hall, 2008.
A social history of rock useful as a text for popular music studies courses for nonmajors. Begins with the late nineteenth century. Comes with a CD compilation. Two iTunes playlists are also available. Good for discussion of the effects of media on American popular culture. In general, not as well organized as Covach, but better for discussion of popular music styles since 1995. Includes a general bibliography, a subject index, and a song index (useful for reference). No musical examples. No discography. Has a companion website. First edition reviewed by

B. Lee Cooper in *Popular Music and Society* 24, no. 2 (Summer 2000): 155–56 and Dave Laing in *Popular Music* 16, no. 2 (May 1997): 223–27.

*9.49 Starr, Larry, and Christopher Waterman. *American Popular Music: From Minstrelsy to MP3,* 2nd ed. New York: Oxford University Press, 2006.

Another text primarily for a popular music survey for nonmajors. Good for discussion of music styles that fed into the development of rock, such as ragtime and blues. Begins earlier than the others discussed here, with the mid-nineteenth century. Not much discussion of very current music. Contains charts and listening guides for songs (without musical examples); however, these are not as descriptive or informative as those in Covach. Comes with a 2-CD anthology. Good index, but table of contents not very descriptive. Covach and Garofalo are more navigable. Includes a glossary, a bibliography, and an index. First edition reviewed by Steven Maxwell in *College Music Symposium* 43 (2003): 178–79 and Daniel Sonenberg in *Institute for Studies in American Music Newsletter* 34, no. 2 (Spring 2005): 12–13.

9.50 Szatmary, David P. *Rockin' in Time: A Social History of Rock-and-Roll.* 6th ed. Upper Saddle River, NJ: Prentice Hall, 2007.

Places rock in the context of the social and political events in the U.S. and Great Britain that surrounded the development of various submovements from 1950 to 2005 in 21 short, chronological chapters. Does not discuss the stylistic precursors to rock in detail as well as does Starr or Covach. Includes neither analysis nor discussion of how the music sounds. No listening is suggested, nor is there an accompanying anthology. Includes a chapter on rock music and the cultural context of the 2004 U.S. Presidential election. Includes a bibliography and an index. First edition reviewed by Craig H. Russell in *American Music* 7, no. 4 (Winter 1989): 467–70.

Women's Music Histories

9.51 Bowers, Jane, and Judith Tick. *Women Making Music: The Western Art Tradition, 1150–1950.* Urbana-Champaign: University of Illinois Press, 1986.

An important early study of women in music that is still useful as a text and as a starting place for research. Consists of 15 chapters by various authors arranged chronologically by style period. Five chapters are devoted to significant women (Barbara Strozzi, Clara Schumann, Ruth Crawford Seeger, etc.). Includes musical examples, illustrations, and an index. Needs updating. Reviewed by Jane Gottlieb in *Notes* 47, no. 1 (Sept. 1990): 56–59 and Ellen Koskoff in *Ethnomusicology* 32, no. 3 (Fall 1988): 474–78.

*9.52 Pendle, Karin. *Women and Music: A History.* 2nd ed. Bloomington: Indiana University Press, 2001.

Similar to Bowers and Tick, including 16 chapters by various authors arranged by style period, but more up-to-date. Intended to be used as a supplement for standard music history courses or on its own. Focuses on Western art music in Europe and North America, but includes a few papers on jazz, non-Western music, and popular styles. Refers to published score anthologies. Includes musical examples, illustrations, a short bibliography and discography, and an index. Reviewed by Catherine Parsons Smith in *Notes* 58, no. 4 (June 2002): 807–10.

Black Music Histories

9.53   Floyd, Samuel A., Jr. *The Power of Black Music: Interpreting Its History from Africa to the United States.* New York: Oxford University Press, 1995.

Floyd's interdisciplinary study focuses on elements of African American music, such as the ring shout and call and response, and traces their influence. Not intended to be all-inclusive, but the lists of anthologies, the bibliography, the discography, and the videography aid its usefulness in the classroom. Reviewed by Guthrie P. Ramsey, Jr., in *American Music* 16, no. 1 (Spring 1998): 95–98.

*9.54   Southern, Eileen. *The Music of Black Americans: A History.* 3rd ed. New York: W. W. Norton, 1997.

A respected text for courses on black music, arranged chronologically, with coverage from 1619 through the mid-1990s. Includes illustrations, musical examples, and chronologies of important events. Has a bibliography, a discography, and an index. See also Southern's *Readings in Black American Music.* Second edition reviewed by Doris E. McGinty in *Black Perspective in Music* 14, no. 2 (Spring 1986): 185–86.

American Music Histories

9.55   Candelaria, Lorenzo, and Daniel Kingman. *American Music: A Panorama.* 3rd concise ed. Belmont, CA: Thomson/Schirmer, 2007.

Focuses on 6 categories of American music: folk music, sacred music, music from the rural South, Broadway, jazz, and art music. Intended as a text for nonmajors. Book allows for a flexible semester organization because each chapter does not rely on the information from previous ones. Much stronger in its discussion of the twentieth century than of earlier periods. Not as comprehensive in scope or scholarship as the Chase, Crawford, Hamm, or Hitchcock. Includes a discography of pieces mentioned in the text. Similar to the text by Jean Ferris, *America's Musical Landscape,* 5th ed. (Boston: McGraw-Hill, 2005). First edition reviewed by Raoul Camus in *Notes* 36, no. 3 (Mar. 1980): 652–53. Second edition reviewed by Douglas A. Lee in *Bulletin of the Sonneck Society* 16, no. 2 (Summer 1990): 87.

9.56   Chase, Gilbert. *America's Music: From the Pilgrims to the Present.* Rev. 3rd ed. Urbana-Champaign: University of Illinois Press, 1987.

Chase was the first to value the differences of American music in comparison with the European art music tradition. Influenced those that followed with his musical pluralism and diversity. Focused on music made and used in America, not just music composed there. Lacks coverage of Anglo-American folk music and of music before the Puritans. Includes a foreword by Richard Crawford and a discographical essay by William Brooks, along with an index. Reviewed by Karl Kroeger in *Notes* 47, no. 2 (Dec. 1990): 381–83.

*9.57   Crawford, Richard. *America's Musical Life: A History.* New York: W. W. Norton, 2001.

Most recent history of American music, by a major scholar in American studies. Differs from previous pillars in the field because Crawford discusses not only composers and performers, but also teachers, instrument builders, sheet music publishers, patrons, and historians. A well-balanced, contextual, chronological look at America's musical life, ranging from the colonial period through the present. Meant to be accessible to the general reader. An appropriate text for upper-level music majors and graduate students. An abridged version with shorter chapters and without musical examples, *An Introduction to America's Music* (New York: W. W. Norton, 2001), is available with a 3-CD set for non-majors. Both titles reviewed by H. Wiley Hitchcock in *American Music* 21, no. 2 (Summer 2003): 236–46 and Thomas L. Riis in *JAMS* 55, no. 3 (Fall 2002): 578–87.

9.58 Hamm, Charles. *Music in the New World.* New York: W. W. Norton, 1983.
A chronological look at American history from music of the Native Americans through the 1970s. Balanced discussion of art and popular music, with about a third devoted to twentieth-century popular music, including jazz and rock. Also includes music from oral tradition and folk song. Includes references to the *Recorded Anthology of American Music* from New World Records. Includes musical examples and illustrations. Useful as a text and as a reference tool for early American music history due to its clear chapter headings and detailed index. Reviewed by H. Wiley Hitchcock in *Journal of Musicology* 2, no. 3 (Summer 1983): 334–39 and Carleton Sprague Smith in *Notes* 41, no. 1 (Sept. 1984): 43–45.

9.59 Hitchcock, H. Wiley, and Kyle Gann. *Music in the United States: A Historical Introduction*, 4th ed. Prentice Hall History of Music Series. Upper Saddle River, NJ: Prentice Hall, 2000.
Hitchcock is a major American music scholar, who coedited *AmeriGrove* (entry 2.1) and has written on twentieth-century American music, especially Charles Ives. An entire chapter of this history is devoted to Ives. The final chapter on music since the mid-1980s was written by critic and composer Kyle Gann. This text focuses on the "cultivated" and "vernacular" traditions. Includes many musical examples in the chronological discussion and references to recording anthologies of American music. Useful text for a one-semester survey course for undergraduate or graduate music majors. Third edition reviewed by J. Bunker Clark in *American Music* 7, no. 4 (Winter 1989): 465–67.

British Music Histories

9.60 Caldwell, John, ed. *The Oxford History of English Music.* 2 vols. New York: Oxford University Press, 1991–1999. Contents: Vol. 1: *From the Beginnings to c. 1715,* 1991; Vol. 2: *From c. 1715 to the Present Day,* 1999.
Two-volume history written by Caldwell, an early music specialist. Well researched, well written, and up-to-date at the time of publication. "English" is defined narrowly; Ireland and Wales are excluded, and Scotland has a single chapter at the end. Little jazz and popular music is included. Caldwell uses the survey approach; he mentions many pieces briefly but does not provide detailed analysis. Filled with musical examples but few other illustrations. The bibliography is substantial. Vol. 1 reviewed by Nicholas Temperley in *Notes* 49, no. 2 (Dec. 1992): 541–43. Vol. 2 reviewed by Arnold Whittall in *Musical Times*

140, no. 1869 (Winter 1999): 71–72 and Hugh Wood in *Times Higher Education Supplement* (London) 30 June 2000.

*9.61 Spink, Ian. *The Blackwell History of Music in Britain.* 5 vols. Cambridge, UK: Blackwell, 1981–1995. Contents: Vol. 1: *The Middle Ages* (never published); Vol. 2: *The Sixteenth Century*, edited by Roger Bray, 1995; Vol. 3: *The Seventeenth Century*, edited by Ian Spink, 1992; Vol. 4: *The Eighteenth Century*, edited by H. Diack Johnstone and Roger Fiske, 1990; Vol. 5: *The Romantic Age: 1800–1914*, edited by Nicholas Temperley, London: Athlone Press, 1981; Vol. 6: *The Twentieth Century*, edited by Stephen Banfield, 1995.

Each of the 5 volumes devoted to a century has a separate editor and a number of specialist contributors. The set was in preparation for a long time. Some sections were written a decade before publication, although they were updated. Began with Volume 5 as the *Athlone History of Music in Britain*, but publication was taken over by Blackwell. The twentieth-century volume, edited by Stephen Banfield, is especially strong. Includes jazz and popular music. Blackwell's individually authored chapters provide more depth than Oxford for the topics covered. More comprehensive than Oxford, although the first volume of the Oxford makes a good companion to these volumes. The first volume of this history (on the Middle Ages) was never published. As mentioned earlier, early music is Caldwell's major area. Vol. 2 briefly reviewed by Peter Williams in *Organ Yearbook* 25 (1995): 164. Vol. 3 reviewed by John Morehen in *Early Music* 22, no. 4 (Nov. 1994): 685–87. Vol. 4 reviewed by Simon McVeigh in *Journal of the Royal Musical Association* 117, no. 2 (1992): 298–304. Vol. 5 reviewed by Alan Walker in *Musical Quarterly* 69, no. 3 (Summer 1983): 446–49. Vol. 6 reviewed by Mervyn Cooke in *Music and Letters* 78, no. 1 (Feb. 1997): 115–18.

Canadian Music Histories

9.62 Kallmann, Helmut. *A History of Music in Canada: 1534–1914.* Toronto: University of Toronto Press, 1960.

Seminal history of Canadian music and still the best on early periods. Used as a model and resource for later histories. Kallman set out to write the social and political history of music, but he also focuses on important musicians. Discusses both secular and sacred music. Includes only a handful of musical examples, and few illustrations overall. Includes a bibliography and an index. See other titles for post–World War I coverage. Reviewed by Irving Lowens in *Notes* 18, no. 3 (June 1961): 428–29. Reprint edition reviewed by Carl Morey in *Notes* 28, no. 2 (Dec. 1971): 231–33.

*9.63 Keillor, Elaine. *Music in Canada: Capturing Landscape and Diversity.* Montreal: McGill-Queen's University Press, 2006.

Most recent and most comprehensive history of Canadian music. Covers various styles of music. Includes illustrations and musical examples. Reviewed by Patrick Watson in *Books in Canada* 35, no. 6 (Sept. 2006): 24.

*9.64 McGee, Timothy J. *The Music of Canada.* New York: W. W. Norton, 1985.

Focused on the post-1918 period to complement Kallmann. McGee includes musical examples and analysis suggestions in boxes to preserve the narrative.

About one-fourth of the book is devoted to an anthology of 16 complete pieces and excerpts. Chronological, except the music of indigenous peoples is discussed in the final chapter. Includes an appendix of "Readings, Recordings, and Films" to make the history more useful as a textbook. Reviewed by R. Dale McIntosh in *University of Toronto Quarterly* 57, no. 1 (Fall 1987): 228–29.

MUSIC SOURCE READINGS

Collections of **source readings** are useful companions to the study of music history. In fact, some of those listed next were intended to be used with a text. Alexander's *To Stretch Our Ears* is geared for use with Crawford's two American music histories. Source readings that include translations of important writings as well as commentary explaining their contexts and significance are the most valuable. Strunk's *Source Readings in Music History*, now edited by Treitler, is a model.

The LC call number for general music source readings is ML160, and the LC subject heading is "Music—History and criticism—Sources." Specialized source readings have call numbers and subject headings appropriate for their topics. The collection of music education source readings has the call number MT2 and the subject heading "Music—Instruction and study—History—Sources."

Additional collections of source readings can be found under the subject heading for the topic and the subdivision "Sources." Examples of other collections of source readings on specific topics include: Edward A. Lippman's *Musical Aesthetics: A Historical Reader*, 3 vols. (New York: Pendragon, 1986–90); David W. Music's *Hymnology: A Collection of Source Readings* (Lanham, MD: Scarecrow, 1996); and Piero Weiss's *Opera: A History in Documents* (New York: Oxford University Press, 2002).

General Music Source Readings

*9.65 Strunk, Oliver, and Leo Treitler. *Source Readings in Music History*. Rev. ed. New York: W. W. Norton, 1998. Also published in 7 volumes. Contents: Vol. 1: *Greek Views of Music*, edited by Thomas J. Mathiesen; Vol. 2: *The Early Christian Period and the Latin Middle Ages*, edited by James McKinnon; Vol. 3: *The Renaissance*, edited by Gary Tomlinson; Vol. 4: *The Baroque Era*, edited by Margaret Murata; Vol. 5: *The Late Eighteenth Century*, edited by Wye J. Allanbrook; Vol. 6: *The Nineteenth Century*, edited by Ruth A. Solie; Vol. 7: *The Twentieth Century*, edited by Robert P. Morgan.

Treitler and a group of specialists compiled a new edition of Strunk's 1950 classic collection of readings. Presented in English translation from writings of theorists, composers, performers, critics, and others; arranged chronologically, offering a sampling of the important musical thought in the Western classical tradition. More inclusive of women and non-Western music, but includes no jazz and very little on popular music. Sources are cited, and each document is preceded by a short introduction. Includes an index. Reviewed by Steven Plank in *Notes* 56, no. 3 (Mar. 2000): 689–91.

9.66 Weiss, Piero, and Richard Taruskin. *Music in the Western World: A History in Documents.* 2nd ed. New York: Schirmer Books, 2008.

A newer but shorter collection (compared to Strunk) covering the gamut of Western art music. Includes about 200 source readings. Intended for the undergraduate major or nonmajor, the commentaries are more generous, illustrations are included (but primarily not in musical notation), and a glossary is provided as well as an index. Reviewed in *Reference and Research Book News* 22, no. 3 (Aug. 2007): 222.

Special Topic Music Source Readings

Ethnomusicology Source Readings

9.67 Shelemay, Kay Kaufman. *The Garland Library of Readings in Ethnomusicology: A Core Collection of Important Ethnomusicological Articles in Seven Volumes.* 7 vols. New York: Garland, 1990. Contents: Vol. 1: *History, Definitions, and Scope of Ethnomusicology*; Vol. 2: *Ethnomusicological Theory and Method*; Vol. 3: *Music as Culture*; Vol. 4: *Musical Transcription*; Vol. 5: *Cross-Cultural Musical Analysis*; Vol. 6: *Musical Processes, Resources, and Technologies*; Vol. 7: *A Century of Ethnomusicological Thought.*

Differs from other source reading collections listed here by providing facsimiles of the 122 articles selected, dating from 1809 to 1987. Within the topical volumes, the articles are arranged primarily chronologically. No introductions or translations are provided (some readings are in German, French, and Spanish), nor is there an index. Some of the illustrations are poor in quality. Reviewed by William P. Malm in *Music and Letters* 73, no. 1 (Feb. 1992): 145–47.

Music Education Source Readings

9.68 Mark, Michael L. *Music Education: Source Readings from Ancient Greece to Today.* 2nd ed. New York: Routledge, 2002.

Includes about 100 source readings related to music education, in three parts: European authors, American authors 1700–1950, and American writings since 1950. Introductions and commentary are minimal. American bias. Includes index. Reviewed by Piers Spencer in *Music Education Research* 6, no. 1 (Mar. 2004): 125–27.

Performance Practice Source Readings

9.69 MacClintock, Carol. *Readings in the History of Music in Performance.* Bloomington: Indiana University Press, 1979.

Includes 66 translated readings dating from the late Middle Ages to the early nineteenth century. The readings are arranged by style periods, with introductions. Designed to aid the study of music history and especially performance practice. Includes musical examples. Does not include an index. Reviewed by Robert Donnington in *Early Music* 8, no. 3 (July 1980): 383, 385, 387.

Jazz Source Readings

9.70 Walser, Robert. *Keeping Time: Readings in Jazz History.* New York: Oxford University Press, 1999.

Intended for classroom use. Walser selected 62 readings on jazz, loosely arranged by decade. Readings date from 1917 to 1995. Those by jazz musicians, critics, and blacks were preferred. Includes a few musical examples, a bibliography, and an index. Reviewed by Sam Miller in *Annual Review of Jazz Studies* 11 (2000–2001): 275–78.

Rock and Pop Music Source Readings

9.71 Brackett, David. *The Pop, Rock, and Soul Reader: Histories and Debates.* New York: Oxford University Press, 2005.

Includes 125 readings dating from 1926 to 1999, ranging in styles from Paul Whiteman's jazz of the 1920s to the Goth revival of the mid-1990s. Brackett provides introductions as well as a bibliography and an index. No musical examples or illustrations. Reviewed by B. Lee Cooper in *Popular Music and Society* 29, no. 1 (Feb. 2006): 136–38.

Women's Music Source Readings

9.72 Neuls-Bates, Carol. *Women in Music: An Anthology of Source Readings from the Middle Ages to the Present.* Rev. ed. Boston: Northeastern University Press, 1996.

Includes 53 source readings, with introductory commentaries for women in art music, primarily composers and performers. Includes illustrations (but no musical examples), a bibliography, and an index. Reviewed by Sophie Fuller in *Times Literary Supplement* (London) 27 Dec. 1996.

African American Music Source Readings

9.73 Southern, Eileen. *Readings in Black American Music.* 2nd ed. New York: W. W. Norton, 1983.

Includes 41 readings dating from 1623 to 1981, although most are from the nineteenth and twentieth centuries. Intended for use with the 2nd edition of Southern's text, *The Music of Black Americans: A History*, although it could be used with the 3rd edition up to 1981 or independently. Arrangement is primarily chronological. Includes musical examples and index. First edition reviewed by Gilbert Chase in *Yearbook for Inter-American Musical Research* 8 (1972): 189–95.

American Music Source Readings

9.74 Alexander, J. Heywood. *To Stretch Our Ears: A Documentary History of America's Music.* New York: W. W. Norton, 2002.

Compilation of 235 source readings dating from the mid-sixteenth century to 1999. Alexander wrote lengthy introductions. No illustrations. Includes an index. Can be used independently or in conjunction with either Crawford's *America's Musical Life: A History* or Crawford's text, *An Introduction to America's Musical Life*. Reviewed by H. Wiley Hitchcock in *American Music* 21, no. 2 (Summer 2003): 236–46.

MUSIC CHRONOLOGIES

Chronologies help place musical events into their historical context. Chronologies vary in the level of detail they provide; some offer day-by-day detail. They also include different degrees of extramusical context, for example, events of note, not only in world history, but in the other arts and humanities as well.

General music chronologies are given the LC call number ML161 and the LC subject heading "Music—History and criticism—Chronology." Specialized titles are classed with the subject. Hall's American music chronology has the call number ML200 and the subject heading "Music—United States—Chronology." Additional chronologies may be found by searching your local library catalog or *WorldCat* using the subject heading for the topic with the subdivision "Chronology."

General Music Chronologies

9.75 Eisler, Paul E., Edith Eisler, and Neal Hatch. *World Chronology of Music History.* 6 vols. Dobbs Ferry, NY: Oceana Publications, 1972–1980. Contents: Vol. 1: *4,000 B.C.–1594 A.D.,* 1972; Vol. 2: *1594–1684,* 1973; Vol. 3: *1685–1735,* 1974; Vol. 4: *Name Index* (Vols. 1–3), 1976; Vol. 5: *1736–1786,* 1978; Vol. 6: *1771–1796,* 1980. Was intended to be an 8- to 10-volume set, but publication stopped after Volume 6. Events are dated as precisely as possible, to the day in the later volumes. Includes musical and nonmusical events in one listing. No index for volumes 5–6. Covers the periods before Hall's *Chronology of Western Classical Music.* Vol. 1 reviewed by Guy A. Marco in *ARBA* 5 (1974): 382. Vol. 2 reviewed by Dominique-René de Lerma in *ARBA* 6 (1975): 495. Vol. 5 reviewed by George L. Mayer in *ARBA* 11 (1980): 941.

*9.76 Hall, Charles J. *Chronology of Western Classical Music,* 2 vols. New York: Routledge, 2002. Contents: Vol. 1: *1751–1900;* Vol. 2: *1901–2000.*
An update and correction of Hall's previous chronologies: *An Eighteenth-Century Musical Chronicle: Events 1750–1799; A Nineteenth-Century Musical Chronicle: Events 1800–1899;* and *A Twentieth-Century Musical Chronicle: Events 1900–1988.* Entries are by year and include historical as well as art and literature summaries. Musical information includes births, deaths, debuts, new positions, prizes/honors, biographical highlights, cultural beginnings, musical literature, and compositions. Focuses only on art music, especially in the U.S. and England. Each volume has two indexes: composition and historical. Slonimsky is recommended for the twentieth century. Reviewed by Timothy J. McGee in *Library Journal* 127, no. 19 (15 Nov. 2002): 60–61.

Special Topic Music Chronologies

Twentieth-Century Music Chronologies

9.77 Burbank, Richard. *Twentieth Century Music.* New York: Facts on File, 1984. Burbank covers 1900 to 1979. Unlike Slonimsky and Kuhn, which is strictly chronological, this book is arranged into categories for each year: opera; dance;

instrumental and vocal music; births, deaths, and debuts; and related events. Includes illustrations and an index. Useful as a supplement to Slonimsky and Kuhn. Reviewed by Rupert Christiansen in *Times Literary Supplement* (London) 26 Oct. 1984.

*9.78 Slonimsky, Nicolas, and Laura Kuhn. *Music Since 1900*. 6th ed. New York: Schirmer Reference, 2001. Available online from Alexander Street Press at http://alexanderstreet.com.

First edition compiled without Slonimsky, who died in 1995. Includes entries for most days between 1 Jan. 1900 and 14 Dec. 2000 concentrating on art music. Focus is on premieres of compositions and significant biographical events for composers and performers. Also provides sections devoted to important letters and documents related to twentieth-century music, a glossary, and an index. Includes documentation and Slonimsky's opinions on music. Reviewed by D. J. Hoek in *Notes* 59, no. 1 (Sept. 2002): 51–53.

Musical Theater Chronologies

9.79 Norton, Richard C. *A Chronology of American Musical Theater*. 3 vols. Oxford: Oxford University Press, 2002.

Includes basic production information on nearly 5,000 musicals dating primarily from the 1850 through 2000 seasons. Information on selected productions from 1750 to 1850 is also given. Off-Broadway productions are excluded. Organized chronologically by season (June–May). Intended as a companion to Gerald Bordman's *American Musical Theatre: A Chronicle*, 3rd ed. (Oxford: Oxford University Press, 2001). Includes indexes for show titles, song titles, and names. Reviewed by Mark Fearnow in *Theatre Survey* 44, no. 2 (Nov. 2003): 303–5.

American Music Chronologies

9.80 Hall, Charles J. *A Chronicle of American Music: 1700–1995*. New York: Schirmer Books, 1996.

Arranged by year, Hall includes historical and cultural highlights worldwide as well as events in American art and literature. Includes musical births, deaths, debuts, biographical information, founding of musical groups/organizations, publications, festivals, etc. Includes a bibliography and an index (including composition titles). Reviewed by Michael Colby in *Library Journal* 122, no. 4 (1 Mar. 1997): 68.

EVALUATION CHECKLISTS

Histories

- What is the history's purpose (reference or text)?
- Who is the audience (graduates/undergraduates, majors/nonmajors)?
- What accompanying materials are provided (scores, recordings, websites, source readings, study guides)?

- How current is it?
- Are materials available for the instructor (a manual, quizzes)?
- Are there illustrations?
- Are a bibliography and a discography for further reading and listening included?
- Is there a glossary?
- Is there a good index?
- What is the cost?
- Does the text match your philosophy (for including non-Western musics, music of marginalized groups, popular/rock music, etc.)?

Source Readings

- Is the scope or purpose clear (topic, date)?
- Are the sources well selected?
- Are original documents fully cited?
- Is it logically organized?
- Are the translations accurate?
- Is it well edited?
- Are the commentaries and introductions useful?
- Is the indexing comprehensive?

Chronologies

- Is the scope clear (dates, places, styles, etc.)?
- What information is included (how detailed is it)?
- Are sources cited?
- Are extramusical contexts included (history, arts, etc.)?
- How high is the quality of the selection process?
- Is the index adequate?
- Are writings about music cited or quoted?

SUGGESTED READINGS

The following readings offer a starting point for discussion about music history and historiography. Kerman's touchstone article started a wave of reconsideration of the canon of Western art music in the 1980s. Randel points out the relationship of the canon to acceptable music scholarship. Four readings examine historiography in traditionally marginalized areas: Holz and Peeples for women, Koskoff for world music, Southern for jazz, and Moore for rock.

The remaining readings relate to Taruskin's *Oxford History of Western Music*. These include Taruskin's introduction to the history itself and an interview about it. The classic reading by Dahlhaus is cited by Taruskin in his introduction for its discussion of a fundamental issue in music historiography. See also the reviews cited earlier in the Taruskin entry.

Dahlhaus, Carl. "The Significance of Art: Historical or Aesthetic?" Chap. 2 in *Foundations of Music History*. Translated by J. B. Robinson. Cambridge: Cambridge University Press, 1983.

Holz, Jennifer, and Georgia K. Peeples. "From Consort to Composer: The Emergence of Clara Wieck Schumann in Music History Texts." *Women of Note Quarterly* 9, no. 1 (Feb. 2005): 24–27.

Kerman, Joseph. "A Few Canonic Variations." *Critical Inquiry* 10, no. 1 (Sept. 1983): 107–25. Reprinted in *Canons*, edited by Robert von Hallberg, 177–95. Chicago: University of Chicago Press, 1984. Also reprinted as Chap. 3 in Kerman's *Write All These Down*. Berkeley: University of California Press, 1994.

Koskoff, Ellen. "What Do We Want to Teach When We Teach Music? One Apology, Two Short Trips, Three Ethical Dilemmas, and Eighty-two Questions." In *Rethinking Music*, edited by Nicholas Cook and Mark Everist, 545–59. New York: Oxford University Press, 1999.

Moore, Allan F. "Issues in Theory." Chap. 1 in *Rock: The Primary Text, Developing a Musicology of Rock*. 2nd ed. Aldershot, UK: Ashgate, 2001.

Randel, Don Michael. "The Canons in the Musicological Toolbox." In *Disciplining Music: Musicology and Its Canons*, edited by Katherine Bergeron and Philip V. Bohlman, 10–22. Chicago: University of Chicago Press, 1992.

Southern, Eileen. "A Study in Jazz Historiography: *The New Grove Dictionary of Jazz*." *College Music Symposium* 29 (1989): 123–33.

Taruskin, Richard. "A History of Western Music? Well, It's a Long Story." Interview with James R. Oestreich, Classical Music: Debriefing, *New York Times*, sec. 2, 19 Dec. 2004.

————. "Introduction: The History of What?" Introduction to *The Oxford History of Western Music*. 6 vols. New York: Oxford University Press, 2005.

CHAPTER 10

Bibliographies of Music
and Music Literature

When you think of a bibliography, you are probably thinking about the list of sources cited or consulted at the end of a research paper or article in an encyclopedia. Bibliographies of music or writings about music can also be documents in themselves, published as articles, books, or websites. This type of bibliography can help you find music for performance or study and help you jump-start your research on a particular topic. Bibliographies are arranged in a variety of ways, but careful cross-references and indexing help the user find information quickly. Major publishers of bibliographies include Routledge, Garland, and Scarecrow Press.

D. W. Krummel, a master bibliographer, has described bibliography as "the bedrock of musical scholarship."[1] The term **bibliography** has different meanings. It is both a research tool and an activity. The class you are taking is probably called "music bibliography." In that sense, the term is virtually synonymous with research. The products of bibliography are also called bibliographies. The most common types are those included in this chapter. Other types of bibliography, more concerned with sources as objects, are described in the Suggested Readings by Krummel ("The Varieties and Uses of Music Bibliography") and Boorman in *New Grove*.

Bibliographies vary in scope. Some attempt to be comprehensive; others are selective. You need to know which you are using in order to discern what additional research you may need to do to complete your literature search. If a comprehensive bibliography on your research topic is available, you may only need to update the research already compiled. Existing bibliographies can also help you determine if a research topic of interest has already been written about, an important factor in selecting a topic for a master's thesis and, especially, a doctoral dissertation. Reading the introduction is helpful in determining a bibliography's scope as well as its arrangement, purpose, and

---

[1]D. W. Krummel, "The Bibliographical Prognosis." *Journal of Musicology* 1, no. 1 (Jan. 1982): 33.

how to use it. A bibliography's value, like that of many research tools, is enhanced by thorough and thoughtful indexing.

Bibliographies of music include indexes, repertory guides, lists of music currently in print, and more comprehensive multi-volume reference tools. Examples are song indexes, guides to music for a particular instrument, music-in-print databases, and RISM, respectively. Some can help you find music in anthologies or libraries, pieces suitable for study or performance, or scores available for purchase. Some are simple to use and understand, while others (RISM, for example) are more complex. Most of RISM is listed in this chapter, although parts are also included in Chapters 8 (Thematic Catalogs) and 13 (Music Directories). A complete listing of RISM is given in Appendix D.

Writings about music also take different forms. Some, like those included at the end of a *Grove Music Online* article, are unannotated. **Annotations** are descriptions of the sources. Good annotations provide evaluation of the source and compare it to similar writings. These distinguish annotations from abstracts (like those in *RILM Abstracts*). However, annotations will vary in quality and length. Yet there is significant value in annotations written by a compiler of a book-length bibliography who has personally considered each source included. For advice on writing annotations, see Chapter 15.

An alternative to the bibliography made up of bibliographic citations and annotations is the bibliographic essay or **literature review** written as a narrative. *The Reader's Guide to Music History, Theory, Criticism, Music Theory from Zarlino to Schenker*, and the *New Handbook of Research on Music Teaching and Learning* are examples of this type. The sections or topics are accompanied by an unannotated bibliography listing the sources.

In this chapter the bibliographies listed are grouped according to whether they include musical scores, musical writings, or both. Also, because of your growing research skills, the bibliographies included are intended to be representative examples. Your ability to search online library catalogs and periodical indexes enables you to find bibliographies useful for your various research topics. Those selected for inclusion are major research tools you will likely be expected to become familiar with (RISM), those for major composers (Bach, Beethoven, etc.), or those for commonly researched topics. Whenever possible, annotated bibliographies in English were preferred and more current bibliographies were chosen over older titles.

The LC subject headings and LC call numbers for bibliographies of music and writings about music are closely related and sometimes identical. The subject headings for both include the subdivision "Bibliography." One of the broadest subject headings, used for comprehensive bibliographies such as RISM, is "Music—Bibliography." "Rock Music—Bibliography" is the subject heading for both Bruce Pollock's *Rock Song Index* (which lists songs) and Frank Hoffmann's *The Literature of Rock* (which lists writings). Bibliographies devoted to particular composers have the subject heading for the composer with the subdivision, i.e., "Brahms, Johannes, 1833–1897—Bibliography." Examples for topical bibliographies include "African Americans—Music—Bibliography," "Music—Great Britain—Bibliography," and "Opera—Bibliography." One exception is the subject heading for song indexes, which is "Songs—Indexes."

The LC call numbers for the following bibliographies are in the range from ML113 to ML128. General bibliographies have the call number ML113 (for example, RISM). Those related to the music of a particular country are assigned ML120. Bibliographies of music in the United States are ML120 .U5, those for Great Britain are ML120 .G7, and those for Canada are ML120 .C2. The topical bibliographies all have the call number ML128, subarranged alphabetically by topic. For example, jazz bibliographies have the call number ML128 .J7; opera bibliographies are assigned ML128 .O4; and piano music repertory guides are under ML128 .P3.

Bibliographies are also related to other types of research tools and indexes. The bibliographies of music research tools listed in Chapter 1 not only are examples of fine bibliographies, but can also help you identify additional bibliographies. See entries 1.10 through 1.16, especially Wingell and Herzog's *Introduction to Research in Music*; Duckles and Reed's *Music Reference and Research Materials: An Annotated Bibliography*; and Crabtree, Foster, and Scott's *Sourcebook for Research in Music*. Library catalogs are a bibliography of the holdings of a particular library. Thematic catalogs are bibliographies of the works of a composer or repertory that include musical incipits. RISM and the *British Catalogue of Music* are examples that, although included here, might have been included with library catalogs as well. The works lists included in the Bio-Bibliographies in Music series are cousins to thematic catalogs.

In this chapter, bibliographies of music are listed first, followed by those of writings about music and those including both music and writings. Next are listed bibliographies devoted to the composers that have been chosen to serve as examples throughout this text; see Appendix C. As throughout this text, major bibliographies are indicated with an asterisk for categories including more than one comparable resource.

BIBLIOGRAPHIES OF MUSIC

General Music Bibliographies

10.1 Jackson, Barbara G. *Say Can You Deny Me: A Guide to Surviving Music by Women from the 16th through the 18th Centuries.* Fayetteville: University of Arkansas Press, 1994.
Identifies extant music by over 600 women composers in European and American libraries. Jackson's research began with sources such as Cohen, Eitner, RISM, etc. Entries include dates, titles, medium, RISM numbers, and RISM library sigla. Includes 5 appendixes, a bibliography, and an index. Reviewed by Deborah Hayes in *Notes* 52, no. 2 (Dec. 1995): 455–56.

10.2 Kellman, Herbert, Charles Hamm, and Jerry Call. *Census—Catalogue of Manuscript Sources of Polyphonic Music 1400–1550.* 5 vols. Renaissance Manuscript Studies, no. 1. Neuhausen-Stuttgart, Ger.: Hänssler, 1979–1988.
This 5-volume set is a product of the Musicological Archives for Renaissance Manuscript Studies of the University of Illinois at Urbana-Champaign and was supported by the National Endowment for the Humanities. It includes extensive descriptions and analyses of over 1,600 manuscript sources of polyphony. Most of the sources are available at the University of Illinois Music Library on microfilm. Lists the contents of each source by genre and the composers represented, and provides a bibliography of secondary literature. Includes extensive indexes. Reviewed by Reinhard Strohm in *JAMS* 48, no. 3 (Fall 1995): 485–90.

10.3 Reese, Donald. *Emusicquest: Music-in-Print.* Lansdale, PA: Emusicquest, 2000–. http://www.emusicquest.com.

Includes the content from the various print volumes of the Music in Print series, which have been standard guides to currently available music since 1965. Includes the "Master Index" as well as separately color-coded subsets, such as piano, string, classical vocal, orchestral, sacred choral, and secular choral. The advanced search is recommended. Search options include instrumentation, period, work duration, and composer nationality; see the search tips. Updated about every 2 weeks. Some print volumes are still available. Also published on CD-ROM. Reviewed by Lisa R. Philpott in *Notes* 60, no. 2 (Dec. 2003): 506–8.

Bibliographies for Particular Repertories

Instrumental Music Bibliographies

Both of the chamber music bibliographies listed next lack an instrumentation index, which would greatly enhance their usefulness for performers. Many guides to literature for solo instruments are included as part of general books on the instrument. For example, see the literature section in Nancy Toff's *The Flute Book*, 2nd ed. (New York: Oxford University Press, 1996), which updates James J. Pellerite's *A Handbook of Literature for the Flute*, rev. 3rd ed. (Bloomington, IN: Zalo Publications, 1978).

10.4 Cobbett, Walter W., and Colin Mason. *Cobbett's Cyclopedic Survey of Chamber Music*, 2nd ed. 3 vols. New York: Oxford University Press, 1963.

A well-respected, though dated guide to significant Western chamber music (three to nine instruments). Arranged alphabetically by composer. Also includes subjects and terms. Most entries are signed. Cobbett was assisted by over 100 contributors. Volume 3 focuses on the period from 1929, as an update to the original two volumes published in 1929–30. Reviewed by Homer Ulrich in *Notes* 21, nos. 1–2 (Winter–Spring 1963–64): 124–26.

*10.5 Cohn, Arthur. *The Literature of Chamber Music.* 4 vols. Chapel Hill, NC: Hinshaw Music, 1997.

First major coverage of chamber music (defined as two to nine instruments) arranged alphabetically by composer since Cobbett. Does not include pieces with voice, and transcriptions are generally omitted. Otherwise the author claims exhaustivity, covering all periods and styles. Includes descriptions and summary analysis in paragraph form, but these do not provide the detail of Cobbett. Reviewed by Paul Orgel in *Notes* 55, no. 4 (June 1999): 897–99.

*10.6 Daniels, David. *Orchestral Music: A Handbook.* 4th ed. Lanham, MD: Scarecrow, 2005.

Includes 6,400 entries for orchestral music by around around 900 composers, listed alphabetically by composer. Includes detailed information about the instrumentation of the works and their durations. Entries incorporate the Orchestra Library Information Service database. Good coverage of contemporary American music. Includes several appendixes (works with chorus, solo voices, solo instruments, etc.). Reviewed by Joseph Boonin in *Notes* 62, no. 4 (June 2006): 949–50.

*10.7 Hinson, Maurice. *Guide to the Pianist's Repertoire*, 3rd ed. Bloomington: Indiana University Press, 2000.

Hinson has compiled several guides to music for the piano, including a second edition of his *The Piano in Chamber Ensemble* (Bloomington: Indiana University Press, 2006). The *Guide* listed here is perhaps the most useful. Hinson used only published works that he examined and decided to include. The largest section of the book is arranged by individual composers. Brief biographies are included for major composers along with a description of their musical style. The annotations for individual pieces include the difficulty, publisher and edition information, and citations for writings about the music. The second section includes anthologies and collections. There are several indexes (black composers, women composers, composers' nationalities, etc.). See also Pamela Youngdahl Dees's *A Guide to Piano Music by Women Composers*, 2 vols. (Westport, CT: Greenwood; Praeger, 2002–2004), which is modeled after Hinson's bibliography. Reviewed by Michael J. Rogan in *Notes* 58, no. 4 (June 2002): 851–52.

Vocal Music Bibliographies

10.8 Carman, Judith E., William K. Gaeddert, Rita M. Resch, and Gordon Myers. *Art Song in the United States, 1759–1999: An Annotated Bibliography*, 3rd ed. Lanham, MD: Scarecrow, 2001.

The most comprehensive guide to American art songs, with over 2,250 entries for songs composed between 1811 and 1999. The descriptions vary from author to author, but none include durations. Includes sections on early music (that needs updating) and songs with foreign texts as well as a discography. Includes indexes. Reviewed by Laurie J. Sampsel in *Notes* 59, no. 4 (June 2003): 921–22.

*10.9 Coffin, Berton. *Singer's Repertoire*, 2nd ed. 5 vols. New York: Scarecrow, 1960–62. Contents: Vol. 1: *Coloratura Soprano, Lyric Soprano, and Dramatic Soprano*, 1960; Vol. 2: *Mezzo Soprano and Contralto*, 1960; Vol. 3: *Lyric and Dramatic Tenor*, 1960; Vol. 4: *Baritone and Bass*, 1960; Vol. 5: *Program Notes for the Singer's Repertoire,* with Werner Singer, 1962.

A guide to the song literature for nine voice types, intended for use by teachers and students. Includes information on the songs' subjects, range, and publisher (dated). Reviewed by Arnold F. Caswell in *Journal of Research in Music Education* 9, no. 1 (Spring 1961): 76.

10.10 Doscher, Barbara, and John Nix. *From Studio to Stage: Repertoire for the Voice*. Lanham, MD: Scarecrow, 2002.

After Doscher's death, her student John Nix transcribed her card file of vocal repertory. About 3,000 songs are included in 12 sections, arranged by composer, with information on language, text author, range, tessitura, tempo, comments, difficulty, voice type, synopsis of text, and common editions. Includes indexes. Reviewed by Debra Greschner in *Journal of Singing* 59, no. 5 (May–June 2003): 440.

10.11 Goleeke, Thomas. *Literature for Voice: An Index of Songs in Collections and Source Book for Teachers of Singing*. 2 vols. Metuchen, NJ: Scarecrow, 1984–2002.

Intended for the new voice teacher or those teaching class voice. The second volume includes an index of 72 song collections in common use, arranged by anthology. Information is given on language, key, and range. Includes composer and title indexes. The first volume is similar, but indexes earlier anthologies. Vol. 1 reviewed by Paula Morgan in *Notes* 41, no. 3 (Mar. 1985): 521–22. Vol. 2 reviewed by Debra Greschner in *Journal of Singing* 59, no. 2 (Nov.–Dec. 2002): 176–77.

10.12 Green, Jonathan D. *A Conductor's Guide to Choral-Orchestral Works.* 4 vols. Metuchen and Lanham, NJ: Scarecrow, 1994–. Contents: Vol. 1: *A Conductor's Guide to Choral-Orchestral Works* (1994); Vol. 2: *A Conductor's Guide to Choral-Orchestral Works, Twentieth Century, Part II: The Music of Rachmaninov through Penderecki* (1998); Vol. 3: *A Conductor's Guide to the Choral-Orchestral Works of J.S. Bach* (2000); Vol. 4: *A Conductor's Guide to Choral-Orchestral Works, Classical Period, Volume I: Haydn and Mozart* (2002).

All together the four volumes published to date include around around 500 works. Information on performing forces, duration, editions, "performance issues," bibliography, and discography are presented. Green's criteria for inclusion varies by volume. All the choral-orchestral works of Bach, Haydn, and Mozart are covered. Vols. 1–2 reviewed by Michael A. Mitchell in *Journal of the Conductors Guild* 18, no. 2 (Summer–Fall 1997): 126–27. Vol. 3 reviewed by Hilary Apfelstadt in *Choral Journal* 41, no. 4 (Nov. 2000): 81–82. Vol. 4 reviewed by C.A. Kolczynski in *Choice* 39, no. 11–12 (July–Aug. 2002): 1930.

10.13 Kagen, Sergius. *Music for the Voice: A Descriptive List of Concert and Teaching Material*, rev. ed. Bloomington: Indiana University Press, 1968.

Repertory lists arranged by type of song, style period, and language. Opera arias are listed by voice type. Well respected but dated. Reviewed by Carol Kimball in *Opera Journal* 30, no. 4 (Dec. 1997): 65.

10.14 Tortolano, William. *Original Music for Men's Voices: A Selected Bibliography.* 2nd ed. Metuchen, NJ: Scarecrow, 1981.

Includes entries for around 800 works, arranged alphabetically by composer. Entries provide information on the voices required, text, accompaniment, and duration. Six essays on male chorus are presented in Part II. There are indexes for authors/text sources and titles/first lines. Reviewed by Walter S. Collins in *Choral Journal* 22, no. 7 (Mar. 1982): 17–18.

10.15 Villamil, Victoria E. *A Singer's Guide to the American Art Song 1870–1980.* Metuchen, NJ: Scarecrow, 1993.

More dated than Carman et al. and covers a narrower time period, but includes biographical and style information on the 144 composers included. Also includes timings and durations as well as range. Many entries list recordings. Includes song title and poet indexes. Reviewed by Richard D. Sjoerdsma in *NATS Journal* 51, no. 5 (May–June 1995): 58.

Song Indexes

10.16 De Charms, Desiree, and Paul F. Breed. *Songs in Collections: An Index.* Detroit: Information Services, 1966.

Continues Sears's index with ca. 9,500 songs from around 410 collections dating from the 1930s through 1957. Arrangement is by composer. Emphasis is on art songs and arias. Reviewed by Ellen Kenny in *Notes* 23, no. 2 (Dec. 1966): 269–70.

*10.17 Ferguson, Gary L. *Song Finder: A Title Index to 32,000 Popular Songs in Collections, 1854–1992.* Music Reference Collection, No. 46. Westport, CT: Greenwood, 1995.
Indexes about 32,000 songs from around 620 collections published 1854–1992. Indexes popular, folk, and art songs. Unlike other indexes, Ferguson does not include first lines of text or chorus, only the song titles. Attempted to include songs not indexed elsewhere. Reviewed by Karen Hovde in *Music Reference Services Quarterly* 4, no. 3 (1996): 79–80 and Pauline S. Bayne in *Notes* 53, no. 2 (Dec. 1996): 449–50.

10.18 Gargan, William, and Sue Sharma. *Find That Tune: An Index to Rock, Folk-Rock, Disco & Soul in Collections.* 2 vols. New York: Neal-Schuman, 1984–88.
Second volume is labeled "second edition." Between the 2 vols. approximately 8,000 songs from around 400 collections dating from 1950 to 1985 are indexed. Vol. 1 reviewed by B. Lee Cooper in *Popular Music and Society* 9, no. 4 (1984): 74–76. Vol. 2, 2nd ed. reviewed by Bruce Rosenstein in *ARSC Journal* 20, no. 2 (Fall 1989): 201–2.

*10.19 Goodfellow, William D. *SongCite: An Index to Popular Songs.* New York: Garland, 1995.
Supplement I was published in 1999. Between the two, around 13,500 songs in about 450 collections published in 1988 or later are indexed. Goodfellow included songs not present in other song indexes in print. Includes a composer index. Main volume reviewed by Pauline S. Bayne in *Notes* 53, no. 2 (Dec. 1996): 449–50. Supplement I reviewed in *Reference and Research Book News* 14, no. 2 (May 1999): 153.

10.20 ———. *Where's That Tune?: An Index to Songs in Fakebooks.* Metuchen, NJ: Scarecrow, 1990.
Goodfellow has compiled several song indexes. This one indexes over 13,500 songs included in 64 fakebooks, dating mostly from the 1980s. Includes a composer index. Reviewed by Monica J. Burdex in *Notes* 49, no. 4 (June 1993): 1525–26.

10.21 Havlice, Patricia P. *Popular Song Index.* Metuchen, NJ: Scarecrow, 1975.
Noncumulative supplements were published in 1978, 1984, 1989, and 2005. All together, Havlice indexes 1,043 song books published from 1940 through 2002. Songs include popular, children's, Christmas, folk, TV, musicals, and jazz standards. Main volume reviewed by Ann Garfield in *ARBA* 7 (1976): 490–91. First supplement reviewed by Patricia Felch in *Notes* 35, no. 3 (Mar. 1979): 637. Second supplement reviewed by Richard Andrewes in *Musical Times* 128, no. 1731 (May 1987): 270–72. Third supplement reviewed by Leslie Troutman in the *Bulletin of the Council for Research in Music Education* 107 (Winter 1991): 81–82. Fourth supplement reviewed in *Reference and Research Book News* 20, no. 3 (Aug. 2005): 216.

10.22 Leigh, Robert. *Index to Song Books: A Title Index to Over 11,000 Copies of Almost 6,800 Songs in 111 Song Books Published between 1933 and 1962.* Stockton, CA: R. Leigh, 1964.

Continues Sears' index by including approximately 7,000 songs (mostly popular) from around 110 songbooks published from the early 1930s through the early 1960s. Includes song titles only, no first lines.

10.23 Luchinsky, Ellen. *The Song Index of the Enoch Pratt Free Library.* 2 vols. Garland Reference Library of Social Science, vol. 1394. New York: Garland, 1998.

Includes about 160,000 entries for both popular and art songs in English and other languages. Indexes over 2,100 anthologies dating mostly from 1900 to 1990 held by the Library in Baltimore. There are some problems with the indexing, likely a result of the number of people and span of years the index was compiled. Includes composer and source (operas, musicals, etc.) indexes. Reviewed by D. Ossenkop in *Choice* 36, no. 6 (Feb. 1999): 1040.

10.24 Sears, Minnie E., and Phyllis Crawford. *Song Index: An Index to More than 12,000 Songs in 177 Song Collections Comprising 262 Volumes and Supplement, 1934.* N.p.: Shoe String, 1966.

Including the supplement, indexes around 19,000 songs from approximately 280 collections dating from the 1880s through the early 1930s. Includes popular and art songs. Both titles and first lines are indexed along with composers and poets.

Rock and Popular Music Bibliographies

10.25 Jasen, David A. *A Century of American Popular Music: 200 Best-Loved and Remembered Songs (1899–1999).* New York: Routledge, 2002.

Arranged by song title, with an earlier and broader focus than *The Rock Song Index.* Entries include composer, publisher, date, and brief description. Has composer, publisher, and date indexes as well as an appendix listing Academy Award winners in the best song category. Reviewed by Barry Zaslow in *Library Journal* 127, no. 9 (15 May 2002): 84.

*10.26 Pollock, Bruce. *The Rock Song Index: Essential Information on the 7,500 Most Important Songs of the Rock and Roll Era: 1944–2000,* 2nd ed. New York: Routledge, 2005.

Arranged by song title. Entries include artist, composer, album, label, producer, date, cover information, and brief description. Has artist and date indexes and a brief bibliography. Reviewed by Diana Kirby in *Booklist* 102, no. 9–10 (Jan. 2006): 153.

10.27 Shapiro, Nat, Bruce Pollock, Barbara Cohen-Stratyner, and Gary Graff. *Popular Music: An Annotated Guide to American Popular Songs. 1964–2004.* Volume for 1900–1919, revised cumulation for 1920–1979, volume for 1980–1984; annually published volumes for 1985–2002.

Annotated list of popular songs from 1900 to 2002. Annotations are generally longer and more informative for songs listed in the 1900–1919 and 1920–1979 volumes. Many annotations in later volumes simply give the album on which a song was featured. Each volume includes a "lyricists & composers" index, an index of important performances, an "awards" index, and a list of publishers. The 1920–1979 Revised Cumulation reviewed by Doris E. McGinty in *Black Perspective in Music* 14, no. 3 (Fall 1986): 309–12. Vols. 20–22 reviewed by B. Lee Cooper in *Popular Music and Society* 24, no. 1 (Spring 2000): 124–25.

American Music Bibliographies

Between them, the bibliographies listed here provide excellent bibliographic control of the early American repertory. Britton, Lowens, and Crawford cover the sacred repertory, while the Sonneck and Upton, along with Wolfe, focus on secular music. Although it includes song lyrics rather than music, see also Irving Lowens's *A Bibliography of Songsters Printed in America before 1821* (Worcester, MA: American Anitiquarian Society, 1976). The general bibliographies titled *American Bibliography* compiled by Charles Evans and Ralph Shaw/Richard Shoemaker should also be consulted. These are available on microform and online.

*10.28   Britton, Allen P., Irving Lowens, and Richard Crawford. *American Sacred Music Imprints 1698–1810: A Bibliography.* Worcester, MA: American Antiquarian Society, 1990.
Comprehensive, scholarly bibliography of the psalmody repertory through 1810, including about 675 tunebooks. Provides good coverage of multiple and variant editions. Arranged by composer/compiler, with short biographies. Includes detailed bibliographic descriptions, contents, and locations of copies. Use in concert with Temperley's *Hymn Tune Index* (entry 8.33). Has appendixes and indexes. Reviewed by Nicholas Temperley in *JAMS* 45, no. 1 (Spring 1992): 123–31.

*10.29   Sonneck, Oscar G. T., and William T. Upton. *A Bibliography of Early Secular American Music (18th Century).* Rev. ed. New York: Da Capo, 1964.
Survey of 40 libraries (public and private) for their holdings of eighteenth-century secular music. Arranged by title, the approximately 3,000 entries include bibliographic descriptions and holding libraries. Includes several indexes (composers, first lines, etc.). The Da Capo publication is a reprint of the 1945 edition published by the Library of Congress. Reviewed by John Tasker Howard in *Notes* 2, no. 1 (Dec. 1944): 59–62.

*10.30   Wolfe, Richard J. *Secular Music in America 1801–1825: A Bibliography.* 3 vols. New York: New York Public Library, 1964.
Includes over 10,350 titles published during the first quarter of the nineteenth century. Arranged by composer, the entries include bibliographic descriptions and holding libraries. Many include short biographies. Appendixes update the Sonneck/ Upton bibliography. Five indexes provide access by title, first line, publisher, plate number, etc. Reviewed by Sigmund Spaeth in *Music Journal* 23, no. 3 (Mar. 1965): 16.

British Music Bibliographies

*10.31   *The British Catalogue of Music.* London, etc.: British Library, etc., 1957–.
Frequency varied, currently published with an annual cumulation by CSA. A 10-volume cumulation covering 1957–85 was published by K. G. Saur in

1988. Includes music published in Great Britain and, available there through a single agent, or published outside Great Britain but not available from a British agent. Music is arranged by Dewey Decimal Classification. There are two indexes: composer/title and subject. Reviewed by Richard Andrewes in *Musical Times* 126, no. 1710 (Aug. 1985): 466–67.

10.32 Schnapper, Edith B. *The British Union-Catalogue of Early Music Printed before the Year 1801.* 2 vols. London: Butterworths Scientific, 1957.
Includes over 55,000 entries for music held in over 100 libraries in the British Isles published through 1800. Does not just include British music. Arranged by composer. Holding libraries are indicated. About 60 percent of the entries are for titles held by the British Library. Reviewed by Richard S. Hill in *Notes* 15, no. 4 (Sept. 1958): 565–68.

Canadian Music Bibliographies

There is a lack of current bibliographies of Canadian music. The Canadian Music Center and the Canadian Association of Music Libraries, Archives, and Documentation Centres (CAML) have published a number of bibliographies of music. Two examples are given here.

10.33 Canadian Music Centre. *Catalog of Chamber Music.* Toronto: Canadian Music Centre, 1967.
Includes brief biographical sketches of the composers as well as information on the pieces (description, duration, level of difficulty, etc.). Includes a title index. In addition to this bibliography, the Centre has published bibliographies of orchestral, keyboard, choral, and vocal music.

10.34 Jarman, Lynne. *Canadian Music: A Selected Checklist 1950–73/La musique canadienne: une liste selective 1950–73.* Toronto: University of Toronto Press, 1976.
Includes music listed in *Fontes artis muiscae* from 1954 to 1973. Standard bibliographic records are enhanced with duration and other notes. Arranged in Dewey Decimal call number order. Includes composer and title indexes. A project of CAML. Reviewed by Richard Andrewes in *Musical Times* 119, no. 1623 (May 1978): 421–24.

BIBLIOGRAPHIES OF MUSIC LITERATURE

General Bibliographies of Music Literature

*10.35 Steib, Murray. *Reader's Guide to Music History, Theory, Criticism.* Chicago: Fitzroy Dearborn, 1999.
Includes around 500 alphabetically arranged bibliographic essays by various authors overseen by the editor and 16 advisors. Topics included are those with at least two books on them in English. Primarily Western art music composers and topics (no performers or individual works). Some non-Western music (Africa, India, and Latin America), jazz, and rock topics are included. Includes

alphabetical and subject lists of entries at the beginning and indexes (books cited and general). Provides a great starting point for research on the topics included because it focuses on the most significant sources. Reviewed by Lois Kuyper-Rushing in *Reference and User Services Quarterly* 39, no. 4 (Summer 2000): 416–18.

Special Topic Bibliographies of Music Literature

World Music/Ethnomusicology Bibliographies

See the bibliography section of the Society for Ethnomusicology website, discussed later (at http://www.ethnomusicology.org), for up-to-date bibliographical references.

10.36 *eHRAF Collection of Ethnography*. New Haven, CT: Human Relations Area Files, 1949–. http://www.yale.edu/hraf/index.html.

Database of over 350,000 pages (books, articles, etc.) on cultural and social life of about 350 cultures. Useful for ethnomusicological studies. Began in paper, moved to microfiche and CD-ROM, and now available online. Created by the nonprofit Human Relations Area Files (HRAF) at Yale University. Reviewed by Tom Gilson in *Charleston Advisor* 1, no. 3 (Jan. 2000): 30–33, 37.

*10.37 Post, Jennifer C. *Ethnomusicology: A Guide to Research*. Routledge Music Bibliographies. New York: Routledge, 2004.

Focusing on the 1990s, Post's bibliography complements Schuursma's. It includes around 1,700 annotated entries for reference and research tools (Part I) and literature (Part II). Also includes recordings and films/videos. About 90 percent of the sources are in English. Each chapter begins with a summary introduction. Annotations are primarily descriptive. Includes name and subject indexes. Lacks a title index. For many years Post has been involved with the bibliographies compiled by the Society for Ethnomuiscology for its journal, *Ethnomusicology*, and since 2000 at the Society's website. Cover title of book is *Ethnomusicology: A Research and Information Guide*. Reviewed by Alec McLane in *Notes* 62, no. 3 (Mar. 2006): 708–11.

*10.38 Schuursma, Ann Briegleb. *Ethnomusicology Research: A Select Annotated Bibliography*. Garland Library of Music Ethnology. New York: Garland, 1992.

Not superseded by Post; Schuursma includes around 470 annotated entries for English-language sources dating from 1960 to 1990. Entries are arranged in five sections (theory, fieldwork, analysis, etc.). Includes name and subject indexes. Reviewed by Tullia Magrini in *Yearbook for Traditional Music* 29 (1997): 142–45.

Theory and Analysis Bibliographies

10.39 Ayotte, Benjamin M. *Heinrich Schenker: A Guide to Research*. Routledge Music Bibliographies. New York: Routledge, 2004.

Includes about 1,500 briefly annotated entries, including Schenker's compositions (with incipits) and writings. Arrangement is by type of document (articles, books, etc.) rather than by topic. Includes an index of pieces analyzed as well as author and title indexes. See also David C. Berry's *A Topical Guide to Schenkerian Literature* (Hillsdale, NY: Pendragon, 2004). A similar bibliography for serial music is John D. Vander Weg's *Serial Music and Serialism: A Research and Information Guide* (New York: Routledge, 2001). Reviewed by Christoph Hust in *Musiktheorie* 19, no. 1 (2004): 89–91.

*10.40 Damschroder, David, and David R. Williams. *Music Theory from Zarlino to Schenker: A Bibliography and Guide*. Harmonologia, no. 4. Stuyvesant, NY: Pendragon, 1990.

The bulk of this work is a "dictionary" of 200 theorists from the period specified. Arranged alphabetically by theorist, each includes a brief bibliographic essay followed by a list of writings by that theorist and secondary literature on him or her. Translations are indicated with a "T," and introductory readings are marked with three dots. The "Literature Supplement" is a bibliography of recent writings on music theory. Reviewed by David Gagné in *Music Theory Spectrum* 14, no. 2 (Fall 1992): 223–26.

*10.41 Diamond, Harold J. *Music Analyses: An Annotated Guide to the Literature*. New York: Schirmer, 1991.

Includes around 4,600 citations for books, articles, and dissertations and theses in English, with analyses of Western art music. Arrangement is by composer. Most entries have brief annotations. Previous edition was titled *Music Criticism: An Annotated Guide to the Literature* (Metuchen, NJ: Scarecrow, 1979). Reviewed by Arthur B. Wenk in *Notes* 48, no. 4 (June 1992): 1307–8.

*10.42 Hoek, D. J. *Analyses of Nineteenth- and Twentieth-Century Music: 1940–2000*. MLA Index and Bibliography Series, no. 34. Lanham, MD: Scarecrow, 2007.

Similar to Diamond, with analyses arranged by composer. Hoek compiled this index incorporating all the entries from Arthur Wenk's earlier title *Analyses of Nineteenth- and Twentieth-Century Music: 1940–1985*. Includes Festschriften in addition to books, articles, and dissertations and theses. Also includes sources in other European languages. The 9,306 entries are unannotated. Over 1,000 composers are represented. Reviewed in *Reference and Research Book News* 22, no. 2 (May 2007): 207.

Music Education Bibliographies

*10.43 Colwell, Richard. *Handbook of Research on Music Teaching and Learning: A Project of the Music Educators National Conference*. New York: Schirmer, 1992.

Includes 55 research and bibliographic essays by different authors arranged in eight sections. Work was directed by an editorial board and a large group of reviewers. Essays are uneven in quality. Reviewed by Douglas S. Medlin in *Notes* 49, no. 4 (June 1993): 1518–21.

*10.44 Colwell, Richard, and Carol Richardson. *The New Handbook of Research on Music Teaching and Learning: A Project of the Music Educators National Conference*. New York: Oxford University Press, 2002.

Similar and complimentary to the *Handbook*, earlier. This *New Handbook* contains 61 literature reviews by over 90 authors organized in 10 sections. Again, the two primary editors were assisted by reviewers. Writing, editing, and content vary in quality. Reviewed by Sandra Stauffer in *Arts Education Policy Review* 104, no. 4 (Mar.–Apr. 2003): 35–37.

Chamber Music Bibliographies

*10.45 Baron, John H. *Chamber Music: A Research and Information Guide*, 2nd rev. ed. Routledge Music Bibliographies. New York: Routledge, 2002.
Includes over 2,200 annotated citations on chamber music, arranged into categories (history, analysis, performance, etc.). Focus is on recent writings (through summer 2001) in English and German. Includes indexes. First edition reviewed by James Dack in *Music and Letters* 69, no. 4 (Oct. 1988): 524–26.

10.46 Parker, Mara E. *String Quartets: A Research and Information Guide*. Routledge Music Bibliographies. New York: Routledge, 2005.
A selectively annotated bibliography of over 1,700 sources, most devoted to quartets by individual composers. Other categories include general sources, histories, and performance. Also includes a section listing critical editions and facsimiles. Languages represented are primarily English and German. Includes two indexes.

Vocal Music Bibliographies

General Vocal Music Bibliographies

10.47 McTyre, Ruthann Boles. *Library Resources for Singers, Coaches, and Accompanists: An Annotated Bibliography, 1970–1997.* Music Reference Collection, no. 71. Westport, CT: Greenwood, 1998.
Highly selective bibliography of around 470 annotated entries for English-language sources intended to be practical in use, with no more than 40 items per section. Includes a general reference section compiled by Ida Reed. Focus is on opera, musical theater, and solo voice. Includes author, title, and subject indexes. Reviewed by John Wagstaff in *Brio* 36, no. 2 (Autumn–Winter 1999): 167–69.

Opera Bibliographies

10.48 Marco, Guy A. *Opera: A Research and Information Guide*, 2nd ed. New York: Garland, 2001.
A model bibliography by an expert compiler. Includes over 2,800 annotated entries focusing on recent books in English published through 1999. Covers opera internationally. The chapter "Composers and Their Operas" is the heart of the volume. Includes four indexes. Reviewed by Tom Kaufman in *Opera Quarterly* 18, no. 3 (Summer 2002): 457–59.

Art Song Bibliographies

10.49 Seaton, Douglass. *The Art Song: A Research and Information Guide*. Garland Reference Library of the Humanities, vol. 673. New York: Garland, 1987.
Most of the 970 entries for books and selected articles and dissertations are annotated. Focus is on individual composers and their works. Coverage is

from 1550 on, with an emphasis on German Lieder. Includes name and subject indexes. Reviewed by Ian Ledsham in *Music and Letters* 70, no. 4 (Nov. 1989): 528–30.

Musical Theater

10.50 Everett, William A. *The Musical: A Research and Information Guide.* Routledge Music Bibliographies. New York: Routledge, 2004.

Has around 1,000 annotated entries for English-language sources covering the musical on stage and screen. Focuses on scholarly sources, and more inclusive of shows from the 1990s and later. Includes index. See also Hubert Wildbihler and Sonja Völklein's *The Musical: An International Bibliography* (New York: K. G. Saur, 1986). Although dated and unannotated, its coverage of European musicals is quite good. Reviewed by Jim Lovensheimer in *Opera Today* (7 Mar. 2005) available from http://www.operatoday.com.

Choral Music Bibliographies

10.51 Sharp, Avery T., and James M. Floyd. *Choral Music: A Research and Information Guide.* Routledge Music Bibliographies. New York: Routledge, 2002.

Has over 500 entries with lengthy annotations for sources dating mostly from 1960 to 2000. Includes chapters on choral technique, surveys of music, choral genres, and individual composers/works. Has subject, author, and title indexes. See also the authors' *Church and Worship Music: An Annotated Bibliography of Contemporary Scholarship* (New York: Routledge, 2005). Reviewed by Patrick K. Freer in *Choral Journal* 44, no. 1 (Aug. 2003): 50–51.

Performance Practice Bibliographies

Both of the following bibliographies are dated. See Roland Jackson's 2005 *Performance Practice: A Dictionary-Guide for Musicians* (entry 3.37) for the more up-to-date bibliographies that accompany most articles.

*10.52 Jackson, Roland. *Performance Practice, Medieval to Contemporary: A Bibliographic Guide.* Music Research and Information Guides, vol. 9. New York: Garland, 1988.

Jackson is a major scholar in the area of performance practice. His now-dated bibliography includes around 1,400 annotated entries arranged chronologically by style period. Was updated in *Performance Practice Review* each fall issue from 1988 through the final issue in 1997. Used Vinquist and Zaslaw as a starting point. Focuses on writings from 1960 to 1986 that discuss period performance and/or including contemporary evidence. Includes indexes. Reviewed by Peter Holman in *Music and Letters* 70, no. 2 (May 1989): 245–47.

10.53 Vinquist, Mary, and Neal Zaslaw. *Performance Practice: A Bibliography.* New York: W. W. Norton, 1971.

This dated listing of about 1,100 unannotated, international citations covering Western art music from 1100 to 1900 began as a bibliography from a graduate seminar taught by William S. Newman at the University of North Carolina. Citations are arranged in 1 alphabetical list by author. Includes index. Also published as Volume 8 (1969) of *Current Musicology*. Supplements were published in Volumes 10 (1970), 12 (1971), and 15 (1973) of the same journal. Reviewed by Frederick Dorian in *ARBA* 4 (1973): 391.

Jazz Bibliographies

10.54 Gray, John. *Fire Music: A Bibliography of the New Jazz: 1959–1990*. Music Reference Collection, no. 31. New York: Greenwood, 1991.

More specialized in scope than Meadows, next, but unannotated. Includes over 7,000 international entries. Includes articles, reviews, interviews, and so. Also includes obvious entries, such as those from standard jazz encyclopedias. Has three indexes, for artists, subjects, and authors. Reviewed by Ingrid Monson in *Notes* 49, no. 3 (Mar. 1993): 1072–73.

*10.55 Meadows, Eddie S. *Jazz Scholarship and Pedagogy: A Research and Information Guide*, 3rd ed. Routledge Music Bibliographies. New York: Routledge, 2006.

Meadows' third edition varies in title from the previous two but includes all the citations from the second edition (1995). He includes over 3,250 annotated entries for books, dissertations, videos, recordings, transcriptions, etc. published between the 1920s and 2004. No articles are included, however. International, but primarily English-language sources are included. Has one index. Second edition (titled *Jazz Research and Performance Materials: A Select Annotated Bibliography*) reviewed by Edward Berger in *Annual Review of Jazz Studies*, no. 9 (1997–98): 391–401.

Rock and Popular Music Bibliographies

See B. Lee Cooper's *Rock Music in American Popular Culture I–III* (New York: Haworth, 1994–99) as an example of combining music and literature. It lists songs by topic with an unannotated bibliography for each.

10.56 Cooper, B. Lee, and Rebecca A. Condon. *The Popular Music Teaching Handbook: An Educator's Guide to Music-Related Print Resources*. Westport, CT: Libraries Unlimited, 2004.

Unannotated, but useful for new teachers of popular music, especially for interdisciplinary studies.

*10.57 Gatten, Jeffrey N. *Rock Music Scholarship: An Interdisciplinary Bibliography*. Music Reference Collection, no. 50. Westport, CT: Greenwood, 1995.

Includes over 930 annotated entries arranged into 10 disciplines with interdisciplinary studies (ethnomusicology, history, etc.). The most scholarly, with detailed annotations. Has author and subject indexes. Reviewed by B. Lee Cooper in *Popular Music and Society* 19, no. 4 (Winter 1995): 105–12.

*10.58 Haggerty, Gary. *A Guide to Popular Music Reference Books: An Annotated Bibliography*. Music Reference Collection, no. 47. Westport, CT: Greenwood, 1995.

Includes around 430 annotated entries for reference and research tools for popular music. Emphasis is on collection biography and discography. Three appendixes provide another approximately 240 unannotated citations for individual musician bibliographies, discographies, and electronic resources. Has a single index of authors, titles, and subjects. Reviewed by Stephen Davison in *Notes* 53, no. 2 (Dec. 1996): 482–83.

10.59 Hoffmann, Frank, B. Lee Cooper, and Lee Ann Hoffmann. *The Literature of Rock*. 4 vols. Metuchen, NJ: Scarecrow, 1981–1995. Contents: Vol. I: 1954–1978, by Frank Hoffmann, 1981; Vols. 2–3: II: 1979–1983, by Frank Hoffmann, B. Lee Cooper, and Lee Ann Hoffmann, 1986; Vol. 4: III: *With Additional Material for the Period 1954–1983*, by Frank Hoffmann and B. Lee Cooper, 1995.

Altogether the four volumes include thousands of unnumbered entries. The first volume is annotated, but the later volumes are unannotated (a few include brief annotations). Arranged in chronological order. Each volume includes appendixes and an index. Vol. I reviewed by B. Lee Cooper in *Popular Music and Society* 8, no. 1 (1981): 60–61. Vol. II reviewed by Kenneth J. Bindas in *Sonneck Society Newsletter* 12, no. 3 (Fall 1986): 90–91. Vol. III reviewed by Rick Anderson in *Library Journal* 120, no. 4 (1 Mar. 1995): 62.

10.60 Shepherd, John, David Horn, Dave Laing, Paul Oliver, Philip Tagg, Peter Wicke, and Jennifer Wilson. *Popular Music Studies: A Select International Bibliography*. London: Mansell, 1997.

While this bibliography is international and includes a relatively high number of citations (around 8,350), it is not annotated. Does not include biographies. Includes citations for books and articles (with a focus on peer-reviewed articles) but not dissertations, liner notes, etc. Served as an introduction to the *Continuum Encyclopedia of Popular Music of the World*. Reviewed in *Reference and Research Book News* 13, no. 2 (May 1998): 137.

Folk Music Bibliographies

10.61 Miller, Terry E. *Folk Music in America: A Reference Guide*. Garland Reference Library of the Humanities, vol. 496. New York: Garland, 1986.

Has around 2,000 entries, mostly for sources in English published since 1900. Miller includes topics such as psalmody and hymnody not generally considered "folk" music today. Citations are arranged topically (Native Americans, Anglo-American folk songs, etc.). While most entries are annotated, they vary in length and quality. Reviewed by Jennifer C. Post in *Ethnomusicology* 32, no. 3 (Fall 1988): 452–53.

Women in Music Bibliographies

10.62 Ericson, Margaret D. *Women and Music: A Selective Annotated Bibliography on Women and Gender Issues in Music, 1987–1992*. New York: G. K. Hall, 1996.

Ericson compiled a selective bibliography of over 1,800 entries and annotated most of them. The 15 chapters include: aesthetics; jazz and popular music; non-Western music; forms of representation; and others in addition to Western art music. Writings on individual women musicians have been excluded. Sources are mostly in English, with some representation of European languages. The annotations vary in length. Includes name and subject indexes. Reviewed by Judy Tsou in *Fontes artis musicae* 43, no. 4 (Oct.–Dec. 1996): 413–14.

*10.63 Pendle, Karin. *Women in Music: A Research and Information Guide*. Routledge
        Music Bibliographies. New York: Routledge, 2005.
        Includes over 2,900 entries on women focusing on English-language sources
        covering Western art music dating from 1980 to 2000. Most of the entries are
        annotated by Pendle or three other annotators (indicated with initials), and many
        are lengthy. Differs from Ericson by including sources devoted to individual
        musicians. Divided into 19 chapters, including ethnomusicology, countries and
        geographical regions, rock and pop, and blues and jazz. Includes some sources
        in Western European languages. Has name, author, and subject indexes, but
        lacks a title index.

Black Music Bibliographies

10.64   de Lerma, Dominique-René. *Bibliography of Black Music*. 4 vols. Westport,
        CT: Greenwood, 1981–84. Contents: Vol. 1: *Reference Materials*, 1981; Vol. 2:
        Afro-American Idioms, 1981; Vol. 3: *Geographical Studies*, 1982; Vol. 4:
        Theory, Education, and Related Studies, 1984.
        Together the 4 vols. include around 19,400 unannotated citations arranged topi-
        cally. Vol. 1 is now the most dated. Vols. 3 and 4 have name indexes, but the
        first 2 vols. do not. Vol. 1 reviewed by Sam Dennison in *American Music* 2,
        no. 2 (Summer 1984): 102–5 and Doris E. McGinty in *Black Perspective in
        Music* 9, no. 2 (Fall 1981): 229–31. Vol. 2 reviewed by Doris E. McGinty in
        Black Perspective in Music 10, no. 1 (Spring 1982): 114–17. Vols. 2–4 reviewed
        by Sam Dennison in *American Music* 6, no. 2 (Summer 1984): 244–46. Vol. 3
        reviewed by Doris E. McGinty in *Black Perspective in Music* 11, no. 1 (Spring
        1983): 79–82. Vol. 4 reviewed by Doris E. McGinty in *Black Perspective in
        Music* 14, no. 2 (Spring 1986): 185–87.

*10.65 Floyd, Samuel A., Jr., and Marsha J. Reisser. *Black Music in the United States:
        Annotated Bibliography of Selected Reference and Research Materials*.
        Millwood, NY: Kraus International, 1983.
        This selective bibliography was intended for use by undergraduates. Like the
        others listed in this section, it is now dated. Includes around 400 annotated
        entries for English-language sources dating mostly from the 1920s to 1980.
        Includes author, title, and subject indexes. Reviewed by Eileen Southern in
        Black Perspective in Music 12, no. 1 (Spring 1984): 137–39.

10.66   Skowronski, JoAnn. *Black Music in America: A Bibliography*. Greenwood
        Encyclopedia of Black Music. Metuchen, NJ: Scarecrow, 1981.
        Includes about 14,300 entries; only a handful are annotated. Now dated, the
        most useful section is probably the first part, which is devoted to 97 individual
        musicians. Focus is on jazz and popular music. Has an author index. Reviewed
        by Samuel A. Floyd, Jr., in *American Music* 3, no. 1 (Spring 1985): 102–3.

American Music Bibliographies

In addition to the titles listed next, see Thomas E. Warner's *Periodical Literature on
American Music, 1620–1920: A Classified Bibliography with Annotations* (Warren,
MI: Harmonie Park Press, 1988). Warner selected about 5,000 articles up to 1920. Other

titles in the Harmonie Park Press series *Bibliographies in American Music* are also of interest. The Institute for Studies in American Music (ISAM) Monographs Series also includes bibliographies.

10.67 Heintze, James R. *Early American Music: A Research and Information Guide.* Garland Reference Library of the Humanities. New York: Garland, 1990.

Heintze's bibliography of over 1,950 entries is almost entirely annotated. He included both reference tools as well as writings (except master's theses, which he included in a separate bibliography) about American music up to 1820. Reviewed by John E. Druesedow, Jr., in *Notes* 47, no. 2 (Dec. 1990): 383–84 and Carol J. Oja in *Music and Letters* 73, no. 4 (Nov. 1992): 597–98.

10.68 Horn, David. *The Literature of American Music in Books and Folk Music Collections: A Fully Annotated Bibliography.* Metuchen, NJ: Scarecrow, 1977.

Horn and Richard Jackson's *Supplement I* was published in 1988; Guy A. Marco's *Literature of American Music III: 1983–1992* was published in 1996; and Marco's *Checklist of Writings on American Music 1640–1992,* published in 1996, provides a cumulative author index to all 3 volumes. Combined, the 3 volumes contain over 4,000 annotated entries for books (primarily in English). The first 2 volumes include additional, unannotated citations in the appendixes. Good coverage of folk and popular music. Original volume reviewed by Irving Lowens in *Fontes artis musicae* 25, no. 1 (Jan.–Mar. 1978): 112–13. *Supplement I* reviewed by John E. Druesedow, Jr., in *Notes* 47, no. 2 (Dec. 1990): 383–84. *Literature of American Music III* and *Checklist* reviewed by B. Lee Cooper in *Popular Music and Society* 23, no. 1 (Spring 1999): 120–21 and David Nicholls in *Music and Letters* 79, no. 3 (Aug. 1998): 459.

*10.69 Krummel, D. W. *Bibliographical Handbook of American Music.* Music in American Life. Urbana-Champaign: University of Illinois Press, 1987.

Still the standard bibliography for American music studies, although in need of updating. Includes over 750 entries, most of which are annotated. Krummel arranged the bibliography into 4 topical themes (chronological, contextual, musical, and bibliographical). Includes an index of names and subjects. Reviewed by Richard Crawford in *Ethnomusicology* 33, no. 2 (Spring–Summer 1989): 324–25.

British Music Bibliographies

10.70 Porter, James. *The Traditional Music of Britain and Ireland: A Research and Information Guide.* Garland Reference Library of the Humanities, vol. 807. New York: Garland, 1989.

Includes both writings about music and music collections, with slightly more emphasis on the recent writings. Has around 1,740 annotated entries for publications dating between 1700 and 1989. There are 2 indexes, names and subjects/ geographical areas. Reviewed by James R. Cowdery in *Ethnomusicology* 35, no. 1 (Winter 1991): 150–52.

10.71 Turbet, Richard. *Tudor Music: A Research and Information Guide.* New York: Garland, 1994.

A selective, annotated bibliography of around 700 entries dating up to 1991, useful for study of Tudor performance practice. One chapter is devoted to various composers, excluding William Byrd. Has an author and musician (i.e., composer) index. Includes an appendix updating *William Byrd: A Guide to Research*, which is now superseded by the second edition of Turbet's *William Byrd: A Guide to Research*, 2nd ed. (New York: Routledge, 2006). Reviewed by Milton H. Crouch in *ARBA* 26 (1995): 542–43.

Canadian Music Bibliographies

*10.72   Morey, Carl. *Music in Canada: A Research and Information Guide*. Garland Reference Library of the Humanities, vol. 1823. New York: Garland, 1997.

Morey includes over 900 annotated citations dating through 1995 and arranged into 13 chapters. Art music is covered most thoroughly. Chapters on native music; folk and ethnic music; popular music and jazz; and education are also included. Has three indexes. Updated by Robin Elliot's "A Canadian Music Bibliography, 1996–2004" in the *Institute for Canadian Music Newsletter* 2, no. 3 (Sept. 2004): [1–32]. Reviewed by Robin Elliott in *CAML Newsletter* 25, no. 2 (Aug. 1997): 20–22.

BIBLIOGRAPHIES OF BOTH MUSIC AND MUSIC LITERATURE

International Inventory of Musical Sources (RISM)

Please note that additional parts of RISM are discussed in Chapters 8 (Thematic Catalogs) and 13 (Music Directories). A complete listing of RISM is available in Appendix D.

RISM A/I

*10.73   Schlager, Karlheinz, and Otto E. Albrecht. *Einzeldrucke vor 1800*. 9 vols. RISM, A/I/1–9. Kassel, Ger.: Bärenreiter, 1971–1981. Kindermann, Ilse, Jürgen Kindermann, and Gertraut Haberkamp. *Addenda et Corrigenda*. 4 vols. RISM, A/I/11–14. Kassel, Ger.: Bärenreiter, 1986–1999. *Register der Verleger, Drucker und Stecher und Register der Orte*. 1 vol. RISM, A/I/15. Kassel, Ger.: Bärenreiter, 2003.

One of the most-used parts of RISM. Bibliography of printed music by a single composers dating before 1800. Arranged alphabetically by composer. Indicates holding libraries. See Figure 10-1. Plans are underway to publish Series A/I on CD-ROM. Vols. 1–2 reviewed by Vincent Duckles in *JAMS* 26, no. 1 (Spring 1973): 153–55. Vols. 1–3 reviewed by Neal Zaslaw in *Notes* 31, no. 1 (Sept. 1974): 42–45. Vol. 4 reviewed by Dale Higbee in *American Recorder* 16, no. 1 (Feb. 1975): 59. Vol. 5 reviewed by Dale Higbee in *American Recorder* 17, no. 1 (May 1976): 39–40. Vol. 6 reviewed by Dale Higbee in *American Recorder* 18, no. 2 (Aug. 1977): 47–48. Vol. 7 reviewed by Dale Higbee in *American Recorder* 19, no. 2 (Aug. 1978): 68. Vols. 8–9 reviewed by A. Hyatt King in *Fontes artis musicae* 30, nos. 1–2 (Jan.–June 1983): 78–80. Vol. 11 reviewed by Richard Schaal in *Die Musikforschung* 42, no. 2 (Apr.–June 1989): 177–78.

INSTRUMENTALWERKE

Sinfonien und Konzerte

Wq 2. Concerto [Es] pour le clavecin, avec accompagnement de deux violons, alto viola et basse. – *Paris, Antoine Huberty (gravé par Ceron).* – St.   [B 43
GB Lbm – S Skma

Wq 11. Concerto [D] per il cembalo concertato accompagnato da 2 violini, violetta e basso. – *Nürnberg, Balthasar Schmid, No. XXVII.* – St.   [B 44
D-brd Kll – D-ddr Bds, HAu, MEIr – DK Kk – GB Lbm – N Ou – US Wc

— *Wq 11 (25, 14).* Concertos [D, B, E] for the harpsicord, or organ, with accompanyments for violins . . . op. 3ª. – *London, John Walsh.* – St.   [B 45
GB Ckc (hpcd, vl I), Ge (hpcd, vl I), Lbm (hpcd, vl I)

Wq 14. Concerto III [E] per il cembalo concertato, accompagnato da II violini, violetta e basso. – *Berlin, G. L. Winter, 1760.* – St.   [B 46
D-brd Kll, Mbs – D-ddr LEIr – DK Kk – F Pc – GB Lbm

— *Wq (11, 25) 14.* Concertos [D, B, E] for the harpsicord, or organ. With accompanyments for violins . . . op. 3ª. – *London, John Walsh.* – St.   [B 47
GB Ckc (hpcd, vl I), Ge (hpcd, vl I), Lbm (hpcd, vl)

Wq 18 (34, 24). A second sett of three concertos [D, G, e] for the organ or harpsichord with instrumental parts. – *London, Longman, Lukey & Co.* – St.   [B 48
GB Lbm (org) – S Skma

Wq (18, 34) 24. A second sett of three concertos [D, G, e] for the organ or harpsichord with instrumental parts. – *London, Longman, Lukey & Co.* – St.   [B 49
GB Lbm (org) – S Skma

Wq 25. Concerto [B] per il cembalo concertato accompagnato da II violini, violetta e basso. – *Nürnberg, Balthasar Schmid, No. XXXVII.* – St.   [B 50
D-brd B, Mh – D-ddr Bds, MEIr – DK Kk – F Pc – GB Ckc, Lbm

— *Wq (11) 25 (14).* Concertos [D, B, E] for the harpsicord, or organ, with accompanyments for violins . . . op. 3ª. – *London, John Walsh.* – St.   [B 51
GB Ckc (hpcd, vl I), Ge (hpcd, vl I), Lbm (hpcd, vl I)

Wq (18) 34 (24). A second sett of three concertos [D, G, e] for the organ or harpsichord with instrumental parts. – *London, Longman, Lukey & Co.* – St.   [B 52
GB Lbm (org) – S Skma

Wq 43. Sei concerti [F, D, Es, c, G, C] per il cembalo concertato accompagnato da due violini, violetta e basso; con due corni e due flauti per rinforza. – *Hamburg, Autor, 1772.* – St.   [B 53
A Wgm (fehlt fl I, fl II; cemb 3 ×) – D-brd Gs (cor II, b, cemb; fl I hs.), Sh (fehlt fl I, fl II) – D-ddr Dlb – DK Kk – F Pc – GB Lbm – I Vc (vl II, vla, b, cor I, cor II, cemb) – N Ou (fehlt fl I, fl II) – US AA, Wc

Wq 177. Sinfonia [e] a II violini, violetta e basso. – *Nürnberg, Balthasar Schmid, [1759].* – St.   [B 54
US CA

Wq 183. [Vier] Orchester-Sinfonien [D, Es, F, G] mit zwölf obligaten Stimmen: 2 Hörnern, Bratsche, 2 Flöten, Violoncell, 2 Hoboen, Fagott, 2 Violinen, Flügel und Violon. – *Leipzig, Schwickert, 1780.* – St.   [B 55
A ST – D-brd Bhm, Gs, Mbs, Rtt – D-ddr LEm, SWl – F Pc, Sim – GB Lbm – I MOe – US AA, NH

Sonatinen für Klavier und verschiedene Instrumente

Wq 106. Sonatina I [C] a cembalo concertato, II flauti traversi, II violini, violetta e basso. – *Berlin, Georg Ludwig Winter, 1764.* – St.   [B 56
A Wgm (3 Ex.), Wst – CS Pk – D-ddr Bds – DK Kk – F Pmeyer (cemb) – GB Lbm – N Ou

Wq 107. Sonatina II [F] a cembalo concertato, II flauti traversi, II violini, violetta e basso. – *Berlin, Georg Ludwig Winter, 1764.* – St.   [B 57
A Wgm (3 Ex.) – CS Pk – D-ddr Bds – DK Kk – F Pc, Pmeyer (cemb) – GB Lbm – N Ou

Figure 10-1 *Einzeldrucke* Example for C. P .E. Bach *(Courtesy of Répertoire Internationale des Sources Musicales)*

RISM B/I and B/II

*10.74   Lesure, François. *Recueils imprimés XVIe-XVIIe siècles.* RISM, B/I. Munich:
         G. Henle, 1960.
         Probably the most frequently used volume of RISM. Includes over 2,700
         published music collections; that is, anthologies of music by more than one
         composer dating from the sixteenth and seventeenth centuries. Arranged
         chronologically with RISM numbers consisting of the year of publication with
         a superscript number. Includes indexes for printers/publishers and authors/titles.
         See Figure 10-2. Reviewed by Daniel Heartz in *JAMS* 14, no. 2 (Summer 1961):
         268–73, Gustave Reese in *Fontes artis musicae* 8, no. 1 (1961): 4–7, and Vincent
         Duckles in *Notes* 18, no. 2 (Mar. 1961): 225–27.

10.75   Lesure, François. *Recueils imprimés XVIIIe siècle.* RISM, B/II. Munich: G.
         Henle, 1964.
         Continuation of B/I, including 1,800 collections published between 1701 and
         1801. Arranged alphabetically by title, rather than chronologically, and with-
         out the numbers included in B/I. Includes indexes for publishers and names.
         Reviewed by Dale Higbee in *American Recorder* 13, no. 2 (1972): 64–65.

RISM B/III

B/III is devoted to music theory writings in Latin manuscripts dating to around 1500.
Each volume covers a different geographical area, and the arrangement is geographical
(by country and city). Each includes an index.

10.76   Smits Van Waesberghe, Joseph. *The Theory of Music from the Carolingian Era
         up to 1400: Descriptive Catalogue of Manuscripts.* RISM, B/III/1. Munich: G.
         Henle, 1961.
         Reviewed by James Coover in *Journal of Music Theory* 6, no. 2 (Winter 1962):
         314–15.

10.77   Fischer, Pieter. *The Theory of Music from the Carolingian Era up to 1400: Italy.*
         RISM B/III/2. Munich: G. Henle, 1968.
         Reviewed briefly by Charles Cudworth in *Musical Times* 111, no. 1523 (Jan.
         1970): 49.

10.78   Huglo, Michel, and Christian Meyer. The *Theory of Music: Manuscripts from
         the Carolingian Era up to c. 1500 in the Federal Republic of Germany (BRD).*
         RISM, B/III/3. Munich: G. Henle, 1986.
         Reviewed by Lawrence Gushee in *Notes* 45, no. 2 (Dec. 1988): 282–83.

10.79   Meyer, Christian, Michel Huglo, and Nancy C. Phillips. *The Theory of Music:
         Manuscripts from the Carolingian Era up to c. 1500 in Great Britain and in
         the United States of America.* RISM, B/III/4. Munich: G. Henle, 1992.
         Reviewed by Darwin F. Scott in *Notes* 51, no. 1 (Sept. 1994): 105–8.

10.80   Meyer, Christian, Elzbieta Witkowska-Zaremba, and Karl-Werner Gümpel.
         *The Theory of Music: Manuscripts from the Carolingian Era up to c. 1500
         in the Czech Republic, Poland, Portugal, and Spain.* RISM, B/III/5. Munich:
         G. Henle, 1997.

[1688]

1688²   XIV. recueil de chansonnettes de différents autheurs à deux et trois parties ... – *Paris, Chr. Ballard,* 1688. 1 vol. in-8º, 77 p.
Anon. (26)
B Br - **F** Pn - **USSR** Lsc

1688³   XXXI. livre d'airs de différents autheurs à deux et trois parties. – *Paris, Chr. Ballard,* 1688. 1 vol. in-8º, 77 p.
Anon. (31)
F CH; Pn - **GB** Lbm - **US** Wc

1688⁴   Di Bernardino Lupachino e di Ioan Maria Tasso il primo libro a due voci di nuovo ristampato. – *Firenze, Stamperia di S. A. S.,* 1688. 2 vol. in-4º, 36 p.
Cf. 1559²⁴
I Bc (S)

1688⁵   Johann-Wilhelm Simlers teutscher Getichten die vierte von ihme selbsten und auss hinterlassenen Schrifften um einen Viertheil vermehrt- un verbesserte Aussfertigung ... – *Zürich, J. W. Simler,* 1688. 1 vol. in-8º, 466-109 p.
A. B. (32), A. T., K. Dietbold (6), D. Friderici (32), I. R., A. Steigleder (54), Anon. (4)
B Bc - **GB** Lbm

1688⁶   The banquet of musick: or, a collection of the newest and best songs sung at court, and at the publick theatres. With a thorow-bass for the theorbo-lute, bass-viol, harpsichord, or organ. Composed by several of the best masters. The words by the ingenious wits of this age. The first book. – *London, E. Jones for H. Playford,* 1688. 1 vol. in-4º, 52 p.
S. Akeroyde, J. Banister (3), J. Blow, J. Hart (2), A. Marsh, D. Purcell (3), H. Purcell (7), J. Roffey, Snow (7), Anon.
EIR Dtc - **GB** Bu; Ctc; En; Ge; Lbm; Lcm; Ob - **US** CA; LA; NYp; Wc; Ws

1688⁷   The banquet of musick: or, a collection of the newest and best songs sung at court, and at the publick theatres. With a thorow-bass, for the theorbo-lute, bass-viol, harpsichord, or organ. Composed by several of the best masters. The words by ingenious wits of this age. The second book ... – *London, E. Jones for H. Playford,* 1688. 1 vol. in-fol., 48 p.
S. Akeroyde, Baptist (2), J. Blow (6), J. Hart (4), R. King, Marsh, Pack, F. Pigott (2), D. Purcell (2), H. Purcell (4), J. Roffey (2), Snow (3), Anon. (5)
EIR Dtc - **F** Pc (mq. p. 1) - **GB** En; Ge; Lbm; Lcm; Ob - **US** Cn; LA; NYp; Wc; Ws

571

Figure 10-2 *RISM* B/I Example *(Courtesy of Répertoire Internationale des Sources Musicales)*

10.81   Meyer, Christian. *The Theory of Music: Manuscripts from the Carolingian Era up to c. 1500, Addenda, Corrigenda*. RISM, B/III/6. Munich: G. Henle, 2003. Reviewed by Marie-Noël Colette in *Revue de musicologie* 90, no. 1 (2004): 133–35.

RISM B/V

10.82   Husmann, Heinrich. *Tropen- und Sequenzenhandschriften*. RISM, B/V/1. Munich: G. Henle, 1964.
Bibliography of manuscripts including tropes and sequences, arranged geographically. Includes indexes. Reviewed by Edward H. Roesner in *JAMS* 21, no. 2 (Summer 1968): 212–15.

RISM B/VI

10.83   Lesure, François. *Écrits imprimés concernant la musique*. 2 vols. RISM, B/VI/1–2. Munich: G. Henle, 1971.
An unannotated bibliography of writings about music. Arranged alphabetically by author. Includes indexes. Reviewed by Gloria Rose in *Notes* 30, no. 1 (Sept. 1973): 54–57.

RISM B/VII

10.84   Boetticher, Wolfgang. *Handschriftlich überlieferte Lauten- und Gitarrentabulaturen des 15. bis 18. Jarhhunderts*. RISM, B/VII/1: Munich: G. Henle, 1978. Bibliography of over 725 manuscripts of lute and guitar tabulature dating from the fifteenth through the eighteenth centuries. Arranged geographically. Includes indexes. Reviewed by Arthur Ness in *JAMS* 34, no. 2 (Summer 1981): 339–45.

RISM B/VIII

10.85   Ameln, Konrad, Markus Jenny, and Walther Lipphardt. *Das deutsche Kirchenlied, DKL: Kritische Gesamtausgabe der Melodien*. 2 vols. RISM, B/VIII/1–2. Kassel, Ger.: Bärenreiter, 1975–80.
Includes German hymns arranged chronologically. Vol. 2 includes indexes. Related to *Das Deutsche Kirchenlied* (*DKL*), a critical edition also published by Bärenreiter. Vol. 1 reviewed by A. Hyatt King in *Erasmus* 28, no. 12 (June 1976): 420–22. Vol. 2 reviewed by Oswald Bill in *Die Musikforschung* 35, no. 1 (Jan.–Mar. 1982): 110.

RISM B/IX

10.86   Adler, Israel. *Hebrew Writings Concerning Music in Manuscripts and Printed Books from Geonic Times up to 1800*. RISM, B/IX/2. Munich: G. Henle, 1975. Differs from other parts of RISM by actually including the 66 texts themselves. Arrangement is alphabetical by author. Includes both manuscripts and printed texts. Reviewed by Michael Ochs in *Notes* 33, no. 1 (Sept. 1976): 56–57 and Eric Werner in *JAMS* 30, no. 3 (Fall 1977): 522–24.

RISM B/X

Bibliography of over 340 texts arranged alphabetically by author. Anonymous writings are in a separate section. Includes a chronological listing, a bibliography, and an index.

10.87 Shiloah, Amnon. *The Theory of Music in Arabic Writings (c. 900–1900): Descriptive Catalogue of Manuscripts in Libraries of Europe and the U.S.A.* RISM, B/X/1. Munich: G. Henle, 1979.
Reviewed by Don Michael Randel in *Ethnomusicology* 26, no. 3 (Sept. 1982): 478–9.

10.88 Shiloah, Amnon. *The Theory of Music in Arabic Writings (c. 900–1900): Descriptive Catalogue of Manuscripts in Libraries of Egypt, Israel, Morocco, Russia, Tunisia, Uzbekistan, and Supplement to BX*. RISM, B/X/2. Munich: G. Henle, 2003.
Reviewed by Michel Huglo in *Revue de musicologie* 90, no. 2 (2004): 357–8.

RISM B/XI

10.89 Mathiesen, Thomas J. *Ancient Greek Music Theory: A Catalogue Raisonné of Manuscripts*. RISM, B/XI/1. Munich: G. Henle, 1988.
Includes about 300 codices dating from the eleventh through the seventeenth centuries by almost 200 authors. Includes indexes. Reviewed by Oliver B. Ellsworth in *Notes* 48, no. 2 (Dec. 1991): 468–71.

RISM B/XIV

Bibliography of chants used for ritual processionals called for in the Roman Mass. Arranged geographically, around 1,200 processionals are included. Has indexes.

10.90 Huglo, Michel. *Les Manuscrits du Processionnal: Volume I Autriche à Espagne*. RISM, B/XIV/1. Munich: G. Henle, 1999.

10.91 Huglo, Michel. *Les Manuscrits du Processionnal: Volume II France à Afrique du sud*. RISM, B/XIV/2. Munich: G. Henle, 2004.

RISM B/XV

10.92 Urchueguía, Cristina. *Mehrstimmige Messen in Quellen aus Spanien, Portugal und Lateinamerika around 1490–1630*. RISM, B/XV. Munich: G. Henle, 2005.
Primarily includes mass settings dating from 1490 to 1630 taken from RISM A/I, B/I, and other bibliographies. Includes a catalog of sources, composers, and index. Reviewed by Stephen Rice in *Early Music* 32, no. 3 (Aug. 2004): 463–65.

COMPOSER BIO-BIBLIOGRAPHIES, GUIDES TO RESEARCH, AND OTHER BIBLIOGRAPHIES

This list is selective. The emphasis is on recent, annotated, English-language bibliographies that are widely held. Examples of composer bibliographies not included are Marc-Aeilko Aris and Werner Lauter's *Hildegard von Bingen: Internationale wissenschaftliche*

Bibliographie (Mainz, Ger.: Gesellschaft für Mittelrheinische Kirchengeschichte, 1998) and the *Mozart-Bibliographie* (Kassel, Ger.: Bärenreiter, 1975–95). Josef Rufer's *The Works of Arnold Schoenberg: A Catalogue of His Compositions, Writings, and Paintings* (London: Faber and Faber, 1962), which was also mentioned in Chapter 8, was omitted here, despite including a list of the composer's writings.

Many of the following bibliographies are primarily "Guides to Research" published by Routledge (previously Garland Press) or "Bio-Bibliographies" published by Praeger or Greenwood Press. The Guides to Research do not include a catalog of the composer's works, while the Bio-Bibliographies do. Other than that, however, they are similar in content. Both include a brief biographical sketch and annotated bibliographies of writings by and about the musician. Some include discographies and reviews. Those for early composers (Josquin, Machaut, and Palestrina) typically include detailed information on sources of the music. Other publishers include Scarecrow Press (Brahms), Oxford University Press (Bach), and Information Coordinators/Harmonie Park Press (Debussy). The quality of these bibliographies and their indexes varies from compiler to compiler. Because of the similarities of these volumes, however, they are not all individually annotated here.

Examples of Single-Composer Bibliographies

Bach, Johann Sebastian

10.93 Melamed, Daniel R., and Michael Marissen. *An Introduction to Bach Studies.* New York: Oxford University Press, 1998.
More of a bibliographic essay than the other volumes listed here. Reviewed by Matthew Dirst in *Music and Letters* 81, no. 3 (Aug. 2000): 444–46.

*10.94 Tomita, Yo. *Bach Bibliography: For the Global Community of Bach Scholars.* Belfast: Queen's University Belfast School of Music and Sonic Arts, 1997–. http://www.mu.qub.ac.uk/~tomita/bachbib.
A free, online bibliography currently including over 23,200 records. Compiled by Tomita and a group of around 80 contributors, including some major Bach scholars. The entries are not annotated, but review citations are included. When an online review is available (most are written by Tomita), a link is provided. The Complex Search is recommended over the Simple Search. Reviewed by Yale Fineman in *Notes* 58, no. 2 (Dec. 2001): 411–14.

Beethoven, Ludwig van

10.95 Ira F. Brilliant Center for Beethoven Studies. *The Beethoven Bibliography Database.* San José, CA: San José State University, 1993–. http://mill1.sjlibrary.org:83.
This annotated, free online bibliography includes over 15,000 records for the Center's holdings. Books, scholarly articles, dissertations and theses, reviews, essays, and newspaper and encyclopedia articles are included. See the *Beethoven Bibliography Database User's Guide and Thesaurus*, 8th ed. (San José, CA: Ira F. Brilliant Center for Beethoven Studies, 2004). Reviewed by Yale Fineman in *Notes* 58, no. 2 (Dec. 2001): 411–14.

Brahms, Johannes

*10.96 Platt, Heather. *Johannes Brahms: A Guide to Research*. Routledge Music Bibliographies. New York: Routledge, 2003.
Differs from Quigley's bibliographies by being selective and providing longer annotations. Reviewed by Camilla Cai in *Choice* 41, no. 7 (Mar. 2004): 1270.

10.97 Quigley, Thomas. *Johannes Brahms: An Annotated Bibliography of the Literature through 1982*. Metuchen, NJ: Scarecrow, 1990.
Between this and the next entry, Quigley is attempting a comprehensive bibliography for Brahms. Annotations are not always given and, when present, are shorter than Platt's. Reviewed by Michael Musgrave in *Music and Letters* 74, no. 4 (Nov. 1993): 601–6 and Margaret Notley in *Notes* 50, no. 2 (Dec. 1993): 577–79.

10.98 Quigley, Thomas, and Mary I. Ingraham. *Johannes Brahms: An Annotated Bibliography of the Literature from 1982 to 1996, with an Appendix on Brahms and the Internet*. Lanham, MD: Scarecrow, 1998.
Reviewed by Heather Platt in *Music and Letters* 83, no. 4 (Nov. 2002): 638–41.

Chopin, Frédéric

10.99 Smialek, William. Frédéric Chopin: A Guide to Research. Composer Resource Manuals, vol. 50. New York: Garland, 2000.
Reviewed by Barbara Milewski in *Notes* 57, no. 3 (Mar. 2001): 611–12.

Debussy, Claude

10.100 Abravanel, Claude. *Claude Debussy: A Bibliography*. Detroit Studies in Music Bibliography, 29. Detroit, MI: Information Coordinators, 1974.
Unannotated bibliography that focuses on earlier writings than Briscoe. Reviewed by François Lesure in *Notes* 31, no. 2 (Dec. 1974): 290–91.

*10.101 Briscoe, James R. *Claude Debussy: A Guide to Research*. Garland Composer Resource Manuals, vol. 27. New York: Garland, 1990.
This annotated bibliography covers the literature dating from 1972 (Abravanel's cutoff date). Reviewed by Richard L. Smith in *Music and Letters* 72, no. 3 (Aug. 1991): 469–70.

Handel, George Frideric

10.102 Parker, Mary Ann. *G. F. Handel: A Guide to Research*, 2nd ed. Routledge Music Bibliographies. New York: Routledge, 2005.
First edition reviewed by C. Steven LaRue in *Notes* 48, no. 3 (Mar. 1992): 867–88.

Haydn, Franz Joseph

10.103 Grave, Floyd K., and Margaret G. Grave. *Franz Joseph Haydn: A Guide to Research*. Garland Composer Resource Manuals, vol. 31. New York: Garland, 1990.
Reviewed by A. Peter Brown in *Music and Letters* 72, no. 4 (Nov. 1991): 595–97.

Ives, Charles

10.104   Block, Geoffrey. *Charles Ives: A Bio-Bibliography*. Bio-Bibliographies in
         Music, no. 14. New York: Greenwood, 1988.
         Reviewed by Thomas D. Winters in *Notes* 49, no. 1 (Sept. 1992): 133–34.

*10.105 Sherwood, Gayle. *Charles Ives: A Guide to Research*. Routledge Music
         Bibliographies. New York: Routledge, 2002.
         Selective bibliography of writings from 1921 to mid-2001. Has some overlap
         with Block. Reviewed by Denise Von Glahn in *Notes* 59, no. 4 (June 2003):
         901–2.

Josquin des Prez

10.106   Charles, Sydney Robinson. *Josquin des Prez: A Guide to Research*. Garland
         Composer Resource Manuals, vol. 2. New York: Garland, 1983.
         Unannotated. Reviewed by Richard Taruskin in *Notes* 42, no. 1 (Sept. 1985):
         39–41.

Liszt, Franz

10.107   Saffle, Michael. *Franz Liszt: A Guide to Research*. 2nd ed. Routledge Music
         Bibliographies. New York: Routledge, 2004.
         Reviewed by János Kárpáti in *Journal of the American Liszt Society* 30 (July–
         Dec. 1991): 85–88.

Machaut, Guillaume de

10.108   Earp, Lawrence. *Guillaume de Machaut: A Guide to Research*. Garland
         Composer Resource Manuals, vol. 36. New York: Garland, 1995.
         Reviewed by Sarah Fuller in *Plainsong and Medieval Music* 6, no. 2 (Oct.
         1997): 180–84.

Monteverdi, Claudio

10.109   Adams, K. Gary, and Dyke Kiel. *Claudio Monteverdi: A Guide to Research*.
         Garland Composer Resource Manuals, vol. 23. New York: Garland, 1989.
         Reviewed by Jeffrey Kurtzman in *Music and Letters* 71, no. 4 (Nov. 1990):
         545–50.

Mozart, Wolfgang Amadeus

10.110   Du Mont, Mary. *The Mozart–Da Ponte Operas: An Annotated Bibliography*.
         Music Reference Collection, no. 81. Westport, CT: Greenwood, 2000.
         Reviewed by E. Thomas Glasow in *Opera Quarterly* 17, no. 2 (Spring 2001):
         288–90.

*10.111 Hastings, Baird. *Wolfgang Amadeus Mozart: A Guide to Research*. Garland
         Composer Resource Manuals. New York: Garland, 1989.
         Reviewed by Malcolm S. Cole in *Journal of Musicological Research* 10,
         no. 1–2 (Oct. 1990): 90–94.

Palestrina, Giovanni Pierluigi da

10.112 Marvin, Clara. *Giovanni Pierluigi da Palestrina: A Guide to Research.* Routledge Music Bibliographies. New York: Routledge, 2002.

Verdi, Giuseppe

10.113 Harwood, Gregory. *Giuseppe Verdi: A Guide to Research.* Garland Composer Resource Manuals, vol. 42. New York: Garland, 1998.
Reviewed by Linda B. Fairtile in *Music and Letters* 80, no. 4 (Nov. 1999): 637–38.

Wagner, Richard

10.114 Saffle, Michael. *Richard Wagner: A Guide to Research.* Routledge Music Bibliographies. New York: Routledge, 2002.
Reviewed by Mike Ashman in *Opera* 54, no. 7 (July 2003): 890–91 and James P. Cassaro in *Notes* 59, no. 4 (June 2003): 916–18.

EVALUATION CHECKLIST

This checklist is for reference bibliographies, not descriptive bibliographies. It is adapted in part from Hunter and from Krummel.[2]

- Is the bibliography annotated?
  - Are annotations descriptive?
  - Are they evaluative?
- Is the scope clearly defined (topic, dates, formats, etc.)?
- Is the compiler's methodology explained?
- Did the compiler examine each source? Are unexamined sources identified?
- Are the citations accurate?
- How many entries are included?
- Is the organization logical (are adequate cross-references included)?
- Are citations for reviews included?
- What is the quality of indexing (author, subject, title)?
- Is there a supplement or update?

---

[2]David Hunter and others, "Music Library Association Guidelines for the Preparation of Music Reference Works," *Notes* 50, no. 4 (June 1994): 1329–38, and D. W. Krummel, "Criteria for Evaluating a Bibliography," Appendix A in *Bibliographies: Their Aims and Methods* (New York: Mansell, 1984).

SUGGESTED READINGS

The reading by Boorman in *Grove* and Krummel's "The Varieties and Uses of Music Bibliography" provide an introduction to music bibliography and its various types. "The Library of the Mind" by Duckles and Krummel's "Introduction" discuss the role of bibliography in musical scholarship and the nature of the bibliographer's work. Finally, Boorman's "What Bibliography Can Do" is an example of a bibliographical study based on the study of early madrigal prints.

Boorman, Stanley. "What Bibliography Can Do: Music Printing and the Early Madrigal." *Music and Letters* 72, no. 2 (May 1991): 236–58.

Duckles, Vincent. "The Library of the Mind: Observations on the Relationship between Musical Scholarship and Bibliography." In *Current Thought in Musicology*, edited by John W. Grubbs, 277–96. Symposia in the Arts and the Humanities, no. 4. Austin: University of Texas Press, 1976.

Krummel, D. W. "Introduction." Chap. 1 in *Bibliographies: Their Aims and Methods*. New York: Mansell, 1984.

————. "The Varieties and Uses of Music Bibliography." In *Foundations in Music Bibliography*, edited by Richard D. Green, 1–25. New York: Haworth, 1993. Simultaneously published in *Music Reference Services Quarterly* 2, nos. 1–2 (1993): 1–25.

Sadie, Stanley, ed. *The New Grove Dictionary of Music of Music and Musicians*, 2nd ed. New York: Grove, 2001. S.v. "Bibliography of Music," by Stanley Boorman. Also available from *Grove Music Online*. http://www.oxfordmusiconline.com.

CHAPTER 11

Discographies

Discographies are essential to the study of music because recorded performances are integral to research and performance. You can use discographies to find recordings of music you are studying or performing. Because sound recordings are often anthologies including several different works, discographies serve a similar function to song indexes for score anthologies. They provide access to all the tracks or titles on a recording, something that may not be included in the catalog record. Recordings are useful for performers for pedagogical purposes. Most musicians use recordings as a way of learning, studying, and analyzing works. Recordings aid with studies of interpretation and performance practice, and serve as models for performance. Historical and musicological studies utilizing recordings include repertory studies, reception histories, and sociological/economical studies. Discographies are also used by record collectors and dealers.

Discography got its start in the mid-1930s, when the first attempts at listing jazz recordings were made. As a genre, jazz depends heavily on recorded performances, in part because of the improvisatory nature of the music. In fact, jazz scholars often refer to recordings as primary sources in their area. Increased emphasis on performers and performances is a characteristic of all discographies. The practice of compiling discographies quickly spread to other genres, styles, and periods of music.

Like bibliographies, several types of discographies exist. Some attempt to be comprehensive; others are selective or list only recommended recordings. Historical discographies differ from those listing only recordings currently in print (available for purchase). Some are devoted to commercial recordings, and others include field recordings. Selective discographies can be limited to a particular performer, recording label, period, composer, place, genre, format, medium of performance, or style. Discographies may list or catalog the holdings of a particular sound recording archive or library collection. Other discographies point indirectly to recordings by listing or indexing published recording reviews.

As a discipline, discography is much younger than bibliography. As a result, discographies are less standardized than other types of reference tools. The citation of sound recordings is covered less extensively in style manuals than other types of sources. Discographies, especially early ones, were often compiled by collectors and amateur musicians. One result is that you will see discographies arranged in a variety of ways. Some of these may not match your research purpose, and some may not seem logical. For instance, some discographies are arranged by the recording label number or by date of release. It is often important to utilize the index of a discography. The composer, performers, and recording details are among the basic information you can expect to find included for each work.

Discographers are also challenged by the special difficulties of recordings. Some examples include the details of reissued recordings and releases of the same recording in different countries. The same recording might be published in different formats, for instance, on LP and CD. Dating sound recordings is often problematic, and it typically includes determining both the date the recording was made and the date the recording was published. Label numbers for recordings can be confusing and may be listed inconsistently in discographies and library catalogs.

In this chapter the discographies are listed by type (comprehensive, in print, etc.). Rather than attempting to be exhaustive, exemplars are provided in each category, as in the bibliographies chapter. Another reason for including only representative examples here is that many tools useful for researching sound recordings have already appeared in other chapters. *WorldCat* (entry 4.12) is one of the best sources for information about LP recordings. Many of the bibliographies listed in Chapter 10 include entries for discographies or have discography sections. This is especially true for the topical and composer bibliographies. Additionally, your research skills have developed to the point where you can search online library catalogs and periodical indexes to find discographies useful for your various research topics.

Discographies, like bibliographies, are published in a variety of formats, both print and electronic. Some are web-based databases on the Internet. Unlike online bibliographies, however, online sound recording dealers have useful websites for currently available recordings. Websites for record labels and dealers like *Amazon.com* and *Tower.com* have made print periodicals like the Schwann catalogs of currently in-print recordings obsolete. Print discographies appear in a variety of formats, including books, periodicals, and journal articles and columns. Bio-discographies are comparable to bio-bibliographies. Recording reviews and indexes to them also function indirectly as discographies. A number of periodicals devoted to recordings fall into this category. See the "Sound Recording Periodicals" article in the *Encyclopedia of Recorded Sound,* edited by Frank W. Hoffmann, which lists over 820 titles.

Book-length and article discographies are among the most common print discographies. The LC subject headings for discographies include the subdivision "Discography" and/or "Catalogs." Two of the broadest subject headings, used for comprehensive titles, such as the *World's Encyclopedia of Recorded Music,* and in-print catalogs, such as *REDMuze Classical Catalogue,* are "Music—Discography," and "Music—Discography—Catalogs," respectively. Discographies for record labels, composers, or performers include the name and the subdivision "Discography." Examples include "Columbia Records—Discography," "Wagner, Richard, 1813–1883—Discography," and "New York Philharmonic—Discography." Topical discographies have subject headings such as "Flute music—Discography," "Music—United States—Discography," and "Jazz—Discography." Reviews and indexes of reviews are given, respectively, the subject headings "Sound recordings—Reviews" and "Sound recordings—Reviews—Indexes." These are typically coupled with a second subject heading with the "Discography" subdivision.

The LC call number range ML156–158 is used for discographies. Both ML156 and ML156.2 are assigned to general and label-specific discographies. Titles devoted to individual library and sound recording archives are given the call number ML156.2. Topical discographies, those for particular instruments, genres, styles, etc., are given the call number ML156.4. Composer discographies are classed in ML156.5, and performer discographies in ML156.7. Those for topics, composers, and performers are subarranged alphabetically by the specific topic. For instance, saxophone discographies are given the call number ML156.4 .S3. Recording reviews and indexes to them are given the call number ML156.9, and miscellaneous discographies (for example, ones devoted to piano rolls) are given ML158. Sometimes periodical discographies are given the general call number for music periodicals, ML1.

BIBLIOGRAPHIES OF DISCOGRAPHIES

The bibliographies of discographies listed here are dated. Some professional associations maintain current listings of discographies. See, for example, the "Current Bibliography" column in each issue of the *Association for Recorded Sound Collections (ARSC) Journal*. A useful listing for ethnomusicologists is the "Current Discographies" section of the Society for Ethnomusicology (SEM) website at http://webdb.iu.edu/sem/scripts/home.cfm. As throughout this text, major bibliographies are indicated with an asterisk for categories including more than one comparable resource.

In addition to the bibliographies listed here, you may also want to consult Brian Rust's *Guide to Discography*. Discographies, no. 4 (Westport, CT: Greenwood Press, 1980), and Lewis Foreman's *Discographies: A Bibliography of Catalogues of Recordings, Mainly Relating to Specific Musical Subjects, Composers, and Performers*. Triad Press Bibliographical Series, no. 1 (London: Triad, 1973).

*11.1 *Bibliography of Discographies*. 3 vols. New York: R. R. Bowker, 1977–1983.
  Contents: Vol. 1: *Classical Music, 1925–1975*, by Michael H. Gray and Gerald D. Gibson, 1977; Vol. 2: *Jazz*, by Daniel Allen, 1981; Vol. 3: *Popular Music*, by Michael H. Gray, 1983.
  The three volumes include a combined total of around 11,000 unannotated entries. Each is arranged in one alphabetical listing by subject and includes an index. Volume 1 updated by Gray. Vol. 1 reviewed by Garrett H. Bowles in *Notes* 35, no. 4 (Jun. 1979): 876–77. Vol. 2 reviewed by Dan Morgenstern in *ARSC Journal* 13, no. 3 (1981): 137–38. Vol. 3 reviewed by David Horn in *Brio* 20, no. 2 (Autumn/Winter 1983): 64.

11.2 Cooper, David E. *International Bibliography of Discographies: Classical Music and Jazz & Blues, 1962–1972: A Reference Book for Record Collectors*,

Dealers, and Libraries. Keys to Music Bibliography, no. 2. Littleton, CO: Libraries Unlimited, 1975.

Unannotated discography including about 1,900 entries arranged as the title indicates. Also includes a listing of discographies, catalogs, and review sources arranged by country. Reviewed by Morris Martin in *Fontes artis musicae* 22, no. 3 (1975): 156–57 and Steve Smolian in *ARSC Journal* 7, no. 3 (1976): 58–63.

11.3 Gray, Michael. H. *Classical Music Discographies, 1976–1988: A Bibliography.* Discographies, no. 34. New York: Greenwood, 1989.

An update to vol. 1 of the *Bibliography of Discographies*, including most of the preceeding updates published in the *ARSC Journal*. Also includes some earlier titles omitted from the previous volume and is more international in scope. Contains 3,800 unannotated entries arranged in one alphabetical list by subject. Includes an index. Reviewed by Jim Farrington in *Fontes artis musicae* 38, no. 3 (Jul.–Sept. 1991): 250.

COMPREHENSIVE AND HISTORICAL DISCOGRAPHIES

No single comprehensive discography exists for historical recordings. A mix of sources must be consulted when attempting to compile a complete recording history. Old issues of "in-print" recordings such as the *Schwann* titles and the *Gramophone Shop Encyclopedia,* are useful. The *WorldCat* database is the most useful for LPs and 78s.

*11.4 Clough Francis F., and G. J. Cuming. *The World's Encyclopædia of Recorded Music.* London: Sidgwick and Jackson, 1952–57. Contents: Vol. 1: Main Vol. and First Supplement (Apr. 1950 to May–Jun. 1951), 1952; Vol. 2: Second Supplement (1951–52), 1953; Vol. 3: Third Supplement (1953–55), 1957.

Known by the nickname *WERM*. Inspired by and modeled after the *Gramophone Shop Encyclopedia*, but comprehensive in scope rather than listing only recordings in print. Arranged by composer, with a section for anthologies. Includes primarily 78s but also 45s and LPs. Does not include dates for recordings or a performer index. Vol. 1 reviewed by Philip L. Miller in *Notes* 10, no. 1 (Dec. 1952): 94–95. Vol. 3 reviewed by Richard S. Hill in *Notes* 14, no. 3 (June 1957): 357–59.

11.5 Reid, Robert H. *The Gramophone Shop Encyclopedia of Recorded Music*, 3rd ed. New York: Crown, 1948.

Includes over 75,000 recordings (78s) available at the time dating from 1925 through Jan. 1948 from European and American labels. Arranged by composer. First edition compiled by R. D. Darrell (New York: Gramophone Shop, 1936) and 2nd edition compiled by George C. Leslie (New York: Simon and Schuster, 1942). Editions are not cumulative; all three must be consulted for a comprehensive search. Third edition includes a performer index. Reviewed by R. D. Darrell in *Notes* 5, no. 4 (Sept. 1948): 563.

CURRENTLY AVAILABLE CATALOGS OF RECORDINGS

Websites such as *Amazon.com*, *Tower.com*, *Ejazzlines.com*, and even *cdbaby.com* have largely replaced print serial publications listing current recordings that are available for purchase. For decades one of the primary publishers of currently available recording catalogs was Schwann Publications. Schwann published a number of titles, including *Schwann Opus*, *Schwann Spectrum*, and the *Schwann Artist Issue*. After those titles ceased publication in 2001, Paratext Publishing began publishing the data online; unfortunately it has not been updated. Not surprisingly, most libraries do not subscribe to it. Another online database with currently available recordings is published by Muze (see the *REDMuze Classical Catalogue*). Recording retailers are the primary subscribers of this service. In addition to the *REDMuze Classical Catalogue*, its German counterpart, the *Bielefelder Katalog Klassik,* should also be mentioned.

*11.6 *REDMuze Classical Catalogue*. London: REDMuze, 2005–.
  Annual publication. Previously titled *RED Classical Catalogue*. The 2005 issue includes over 60,000 classical recordings. Based on data from *Gramophone Magazine*. Focuses on recordings released in the United Kingdom that are currently in the record labels' catalogs and available for sale. Also includes DVDs. Has title, composer, and performer indexes as well as operas and concert recordings.

11.7 *Schwann Online: The Source for Music Reference*. Austin, TX: Paratext, 2001–.
  http://www.paratext.com.
  Subscription-based database including the Schwann information from 1996 to 2001. Has information on over 3 million tracks, classical and popular. Currently not being updated. Reviewed by Lois Kuyper-Rushing in *Charleston Advisor* 3, no. 1 (July 2001): 32–35.

RECOMMENDED RECORDINGS AND BUYER'S GUIDES

Discographies in this category are intended to help listeners build a recording collection and to guide those new to a particular genre. They are typically less scholarly than many, with less discographical detail. Because of their audience, they focus on recordings available for purchase. For that reason, currency is important.

In addition to the two titles listed here, others are available for specific styles and types of music. In addition to the classical *Penguin* guide listed here, jazz musicians may want to consult *The Penguin Guide to Jazz Recordings*, 8th ed. (London: Penguin, 2006). The *All Music Guides*, *Rough Guides*, and *Blackwell Guides* to recordings are also popular. All three have also published guides to jazz along with other styles.

Older buyer's guides can also be helpful in your research. The reviews may be useful in reception histories as well as the listings of recommended recordings themselves. One example is Arthur Cohn's *Recorded Classical Music: A Critical Guide to Compositions and Performances* (New York: Schirmer Books, 1981).

*11.8 Jolly, James. *Gramophone Classical Good CD, DVD, & Download Guide*. Harrow, UK: Gramophone, 2007–.

Annual publication. Previously titled *Gramophone Classical Good CD & DVD Guide* and *Gramophone Classical Good CD Guide*. Based on the *Gramophone* reviews. Main section arranged by composer, with brief bios from the *Concise Grove Dictionary of Music*. The 2007 issue includes around 3,000 reviews. Recommended recordings are indicated. Includes composer and performer indexes. The 2004 edition reviewed by Daniel Zager in *ARSC Journal* 36, no. 1 (Spring 2005): 58–59.

11.9   March, Ivan, Edward Greenfield, and Robert Layton. *Penguin Guide to Compact Discs & DVDs*. London: Penguin, 2004–.

Previously titled *Penguin Guide to Compact Discs*. Updated by the annual *Penguin Guide to Compact Discs & DVDs Yearbook*. Similar to *Gramophone* guide in arrangement and offering recommendations. The 2005/06 edition includes 11,500 listings. Reviews are written by the three authors and are typically longer than *Gramophone's*. Not indexed. The 2005/06 ed. reviewed by Mark Pappenheim in *BBC Music* 14, no. 6 (Feb. 2006): 109.

LIBRARY AND SOUND ARCHIVE CATALOGS

Sound recordings are included in library catalogs (local, consortial, national, and bibliographic utilities) along with other music materials. Library catalogs are covered in more detail in Chapter 4. Remember to use format limits, when available, to restrict your search results to recordings when appropriate. Also, keep in mind that in many libraries, not all sound recordings are included in the online catalog. You may need to consult card catalogs or print catalogs, especially for recordings issued before the 1980s. Some libraries and archives have a mix of online and print catalogs plus finding aids for archival/special collections of recordings (the New York Public Library is one example). Sometimes libraries and sound archives have separate catalogs for their recordings. These catalogs are the focus in this chapter.

Local Libraries

The New York Public Library and Sibley Music Library catalogs are examples of local library catalogs that represent extensive sound recording collections. Both libraries were chosen as examples in Chapter 4, and both also have separate catalogs for their audio collections. Both provide access to their recorded sound collections through a mix of online and card or paper catalogs along with archival finding aids. Not all the sound recordings are included in the libraries' online catalogs, a situation typical for many libraries.

11.10 [New York Public] Library & Museum of the Performing Arts. *Dictionary Catalog of the Rodgers and Hammerstein Archives of Recorded Sound*. 15 vols. Boston: G. K. Hall, 1981.

The Rodgers and Hammerstein Archives of Recorded Sound at the New York Public Library includes about half a million recordings in virtually every format ever made. Recordings can be found by searching their online catalog (*CATNYP*), card catalog, and various archival finding aids and catalogs. In addition, NYPL is one of five libraries that contributed to the *Rigler and Deutsch Index* of pre-1950 commercial recordings, discussed later. In Chapter 4 the *Dictionary Catalog of the NYPL* was described. The companion print catalog for recordings is cited here.

11.11   Sibley Music Library. *Catalog of Sound Recordings: The University of Rochester, Eastman School of Music.* 14 vols. Boston: G. K. Hall, 1977.
The Sibley Music Library at the University of Rochester's Eastman School of Music also provides access to its extensive recording collection via multiple catalogs and finding aids. For a comprehensive search, the card catalog must be consulted along with the online *Voyager* catalog. Recordings in the Watanabe Special Collections are included in finding aids. Like NYPL, the recording card catalog has been reproduced in print.

Library Consortia

11.12   Research Libraries Group. *Rigler and Deutsch Index.* http://www.oclc.org/worldcat.
Although not an actual consortium, the five libraries that collaborated to create the *Rigler and Deutsch Index* of recordings achieved a similar result. A project of the *Association for Recorded Sound Collections* (*ARSC*) in the early 1980s, the five libraries (Library of Congress, New York Public Library, Syracuse University, Stanford University, and Yale University) created an index of their combined holdings of about 615,000 78 RPM commercial recordings released before 1950. The index was first published on microfilm but is now becoming available online as part of *WorldCat*. The microfilm version of the *Rigler and Deutsch Index* was reviewed by Richard Koprowski in *Notes* 42, no. 3 (Mar. 1986): 535–37.

National Libraries

The national libraries of the United States, United Kingdom, and Canada all have extensive sound recording collections. The online catalogs of these three libraries are discussed in Chapter 4. This chapter describes their catalogs specifically devoted to recordings.

11.13   Library of Congress. *SONIC: Sound Online Inventory and Catalog.* http://www.loc. gov/rr/record/Sonicintro.html.
The Library of Congress (LC) has a number of catalogs discussed in Chapter 4 that include sound recordings. LC's sound recording collection, including about 2.5 million recordings, is only about half cataloged. Some are included in the LC online catalog, some are available through the sound recording catalog (*SONIC*), others are included in the *Rigler and Deutsch Index*, and the remainder can only be found by consulting LC staff. See the SONIC Music Only Search in Figure 11-1. Reviewed by the *Scout Report* 7, no. 7 (Mar. 2001). http://scout.wisc. edu/Archives/SPT--FullRecord.php?ResourceId=7717.

11.14   British Library. *National Sound Archive Catalogue* (*Cadensa*). http://cadensa.bl.uk.
The British Library's National Sound Archive Catalogue provides access to about 3.5 million recordings. See the Advanced search screen in Figure 11-2. Reviewed

Figure 11-1 LC's *Sonic Catalog* Music Only Search Screen *(Courtesy of Library of Congress, Recorded Sound Section)*

by the *Scout Report* 7, no. 32 (Feb. 2001). http://scout.wisc.edu/Archives/SPT--FullRecord.php?ResourceId=7559.

11.15 Library and Archives Canada. *Disc-O-Logue*. http://www.collectionscanada.ca/discologue.
       Disc-O-Logue is an index of over 90,000 French-language popular songs available in Canada in the 1960s and '70s. The sound recording holdings of the Canadian national library are available through the *Amicus* and *ArchiviaNet* catalogs described in Chapter 4. Reviewed by the *Scout Report* 5, no. 15 (Aug. 1998). http://scout.wisc.edu/Archives/SPT--FullRecord.php?ResourceId=3570.

Bibliographic Utilities

11.16 Online Computer Library Center (OCLC). *WorldCat*. http://www.oclc.org/worldcat.
       The major fee-based bibliographic utility *WorldCat* includes the most bibliographic information on LPs and 78 RPM recordings. See the description in Chapter 4. (entry 4.12).

Figure 11-2 National Sound Archive Catalogue Advanced Search Screen *(Courtesy of the British Library, National Sound Archive)*

SPECIAL TOPIC DISCOGRAPHIES

Discographies for Instruments and Ensembles

A model instrument-specific discography is James Creighton's *Discopaedia of the Violin: 1889–1971* (Toronto: University of Toronto Press, 1974), which includes the recordings of around 17,000 violinists. The first edition is too early to include CDs, and the second edition, 4 vols. (Burlington, ON: Records Past, 1994) is not widely held.

11.17 Nelson, Susan. *The Flute on Record: The 78 RPM Era: A Discography.* Lanham, MD: Scarecrow, 2006.

Includes historical recordings, primarily on 78s, dating from 1889 to 1954. Solo, chamber, and large ensembles are included. Over 200 flutists are represented, and brief biographical information is provided for most of them. Includes two indexes (composers/titles and additional performers) and bibliography. Reviewed by Annette B. Farrington in *ARSC Journal* 37, no. 2 (Fall 2006): 223–25.

11.18 Stoffel, Lawrence F. *A Discography of Concert Band Recordings on Compact Disc: Promoting the Artistry of Band Composition.* Lewiston, NY: E. Mellen Press, 2006.

Includes recordings dating from 1978 on, but primarily CDs from the 1990s are listed for seventy-three core works for wind band. Arrangement is by composer, then title. Includes analysis of the recordings, interviews with six conductors, bibliography, and index. Reviewed in *Reference and Research Book News* 21, no. 3 (Aug. 2006): 250.

Opera Discographies

In addition to the sources listed next, you may want to consult Alan Blyth's *Opera on CD: The Essential Guide to the Best CD Recordings of 100 Operas* (London: K. Cathie, 1994) and his earlier *Opera on Record*, 3 vols. (place and publisher vary, 1979–1984). For musicals, see Kurt Gänzl's *The Blackwell Guide to the Musical Theatre on Record* (Oxford, UK: Blackwell Reference, 1990).

11.19   Gruber, Paul. *The Metropolitan Opera Guide to Recorded Opera.* New York: Metropolitan Opera Guild; W. W. Norton, 1993.
   Includes reviews of recordings of 150 operas by 72 composers written by 20 critics. Arranged alphabetically by composer. All recordings of an opera are included, with a few of them recommended for each opera. Omits almost all recordings of opera selections, those not in the original language or English, and pirated recordings. The recording dates range from the 1920s up to the early 1990s. Formats include 78s, LPs, and CDs; CD reissues are noted next to the entries. There is a table of contents by title and a performer index. Reviewed by Frederick Maliphant in *Music Review* 55, no. 1 (Feb. 1994): 79–81.

*11.20   Parsons, Charles H. *Recent International Opera Discography.* 7 vols. Mellen Opera Reference Index, vols. 22–23. Lewiston, NY: E. Mellen Press, 2003–2004.
   Part of Parson's monumental *Mellen Opera Reference Index*, these volumes are updated by later volumes in the series: volumes 24–25, titled *2003 Update* and *2004 Update*. Includes mostly LPs and CDs. Vol. 22, in 4 volumes, includes composer entries, arranged alphabetically and then chronologically. Vol. 23 is arranged similarly but includes performers. Preferred recordings are indicated. Vols. 10–12 of the *Mellen Opera Reference Index* represent a first edition of the discography. Volume 25 reviewed in *Reference and Research Book News* 21, no. 2 (May 2006): 248.

Jazz Discographies

*11.21   Bruyninckx, Walter, and Domi Truffandier. *85 Years of Recorded Jazz (1917–2002, A–Z Complete).* CD-ROM. Mechelen, Belgium: Bruyninckx, 2004.
   One of the most comprehensive jazz discographies. Comparable in size to Lord but broader in scope, with the inclusion of blues and gospel recordings. Includes brief bios and more information about the recordings than Lord. The format, PDF files, is cumbersome to use, and CD-ROM is not currently fully compatible with Macs. Lacks the chronological lists included by Lord. Was first available in print. An update is anticipated. Reviewed by Tim Brooks in *ARSC Journal* 33, no. 2 (Fall 2002): 260–66 and Eric Charry in *Notes* 61, no. 3 (Mar. 2005): 833–37. Earlier edition reviewed by Barry Kernfeld and Howard Rye in *Notes* 51, no. 3 (Mar. 1995): 865–91.

11.22   Jepsen, Jørgen G. *Jazz Records: 1942–1965 to 1942–1969.* 11 vols. in 8. Holte, Denmark, and Copenhagen: K. M. Knudsen; Copenhagen: Nordisk Tidsskrift, 1963–1970. Contents: Vol. 1: *A–BL 1942–1965*, Knudsen, 1966; Vol. 2: *BL–CO 1942–1965*, Knudsen, 1966; Vol. 3: *CO–EL 1942–1965*, Knudsen, 1967; Vol. 4a: *ELL–GOO 1942–1967*, Knudsen, 1968; Vol. 4b: *GOO–IWR*

1942–1967, Knudsen, 1969; Vol. 4c: *J–KI 1942–1968*, Knudsen, 1970; Vol. 4d: *KL–L 1942–1968*, Knudsen, 1970; Vol. 5: *M–N 1953–1962*, Nordisk Tidsskrift, 1963; Vol. 6: *O–R 1942–1962*, Nordisk Tidsskrift, 1963; Vol. 7: *S–TE 1942–1962*, Knudsen, 1964; Vol. 8: *TE–Z 1942–1962*, Knudsen, 1965.

Published out-of-order, this discography continues Rust's work into the 1960s. The dates of coverage vary by volume. Arranged like Rust, by performer and then chronologically. Includes primarily 78s and LPs. Scholarly and detailed. Includes cross-references, but no index. Reviewed by Barry Kernfeld and Howard Rye in *Notes* 51, no. 2 (Dec. 1994): 501–47.

*11.23 Lord, Tom. *The Jazz Discography.* CD-ROM version 7.0. West Vancouver, BC: Lord Music Reference, 2006.

Another of the most comprehensive jazz discographies, covering the period from 1896 onwards. Provides information on about 170,000 recording sessions. Earlier in coverage than Bruyninckx, but does not include blues or gospel. The relational database is easier to use and print than Bruyninckx, but records include less information. Also includes useful chronological lists. Largely compiled from other sources, some of which are not credited. Was also first available in print. Version 6.0 reviewed by Russ Chase in *International Association of Jazz Record Collectors Journal* 39, no. 2 (May 2006): 102. Earlier versions reviewed by Tim Brooks in *ARSC Journal* 33, no. 2 (Fall 2002): 260–66; Eric Charry in *Notes* 61, no. 3 (Mar. 2005): 833–37; and Barry Kernfeld and Howard Rye in *Notes* 51, no. 3 (Mar. 1995): 865–91.

11.24 Raben, Erik. *Jazz Records: 1942–80: A Discography.* 8 vols. Copenhagen: JazzMedia Aps, 1989–2004. Contents: Vol. 1: *A–Ba*, 1989; Vol. 2: *Bar–Br*, 1990; Vol. 3: *Bro–Cl*, 1991; Vol. 4: *Cla–Da*, 1993; Vol. 5: *Dav–El*, 1995; Vol. 6: *Duke Ellington*, edited by Ole J. Nielsen, 1992; Vol. 7: *Ell–Fr*, 1999; and Vol. 8 [on CD-ROM] *Fre–Gi*, 2004.

Scholarly update of Jepsen that was not completed. Compiled by a team of contributors. Includes primarily commercial 78s, 45s, LPs, and CDs for recordings made from 1942 to 1980. Includes some reissues as well as live and broadcast recordings. International in scope. Does not include blues or rhythm and blues. Each volume includes an artist index. Reviewed by Barry Kernfeld and Howard Rye in *Notes* 51, no. 2 (Dec. 1994): 501–47.

11.25 Rust, Brian. *Jazz Records: 1897–1943.* 4th ed. 2 vols. New Rochelle, NY: Arlington House, 1978.

The definitive discography of early jazz. Includes primarily 78s, but some LPs are listed as well. Arranged by performer(s) and then chronologically. Scholarly and detailed. Includes two indexes for artists and titles. Later editions (5th from 1983 and rev. from 2002) are basically reprints. Supplemented by other discographies by Rust, for example, *The American Dance Band Discography: 1917–1942*, 2 vols. (New Rochelle, NY: Arlington House, 1975), and Rust and Allen G. Debus's *The Complete Entertainment Discography* from the mid-1890s to 1942 (New Rochelle, NY: Arlington House, 1973). Reviewed by Donald McCormick in *Notes* 35, no. 3 (Mar. 1979): 638, Dan Morgenstern in *Journal of Jazz Studies* 5, no. 2 (Spring–Summer 1979): 91–93, and Barry Kernfeld and Howard Rye in *Notes* 51, no. 2 (Dec. 1994): 501–47.

Rock Music Discographies

11.26 Strong, Martin C. *The Essential Rock Discography*. Edinburgh: Canongate Books, 2006.

Previous seven editions were titled *The Great Rock Discography*. Selective discography of rock (largely excludes pop and indie rock) including 600 entries. Includes 100 performers each from the 1950s, '60s, '70s, '80s, etc. Arranged alphabetically by performer/group, with subentries. If included, a complete chronological discography with both UK and US release information as well as a critical biography and career summary is presented. Formats include primarily LPs and CDs. No indexes. Reviewed by Sean Guthrie in the *Glasgow Herald* (11 Nov. 2006): 10.

Folk and World Music Discographies

11.27 Cohen, Norm. *Traditional Anglo-American Folk Music: An Annotated Discography of Published Sound Recordings*. Garland Library of Music Ethnology. New York: Garland, 1994.

Selective discography including around 500 recordings. Organized by type of recording, such as field recordings of a single artist or ensemble, field anthologies, and commercial hillbilly recordings by a single artist or ensemble. Biographical and critical commentary is included. Has indexes for performers, titles, Child Ballads, Laws Ballads, and label numbers. Includes LPs, cassettes, and CD reissues of commercial 78s and field recordings. Reviewed by Kip Lornell in *Notes* 52, no. 3 (Mar. 1996): 826–27.

*11.28 Keefer, Jane. *Folk Music Index*. http://www.ibiblio.org/folkindex.

Also titled *Folk Music: An Index to Recorded Resources*, this free online database includes about 4,000 recordings, mostly LPs. Browsable by title, performer, or publisher. Also has a keyword search. Both commercial and noncommercial recordings are included.

11.29 Spottswood, Richard K. *Ethnic Music on Records: A Discography of Ethnic Recordings Produced in the United States, 1893–1942*. 7 vols. Music in American Life. Urbana-Champaign: University of Illinois Press, 1990.

Arranged geographically, then by language and performer. Includes primarily commercial foreign-language records made in the U.S. and its possessions during the period 1883–1942 (mostly 78s, with information about reissues). Exceptions include classical music and opera, language instruction records, humorous material, Hawaiian music, reissues of foreign labels, instrumental recordings, and Native American recordings of private or institutional origin. Vols. 6–7 are indexes for performers, titles, and label or matrix numbers. Genre and instrumentation are not indexed. Reviewed by Philippe Varlet in *Ethnomusicology* 35, no. 3 (Fall 1991): 433–36.

11.30 Stradling, Rod. *A Discography of Recorded Traditional Music.* http://www.mustrad.org.uk/discos/tradisco.htm.

Published by *Musical Traditions* magazine, this free online discography includes around 2,500 currently available (in the UK) CDs of traditional music from about 140 labels. Arranged by publisher and then label number, database can be browsed online or can be downloaded and searched. Includes links to full text reviews from *Musical Traditions*, when available.

11.31 Wright-McLeod, Brian. *The Encyclopedia of Native Music: More Than a Century of Recordings from Wax Cylinder to the Internet.* Tucson: University of Arizona Press, 2005.

Includes approximately 1,800 entries on commercial recordings in many styles made by reservation-based Native Americans over the course of the last 100 years. Comprehensive in its inclusion of folk, popular, jazz, as well as native music. Divided into seven sections for regions (arctic/circumpolar region), styles (chicken scratch), or periods (contemporary music). The contemporary music section is by far the largest and most detailed. Entries for some artists contain biographical material. Includes a bibliography and index of performers. Reviewed by Tara Browner in *ARSC Journal* 37, no. 2 (Fall 2006): 244–45.

Discographies of Women in Music

Both of the following two discographies cover art music composed by women. Little overlap exists between the two, and both need updating. For more recent recordings, see, for example, the column published in *Women of Note Quarterly* as well as discographies published as articles, in theses or dissertations, etc.

*11.32 Cohen, Aaron I. *International Discography of Women Composers.* Discographies, no. 10. Westport, CT: Greenwood, 1984.

A companion to Cohen's *International Encyclopedia of Women Composers* (entry 3.11). Includes LPs and 45s for 468 women composers. Arrangement is by composer, then title. Includes performers and nationality of women, and is more international than Frasier. Includes indexes of titles, genres, and nationality. Recording labels are listed. Reviewed by Ann P. Basart in *American Music* 4, no. 2 (Summer 1986): 227–28.

11.33 Frasier, Jane. *Women Composers: A Discography.* Detroit Studies in Music Bibliography, no. 5. Detroit, MI: Information Coordinators, 1983.

Includes around 1,030 discs (78s and LPs) by 337 women composers. Arranged similarly to Cohen, but does not include information on performers. About two-thirds of the book is devoted to indexes by title, genre, and recording company. Has a short bibliography. Reviewed by Ann P. Basart in *American Music* 4, no. 2 (Summer 1986): 227–28.

SINGLE-COMPOSER DISCOGRAPHIES

The state of current composer discographies is surprisingly poor. There are few current discographies for the composers selected as examples throughout this text. The compilation of an exhaustive discography for major composers such as Bach, Beethoven, and Mozart would be a daunting task indeed. One of the books listed next is a discography of a single Wagner opera, *Tristan und Isolde*. Its author, Jonathan Brown, has also compiled a similar discography for *Parsifal*.

The focus here is on discographies current enough to include CD recordings, because these are likely the first choice for your listening and study needs. Older discographies, such as Richard Warren Jr.'s *Charles E. Ives: Discography* (New Haven, CT: Yale University Library, 1972) are not listed here. Students working on historical projects or compiling comprehensive discographies, for example, will benefit from older discographies including recordings on formats such as 78s, LPs, etc. Book-length discographies can be found by searching the subject heading for the appropriate composer with the subdivision "Discography." For example, the LC subject heading for the Warren discography of Ives is "Ives, Charles, 1874-1954—Discography."

Discographies are sometimes included in composer bio-bibliographies and guides to research, such as those included in Chapter 10. Some compilers include a discography chapter or section in their bibliography. Two excellent examples are included in the Machaut (entry 10.108) and Palestrina (entry 10.112) guides to research by Earp and Marvin, respectively. Others include a bibliography of discographies on the composer. See Quigley's 1998 bibliography of Brahms (entry 10.97) for an example of this type.

Major composers are included in the general discographies listed in this chapter as well. Also keep in mind that discographies, like bibliographies, are published in other formats besides books. Those with a narrow scope are often published as articles. The *ARSC Journal* frequently publishes composer-specific discographies. Discographies are available on the web as well. See the Hildegard discography included by the Medieval Music & Arts Foundation website at http://www.medieval.org/emfaq/composers/hildegard.html.

Schoenberg, Arnold

11.34 Shoaf, R. Wayne. *The Schoenberg Discography.* 2nd ed. Fallen Leaf Press Reference Books in Music, 18. Berkeley, CA: Fallen Leaf, 1994.
Includes around 1,500 commercial recordings in a variety of formats arranged by title (those with opus numbers, then those without them) and then chronologically, recorded from 1922 to 1994. Includes a chronology, a bibliography, and three indexes (name; label and review; and title). Review index includes about 2,300 citations. Reviewed by William E. Studwell in *Music Reference Services Quarterly* 3, no. 4 (1995): 75–76.

Stravinsky, Igor

11.35 Stuart, Philip. *Igor Stravinsky: The Composer in the Recording Studio, A Comprehensive Discography.* Discographies, no. 45. Westport, CT: Greenwood, 1991.
Includes around 200 studio recordings in a variety of formats that Stravinsky conducted or was involved with. Arrangement is chronological from 1923 to 1967. Includes appendixes and a short index. Reviewed by Claudio Spies in *Notes* 50, no. 1 (Sept. 1993): 157–58.

Wagner, Richard

11.36 Brown, Jonathan. *Tristan und Isolde on Record: A Comprehensive Discography of Wagner's Music with a Critical Introduction to the Recordings*. Discographies, no. 85. Westport, CT: Greenwood, 2000.

Includes around 600 recordings made from 1901 to 1999 on LP, CD, and some videos. Complete recordings are listed first, followed by excerpts. Includes a lengthy introduction discussing significant recordings and performers. Includes a performer index. Reviewed by Gary A. Galo in *Notes* 58, no. 1 (Sept. 2001): 64–65.

PERFORMER DISCOGRAPHIES

The next two titles are recent examples of performer discographies. Many others are available. Additional excellent examples for jazz musicians include W. E. Timmer's *Ellingtonia: The Recorded Music of Duke Ellington and His Sidemen*, 4th ed. (Lanham, MD: Scarecrow, 1996), and J. Wilfred Johnson's *Ella Fitzgerald: An Annotated Discography* (Jefferson, NC: McFarland, 2001).

11.37 North, James H. *New York Philharmonic: The Authorized Recordings, 1917–2005: A Discography*. Lanham, MD: Scarecrow, 2006.

Includes about 1,500 recordings in a variety of formats, arranged chronologically. Includes appendixes (composers, conductors, soloists, etc.) and a bibliography. Reviewed in *Reference and Research Book News* 21, no. 4 (Nov. 2006): 245.

11.38 Willems, Jos. *All of Me: The Complete Discography of Louis Armstrong*. Studies in Jazz, no. 51. Lanham, MD: Scarecrow, 2006.

Comprehensive Armstrong discography including a variety of recording formats made from 1923 to 1971, arranged chronologically. Includes song title and performer indexes and a bibliography. Reviewed by A. J. Adam in *Choice* 44, no. 3 (Nov. 2006): 453.

RECORDING LABEL DISCOGRAPHIES

The next two listings are examples of good discographies for a major classical and a major jazz recording label.

11.39 Brooks, Tim, and Brian Rust. *The Columbia Master Book Discography*. 4 vols. Discographies, no. 78. Westport, CT: Greenwood, 1999.

A model label discography compiled by major discographers. Brooks wrote vol. 1, Rust vols. 2–3, and both contributed to vol. 4. Arranged chronologically, with all recordings from 1901 to 1934 included. A history of the label is included in vol. 1. All volumes have artist and title indexes; vols. 1 and 4 also have a label index. No composer index is included. Reviewed by Jerome F. Weber in *ARSC Journal* 31, no. 1 (Spring 2000): 122–24.

11.40 Cuscuna, Michael, and Michel Ruppli. *The Blue Note Label: A Discography, Revised and Expanded*. Discographies, no. 88. Westport, CT: Greenwood, 2001.

Comprehensive discography of commercial releases from 1939 to 1999 on Blue Note. Basically a second edition to the authors' 1988 discography. Arranged chronologically, with separate sections for purchased sessions, reissues, etc. Includes a performer index. Reviewed by Brian Davis in *Jazz Journal International* 54, no. 10 (Oct. 2001): 16.

AMERICAN MUSIC DISCOGRAPHIES

See entry 14.14 on the *Database of Recorded American Music (DRAM)*. This database makes Elizabeth A. Davis's Index to the New World Recorded Anthology of American Music: A User's Guide to the Initial One Hundred Records (New York: W. W. Norton, 1981) largely obsolete.

11.41 Heintze, James R. *American Music before 1865 in Print and on Records: A Biblio-Discography*. Rev. ed. I.S.A.M. Monographs, No. 30. Brooklyn, NY: Institute for Studies in American Music, 1990.

A companion to Heintze's bibliography of early American music (entry 10.67), listing both scores and recordings. About half the book (Chapter 3) is a discography listing over 1,100 tracks of early American music released through 1987. Most recordings are LPs. Arrangement is by composer or title for anonymous works or anthologies (i.e., tunebooks). Includes a label index as well as one for composers, compilers, and titles. No performer index. Reviewed by John E. Druesedow, Jr., in *Notes* 47, no. 3 (Mar. 1991): 770.

11.42 Oja, Carol J. *American Music Recordings: A Discography of 20th-Century U.S. Composers*. Brooklyn, NY: Institute for Studies in American Music, 1982.

"A Project of the Institute for Studies in American Music for the Koussevitzky Music Foundation." Includes over 13,000 commercial recordings (78s, 45s, and LPs) released before June 1980. Over 8,000 titles of art music by around 1,300 American composers are represented. Arrangement is alphabetical by composer, then title. Includes indexes of performers (ensembles, conductors, singers, and instrumentalists) and a bibliography. Reviewed by Steven Ledbetter in *American Music* 5, no. 3 (Autumn 1987): 346–48.

CANADIAN MUSIC DISCOGRAPHIES

11.43 Moogk, Edward B. *Roll Back the Years: History of Canadian Recorded Sound and Its Legacy, Genesis to 1930*. Ottawa, ON: National Library of Canada, 1975.

Over half of this book (Chapter 6) is a discography of recordings issued in Canada during the period covered, in a variety of formats. The performers, composers, and lyricists represented were either born or educated in Canada. Arranged in three sections: composer, composer/lyricist, and recording label. Reviewed by Robert Philip in *Musical Times* 117, no. 1600 (Jun. 1976): 493.

RECORDING REVIEWS AND INDEXES TO REVIEWS

*11.44 Gramophone. *Gramofile.* http://www.gramophone.co.uk.
Free online database including full text for over 30,000 classical CD and DVD reviews from *Gramophone* magazine. Searchable by composer, title, performers, label, and keyword. Also searchable by label number and bar code. Updated monthly. Site requires registration. Reviewed by the *Scout Report* 7, no. 32 (Aug. 2001). http://scout.wisc.edu/Archives/SPT--FullRecord.php?ResourceId=8455.

11.45 Grimes, Janet, ed. *CD Review Digest Annual.* Voorheesville, NY: Peri, 1989–1994.
Annual volumes for classical and jazz/popular music were published. It was continued in 1995 as the *Schwann CD Review Digest* but then ceased. Includes excerpts of CD reviews published in around 30 English-language periodicals. (More were indexed initially.) Arrangement is by composer for the classical volumes and by artist for the popular ones. Several indexes were included, for example, label, reviewer, performer, and awards. Volume 1 reviewed by Stephen Ellis in *Fanfare* 12, no. 6 (1989): 419–20.

11.46 Palkovic, Mark, and Paul Cauthen. *Index to CD and Record Reviews, 1987–1997: Based on Material Originally Published in Notes, Quarterly Journal of the Music Library Association, between 1987 and 1997.* 3 vols. New York: G. K. Hall, 1999.
Based on the *Notes* column "Index to Record Reviews," which ceased with the Sept. 1997 issue. Indexes classical CD reviews from 23 periodicals for around 37,000 recordings. Arrangement is by label name and number. Volume 3 includes indexes by composer, anthology, and performer. Reviews are characterized as excellent, adequate, or inadequate in their assessment. Previous titles based on the *Notes* column compiled by Kurtz Myers and published by G. K. Hall were titled *Index to Record Reviews,* with compilations for 1984–1987 (1989), 1978–1983 (1985), and 1949–1977 (5 vols., 1978–80). The first compilation, titled *Record Ratings*, was compiled by Myers and Richard S. Hill (New York: Crown, 1956). Reviewed by Brad Short in *Fontes artis musicae* 46, nos. 3–4 (July–Dec. 1999): 357–58.

EVALUATION CHECKLIST

The following checklist was adapted in part from Brooks and Hunter.[1]

• Is the scope clear (recording formats, date range, number of entries)?
• Are reissues included?

---

[1]Tim Brooks, "Guidelines for Discographies in the *ARSC Journal*," *ARSC Journal* 37, no. 1 (Spring 2006): 14–20, and David Hunter and others, "Music Library Association Guidelines for the Preparation of Music Reference Works," *Notes* 50, no. 4 (June 1994): 1329–38.

- Is the discography exhaustive or selective (are the criteria for inclusion explained)?
- Is the arrangement logical?
- What is the discographer's methodology (were recordings examined, or is it based on other discographies, what process was used to date recordings, are sources listed, etc.)?
- Is it thoroughly indexed (performer, composer, etc.)?
- Are the entries annotated, or are recordings reviewed or rated?
- What is the discography's purpose (is it a purchasers' guide, scholarly, etc.)?
- What type of discography is it (label, artist/composer, or subject)?
- Is a bibliography included?
- Do the entries include:
  - Recording title(s)?
  - Recording company and place?
  - Date of recording, publication, reissue, and/or deletion?
  - Label, label number, matrix number, take number, etc.?
  - Format(s) of recording?
  - Producer, director, recording engineer?
  - Presence of notes, author, etc.?
  - Title of work(s) with opus number, thematic catalog number, key, etc.?
  - Composer(s)?
  - Performer(s) and instrumentation/roles/voices, couplings?
  - Language of performance?
- Is information on composers or performers provided?
- Is the discography ongoing? Are supplements or updates provided?

SUGGESTED READINGS

The readings listed here fall into three categories: those that provide an overview of discography, examples of or discussions about discographical studies, and information about how to compile a discography. All are written by respected discographers. The "Discography" entries in the *Encyclopedia of Recorded Sound* and *New Grove* provide an overview and introduction of major discographies. The first chapter of Brian Rust's *Guide to Discography* has a similar purpose. Cuming describes the genesis and creation of *WERM*. Kernfeld and Rye present a series of reviews of major jazz discographies while also explaining some of the challenges of compiling them. Hall presents a chronological survey of major titles and also introduces suggested elements to be included in a discography. Rust's Chapter 3 and the recent *ARSC Journal* guidelines by Brooks are similar. The latter is the most current and authoritative. Finally, Brooks's study of recordings from *Florodora* provides an example of a well-executed discographical study.

Brooks, Tim. "Early Recordings of Songs from *Florodora*: Tell Me, Pretty Maiden . . . Who Are You?—A Discographical Mystery." *ARSC Journal* 31, no. 1 (Spring 2000): 51–69.

———. "Guidelines for Discographies in the *ARSC Journal.*" *ARSC Journal* 37, no. 1 (Spring 2006): 14–20.

Cuming, G. J. "*The World's Encyclopaedia of Recorded Music*: Some Reminiscences." *ARSC Journal* 19, no. 1 (1987): 11–15.

Hall, David. "Discography: A Chronological Survey." In *Modern Music Librarianship: Essays in Honor of Ruth Watanabe*, edited by Alfred Mann, 173–84. Stuyvesant, NY: Pendragon, 1989.

Hoffmann, Frank, ed. *Encyclopedia of Recorded Sound*, 2nd ed. 2 vols. New York: Routledge, 2005. S.v. "Discography."

Kernfeld, Barry, and Howard Rye. "Comprehensive Discographies of Jazz, Blues, and Gospel." Pts. 1 and 2. *Notes* 51, no. 2 (Dec. 1994): 501–47; 51, no. 3 (Mar. 1995): 865–91.

Rust, Brian. "Purpose and Function of Discography." Chap. 1 in Brian Rust's *Guide to Discography*. Westport, CT: Greenwood, 1980.

———. "The Creation of a Discography." Chap. 3 in Brian Rust's *Guide to Discography*. Westport, CT: Greenwood, 1980.

Sadie, Stanley, ed. *The New Grove Dictionary of Music and Musicians*, 2nd ed. New York: Grove, 2001. S.v. "Discography," by Jerome F. Weber. Also available from *Grove Music Online*. http://www.oxfordmusiconline.com.

CHAPTER 12

Music Iconographies

Images are valuable for many purposes in music research. You may embark on research projects that have art depicting music at the heart of the study. Or you may need images as illustrations in your papers or presentations. Perhaps you want to include illustrations in your teaching for their educational value, especially for visual learners. Finding images may not be as central to your musical life as finding scores, recordings, and writings about music; you may instead simply enjoy iconographies because of their beauty.

Like discography, musical **iconography** has only been practiced since the twentieth century, so it is not well established as a discipline. Some would suggest that iconography is a branch of musicology; others describe it as an interdisciplinary study with art history. Either way, the methodology of iconographical studies is still evolving. Unlike discography, however, iconography requires special knowledge and attention to the medium. The Suggested Readings by Barbara Renton and Emanuel Winternitz point out how misinterpretations can easily be made when musicians interpret art.

The compilation of a database of accurately cataloged images has been discussed for decades. This project is finally coming to fruition in a web-based database sponsored by Répertoire International d'Iconographie Musicale, or RIdIM (International Repertory of Musical Iconography), discussed later.

Misinterpretations in iconographical studies can result for a number of reasons. The intent of the artist may not have been a realistic portrayal of the subjects involved. Artistic decisions based aesthetics or individual style, social conventions, symbolism, and limitation of the artistic media all need to be considered. The representation may have been based the artist's imagination rather than on a model. For these reasons, comparison of a number of artworks is important, as is working with an art historian if that is not your area of specialization.

Music in art can tell us about musical instruments, musicians, performance practice, and social or historical context of music making, among other topics. From periods before photography, art is often the only surviving visual evidence of certain composers or instruments. Art in various media are used in iconography, including paintings, sculpture, photographs, tapestries, woodcuts, sheet music illustrations, and record jackets. Common subjects for iconographical music studies are biography and **organology**. Other types of iconographical studies might involve musical sources such as manuscripts or signatures. Studies of musical synesthesia, music inspired by art, and art created by musicians (for example, Mendelssohn, Schoenberg, and David Byrne) also fall into the broad category of iconographies.

Images can be found in a variety of places, and most musical writings include some illustrations. Histories, biographies, and encyclopedias are good examples. For this reason, consider titles included in other chapters of the text when searching for images. Examples include encyclopedias and dictionaries covered in Chapters 2 and 3, histories mentioned in Chapter 9, and the online image search engines and databases listed in Chapter 14. The titles listed here are primarily in the following categories: comprehensive iconographies, illustrated histories, musical instruments, and composers. Exhibition catalogs have been largely excluded.

Both the Répertoire International d'Iconographie Musicale (International Repertory of Musical Iconography) (RIdIM) and the Research Center for Music Iconography (RCMI) are leaders in musical study of art. RIdIM (http://www.ridim.org) is the fourth and final international, cooperative "R" project to be discussed in this text. See Figure 12-1. The others are RILM, RIPM, and RISM. Currently centered in Paris, RIdIM was founded in 1971 with the goal of fostering musical iconography studies by establishing

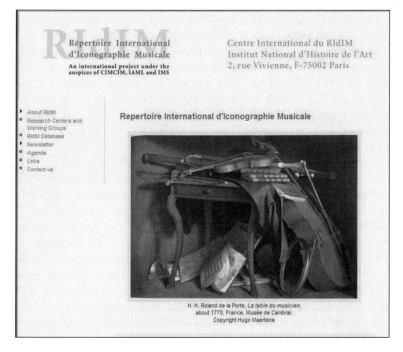

Figure 12-1 RIdIM Homepage *(Copyright © Répertoire International d'Iconographie Musicale, 2007)*

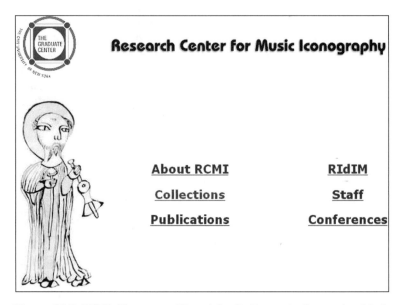

Figure 12-2 RCMI Homepage (*Copyright © Research Center for Music Iconography, CUNY Graduate Center*)

methodology, forming research centers, and cataloging images with musical content. RIdIM is a joint project of the International Association of Music Libraries, Archives and Documentation Centres (IAML), the International Musicological Society (IMS), the International Committee of Musical Instrument Museums and Collections (CIMCIM), and the International Council of Museums (ICM). Although for many years RIdIM was not very active, it has become more active since 2004.

The RCMI was established in 1972. Located at the City University of New York (CUNY) Graduate Center, it is the U.S. national center of RIdIM. Other national centers have also been established. It maintains an iconographical collection and contributes bibliographic entries to its sister bibliographic project RILM. See the RCMI website at http://web.gc.cuny.edu/rcmi. See Figure 12-2.

The projects and publications of both RIdIM and RCMI, which are intended to help musicians use visual materials, are discussed here. The two organizations have collaborated on publications and conferences, in addition to working independently. Currently, each publishes a scholarly journal, and RIdIM has recently begun issuing a newsletter. The "old" *RIdIM/RCMI Newsletter* was published from 1975 to 1997 and then became the journal *Music in Art* (1998–). Both were published by the RCMI at CUNY. The parent organization, RIdIM, also publishes a scholarly journal, titled *Imago musicae* (1984–). Both journals include articles in a variety of European languages in addition to English. Both include black-and-white illustrations, although those in *Imago musicae* are generally of higher quality. In 2006, RIdIM began publishing a "new" *RIdIM Newsletter* in Paris. In addition to *Music in Art*, the RCMI has published five *RIdIM/RCMI Inventories of Music Iconography* (1987–), which are catalogs of the musical images of major U.S. art museums.

At present, RIdIM's major project is creating an online searchable database of cataloged images that is under development. It will be part of the RIdIM website (http://www.ridim.org) and will require users to register. Initially, the database is expected to include around 2,000 records for musical images, with links to reproductions of the artwork for about one-third of the records hosted at the various museums, libraries, and other collections that own them. The hope is that institutions owning art objects and images of musical interest will contribute to the database and that it will grow quickly.

In addition to the projects and publications already mentioned, both RIdIM and the RCMI sponsor international conferences (sometimes jointly) related to musical iconography. Information about conferences, publications, and projects is available at the centers' websites. A report of RIdIM activities is also published irregularly in journals such as *Music in Art* and *Fontes artis musicae.*

Like other writings on music included in this text, iconographies vary in scope and format of publication. Thomas F. Heck has described the body of literature as international and multilingual, interdisciplinary, and very narrow in scope overall.[1] Furthermore, many are published in multiple languages and editions. The cataloging and indexing of these studies, discussed later, is often inconsistent. They are published in a variety of formats, ranging from comprehensive, multi-volume sets published over many years to essays in collections and journal articles. Book-length iconographies include pictorial biographies, illustrated histories, and exhibition catalogs. Major publishers of iconographies include Bärenreiter, Thames and Hudson, Schott, and Hirmer. Some consist almost entirely of images; others do not even include images. Many are dated. Because of the wide appeal of art, many iconographies are popular rather than scholarly, and these might best be described as picture or coffee table books. All of these factors combine to make iconographies challenging bibliographically.

Searching for iconographies in online catalogs can also be difficult. Books that consist primarily of pictures may not even have a subject heading or call number related to iconographies. All should, however, have "ill." in the physical description of the bibliographic record. Also be aware that iconographies may be housed in your library's circulating, reference, or special collections. They may also be located in your institution's art library if one exists.

The primary LC classification numbers for iconographies are in the ML85–89 range. The most common subject headings are the subdivisions "Pictorial works," "Portraits," and "Iconography." The most common call numbers are ML85 (corresponding to the LC subject heading "Music in art"); ML87 for portraits of groups of musicians ("Composers—Portraits"); ML88 for portraits of individual musicians ("Chopin, Frédéric, 1810–1849—Pictorial works"); and ML89 for general pictorial works ("Music—Pictorial works" and "Music—History and criticism—Pictorial works"). Sometimes iconographies for individual composers are classed in ML410 with biographies or in M3 if they are published as part of a complete works edition.

Other LC call numbers and subject headings include the following: ML112.5 is assigned for reproductions of title pages; ML140–141 are assigned for catalogs of portraits and exhibition catalogs, respectively; ML460–1093 are used for "Musical instruments in art" and are classified by the individual instrument. General works and collections are given the call numbers ML460–462. Other iconographies are classified by their primary topic. For example, ML3556 for "African Americans—Music—Pictorial works."

---

[1]Thomas F. Heck, *Picturing Performance: The Iconography of the Performing Arts in Concept and Practice* (Rochester, NY: University of Rochester Press, 1999), 218.

BIBLIOGRAPHIES OF ICONOGRAPHIES

The following bibliography, compiled by Frederick Crane, is updated in several ways. The RCMI maintains a bibliography of scholarly writings and submits that information to *RILM Abstracts*. The RCMI website also includes a bibliography of writings published under the auspices of RIdIM as well as writings about the organization. RIdIM itself publishes bibliographies irregularly in *Imago musicae*. Thomas F. Heck included a brief bibliography of music iconography (around 90 entries dating from 1973 through 1998) in *Picturing Performance: The Iconography of the Performing Arts in Concept and Practice* (Rochester, NY: University of Rochester Press, 1999). Also see the bibliography of the *New Grove* article listed in the Suggested Readings.

*12.1 Crane, Frederick. *A Bibliography of the Iconography of Music.* Iowa City: University of Iowa, 1971. Also available online from the Research Center for Music Iconography at http://web.gc.cuny.edu/rcmi/CraneBibliography1971.pdf. Dated, unannotated bibliography including around 700 entries arranged by categories (illustrated histories, pictorial biographies, iconographical studies, etc.).

GENERAL MUSIC ICONOGRAPHIES
AND ILLUSTRATED HISTORIES

*12.2 Besseler, Heinrich, and Max Schneider. *Musikgeschichte in Bildern.* 26 vols. Leipzig, Ger.: VEB Deutscher Verlag für Musik, 1961–1989. Contents: Vol. 1: *Musikethnologie*: Pt. 1: *Ozeanien*, edited by Paul Collaer, 1965; Pt. 2: *Amerika: Eskimo und indianische Bevölkerung*, edited by Paul Collaer, 1967; Pt. 3: *Südostasien*, edited by Paul Collaer, Emmy Bernatzik, et al., 1979; Pt. 4: *Südasien: Die indische Musik und ihre Traditionen*, edited by Alain Daniélou, translated by Fritz Bose, 1978; Pt. 8: *Nordafrika*, edited by Paul Collaer, Jürgen Elsner, et al., 1983; Pt. 9: *Zentralafrika*, edited by Jos Gansemans, Barbara Schmidt-Wrenger, et al., 1986; Pt. 10: *Ostafrika*, edited by Gerhard Kubik, Jim de Vere Allen, et al., 1982; Pt. 11: *Westafrika*, edited by Gerhard Kubik, Danhim Amagbenyõ, et al., 1989; Vol. 2: *Musik des Altertums*: Pt. 1: *Ägypten*, edited by Hans Hickmann, 1961; Pt. 2: *Mesopotamien*, edited by Subhi Anwar Rashid, 1984; Pt. 4: *Griechenland*, edited by Max Wegner, 1963; Pt. 5: *Etrurien und Rom*, edited by Günter Fleischhauer, 1964; Pt. 7: *Alt-Amerika: Musik der Indianer in präkolumbischer Zeit*, edited by Samuel Martí, 1970; Pt. 8: *Altindien*, edited by Walter Kaufmann, Joep Bor, et al., 1981; Pt. 9: *Mittelasien*, edited by F. M. Karomatov, V. A. Meškeris, et al., 1987; Vol. 3: *Musik des Mittelalters und der Renaissance*: Pt. 2: *Islam*, edited by Henry George Farmer, 1966; Pt. 3: *Musikerziehung: Lehre und Theorie der Musik im Mittelalter*, edited by Joseph Smits van Waesberghe, 1969; Pt. 4: *Schriftbild der einstimmigen Musik*, edited by Bruno Stäblein, 1975; Pt. 5: *Schriftbild der mehrstimmigen Musik*, edited by Heinrich Besseler and Peter Gülke, 1973; Pt. 8: *Musikleben im 15. Jahrhundert*, edited by Edmund A. Bowles, 1977; Pt. 9: *Musikleben im 16. Jahrhundert*, edited by Walter Salmen, 1976; Vol. 4: *Musik der Neuzeit*: Pt. 1: *Oper: Szene* *und Darstellung von 1600 bis 1900,* edited by Hellmuth Christian Wolff, 1968; Pt. 2: *Konzert: Öffentliche Musikdarbeitung vom 17. bis 19. Jahrhundert,* edited by Heinrich W. Schwab, 1971; Pt. 3: *Haus- und Kammermusik: Privates Musizieren im gesellschaftlichen Wandel zwischen 1600 und 1900,* edited by Walter Salmen, 1969; Pt. 4: *Tanz im 17. und 18. Jahrhundert,* edited by Walter Salmen, 1988; Pt. 5: *Tanz im 19. Jahrhundert,* edited by Walter Salmen, 1989.

Intended to cover all cultures of world music and all time periods of Western music history. Not all parts that were planned were completed. Each book includes many plates, nearly all of which are black-and-white. Pictures are accompanied by detailed commentary, a bibliography, examples in musical notation, chronological tables, and indexes. Vol. 1, Part 1 reviewed by Bruno Nettl in *Notes* 23, no. 2 (Dec. 1966): 276. Vol. 1, Part 2 reviewed by Bruno Nettl in *Notes* 24, no. 4 (June 1968): 717–18. Vol. 1, Part 3 reviewed by Andrew Toth in *Ethnomusicology* 25, no. 3 (Sept. 1981): 541–42. Vol. 1, Part 4 reviewed by Bruno Nettl in *Ethnomusicology* 25, no. 2 (May 1981): 337–38. Vol. 1, Part 9 reviewed by V. Kofi Agawu in *Music and Letters* 70, no. 1 (Feb. 1989): 74–76. Vol. 1, Part 10 reviewed by Rupert Mayr in *African Music* 6, no. 3 (1983): 126–27. Vol. 2, Part 1 reviewed by Caldwell Titcomb in *JAMS* 17, no. 3 (Fall 1964): 386–89. Vol. 2, Part 4 reviewed by Emanuel Winternitz in *JAMS* 19, no. 3 (Fall 1966): 412–15. Vol. 2, Part 7 reviewed by Christian Ahrens in *Die Musikforschung* 28, no. 4 (Oct.–Dec. 1975): 452–53. Vol. 2, Part 8 reviewed by Jonathan Katz in *Music and Letters* 64, nos. 1–2 (Jan.–Apr. 1983): 67–68. Vol. 3, Part 2 reviewed by Ella Zonis in *JAMS* 22, no. 2 (Summer 1969): 293–96. Vol. 3, Part 3 reviewed by Dale Higbee in *American Recorder* 13, no. 2 (May 1972): 64. Vol. 3, Part 4 reviewed by Ruth Steiner in *Musical Quarterly* 63, no. 2 (Apr. 1977): 283–86. Vol. 3, Part 5 reviewed by David Fallows in *Musical Times* 117, no. 1605 (Nov. 1976): 909. Vol. 3, Part 8 reviewed by Howard Mayer Brown in *Music and Letters* 62, no. 1 (Jan. 1981): 71–74. Vol. 3, Part 9 reviewed by Richard D. Leppert in *JAMS* 32, no. 2 (Summer 1979): 339–43. Vol. 4, Part 1 reviewed by Elvidio Surian in *JAMS* 24, no. 2 (Summer 1971): 306–308. Vol. 4, Part 3 reviewed by Dale Higbee in *American Recorder* 13, no. 2 (May 1972): 422.

*12.3 Blackwood, Alan. *Music of the World.* Englewood Cliffs, NJ: Prentice Hall, 1991. Beautiful and relatively recent. Intended for a general audience. Replete with images of instruments and musicians from cultures around the world, including non-Western music as well as the Western classical tradition. Includes portraits, instruments, line drawings, and other images, many in color. Book was also issued by other publishers (for example, Mallard Press), with slightly different titles.

12.4 Bosseur, Jean-Yves. *Music: Passion for an Art.* Geneva: Skira; New York: Rizzoli, 1991. Focuses on the relationship between the visual arts and music. Nearly all images are color. Most of the book focuses on twentieth-century art. The text, focusing on both art history and music history, was not intended for a scholarly audience. Includes a list of illustrations featuring dimensions. No index. A similar (but less lavishly illustrated) title is Tom Phillips's *Music in Art: Through the Ages* (New York: Prestel, 1997). Reviewed by Tilman Seebass in *Notes* 49, no. 2 (Dec. 1992): 596–98.

12.5 Collaer, Paul, and Albert Vander Linden. *Historical Atlas of Music: A Comprehensive Study of the World's Music, Past and Present.* Translated by Allan Miller. Cleveland: World, 1968.

Illustrated survey of music history. After a brief survey of world music cultures, the book concentrates primarily on Western music history, subdivided into standard historical periods. Includes summary discussions, 15 full-page color maps, and about 675 mostly small, black-and-white illustrations. Some maps are now out-of-date. Reviewed by Guy Oldham in *Musical Times* 109, no. 1508 (Oct. 1968): 924.

12.6 Kinsky, Georg, Robert Haas, and Hans Schnoor. *A History of Music in Pictures.* New York: Dover, 1951.

A classic illustrated history, first published in English in 1930. Consists almost entirely of images, without text or commentary. Arranged chronologically, beginning with antiquity and ending with the early twentieth century. The approximately 1,550 reproductions are relatively small, and all are black-and-white. Images include portraits, artwork, facsimiles, etc. Includes a brief section on non-Western musical cultures. Reviewed by William Lichtenwanger in *Notes* 9, no. 3 (June 1952): 422.

12.7 Lang, Paul Henry, and Otto Bettmann. *A Pictorial History of Music.* New York: W. W. Norton, 1960.

The text of this illustrated history is taken from Lang's *Music in Western Civilization* (entry 9.64). Organized chronologically, with a section devoted to each standard period of Western music history. All images are black-and-white. Some images are full page, but many are reproduced at too small a size to be useful. Image captions lack detail. Reviewed by J. A. Westrup in *Music and Letters* 45, no. 3 (July 1964): 263–64.

12.8 Lesure, François. *Music and Art in Society.* Translated by Denis and Sheila Stevens. University Park: Pennsylvania State University Press, 1968.

Includes a mixture of black-and-white and color plates. Images are divided into sections, by topic. Each section is prefaced by a well-written introduction. Focuses on images of music making, and includes artworks not reproduced elsewhere. Images are annotated, but some lack dates. Reviewed by J. A. Westrup in *Music and Letters* 49, no. 4 (Oct. 1968): 382–84.

12.9 Pincherle, Marc. *An Illustrated History of Music.* Translated by Rollo Myers. New York: Reynal, 1959.

Includes 200 black-and-white illustrations and 40 in color; many are large. Has a wide variety of images, including portraits, photos of paintings, manuscript facsimiles, and pictures of instruments. Although intended as an introductory text, the level of accuracy is high and critical commentary is good. No bibliography. Reviewed by Denis Stevens in *Musical Times* 101, no. 1410 (Aug. 1960): 493.

MUSICAL INSTRUMENT ICONOGRAPHIES

In addition to the titles listed next, be sure to check the musical instrument encyclopedias and dictionaries listed in Chapter 3. Many are well illustrated. Also consider exhibition catalogs for images of instruments. Examples include Marie-Thérèse Bringard's *Sounding Forms: African Musical Instruments* (New York: American Federation of Arts, 1989); Mitchell Clark's *Sounds of the Silk Road: Musical Instruments of Asia* (Boston: Museum of Fine Arts Publications, 2005); Laurence Libin's *American Musical Instruments* (New York: Metropolitan Museum of Art; W. W. Norton, 1985); and Leo Mazow and Sarah Burns's *Picturing the Banjo* (University Park: Pennsylvania State University Press, 2005).

General Musical Instrument Iconographies

12.10 Buchner, Alexander. *Musical Instruments through the Ages*. Translated by Iris Urwin. London: Spring Books, 1956.

Consists almost entirely of images of both Western and non-Western instruments, with very little text. The vast majority are black-and-white, but a few are in color. Arrangement is chronological. Based on collections in Prague (the National Museum, Museum of Art, and University Library). Reviewed by Anthony Baines in the *Galpin Society Journal* 10 (May 1957): 93–94.

12.11 Dearling, Robert. *The Illustrated Encyclopedia of Musical Instruments*. New York: Schirmer Books, 1996.

Far better illustrations—many in color—than *Grove Instruments* (entry 3.28) or *The Oxford Companion to Musical Instruments* (entry 3.25). Less scholarly, however, than these two titles. Arranged by instrument families, i.e., winds, strings, etc. Language used for non-Western instruments is value laden. Intended for a general audience. Reviewed by Michael Colby in *Library Journal* 122, no. 2 (1 Feb. 1997): 72 and Judith Gray in *Ethnomusicology* 41, no. 3 (Fall 1997): 574.

*12.12 Diagram Group. *Musical Instruments of the World*. [New York]: Paddington Press, 1976. Reprint, New York: Sterling, 1997.

Arranged by the Hornbostel and Sachs system (aerophones, etc.). Most useful for its approximately 4,000 illustrations (contains more illustrations than text); of those the halftones are the best. Contains errors. Includes a brief bibliography and index. Reviewed by Laurence Libin in *Notes* 34, no. 2 (Dec. 1977): 336–40.

Western Musical Instrument Iconographies

*12.13 Bragard, Roger, and Ferdinand J. de Hen. *Musical Instruments in Art and History*. Translated by Bill Hopkins. New York: Viking; London: Barrie, 1968.

Most useful as a source of excellent color photos of Western instruments. The accompanying text is uneven and is particularly weak in the early music chapters. Bragard is curator of the Instrument Museum at the Brussels Conservatory, but this is not a scholarly volume. Reviewed by Mary Remnant in *Music and Letters* 50, no. 2 (Apr. 1969): 301–3.

12.14 Buchner, Alexander. *Musical Instruments: An Illustrated History*. Translated by Borek Vancura. New York: Crown, 1973.

A major revision of Buchner's earlier *Musical Instruments Through the Ages* that removed the non-Western instruments. This volume includes more text that, as in his other volumes, is not accurate. More photographs of early and modern instruments are added. Most of the 300 plus illustrations are black-and-white, and the arrangement is basically chronological. Reviewed by Robert A. Warner in *Music Educators Journal* 61, no. 3 (Nov. 1974): 75–79.

12.15 Winternitz, Emanuel, and Lilly Stunzi. *Musical Instruments of the Western World*. New York: McGraw-Hill 1967.

Mixture of color and black-and-white photos and other illustrations. The 100 or so instruments were chosen not necessarily for their typicality, but for their beauty. The instruments represent fine collections in Europe, England, and the U.S. Concerned primarily with older instruments, dating from the eighteenth century and earlier. Contains early examples of many major Western instruments as well as examples of more unusual instruments, such as the Geigenwerk and the orpheoreon. Includes several short introductory essays on aspects of organology and instrument collection. See also Winternitz's collection of essays, *Musical Instruments and Their Symbolism in Western Art*, 2nd ed. (New Haven, CT: Yale University Press, 1979). Reviewed by Howard Mayer Brown in *Notes* 25, no. 2 (Dec. 1968): 223–25.

Non-Western Musical Instrument Iconographies

12.16 Buchner, Alexander. *Folk Music Instruments*. Translated by Alžběta Nováková. New York: Crown, 1972.

Most of the photographs show the instruments in performance. As a result the instruments are not museum pieces, as in Buchner's other volumes listed here. The text includes dated and inaccurate terminology and is less useful than the images. Some of these are in color, but most are black-and-white. Full citations of images are lacking. Reviewed by Ani Apelian in *Ethnomusicology* 17, no. 3 (Sept. 1973): 545–47.

*12.17 Rault, Lucie. *Musical Instruments: Craftsmanship and Traditions from Prehistory to the Present*. Translated by Jane Brenton. New York: H. Abrams, 2000.

Includes over 200 beautiful, large photos; most are in color. Includes primarily non-Western instruments. Rault is an ethnomusicologist at the Musée l'Homme, and the text reflects modern viewpoints and scholarship in the area. Strongest in coverage of Africa, the Middle East, and Asia. Some images lack full citation details. Reviewed by R. Knight in *Choice* 38, no. 8 (Apr. 2001): 1472.

MULTIPLE-COMPOSER ICONOGRAPHIES

*12.18 Buettner, Stewart, and Reinhard G. Pauly. *Great Composers, Great Artists: Portraits*. Portland, OR: Amadeus Press, 1992.

Typically features one famous portrait or photograph per composer for more than 60 composers. Most are paintings, but sculptures and drawings are included as well. Each image is accompanied by a short essay on the relationship of the artist to the composer being profiled. Most images are in color and are well cited. Contains a list of plates, a list of illustrations, a bibliography, and an index. Reviewed by Alain Frogley in *Musical Times* 134, no. 1803 (May 1993): 273.

12.19 Camner, James. *Great Composers in Historic Photographs: 244 Portraits from the 1860s to the 1960s.* New York: Dover, 1981.

Black-and-white photos of composers are arranged in alphabetical order. Multiple images are included for some. Most of the reproductions are small and lack dates. The accompanying text is not scholarly. See also Erich Auerbach's similar twentieth-century collection, *Images of Music* (Cologne, Ger.: Könemann, 1996). Reviewed by Ellen Sisco in *School Library Journal* 28, no. 4 (Dec. 1981): 88–89.

SINGLE-COMPOSER ICONOGRAPHIES

Iconographies and/or highly illustrated biographies do not exist for all the composers selected as examples in this text; see Appendix C. Some, for example, Chopin and Liszt, have several. Scholarly iconographies in English that are widely held were chosen for inclusion here. Additionally, preference was given to iconographies published as part of a composer's complete works edition, more recent scholarship, and those with both high-quality images (especially large images and those in color) and text. Comprehensive titles were selected over those with narrower scope. Major iconographers in this category are Ernst Burger, Robert Bory, Otto Erich Deutsch, and H. C. Robbins Landon.

Bach, Johann Sebastian

*12.20 Neumann, Werner. *Bilddokumente zur Lebensgeschichte Johann Sebastian Bachs/Pictorial Documents of the Life of Johann Sebastian Bach.* Translated by Anne Wyburd. Bach-Dokumente, 4. Kassel, Ger.: Bärenreiter, 1979.

Part of the supplement to the *Neue Ausgabe sämtlicher Werke* (entry 7.2). Contains reproductions of an assortment of images and documents from Bach's life, including portraits, paintings of places, manuscripts, concert programs, and letters. Nearly all of the approximately 675 images are black-and-white. Images are annotated in a section at the back of the book. Contains an index of names, an index of places, and an index of works referenced. See also Neumann's earlier illustrated biography, *Bach and His World*, rev. ed. (New York: Viking, 1970). Reviewed by Robert Cammarota in *Notes* 37, no. 4 (June 1981): 857–58.

12.21 Schwendowius, Barbara, and Wolfgang Dömling, eds. *Johann Sebastian Bach: Life, Times, Influence.* Translated by John Coombs, Lionel Salter, and Gaynor Nitz. New Haven, CT: Yale University Press, 1984.

Translation of an illustrated anthology of essays on a variety of subjects pertaining to the life and music of J. S. Bach. Originally published as an accompaniment to a series of Deutsche Gramophon Archiv records in the mid-1970s. Includes portraits of important personages, paintings of important places, reproductions of manuscripts, and pictures of period musical instruments. Nearly all images are black-and-white. Some articles are better written than others; particularly of interest are those by Christoph Wolff. The 1977 Bärenreiter edition reviewed by Michael A. Keller in *Notes* 35, no. 4 (June 1979): 888.

Beethoven, Ludwig van

12.22   Bory, Robert. *Ludwig van Beethoven: His Life and Work in Pictures*. Translated by Winifred Glass and Hans Rosenwald. New York: Atlantis Books, 1960.
Bory was widely considered to be the greatest music iconographer of his generation. His volume on Liszt, *La vie de Franz Liszt par l'image* is considered a defining benchmark in the field of music iconography. His volumes on that composer, as well as ones on Wagner, Chopin, Mozart, and Beethoven were unparalleled until recently, with books by Ernst Burger and others. This particular iconography, Bory's last, was also published in French and German. Consists almost entirely of images, prefaced by an essay on the life of the composer. All images (over 600 of them) are black-and-white, but the variety and quality of the images selected are good. Bory's scholarship is strong, but the English translation of this volume is weak. Includes an index of names, places, and images and a works list. Reviewed by Donald W. MacArdle in *Notes* 20, no. 1 (Winter 1962–63): 64–65.

*12.23   Schmidt-Görg, Joseph, and Hans Schmidt, eds. *Ludwig van Beethoven*. Translated by the editorial department of the Deutsche Grammophon Gesellschaft. New York: Praeger, 1970.
An anthology of 14 iconographical essays, each on a different Beethoven-related subtopic by members of the staff of the Beethoven-Archiv in Bonn. Many essays are devoted to compositional genres or individual pieces, with the remaining ones being strictly biographical. Wide variety of images (over 250 total), including portraits of Beethoven and his contemporaries and manuscripts in Beethoven's hand. Features about 200 color reproductions. Contains an index of names and illustrations, a list of compositions, and a selected bibliography. A similar volume, also published for the bicentennial of Beethoven's birth, is H. C. Robbins Landon's *Beethoven: A Documentary Study* (New York: Macmillan, 1970). Reviewed by Alan Tyson in *Musical Times* 111, no. 1532 (Oct. 1970): 999–1001.

Brahms, Johannes

*12.24   Boeck, Dieter. *Johannes Brahms: Lebensbericht mit Bildern und Dokumenten*. Kassel, Ger.: Georg Wenderoth, 1998.
Rare example of a recent iconographical study of Brahms. Contains over 300 images arranged chronologically, about 50 in color. Includes portraits and photographs of the composer, his family, and his colleagues as well as samples of autograph manuscripts, concert posters, landscape paintings and photographs of important places in his life, and other images. Includes indexes. Reviewed by Martin Wulfhorst in *Das Orchester* 47, no. 9 (Sept. 1999): 74.

12.25 Miller zu Aichholz, Viktor von, and Max Kalbeck. *Ein Brahms-Bliderbuch.* Vienna: R. Lechner, 1905.

This picture book includes small black-and-white photos of Brahms, his family, his apartment, etc. Also contains reproductions of concert programs, musical manuscripts, and letters.

Chopin, Frédéric

*12.26 Burger, Ernst. *Frédéric Chopin: Eine Lebenschronik in Bildern und Dokumenten.* Munich: Hirmer, 1990.

Like Burger's iconographies of Liszt and Schumann, this book is arranged in chronological order, with accompanying lists of biographical events and compositional works from the relevant year. Scholarship is excellent. Images included vary from beautifully reproduced color portraits of Chopin and his contemporaries to facsimiles of manuscripts in the composer's hand. Also included are images (some of them recent photographs) of important places that Chopin lived or visited. Includes an index of sources, names, and compositional works. Reviewed by Jeffrey Kallberg in *Notes* 50, no. 3 (Mar. 1994): 963–64.

12.27 Kobylańska, Krystyna. *Chopin in His Own Land: Documents and Souvenirs.* Translated by Claire Grece-Dabrowska and Mary Filippi. Kraków: Polish Music Publications, 1955.

Older than Burger and focuses on Chopin's time in Poland. Images are excellently chosen for relevancy but are not reproduced as well as those in Burger. None are in color. Well indexed. Includes indexes of people whose portraits are included, illustrators and artists, and places. Includes a bibliography. See also Robert Bory's *La vie de Frédéric Chopin par l'image* (Paris: Horizons de France, 1951). Reviewed by Harald Heckmann in *Musica* 10, no. 12 (Dec. 1956): 882–83.

Debussy, Claude

12.28 Lesure, François. *Claude Debussy.* Iconographie Musicale, vol. 4. Geneva: Editions Minkoff, 1975.

This book, by a noted Debussy scholar, consists almost entirely of images, with little accompanying text. Laid out chronologically, with portraits and photographs of Debussy interspersed with images of his contemporaries, set designs from *Pelléas et Mélisande*, and other relevant period artwork. Contains around 165 images; only a handful are in color, and the reproduction quality is mediocre. Also includes a chronology, samples of Debussy's signature, a table of illustrations, and a short index. Reviewed by Richard L. Smith in *Music and Letters* 57, no. 2 (Apr. 1976): 189–90.

Handel, George Frederic

*12.29 Rackwitz, Werner. *Il Caro Sassone: Georg Friedrich Händel, Lebensbeschreibung in Bildern.* Wiesbaden, Ger.: Breitkopf and Härtel, 1986.

Includes portraits of the composer and his contemporaries, numerous maps and landscape paintings, and reproductions of manuscripts in the composer's hand

and other period documents. Over 50 images are in color. Little accompanying text by the author, apart from the biographical introduction. Includes a bibliography and an index of names. Reviewed by Renate Steiger in *Musik und Kirche* 57, no. 6 (Nov.–Dec. 1987): 301.

12.30 Rackwitz, Werner, and Helmut Steffens. *George Frideric Handel: A Biography in Pictures*. Leipzig, Ger.: VEB Edition, 1962.

All images are black-and-white, although most are very high quality. Includes images of the composer and important historical personages from Handel's time. Also includes reproductions of pages of manuscript in the composer's hand as well as numerous images of important places in the composer's life. Commentary and image selection are influenced by authors' political leanings, and the translation is poor. Includes a list of illustrations and a list of portraits of the composer. See also H. C. Robbins Landon's illustrated biography, *Handel and His World* (Boston: Little, Brown, 1984), which is also in English. Reviewed by Paul Henry Lang in *Notes* 22, no. 1 (Fall 1965): 723–25.

Haydn, Franz Joseph

*12.31 Landon, H. C. Robbins. *Haydn: A Documentary Study*. New York: Rizzoli, 1981. Includes over 200 images, with more than 40 in color. Images cover diverse aspects of the composer's life, including paintings of members of the Esterházy family, autographs, and modern pictures of places that Haydn frequented. Contains a chronology and a short bibliography. Based on Landon's 5-volume set *Haydn: Chronicle and Works*. Lacks a good index of the images. Reviewed by A. Hyatt King in *Early Music* 10, no. 4 (Oct. 1982): 535–37 and Stanley Sadie in *Musical Times* 123, no. 1669 (Mar. 1982): 187.

12.32 Somfai, László. *Joseph Haydn: His Life in Contemporary Pictures*. Translated by Mari Kuttna and Károly Ravasz. New York: Taplinger, 1969.

Contains nearly 400 images, including portraits, landscapes, excerpts of musical manuscripts, concert playbills, early publications of Haydn's music, correspondence, and even architectural plans for Haydn's house. Unlike the Landon, contains no color plates. Images are not annotated, but sections are instead accompanied by written text that places the many personages and locations in an appropriate historical context. Reviewed by J. A. Westrup in *Music and Letters* 51, no. 3 (July 1970): 295–96.

Liszt, Franz

12.33 Bory, Robert. *La vie de Franz Liszt par l'image*. Paris: Éditions des Horizons, 1936.

Classic, well-organized, remarkably detailed iconography. All images are black-and-white. Contains numerous portraits of the composer at all stages of his life as well as portraits of his friends, colleagues, and important contemporaries. Also contains reproductions of pages from manuscripts in the composer's hand, his letters, and paintings and photographs of important places the composer visited and lived. Contains an index of names, illustrations arranged by artistic medium, places, and documents/materials. Reviewed by Thérèse Marix in *Revue de musicologie* 20, no. 60 (Nov. 1936): 194–95.

*12.34 Burger, Ernst. *Franz Liszt: A Chronicle of His Life in Pictures and Documents.* Translated by Stewart Spencer. Princeton, NJ: Princeton University Press, 1989. Whereas Burger's most recent Liszt iconography focuses solely on photographs of Liszt, this volume has a greater quantity (around 650) and variety of images, including portraits, reproductions of letters, and photographs. Images (some in color) are laid out in roughly chronological order and are accompanied by a chronology of events in the composer's life. Quality of scholarship and images is excellent. Includes an index of names and an index of compositions. Reviewed by Michale Saffle in *Notes* 47, no. 4 (June 1991): 1133–35 and Derek Watson in *Music and Letters* 72, no. 1 (Feb. 1991): 126–29.

12.35 ———. *Franz Liszt in der Photographie seiner Zeit: 260 Portraits, 1843–1886.* Munich: Hirmer, 2003. An excellent example of contemporary iconographical study. Contains 260 daguerreotypes and other types of early photographic images of Liszt spanning the last 43 years of his life. Nearly all images are accompanied by annotations that include the approximate date of the image and the photographer (when available). For the years for which there are portraits, Burger provides a brief synopsis of the important events of Liszt's life. Reviewed by David B. Cannata in *Journal of the American Liszt Society* 52–53 (Fall 2002–Spring 2003): 139–54.

Mozart, Wolfgang Amadeus

12.36 Bory, Robert. *The Life and Works of Wolfgang Amadeus Mozart in Pictures.* Geneva, Switzerland: Éditions contemporaines, 1948. Divided into a dated biographical section and a section containing plates. Contains a variety of images, including portraits of the composer and his contemporaries, landscape paintings and photographs of important places in the composer's life, reproductions of manuscripts, and period images depicting scenes from Mozart's operas. All are black-and-white; quality of some is weaker than in Bory's other iconographies. Includes an index of names, illustrations arranged by artistic medium, places, subjects, and compositions.

*12.37 Deutsch, Otto Erich, and Maximilian Zenger. *Mozart and His World in Contemporary Picutres.* Neue Ausgabe sämtlicher Werke. Series 10. Supplement. Werkgruppe, 32. Kassel, Ger.: Bärenreiter, 1961. Divided into several sections, including one containing all of the historical portraits of the composer, one devoted to the people and places of Mozart's life, and one dedicated to Mozart relics. Almost all images are black-and-white and are printed clearly on heavy paper. Images are numbered and annotated—in German and English—in a commentary section near the back of the book. Contains a comprehensive index and a list of the works by Mozart that are referenced in the book. Reviewed by Karl Geiringer in *Notes* 19, no. 3 (June 1962): 432–34.

Palestrina, Giovanni Pierluigi da

12.38 Bianchi, Lino, and Giancarlo Rostirolla. *Iconografia palestriniana: Giovanni Pierluigi da Palestrina, immagini e documenti del suo tempo.* L'arte armonica, Serie 4. Iconografia e cataloghi, 1. Lucca, It.: Libreria Musicale Italiana, 1994.
Beautiful book containing about 500 well-documented images, arranged chronologically. Includes portraits of the composer and of contemporary figures in the Catholic Church, reproductions of covers and pages of part books of Palestrina's compositions, letters in the composer's hand, historical maps, and important period artwork. Mainly black-and-white, but some color images. Contains an index of names and artists. Reviewed by Noel O'Regan in *Music and Letters* 77, no. 3 (Aug. 1996): 455–56 and Richard Sherr in *Notes* 53, no. 1 (Sept. 1996): 66–67.

Schoenberg, Arnold

12.39 Nono-Schoenberg, Nuria. *Arnold Schönberg 1874–1951: Lebensgeschichte in Begegnungen.* Klagenfurt, Aus.: Ritter Klagenfurt, 1992.
Extensive coverage, compiled by the composer's daughter. Contains over 1,400 images, including numerous photographs of the composer and other important personages, reproductions of pages from scores and manuscripts, reprints of letters, and examples of Schoenberg's own art. Most images are small and black-and-white. Contains chronologies, one appearing before each section. Index of names. Reviewed by Peter Gradenwitz in *Musica* 47, no. 5 (Sept.–Oct. 1993): 303–4.

Schubert, Franz

12.40 Deutsch, Otto Erich. *Franz Schubert: Die Dokumente seines Lebens und Schaffens.* Vol. 3, Sein Leben in Bildern. Munich: G. Müller, 1913.
Pioneering Schubert iconography consisting entirely of images (over 600) with captions. All are small and black-and-white. Includes primarily portraits (most are not Schubert) but also other art and documents. Still useful, although dated and not widely held. Includes index.

*12.41 Hilmar, Ernst. *Schubert.* Graz, Aus.: Akademische Druck- u. Verlagsanstalt, 1989.
Most of the 350 images are black-and-white, but about 50 are color. Includes portraits of Schubert and his contemporaries as well as images of places and reproductions of manuscripts, correspondence, and period sheet music covers. Some of the captions and attributions have errors. Includes an index. See also Joseph Wechsberg's illustrated biography *Schubert: His Life, His Work, His Time.* (New York: Rizzoli, 1977). Reviewed by Ewan West in *Journal of Musicological Research* 12, nos. 1–2 (1992): 132–34.

Schumann, Robert

12.42 Burger, Ernst, Gerd Nauhaus, and the Robert Schumann House. *Robert Schumann: Eine Lebenschronik in Bildern und Dokumenten.* Mainz, Ger.:

Schott, 1999. Also published as *Eine Lebenschronik in Bildern und Dokumenten.* Neue Ausgabe sämtlicher Werke. Series 8. Supplement, Band 1. Mainz, Ger.: Schott, 1999.

Organized chronologically and much like Burger's earlier iconography of Liszt. Includes over 600 beautifully reproduced color and black-and-white images of Schumann and his contemporaries, landscape paintings illustrating relevant locations in the composer's life, as well as facsimiles of excerpts from Schumann's compositions, and pages from *Neue Zeitschrift für Musik.* Includes a source bibliography, and an index of names and compositions. Reviewed by David B. Cannata in *Journal of the American Liszt Society* 52–53 (Fall 2002– Spring 2003): 139–54 and Claudia Macdonald in *Notes* 56, no. 2 (Dec. 1999): 409–411.

Stravinsky, Igor

12.43 Craft, Robert. *A Stravinsky Scrapbook: 1940–1971.* Illustrations chosen by Patricia Schwark. New York: Thames and Hudson, 1983.

Primarily a picture book, but contains a small amount of accompanying text. Most images have some sort of caption. Nearly all images are black-and-white. Includes Stravinsky's complete medical diaries. No index. Robert Craft was involved in compiling several Stravinsky iconographies, including *Stravinsky in Pictures and Documents* (New York: Simon and Schuster, 1978). Reviewed by James Keolker in *Opera Quarterly* 2, no. 4 (Winter 1984–85): 171–73.

Verdi, Giuseppe

12.44 Weaver, William. *Verdi: A Documentary Study.* London: Thames and Hudson, 1977.

Divided into a section containing images and a section containing documents. Some color plates, but most of the approximately 320 images are black-and-white. Images include portraits, set designs, facsimiles of manuscripts, and other important documents. All images are numbered and have captions. Contains an index of names and works. Reviewed by Julian Budden in *Musical Times* 119, no. 1619 (Jan. 1978): 39–41.

Wagner, Richard

12.45 Barth, Herbert, Dietrich Mack, and Egon Voss. *Wagner: A Documentary Study.* New York: Oxford University Press, 1975.

About half the images are in color. Includes portraits of Wagner, his friends, and contemporaries, illustrations of set designs from early staging of Wagner's operas, excerpts from scores, and reproductions of advertisements for performances. More text than images. Also includes a brief chronology and a short index. Reviewed by Robert Anderson in *Musical Times* 117, no. 1596 (Feb. 1976): 133–34.

*12.46 Bory, Robert. *La vie et l'oeuvre de Richard Wagner par l'image*. Geneva, Switzerland: Éditions A. Jullien, 1938.

Includes paintings and photographs of the composer and contemporaries as well as images of opera singers dressed for their famous roles in Wagner's operas and a whole section of Wagner caricatures. All images are black-and-white. Includes an index of names, illustrations arranged by artistic medium, places, and materials/documents.

EVALUATION CHECKLIST

- What kind of iconography is it? What purpose does this book serve?
  - Illustrated history?
  - Illustrated chronology?
  - Illustrated biography?
  - Documentary biography?
  - Iconographical study?
  - Iconography of instruments?
- What kinds of images does it include?
  - Paintings (oil, watercolor, etc.) ?
  - Photographs (kaleotype, daguerreotype, film photography, digital)?
  - Reproductions of playbills and concert programs?
  - Manuscripts or early editions (in facsimile)?
  - Stage design schematics?
  - Sheet music reproductions?
  - Handwriting/autograph samples?
  - Other mediums (statues, medallions, etc.)?
- What are the qualifications of the author or iconographer?
  - Is the author qualified with training in art history, or did he or she work with someone with a background or training in art history?
  - Is the study methodologically sound? For example, is the approach suit able to the material that is covered?
  - Did it consider the artist's intent? Did it consider the intent of the subject if it was a commissioned portrait? Did it look at many examples of art?
- What is the quality of the reproductions?
  - Is information on the original included (medium, dimensions, date, artist)?
  - Are the sources of images indicated (location)?
  - Have images been altered?
  - Are images copies of photos or copies of originals?

- Are images in black-and-white or color?
- How many images are included?
- How large are the images?
- Is the indexing adequate?
- Are images available for reproduction and use (licensing)?
- Who is the intended audience (scholarly or general)?
- What is the quality of the text?
  - What is the level of scholarship?
  - What language is it in? Is it a translation or does it appears in the original language?

SUGGESTED READINGS

The following suggested readings are, with the exception of the reviews, written by iconographers. They cover different types of iconographical studies as well as methodology. The *New Grove* article by Tilman Seebass provides an overview of the field's themes and sources as well as an extensive bibliography. Another recent article is Antonio Baldassarre's discussion about iconography methodology and theory, which points out continuing disagreements and challenges and is presented as a framework for those discussions. The other selection by Seebass discusses uses of iconography in ethnomusicology. H. Colin Slim's reading, though an introduction to his book of essays on musical inscriptions (musical scores in paintings), describes the relationship between art historians and musicologists in iconographical studies along with the potential benefits for both disciplines. Potential problems and misinterpretations in musical iconography are described by Emanuel Winternitz and Barbara Renton. Howard Mayer Brown and Joan Lascelle provide a good history of iconographical work in music focusing on organology using art from the Middle Ages and Renaissance. This reading is the first chapter in their important book on cataloging musical art. Eileen Southern discusses the goals and methodology used by her and Josephine Wright in their study of music in African American culture. Finally, the reviews by David B. Cannata and Alan Tyson point out special evaluation criteria for composer iconographies as well as their value in musicology.

Baldassarre, Antonio. "Reflections on Methods and Methodology in Music Iconography." *Music in Art* 25, no. 1–2 (Spring–Fall 2000): 33–38.

Brown, Howard Mayer, and Joan Lascelle. "What Can Works of Art Teach Us about Music?" Chap. 1 in *Musical Iconography: A Manual for Cataloguing Musical Subjects in Western Art before 1800*. Cambridge, MA: Harvard University Press, 1972.

Cannata, David B. "Review: *Franz Liszt in der Photographie seiner Zeit: 260 Portraits 1843–1886* [and] *Robert Schumann, Eine Lebenschronik in Bildern und Dokumenten.*" *Journal of the American Liszt Society* 52–53 (Fall 2002–Spring 2003): 139–54.

Renton, Barbara H. "Musical Iconography '...Worth a Thousand Words?'" *College Music Symposium* 19, no. 1 (Spring 1979): 247–51.

Sadie, Stanley, ed. *The New Grove Dictionary of Music and Musicians.* 2nd ed. New York: Grove, 2001. S.v. "Iconography," by Tilman Seebass. Also available from *Grove Music Online.* http://www.oxfordmusiconline.com.

Seebass, Tilman. "Iconography." In *Ethnomusicology: An Introduction*, edited by Helen Myers, 238–43. New York: W. W. Norton, 1992.

Slim, H. Colin. "Introduction: Some Thoughts on Musical Inscriptions." Chap. 1 in *Painting Music in the Sixteenth Century: Essays in Iconography.* Aldershot, UK: Ashgate, 2002.

Southern, Eileen. *Introduction to Images: Iconography of Music in African-American Culture, 1770s–1920s*, by Eileen Southern and Josephine Wright. Music in African-American Culture. New York: Garland, 2000.

Tyson, Alan. "Book Reviews: Pictorial Beethoven." *Musical Times* 111, no. 1532 (Oct. 1970): 999–1001.

Winternitz, Emanuel. "The Iconology of Music: Potentials and Pitfalls." In *Perspectives in Musicology*, edited by Barry S. Brook, Edward O. D. Downes, and Sherman Van Solkema, 80–90. New York: W. W. Norton, 1972.

CHAPTER 13

Music Directories

Directories are useful for getting information about a wide variety of musical topics. Some will give you information about performance opportunities or competitions. Directories to schools of music and conservatories can help you when looking for a place to study music or help you locate particular music faculty. Others will provide basic information about music libraries and collections. Information about various segments of the music business is included in others, for example, musical instruments, equipment, publishers, and record labels. Because directories are judged on their ease of use for quick reference, they are relatively easy research tools to use—similar to a phone book in many cases.

The common denominator is the inclusion of contact information, such as name, address, phone, e-mail, and website. For this reason, currency is important. Many directories are compiled from responses to questionnaires or surveys. As a result, the accuracy and scope of information may be inconsistent from entry to entry in some cases.

While there are a wide variety of directories for music, directories are not available in all of the categories included in other chapters of this text. For instance, no directory is currently available specifically devoted to black musicians. The examples included here were selected on the basis of their usefulness for music research and study as well as their currency.

Some research tools from other chapters are also useful for finding contact information, especially some listed in Chapters 3 and 4. The *International Who's Who in Classical Music* (entry 3.2) and *International Who's Who in Popular Music* (entry 3.41) include contact information for the living musicians included and are based on questionnaire responses. The union catalogs listed in Chapter 4, for example, *WorldCat* (entry 4.12), as well as some of the bibliographies in Chapter 10 (*British Union-Catalogue of Early Music* (entry 10.32), are similar to titles like *Resources of American Music History*, which include holding libraries for research materials.

Additional sources of contact information for individuals include association membership directories, which are typically issued annually. The *Directory* of the American Musicological Society is a good place to find U.S. musicologists, for instance. Sometimes journals publish directories as supplements. *Chamber Music* magazine includes a directory of summer chamber music festivals, schools, and workshops each year in the April issue.

Very specialized directories are omitted here, as are those intended for use by travelers or concertgoers. One fine example of a specialized directory is the *Film Composers Directory* (Los Angeles: Lone Eagle, 2000–). Examples of guides intended for the musician traveler include Lewis and Susan Foreman's *London: A Musical Gazetteer* (New Haven, CT: Yale University Press, 2005) and Steve Cheseborough's *Blues Traveling: The Holy Sites of Delta Blues* (Jackson: University Press of Mississippi, 2001). A directory for the concertgoer, including programming and venue information, is *Music & Opera Around the World* (Paris: Editions le fil d'Ariane, 1996–). Also excluded are those intended for the job seeker and those useful primarily to music librarians. For example, *Career Guide for Singers* (Washington, DC: Opera America, 1992–) and *Music Publishers' International ISMN Directory* (Munich: K. G. Saur, 1996–), respectively.

These and other directories can be found by using the appropriate LC subject headings and browsing the associated LC call number range, ML12–21. The subdivision "Directories" is used with other subject headings. Examples include "Music—Directories," "Music libraries—Directories," "Music—Instruction and study—Directories," and "Music—Great Britain—Directories." International directories are given the call number ML12; U.S. directories are in the range ML13–20; and ML21 is used for other individual regions or countries.

DIRECTORIES OF MUSIC LIBRARIES AND COLLECTIONS

International Music Library Directories

RISM Series C

13.1 Benton, Rita, and Elizabeth A. Davis. *Directory of Music Research Libraries.* RISM, C. Kassel, Ger.: Bärenreiter, 1967–.
   RISM C is the third printed series of RISM included here. The usefulness of the directories vary with their currency. Some volumes have had a second edition prepared. Supplements to some have also appeared as periodical articles. Arranged geographically with introduction for each country. Includes information on holdings, hours, services, etc. useful for researchers. See also the guides to libraries' online catalogs discussed in Chapter 4.

13.2 Kahn, Marian, Helmut Kallmann, and Charles Lindahl. *Directory of Music Research Libraries.* Volume 1: *Canada and the United States.* 2nd rev. ed. RISM, C/I. Kassel, Ger.: Bärenreiter, 1983.
   Reviewed by Geraldine Ostrove in *Fontes artis musicae* 31, no. 2 (Apr.–June 1984): 134–35.

13.3 Davis, Elizabeth A. *Directory of Music Research Libraries.* Volume 2: *Sixteen European Countries.* 2nd rev. ed. RISM, C/II. Kassel, Ger.: Bärenreiter, 2001.

Includes Austria, Belgium, Switzerland, Germany, Denmark, and Spain. First edition reviewed by Vincent Duckles in *Journal of Research in Music Education* 20, no. 2 (Summer 1972): 293–94 and Eugene K. Wolf in *JAMS* 29, no. 3 (Fall 1976): 484–86.

13.4 ———. *Directory of Music Research Libraries*. Volume 3: *Sixteen European Countries*. 2nd rev. ed. RISM, C/III/1. Kassel, Ger.: Bärenreiter, 2001.

Includes France, Finland, Great Britain, Ireland, Luxembourg, Norway, Netherlands, Portugal, and Sweden. C/III/2, which is in preparation, will include Italy. First edition reviewed by Eugene K. Wolf in *JAMS* 29, no. 3 (Fall 1976): 484–86.

13.5 Hill, Cecil, Katya Manor, James Siddons, and Dorothy Freed. *Directory of Music Research Libraries*. Volume 4: *Australia, Israel, Japan, and New Zealand*. RISM, C/IV. Kassel, Ger.: Bärenreiter, 1979.

Reviewed by Harold J. Diamond in *Notes* 36, no. 3 (1980): 660–61.

13.6 Pruett, Lilian, and James B. Moldovan. *Directory of Music Research Libraries*. Volume 5: *Czechoslovakia, Hungary, Poland, and Yugoslavia*. RISM, C/V. Kassel, Ger.: Bärenreiter, 1985.

Reviewed by FWD in *Musikhandel* 37, no. 8 (1986): 398.

United States Music Library Directories

13.7 Krummel, D. W., Jean Geil, Doris J. Dyen, and Deane L. Root. *Resources of American Music History: A Directory of Source Materials from Colonial Times to World War II. Music in American Life*. Urbana-Champaign: University of Illinois Press, 1981.

Geographically arranged directory of Americana in many formats in library collections (primarily in the U.S.). Known as *RAMH*. Result of a project funded by the National Endowment for the Humanities. Entries compiled primarily from survey responses. Arrangement is alphabetical by state, then city, and finally institution name. Includes index. Updated in part by more recent works, for example, Henry Bloch's *Directory of Conductors' Archives in American Institutions* (Lanham, MD: Scarecrow, 2006) and Tina M. Schneider's *Hymnal Collections of North America* (Lanham, MD: Scarecrow, 2003). A new edition is being planned. Reviewed by Charles Hamm in *American Music* 3, no. 2 (Summer 1985): 232–35.

British Music Library Directories

13.8 Penney, Barbara. *Music in British Libraries: A Directory of Resources*, 4th ed. London: Library Association Publishing, 1992.

Includes around 350 entries arranged alphabetically. Information was compiled from questionnaires and is somewhat inconsistent. Has limited information about special collection holdings. Includes appendixes and indexes. Reviewed by Lenore Coral in *Fontes artis musicae* 40, no. 2 (Apr.–June 1993): 166.

Canadian Music Library Directories

13.9 Ohlers, Carol. *Directory of Music Collections in Canada*. York, ON: Canadian Association of Music Libraries, Archives and Documentation Centres, 2001–. http://www.yorku.ca/caml/dmcc/dmcc.asp.

Free online directory includes information on about 70 library collections. Based on survey responses. Updates are irregular. Searchable by province, type of library, and institution name. Entries include address, contact information, collection description, and services. Originally published in print in 2000 in both English and French. See also the general, subscription-based *Directory of Libraries in Canada* database, available from ProQuest.

MUSIC EDUCATION DIRECTORIES

*13.10 Bartle, Graham. *International Directory of Music and Music Education Institutions.* Rev. 3rd ed. Nedlands, Australia: Callaway International Resource Centre for Music and Education (CIRCME), 2000.
Published irregularly with the subtitle "Details of Higher Music and Music Education Qualifications at 3,331 Institutions in 157 Countries." Arranged alphabetically by country and city. Entries include name, address, phone number, e-mail address, website, description, and degrees offered. There are two indexes: one for less common degrees offered and one for institution names. Nancy Uscher's older title, *The Schirmer Guide to Schools of Music and Conservatories throughout the World* (New York: Schirmer Books, 1988), includes similar information. Reviewed by Martin D. Jenkins in *Fontes artis musicae* 44, no. 3 (July–Sept. 1997): 292.

*13.11 College Music Society. *Directory of Music Faculties in Colleges and Universities, U.S. and Canada.* Missoula, MT: College Music Society, 1967–. *Directory of Music Faculties.* Missoula, MT: College Music Society, 1998–. http://www.music.org/cgi-bin/showpage.pl?tmpl=/infoserv/facdir/facdirhome&h=63.
Annual publication currently listing over 30,000 faculty at over 1,800 schools of music. Arranged geographically by state, but Canadian provinces are listed first. Entries include institution name, address, phone, website, e-mail address, type of school, administration, and faculty. Information about the faculty includes rank, highest degree, and area of specialization. Includes four indexes: faculty by area, faculty alphabetically, graduate degrees offered, and an alphabetical list of institutions. Online database has some information available free of charge (school name, phone, e-mail, and website). Remaining information is only available to personal members of the CMS. Online version is updated annually. See the College Music Society homepage in Figure 13-1. Reviewed by Rey M. Longyear in *Journal of Research in Music Education* 16 (1968): 220–21.

13.12 National Association of Schools of Music (NASM). *Directory.* Reston, VA: NASM, 1967–. Searchable NASM Directory Information. Reston, VA: NASM, 2005–. http://nasm.arts-accredit.org.
Annual publication including schools accredited by NASM, currently over 600. Arranged alphabetically by institution name. Entries include school name, address, phone, website, description, chief administrator, and degrees. Online version is updated annually with new schools and weekly with changes to existing entries.

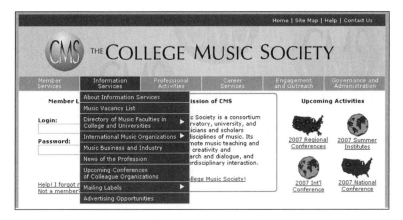

Figure 13-1 College Music Society Homepage *(Copyright © 2007 The College Music Society)*

PERFORMING ARTS DIRECTORIES

*13.13 *British and International Music Yearbook*. 2 vols. London: Rhinegold, 1999–.
Annual publication that includes over 18,000 entries. Similar to *Musical America*. Formerly titled *British Music Yearbook*. Primarily devoted to the United Kingdom. Includes publishers, instrument makers, record companies, libraries, museums, and organizations. Entries are arranged alphabetically and include contact information. Includes indexes. Earlier editions were in one volume, and some were available on CD-ROM. The 1990/91 ed. of the *British Music Yearbook* reviewed by Andrew Peggie in *British Journal of Music Education* 8, no. 2 (July 1991): 194–95.

*13.14 *International Music Directory*. 2 vols. Munich: K. G. Saur, 2005–.
Annual publication, formerly titled *European Music Directory*. Comparable to *Musical America*, *Purchaser's Guide* and Billboard's *International Buyer's Guide*. Over 35,000 entries, including name, address, phone, e-mail, web site, etc. First volume includes orchestras, competitions, festivals, libraries, museums, and so on. Second volume devoted to the music industry, recording companies, and music publishers. Especially good for Eastern Europe and South America. Arranged geographically. Includes indexes for names and institutions. Reviewed in *Choice* 42, no. 1 (Sept. 2004): 62.

*13.15 *Music Directory Canada*, 8th ed. St. Catharines, ON: Norris-Whitney Communications, 2001.
Irregular publication first published in 1983. Includes entries in 60 categories, arranged alphabetically by name. Similar to *Musical America*, but devoted entirely to Canada. Information includes name, contact, address, phone, e-mail, website, and description. Includes appendixes but no index. Reviewed by Janneka L. Guise in *CAML Review* 29, no. 2 (Aug. 2001): 43–44.

*13.16 *Musical America International Directory of the Performing Arts*. New York: Musical America, etc., 1898–. *MusicalAmerica.com: The Business Source* *for the Performing Arts.* East Windsor, NJ: Commonwealth Business Media, 1998–. http://www.musicalamerica.com.

Print version is annual; the recommended online version is updated daily (Industry News) and quarterly (Listings). Print version contains two listings sections: United States and Canada, and International. Each section is divided into categories such as: Orchestras, Opera Companies, Music Festivals, Music Schools, Contests, Music Publishers, Professional Organizations, and Music Critics. International section is more limited. Includes many artists management ads, with indexes listing individual artists. Online version is preferred and includes Industry News. Online version is subscription based, but free access to some information is available (Calendar of Events, Directory Articles, etc.). See the Advanced Site Search screen in Figure 13-2. Reviewed by Bonnie Houser in *Notes* 63, no. 2 (Dec. 2006): 398-400.

Figure 13-2 *MusicalAmerica.com* Advanced Site Search Screen (*Courtesy of Musical America Worldwide*)

13.17 *Performing Arts Yearbook for Europe (PAYE): The Definitive and Indispensable Directory.* London: Alain Charles Arts, 1991–.

Similar to the *European Music Directory,* but with broader coverage of the arts. Includes radio, TV, drama, and other arts in addition to music. Does not include music schools or libraries, however. Arranged by categories and then geographically. Entries include name, address, phone, e-mail, website, etc. Also published on CD-ROM. See also the companion volume, *Music, Opera, Dance and Drama in Asia, the Pacific and North America (MOD)* (London:

Alain Charles Arts, 1996–.). Reviewed by Deidre Tilley in *Opera* 43, no. 7 (July 1992): 877.

MUSIC INDUSTRY AND MUSIC COMPANY DIRECTORIES

13.18 Billboard. *International Buyer's Guide*. New York: Billboard, 1959–. http://www.billboard.com/directories.

Annual publication, with over 13,000 entries, divided by type. Under each section (except International) listings are either alphabetical by company name or alphabetical by state, then by company name. International listings are arranged by country. Some sections are also broken down by broad commodity categories. Entries usually give complete information on address, website, e-mail address, phone number, and contact person. Online version is updated daily.

*13.19 Music Trades. *Purchaser's Guide to the Music Industries*. Englewood, NJ: Music Trades, 1897–.

An annual "who makes it" and "where to buy it" guide for all sorts of musical items, from autoharps to Zildjian cymbals. Includes over 5,000 entries. Mostly U.S. and Canadian companies, but a section at the back gives a selected list of foreign manufacturers and dealers. Gives names, address, website, e-mail address, telephone number, and, in many cases, the company president or sales manager. Published as a supplement to *Music Trades* magazine.

MUSIC ORGANIZATIONS AND MUSIC COMPETITIONS DIRECTORIES

13.20 College Music Society. *International Directory of Music Organizations*. Missoula, MT: College Music Society, 1995–2001. *International Music Organizations*. Missoula, MT: College Music Society, 2002–. http://www.music.org/cgi-bin/showpage.pl?tmpl=/infoserv/imo/imohome&h=62.

Includes contact information for the business offices of over 360 organizations, including mailing address, phone number, e-mail address, and website free of charge. Additional information for members includes business hours, purpose of the group, officers, publications, committees, conferences, etc. Searchable by organization name, city, state/province, country, and area code. Updated annually.

13.21 Concert Artists Guild. *Guide to Competitions*. New York: Concert Artists Guild, 1996–. Also available online at http://www.concertartists.org.

Annual publication. Arranged in two sections, U.S. and foreign, then arranged alphabetically by competition name. Has over 500 entries, including category, entry requirements, and contact information. Index arranged by type of competition (piano, string quartet, composition, etc.) The 8th ed. (1994) reviewed by Jean Morrow in *Notes* 52, no. 2 (Dec. 1995): 450–51.

EVALUATION CHECKLIST

- What is the format (print or online)?
- Is the directory current or frequently updated?
- Is it logically arranged or browsable?
- Is it well indexed? Is the database easily searchable?
- Is the content unique?
- What is the directory's scope or purpose?
- Is subscription, membership, or registration required?
- If subscription based, is some information available free?

SUGGESTED READING

Krummel's article, like his Introduction to *Resources of American Music History*, relates some of the interesting experiences concerning the creation of this directory.

Krummel, D. W. "Little *RAMH*, Who Made Thee?: Observations on an American Music Census." *Notes* 37, no. 2 (Dec. 1980): 227–38.

CHAPTER 14

Internet Resources for Music

Perhaps the two greatest advantages of web-based research tools are their increased search capability and greater availability. Searching the full text of *Grove Music Online* (*GMO*) (entry 2.2) far surpasses use of the print *New Grove* index. Electronic resources are available around the clock and from multiple locations. Additionally, web-based research tools can be updated more easily and frequently than other publications. *GMO* is a good example; articles can be updated much more frequently than the entire encyclopedia can be revised.

Internet resources have been included throughout this textbook as appropriate. For example, *GMO* is included in Chapter 2 with print encyclopedias of music. Internet research tools are sometimes an electronic version of a print resource, like *GMO*. Others, for instance, *International Index to Music Periodicals* (entry 5.1), were born electronic. While these two are fee based and are paid for through subscriptions, others, like the *Encyclopedia of Music in Canada* (entry 2.3), are free.

Topics covered especially well on the Internet include contemporary (especially living) composers, cutting-edge music technology, popular and rock music, and the music business. Many composers have websites with more information about their works than is available through print resources. Other frequent scholarly uses of the Internet by graduate music students include searching for online journals, texts, scores, audio, video, and images. Additionally, purchasing scores, recordings, equipment, and software online is common. Sites like *Amazon.com* have made print resources such as the *Schwann* catalogs of currently in-print recordings obsolete.

The Internet has also given rise to resources previously unavailable in other formats as well as those that are much easier to use in electronic format. There are also new types of publications, such as **web logs (blogs)**, that do not have a print equivalent. While scholarly blogs have been slow in taking off, some are available. David Byrne's blog (http://journal.davidbyrne.com) is one that might be useful for rock music studies. Podcasting is another example that is beginning to gain popularity in higher education.

Some of the most exciting websites available for researchers are those offering digital content. Websites that provide scanned scores or streamed audio are valuable for research, but they do not fit into any of the earlier chapters of this text. Rather, they are examples of the types of content most of the research tools in this book are intended to help you find. These websites and ways to find them are included here. Websites offering transcribed rather than scanned texts, for example, *Thesaurus musicarum latinarum* and its companions, are included at this text's companion website.

The negative aspect of the increased fluidity of the web for distributing information is its mercurial nature. For that reason a more comprehensive listing of websites, for instance, databases, in more specific topical categories (opera, theory, etc.) as well as the composers used as examples are provided at the companion website. Like the titles listed next, this textbook's companion website can be much more frequently updated than the published book. Lists of links in the categories included throughout are given at the companion website. These include those that do not fit in the chapters of the text but are useful in research. One example is Emily Ezust's *Lied and Art Song Texts Page*.

This chapter focuses on providing examples of high-quality, stable websites providing scholarly digital content as well tools useful for finding websites (search engines, music library subject directories, and professional association websites). The final category includes suggestions for staying current. Keep in mind that while critical evaluation is important with all types of materials, it is especially crucial with websites because much of the content available is unfiltered. See this chapter's Evaluation Checklist.

DIGITAL CONTENT WEBSITES

The focus of this chapter is on sites useful for academic purposes that are either free sites (typically music library sites) or commercial sites that are marketed primarily to libraries. Online music dealers geared primarily for individual use, such as *Schubertline* for scores and *Emusic* for audio, have been excluded. Sites marketed to individuals may be useful, but they are unlikely to be sponsored by your local library. While the focus here is on music-specific websites, keep in mind that general research tools with digital content, for example, *Early English Books Online* (*EEBO*), also include musical content. The following categories are provided: multimedia sites, musical scores, digital audio, and images. See the companion website for additional websites and updated information on those mentioned here. As in previous chapters asterisks indicate recommended titles.

Multimedia Websites

The websites listed here are all the products of major libraries (all but the New York Public Library are national libraries) with wide-ranging collections. While all are general or include digital content in many subject areas, they all have fine music collections that are well represented on their websites. The four listed include multiple types of digital content, for instance, scores, audio, video, and art images.

14.1   British Library. *Online Gallery.* http://www.bl.uk/onlinegallery/homepage.html.

Digital collections with musical content include: Turning the Pages: Leaf through 15 Great Books and Magnify the Details (including Mozart's diary); Musical Manuscripts (including sketches for Beethoven's sixth symphony); Images Online (including sheet music covers and composer portraits); and Archival Sound Recordings (including wax cylinders). Digitized audio is only available within the UK. Reviewed in the *Scout Report* (Nov. 27, 2002), http://scout.wisc. edu/Archives/SPT--FullRecord.php?ResourceId=11381.

14.2 Library and Archives Canada. *Digital Collections*. http://www.collectionscanada. ca/music/index-e.html#h.

See especially *Sheet Music from Canada's Past*, which includes audio as well, and the *Virtual Gramophone: Canadian Historical Sound Recordings*. See also the Virtual Exhibits, including Glenn Gould and Oscar Peterson. *Sheet Music from Canada's Past* reviewed in *Scout Report* (May 29, 2001), http://scout. wisc.edu/Archives/SPT--FullRecord.php?ResourceId=8213. *Virtual Gramophone* reviewed in the *Scout Report* (Apr. 7, 2006), http://scout.wisc.edu/Archives/ SPT--FullRecord.php?ResourceId=24127.

*14.3 Library of Congress. *American Memory*. http://memory.loc.gov.

A major digital collection, with over 7.5 million objects, primarily from LC's collections in various formats. Over 30 collections in music and the performing arts have been mounted. These include scanned scores (including sheet music), digital audio (including folk recordings), photographs (for example, jazz musicians), video (vaudeville performances), images of instruments (Dayton Miller Flute Collection), and archival collections (including Leonard Bernstein and Aaron Copland). See Figure 14-1 for the Performing Arts, Music homepage. See also LC's companion websites, *The Library of Congress Presents . . . Music, Theater & Dance: A Performing Arts Digital Library* (previously titled *I Hear America Singing*) at

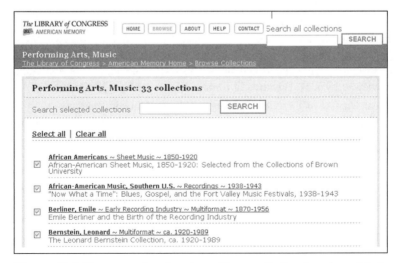

Figure 14-1 Homepage for *American Memory* Performing Arts, Music *(Courtesy of the Library of Congress, American Memory)*

http://www.loc.gov/rr/perform/ihas/index.html and *Prints & Photographs Online Catalog* at http://www.loc.gov/rr/print/catalog.html. *American Memory* reviewed by D. D. Siles in *Choice* 43, Special Issue Web 10 (Aug. 2006): 19 and Judy Tsou in *Notes* 57, no. 2 (Dec. 2000): 453–57. *Music, Theater & Dance* reviewed by M. Goldsmith in *Choice* 43, Special Issue Web 10 (Aug. 2006): 115–16.

14.4　New York Public Library. *NYPL Digital.* http://www.nypl.org/digital.
Smaller in size than LC's digital collection, but similar in format of digital content. Collections of musical interest include: Performing Arts in America, 1875–1923 (including scores and sheet music); Louis Armstrong Jazz Oral History Project (including audio); and NYPL Digital Gallery (including over half a million images from the NYPL collections). Digital Gallery collections of musical interest include "American Popular Song Sheet Covers, 1890–1922" and "Joseph Muller Collection of Music and Other Portraits." Performing Arts in America, 1875–1923 reviewed by A. Courtney in *Choice* 40, Special Issue Web 7 (Aug. 2003): 112. NYPL Digital Gallery reviewed by M. Nilsen in *Choice* 43, Special Issue Web 10 (Aug. 2006): 80.

Online Scores Websites

The sites listed here are all stable, free, digital score collections. With the exception of the *Choral Public Domain Library,* all are library sponsored. The *Sheet Music Consortium* is an example of a cooperative multi-library project. Additional library score digitization sites include those of the Sibley Music Library at the Eastman School of Music, the Loeb Music Library of Harvard College, and the Variations Project at Indiana University. Vendors also publish music score collections. Your library might provide musical scores via Ebrary's *Online Sheet Music*, Alexander Street Press's *Classical Scores Library*, or Sheet Music Now's bundle with *Naxos Music Library* (described later). For additional websites, see the companion website.

14.5　Ornes, Rafael. *Choral Public Domain Library.* http://www.cpdl.org.
Maintained by a church musician as part of *ChoralWiki*. Includes thousands of pieces of free choral music in a variety of formats submitted by hundreds of contributors. Searchable and browsable. Also includes texts and translations. Reviewed by J. M. Edwards in *Choice* 40, no. 1 (Sept. 2002): 108.

14.6　*Sheet Music Consortium.* http://digital.library.ucla.edu/sheetmusic.
Collaborative project that allows you to search multiple digital sheet music collections (over 120,000 titles) with a single search. Not all the titles have been digitized, and the quality varies from library to library. Participating libraries include the Library of Congress, Duke University, Indiana University, and Johns Hopkins University. Website and database are hosted by UCLA. Reviewed by Laurie J. Sampsel in *Notes* 63, no. 3 (Mar. 2007): 663–67.

14.7　University of Chicago Library. *Chopin Early Editions.* http://chopin.lib.uchicago.edu.
Scholarly site including over 400 digitized first and early Chopin editions. Searchable and browsable. Two sizes of images are available. Reviewed in *Scout Report* (July 6, 2005). http://scout.wisc.edu/Archives/SPT--FullRecord.php?ResourceId=23200.

14.8 University of North Texas Music Library. *The Jean-Baptiste Lully Collection.* http://www.unt.edu/lully.

Another scholarly site with a great deal of background information. Includes digitized versions of the collection's Lully opera manuscripts as well as first and early editions. Some audio files are also available. See also UNT's Virtual Rare Book Room, with full text of public domain scores from their music special collections. Reviewed in *Scout Report* (May 23, 2003). http://scout.wisc.edu/Archives/SPT--FullRecord.php?ResourceId=17539.

Digital Audio Streaming Services

The **streaming audio** services listed here are included because they either target the music library market (the Alexander Street Press and Naxos titles) or are becoming increasingly used by libraries (iTunes University for course reserves and podcasting). Audio services marketed primarily to individuals, such as Andante and Rhapsody, are included at the companion website. Napster and Cidigix's *Ctrax* are also listed at the website; they are sometimes subscribed to by universities primarily for students' recreational listening.

Naxos and Alexander Street Press are the leaders in this area. Both support educational uses, including the creation of playlists. Both vendors are exploring adding additional audio and textual content to their services. Alexander Street Press's *Music Conductor* product allows students to search multiple databases offered by the company. These services will continue to grow in size and usefulness.

14.9 Alexander Street Press. *African American Song.* http://www.alexanderstreet.com.

Includes about 17,500 tracks from various labels (including Document Records and Rounder Records) and over 2,300 performers, some previously unreleased. Styles include jazz, blues, gospel, ragtime, and folk. Liner notes are available as PDFs but are not searchable. Reviewed by Edward Komara in *Notes* 64, no. 1 (Sept. 2007): 117–21.

*14.10 ———. *Classical Music Library.* http://www.alexanderstreet.com.

Includes about 55,000 tracks of art music, ranging from the Middle Ages to the present from about 40 labels, including EMI Classics and Hyperion. Much smaller database than Naxos Music Library and offers a narrower repertory. Does not always include an entire label's catalog. Strongest in Baroque and twentieth-century music. Offers two streaming rates. No liner notes are included. Searching is cumbersome; browsing the works list feature is recommended. See the homepage in Figure 14-2. Links to *GMO* and Wilson's *Biography Reference Bank* are available for libraries who subscribe to both. Reviewed by Paul Cary in *Notes* 61, no. 4 (June 2005): 1057–59 and by Michael Duffy in *Choice* 43, Special Issue Web 10 (Aug. 2006): 114.

14.11 Apple. *iTunes.* http://www.apple.com/itunes.

Apple Computer's audio software and online store are extremely popular. Store includes over 3.5 million songs, including art music, available for purchase. Store is not especially extensive in classical music. The iTunes University is becoming popular as a way of distributing audio for class reserves. The iTunes

Figure 14-2 *Classical Music Library* Homepage *(Copyright © 2007, Alexander Street Press)*

Music Store reviewed by Gail Golderman and Bruce Connolly in *Library Journal netConnect* 131, supplement (Spring 2006): 24–34.

*14.12   Naxos. *Naxos Music Library.* http://www.naxosmusiclibrary.com.
Largest streaming service, with around 250,000 tracks (approximately 17,000 CDs) representing about 7,000 composers. Has the complete catalogs of Naxos and Marco Polo labels. Also has music from some independent labels, including Chandos. Styles include classical, jazz, blues, world, folk, and some rock and pop music. Offers three streaming rates, including one at CD quality. Playlists are not as easy to create as with the Alexander Street Press services. Some features do not work as well on Macs. Liner notes are available and are searchable. Offers a package providing digital scores from *Sheet Music Now.* Reviewed by Darwin F. Scott in *Notes* 62, no. 1 (Sept. 2005): 192–98 and by Michael Duffy in *Choice* 43, Special Issue Web 10 (Aug. 2006): 116.

14.13   Naxos. *Naxos Music Library Jazz.* http://www.naxosmusiclibrary.com/jazz.
A distinct collection from the *Naxos Music Library*, including around 20,000 tracks of jazz by approximately 500 musicians from about 2,300 albums. The labels include Naxos Jazz and Fantasy Jazz. Functionality is the same as the larger *Naxos Music Library.* Reviewed by Gail Golderman and Bruce Connolly in *Library Journal netConnect* 131, supplement (Winter 2006): 24.

14.14   New World Records. *Database of Recorded American Music (DRAM).* http://dram.nyu.edu.

A nonprofit audio service hosted by New York University. Provides about 2,000 CDs (over 18,000 tracks) on the New World Records label, CRI, Albany Records, and others specializing in American music. Includes recording liner notes. Not as technically sophisticated as the other streaming services listed here. Reviewed by D. E. Levinson in *Choice* 44, no. 6 (Feb. 2007): 952.

14.15 Smithsonian Folkways Recordings and Alexander Street Press. *Smithsonian Global Sound (SGS)*. http://www.smithsonianglobalsound.org or http://www.alexanderstreet.com.

Includes about 40,000 tracks of music, spoken word, and natural and man-made sound recordings, primarily from Folkways as well as a few other labels and archives. Especially strong in American folk and traditional music. Collection can be browsed, and there are both regular and advanced searches. The browse is recommended. Audio quality is not as high as for some of the other services listed here, but many of the originals are field recordings. Folkways liner notes can be viewed but not searched. Reviewed by Gail Golderman and Bruce Connolly in *Library Journal netConnect* 131, supplement (Spring 2006), 24–34, Martin D. Jenkins in *Choice* 43, Special Issue Web 10 (Aug. 2006): 116, and Alec McLane in *Notes* 62, no. 3 (Mar. 2006): 776–80.

14.16 University of California, Santa Barbara. *Cylinder Preservation and Digitization Project*. http://cylinders.library.ucsb.edu.

Digital collection of nearly 7,000 cylinder recordings that can be downloaded or streamed. Includes both musical and spoken word recordings. Includes scholarly information on history of cylinders, recording labels, and a bibliography. Reviewed by Jim Farrington in *Notes* 64, no. 1 (Sept. 2007): 121–23.

Image Websites

Images are useful for a variety of purposes. The most obvious is an iconographical study in music, such as those discussed in Chapter 12. Other uses include incorporating illustrations into your teaching, papers, and presentations.

In addition to the websites listed in this section, see those listed earlier that include images, for example, some of the LC *American Memory* collections, the NYPL *Digital Gallery*, and the British Library's *Images Online*. The most exciting online collection of musical images, the free online database of the Répertoire International d'Iconographie Musicale (RIdIM), discussed in Chapter 12, was not yet available at the time of writing. It will be posted at the companion website when it is live. See also the companion website for more musical instrument image sites, for instance, Yale University's Collection of Musical Instruments.

14.17 *ARTstor*. New York: ARTstor, 2004–. http://www.artstor.org.

A sister database to *JSTOR* (entry 5.42), also nonprofit and founded by the Andrew W. Mellon Foundation. Includes over half a million images intended for noncommercial education and scholarship purposes. Images are drawn from museums, libraries, archives, and personal collections. Includes browse as well as basic and advanced search options. You can zoom, pan, and compare images. They can also be saved in groups that may be accessed offline. Includes the previously separate *Art Museum Image Consortium* (*AMICO*). Reviewed by C. S. Dunham in *Choice* 43, Special Issue Web 10 (Aug. 2006): 88 and Ashley Pillow in *Charleston Advisor* 6, no. 4 (Apr. 2005): 38–40.

14.18 *Google Image Search: The Most Comprehensive Image Search on the Web.* http://images.google.com.
Claims to be the largest image database on the web, including billions of images. A great place to begin your search for visual material. Has an advanced search option. Reviewed in the *Scout Report* (June 29, 2001). http://scout.wisc.edu/Archives/SPT--FullRecord.php?ResourceId=8305.

14.19 Kuan, Christine. *Grove Art Online.* Oxford: Oxford University Press, 1998–. http://www.groveart.com.
Grove Art Online is a major scholarly encyclopedia for art, similar in several ways to *GMO*. It is listed here, however, because of the wealth of fine art images it includes. Both *Art Resource* (with over 250,000 images) and *Bridgeman Art Library* (with over 100,000 images) are included, along with links to over 40,000 museum- and gallery-hosted images as well as the illustrations in the articles themselves (over 3,000). Search interface is similar to that for *GMO* (entry 2.2). Reviewed by Mary Kate Boyd-Byrnes in *Charleston Advisor* 7, no. 3 (Jan. 2006): 25–27 and M. Nilsen in *Choice* 43, Special Issue Web 10 (Aug. 2006): 89.

14.20 The Metropolitan Museum of Art. http://www.metmuseum.org.
Digital collection of 6,500 images from the largest art museum in the U.S. Includes a nice collection of musical instruments. Collection can be browsed by subject or searched. You can create a group of images using the "My Met Gallery" feature. Reviewed by A. R. Stanton in *Choice* 43, Special Issue Web 10 (Aug. 2006): 89–90.

14.21 Museum of Fine Arts, Boston. http://www.mfa.org.
Website has over 300,000 images. Musical instrument collection (Francis W. Galpin) is distinguished by audio clips of some of the instruments being played. It includes European and non-Western instruments. The site has search, browse, and advanced search options. Also includes a "My Gallery" feature. Reviewed by J. A. Day in *Choice* 43, Special Issue Web 10 (Aug. 2006): 92.

14.22 Tate Gallery. *Tate Online.* http://www.tate.org.uk.
Online gallery of the national collection of British art. Includes information on each of the approximately 65,000 items in the collection; most include images. Can be browsed or searched. Includes an advanced search option as well as "My Selection" for saving images. Currently includes about 700 images with the subject music. Reviewed by W. B. Maynard in *Choice* 43, Special Issue Web 10 (Aug. 2006): 92–93.

FINDING MUSIC WEBSITES

Finding Internet resources of interest can be challenging. Even more difficult is finding "deep content," for example, specific sheet music titles included as part of a library's digital collection. Three common ways to find websites of interest include search engines, music subject directories, and professional association websites. In addition, articles and books of links can be helpful. One example is Elizabeth C. Axford's *Song Sheets to Software: A Guide to Print Music, Software, and Web Sites for Musicians*, 2nd ed. (Lanham, MD: Scarecrow, 2004).

Search Engines

Internet search engines are a popular and effective way to find websites of interest. Search engine software is improving all the time, and search engines are big business. Many times students and faculty adopt a favorite search engine, perhaps *Google*, and then always use it. While there is nothing wrong with having a favorite that you become familiar with and learn the advanced search options for and so on, it is often helpful to use more than one search engine if you do not find what you are looking for with your favorite. Search engines, like periodical indexes, vary in the scope and volume they index, and each has strengths and weaknesses. The following list includes the current leaders in search engines. A few popular metasearch engines, software that searches multiple search engines at a time, are also provided.

Despite improvements in relevance and usefulness rankings, search engines are software, and results are provided without a human evaluator. Additional ways of finding websites that do incorporate recommendations include music library subject directories of links and professional association websites that provide relevant lists of links. A few outstanding examples of each are listed here.

The four search engines listed here were (as of December 2006) considered the best by Greg R. Notess. Search engines, like periodical indexes, have less overlap than you might expect. If you do not find what you are looking for, try another search engine. Using the advanced search options available for each is recommended. Only *Google* has a link to its advanced search screen on its homepage. The others have advanced search options only after a search has been entered.

14.23 *Ask*. http://www.ask.com.
Used to be called *Ask Jeeves*. Good for finding metasites, but has a smaller database and limited advanced search capability. Reviewed by Greg R. Notess at *Search Engine Showdown* (Oct. 10, 2006). http://www.searchengineshowdown.com/features/ask/review.html.

*14.24 *Google*. http://www.google.com.
Extremely popular, in part because of the online applications available (mail, calendar, maps, etc.) and other search databases (especially *Google Image* and *Google Scholar*). Has the largest database and best advanced search of the engines listed here. Reviewed by Greg R. Notess at *Search Engine Showdown* (Oct. 10, 2006). http://www.searchengineshowdown.com/features/google/index.shtml.

14.25 *Live Search*. http://www.live.com.
The new *MSN Search* (Microsoft Network). Newest of those listed here. Has an image search. Least sophisticated advanced search of the four listed here. Reviewed by Greg R. Notess at *Search Engine Showdown* (Oct. 21, 2006). http://www.searchengineshowdown.com/features/live/review.html.

14.26   *Yahoo! Search.* http://www.yahoo.com/.
        Includes a search database and a directory. Has audio, image, and video
        searches as well. Advanced search options are not as good as those of *Google.*
        Yahoo! Directory (http://dir.yahoo.com/Entertainment/Music) is not academic,
        but it is popular. *Yahoo! Search* reviewed by Greg R. Notess at *Search Engine
        Showdown* (Oct. 10, 2006). http://www.searchengineshowdown.com/features/
        yahoo/review.html.

Metasearch Engines

Metasearch engines are also called *metacrawlers* and *multiple search engines.* Rather
than searching the Internet, they send your search to several different search engines so
that you can see the results from each.

14.27   *Clusty.* http://clusty.com/.
        Differs from other metasearch engines by grouping (clustering) results into sub-
        topics. Queries *Ask* and *MSN,* among others. Reviewed by Mick O'Leary in
        Information Today 23, no. 7 (July–Aug. 2006): 35, 39.

*14.28 *Dogpile: All the Best Search Engines Piled into One.* http://www.dogpile.com/.
        Often considered to be one of the best metasearch engines and the oldest of
        those listed here. *Dogpile* searches the top four: *Google, Yahoo!, MSN,* and *Ask,*
        among others. Has separate searches for images, audio, and video as well. See
        Figure 14-3 for the *Dogpile* homepage. Reviewed in *Voice of America* (Mar. 10,
        2006).   http://www.voanews.com/english/archive/2006-03/2006-03-10-voa65.
        cfm?CFID=66785982&CFTOKEN=32016907.

Figure 14-3 *Dogpile* Homepage (*Copyright © 2007 InfoSpace, Inc. All rights
reserved*)

14.29   *KartOO.* http://www.kartoo.com/.
        French metasearch engine; select English on the homepage. Unique presenta-
        tion of search results visually as "maps." Of the top four search engines, only
        MSN is included among the search engines queried.

Music Subject Directories

Many music libraries maintain lists of music website links useful for their students and faculty. These have the advantage that a librarian selects them for recommendation and sometimes annotates their lists of links. Some libraries catalog websites in their local online catalogs; others do not. Use your local library's guides to web resources as well as those listed here. Although the libraries listed next are academic music libraries, others also include music links. The Library of Congress, for example, maintains a list of Internet resources in the performing arts. See also the *Yahoo! Directory*, previously mentioned with *Yahoo! Search* as an example of a nonscholarly music directory.

14.30 Cook Music Library. Indiana University. *Worldwide Internet Music Resources.* http://www.music.indiana.edu/music_resources.

   Over 10 years old, Indiana's metasite is also one of the largest. This searchable site offers a wide range of web resources, including commercial and personal web pages. Emphasizes links useful for performers. Includes popular music. Reviewed by B. Cressman in *Choice* 40, Special Issue Web 7 (Aug. 2003): 94.

*14.31 Loeb Music Library. Harvard University. *Online Resources for Music Scholars.* http://www-hcl.harvard.edu/research/guides/music/resources/.

   Most useful for research. Includes about 600 art music links; some are annotated briefly. Updated regularly. Reviewed by B. J. Murray in *Choice* 43, Special Issue Web 10 (Aug. 2006): 115.

Professional Association Websites

Professional associations often provide lists of links useful for their members. The four listed here are good examples that represent the broad disciplines of musicology, ethnomusicology, theory, and music education. For additional society homepages, see this text's companion website.

14.32 American Musicological Society (AMS). *Web Sites of Interest to Musicologists.* http://www.ams-net.org/musicology_www.php.

14.33 National Association for Music Education (MENC). http://www.menc.org/.

14.34 Society for Ethnomusicology (SEM). *Link Categories.* http://webdb.iu.edu/sem/scripts/links/linkcategories.cfm.

14.35 Society for Music Theory (SMT). *Resources.* http://www.societymusictheory.org/index.php?pid=109.

WEBSITES FOR STAYING CURRENT

Keeping current with Internet resources is more challenging than keeping up with other formats, because the online landscape changes more rapidly than other formats of music materials. One great way to keep up with new content on websites is to use **Real Simple Syndication (RSS) feeds**; hopefully these will become more widely offered on scholarly music websites. For online resources offered by vendors, publishers, and organizations, see the relevant websites (RILM, *GMO*, RISM, etc.) for updates on content and functionality. Another way is to check reviews, for example, the "Digital Media

Reviews" column in *Notes* and the "Electronic Resources Column" in *Music Reference Services Quarterly*. For news, search tips, and reviews of search engines, see sites such as *Search Engine Showdown* and *Search Engine Watch*.

14.36 Internet Scout Project. *Scout Report*. http://scout.wisc.edu/Reports/ScoutReport/ Current/.

Hosted by the University of Wisconsin–Madison, the weekly online publication *Scout Report* (published since 1994) includes reviews of many Internet resources not reviewed elsewhere. Discussed by Danianne Mizzy in *College and Research Libraries News* 65, no. 2 (Feb. 2004): 84–85.

*14.37 Notess, Greg R. *Search Engine Showdown*. http://www.searchengineshowdown. com.

Site for searchers maintained by a librarian at Montana State University. Notess is also a musician. "Search Engine Statistics," "Search Engine Features Chart," and the reviews are especially useful. See also Notess's columns in *Online* and his book *Teaching Web Search Skills* (see Suggested Readings). Reviewed by the *Scout Report* (June 11, 1999). http://scout.wisc.edu/Archives/SPT--FullRecord. php?ResourceId=14618.

14.38 *Search Engine Watch*. http://www.searchenginewatch.com.

Intended primarily to help with search engine marketing, but includes information useful for searchers as well. Was edited by expert Danny Sullivan until he resigned in 2007. See especially the "Search 101," and "Ratings and Stats." Some content is free and some is fee-based. Web Search Tips section reviewed by the *Scout Report* (Nov. 21, 2003). http://scout.wisc.edu/Archives/ SPT--FullRecord.php?ResourceId=19223, and Search Engine Tips section reviewed by the *Scout Report* (June 18, 2004). http://scout.wisc.edu/Archives/ SPT--FullRecord.php?ResourceId=20776.[1]

EVALUATION CHECKLISTS

With Internet resources, verification of information is especially important. For more information and additional criteria for consideration, see Cornell University's website on Internet evaluation.[1]

• Is usability affected by pop-ups or advertising?
• Is the site computer intensive (graphics, audio, etc.)?
• How stable is the site (what type of domain)?
• Is the author's or publisher's identity and authority readily available?
• Is the author's or publisher's contact information provided?
• Does it work with all major browsers (Internet Explorer, Firefox, etc.)?

---

[1]Michael Engle, "Evaluating Web Sites: Criteria and Tools." Olin and Uris Libraries, Cornell University. http://www.library.cornell.edu/olinuris/ref/research/webeval.html (accessed 30 Mar. 2007).

- Is there a way to report problems and errors or to submit questions?
- Is support provided in an effective and timely manner?
- Who is the publisher? Is it a name you recognize?
- Is it scholarly (are sources cited or are links provided)?
- What is the site's purpose or bias (is the intent to sell you something)?
- Is the site a spoof or joke?
- Is the content factual or opinion/editorial?
- Is the website well designed and organized?
- How high is the quality of information or digital content (CD-quality audio, high-resolution images, PDFs of text, etc.)?
- Is it current (do the links work, is the content updated frequently)?
- Are the links provided to reliable and useful sites?
- Are the links evaluated or annotated?
- Is software required (is it available free or are relevant links provided)?
- Is the content free or subscription based?
- Is membership or registration required for full use?
  - Has it been evaluated?
  - Has it been reviewed?
  - Is it included in subject directories?
  - Is it linked to by reputable sites?

Digital Audio Streaming Services

- Who is the intended audience?
- What is the cost and pricing model?
- What is the quality of the original audio being digitized?
- How many tracks or works are included?
- Is the quality of audio sufficient (bandwidth or streaming rate)?
- Can you adjust the audio quality?
- How powerful is the search engine (can you search by instrumentation, opus number, title, etc.)?
- How useful are the browse options (by composer, genre, instrumentation, etc.)?
- Is the functionality of the player good (can you adjust volume, move within track, skip tracks, etc.)?
- Can you continue with other tasks while listening to audio?
- Are playlists easy to create?
- Is it compatibile with major operating systems and browsers?
- Are supplemental materials present or linked to (reference, scores, etc.)?
- Are "Help" screens or tutorials provided?

SUGGESTED READINGS

The following readings are sure to become dated quickly. See the companion website for more current readings. Cohen discusses using several different techniques for finding scholarly information, including RSS feeds and A9 book searching available from *Amazon.com*. Dunn et al. discuss the Variations2 Project at Indiana University's Cook Music Library, while Fineman describes the former DW3 web portal at Duke. Jenkins discusses some of the sites and software needed for downloading free scores. The book by Notess, while intended for web trainers, includes a chapter on terminology that will help those less familiar with the Internet. For keeping current, see the websites and columns listed earlier.

Cohen, Laura B. "Finding Scholarly Content on the Web: From Google Scholar to RSS Feeds." *Choice* 42, Special Issue Web 9 (Aug. 2005): 7–17.

Dunn, Jon W., Donald Byrd, Mark Notess, Jenn Riley, and Ryan Scherle. "Variations2: Retrieving and Using Music in an Academic Setting." *Communications of the ACM* 49, no. 8 (Aug. 2006): 53–58.

Fineman, Yale. "DW3 Classical Music Resources: Managing Mozart on the Web." *Portal: Libraries and the Academy* 1, no. 4 (Oct. 2001): 383–89.

Jenkins, Martin D. "Free (Mostly) Scores on the Web." *Notes* 59, no. 2 (Dec. 2002): 403–407. See update on Jenkins's website at http://www.wright.edu/~martin.jenkins/printmusic.html.

Notess, Greg R. "Terminology." Chap. 6 in *Teaching Web Search Skills: Techniques and Strategies of Top Trainers*. Medford, NJ: Information Today, 2006.

PART TWO

Writing, Style Manuals, and Citation

CHAPTER 15

Writing

In some ways writing is very much like musical performance. You can always improve your writing, regardless of how much "natural talent" you have. Also like performance, practice is essential to writing. In writing, the equivalent of practice is revision. Just as performers need a coach, writers need an editor. An important step toward becoming a better writer is reading good writing. Most of you have performers you admire, but do you have writers you emulate? This chapter is intended to introduce tools helpful for beginning the journey toward better writing.

Other books with sections on writing are covered in Chapters 1 and 16 of this textbook. There is a great deal of overlap among the books listed next as well as between those listed here and in Chapter 16. Books covering both general and music-specific writing style in terms of rhetoric, grammar, spelling, punctuation, and usage are listed here. Those focusing on documentation (i.e., citation) style are listed in Chapter 16. Some of the following writing books include guides to the various citation styles. For that reason, a brief overview of documentation styles is needed here.

The leading style manual for music is the *Chicago Manual of Style* (Chicago). *A Manual for Writers of Term Papers, Theses, and Dissertations* (Turabian) is a concise version of Chicago for students. Two additional style manuals used in some music publications are the *Publication Manual of the American Psychological Association* (APA) and the style manual of the Modern Language Association (MLA). Another mentioned here is the "Harvard" style, which is an author-date citation style similar to that of APA. Additional overlap exists between writing, research methodology, and research tools. Books have been placed in this text according to their primary focus and strengths.

Two important tools in the writer's toolbox are a good dictionary and a good thesaurus. One widely used dictionary is *Merriam-Webster's Collegiate Dictionary*, 11th ed. (Springfield, MA: Merriam-Webster, 2003). Good dictionaries are also available from American Heritage, Oxford University Press, and Random House. *Roget's International Thesaurus*, 6th ed., (New York: HarperCollins, 2001), edited by Barbara

Ann Kipfer and Robert L. Chapman, is recommended. Other publishers of fine thesauri include Little, Brown; Houghton Mifflin; and Oxford University Press. Free versions of writing tools, including dictionaries, thesauri, and the 1918 edition of Strunk and White's *Elements of Style*, are available from http://www.bartleby.com. Links to online writing tools are also provided by the Internet Public Library at http://www.ipl.org.

Some of the writing books included here are useful as "quick reference" books, for looking up rules as you need them. These include the comprehensive books on grammar, punctuation, writing style, and the citation formats. Others, for example, Zinsser's titles, are "reading" books and are more useful when you are not on deadline or actively writing. They provide information on the writing process but are not likely to answer specific questions such as whether to use "which" or "that" in a particular situation.

There are many useful books about writing, grammar, punctuation, etc. Those listed here are only suggestions. You might already have one or more books like these from an undergraduate writing class. Students learning English as a second language (ESL) might benefit from a book specifically designed to help them. Some of the music-specific writing books intended for undergraduates are also helpful for ESL students, and some general writing books include sections specifically intended for the writer new to English.

Although not listed here, you should have the information about your particular assignment or writing exercise available when you write. For larger projects, such as a thesis or dissertation, have your school's guidelines for those documents at hand. Keep in mind that your institution may require the electronic submission of your thesis or dissertation. See Chapter 6 for more information on electronic theses and dissertations (ETDs).

For those transitioning to publication, the following are helpful in identifying opportunities. Although dated, Ann Basart's *Writing about Music: A Guide to Publishing Opportunities for Authors and Reviewers* (Berkeley, CA: Fallen Leaf, 1989), provides information about journal scope, submission guidelines, and peer review. The College Music Society's *International Directory of Music Organizations* (entry 13.11) provides much more up-to-date information, including society websites that typically include information about association publications. Also see Beth Luey's *Handbook for Academic Authors*, 4th ed. (Cambridge: Cambridge University Press, 2002). Luey discusses journal articles, revising a dissertation as a book, finding a publisher for a book or textbook, and so on.

The LC call numbers for the general writing books listed here are in the PE ranges (mostly PE1408) that correspond to various aspects of the broad subject headings "English philology" and "English language." Books on general bibliographies are given the LC call number Z1001 and the subject heading "General bibliography." The music-specific books on writing are mostly found under the LC call number ML3797, which corresponds to the subject heading "Musicology—Handbooks, manuals, etc." "Musical criticism—Handbooks, manuals, etc." is also used. Many of these books have maddeningly similar titles that are variations on "Writing about Music." These call numbers and subject headings are also used for the music-specific style manuals included in Chapter 16. Additional, nonmusical subject headings include "Academic writing—Handbooks, manuals, etc." and "Dissertations, Academic—Handbooks, manuals, etc."

Common graduate-level music writing tasks run a wide range in terms of audience, tone, purpose, style, and length. Many are specific to a particular course, such as a research paper, a book review, a concert report, or a seminar presentation. Others are more independent of course work, for instance, program notes, a lecture recital, a thesis, or a dissertation. For bibliography and research methodology classes, annotated bibliographies, bibliographic essays, or state of the research projects are common. For these projects, keep in mind the distinction between annotations and abstracts, and understand what you are being asked to write. Annotations include both summary and evaluation of the source being described. Abstracts, on the other hand, such as those in *RILM Abstracts*, only provide summary. References to these types of writing are included in the following annotations.

The asterisks in the following indicate recommended titles. See the companion website for updated information on new titles or editions.

MUSIC-SPECIFIC WRITING BOOKS

Those writing program notes should see the following sources as well as the Suggested Readings on this topic. Sources on creating the concert program itself are included in Chapter 16; see entries 16.7 and 16.8.

*15.1 Bellman, Jonathan D. *A Short Guide to Writing about Music.* 2nd ed. New York: Longman, 2007.

Intended for the undergraduate, Bellman focuses on introducing a wide variety of common musical writing tasks and types of contextual criticism. Includes student writing samples, with a research paper and commentary. Contains a special section on writing about world and popular music as well as writing by and for nonmusicians. Encourages students to improve their writing. Citation examples, however, do not follow Chicago, APA, or MLA style. Has a companion website. First edition reviewed by Richard Griscom in *Notes* 57, no. 3 (Mar. 2001): 598–600.

15.2 Boyle, J. David, Richard F. Fiese, and Nancy Zavac. *A Handbook for Preparing Graduate Papers in Music.* 2nd ed. Houston: Halcyon, 2004.

Originally written as a guide for graduate music students at the University of Miami. Devoted to typical graduate writing, including recital, project, and DMA papers as well as theses and dissertations. Includes detailed instructions on the mechanics of paper writing (formatting musical examples, tables, etc.) that may not be applicable at all schools. Includes citation examples using Turabian and APA. Not indexed.

15.3 Herbert, Trevor. *Music in Words: A Guide to Researching and Writing about Music.* London: Associated Board of the Royal Schools of Music, 2001.

Intended primarily for performers, including sections on writing exams, recording notes, program notes, reviews, and presentations. Includes a short chapter on writing theses and dissertations. Citation format examples are in the humanities short-title (similar to MLA) and author-date (Harvard) styles. Has a companion website. Reviewed by Nicholas Bannan in *British Journal of Music Education* 19, no. 2 (July 2002): 209–210.

15.4   Irvine, Demar, and Mark A. Radice. *Irvine's Writing about Music*. 3rd ed.
       Portland, OR: Amadeus Press, 1999.
       Although Radice updated Irvine's text, it still retains much of its dated discus-
       sion of writing. Does not include as many examples as Wingell or Bellman, nor
       is it as encouraging in tone. A sample paper written by the author is included as a
       model. Citation examples are not in Chicago, APA, or MLA style. Also includes
       a brief appendix on copyright. Reviewed by Richard Griscom in *Notes* 57, no. 3
       (Mar. 2001): 598–600.

15.5   Schick, Robert D. *Classical Music Criticism: With a Chapter on Reviewing
       Ethnic Music*. Perspectives in Music Criticism and Theory, vol. 2. New York:
       Garland, 1996.
       Unlike the other titles listed here, Schick focuses on writing criticism, specifi-
       cally reviews for newspapers and popular magazines. Includes examples through-
       out. Relevant for scholarly reviews, too, especially reviews of performances and
       recordings. Includes discussion of reviewing non-Western music, but not jazz,
       rock, or pop. See Schick's "Postscript: A Summary of What Critics Consider."
       Schick is a critic himself and he surveyed other critics while writing this book.
       Reviewed by John Harley in *Brio* 34, no. 1 (Spring–Summer 1997): 57–58.

*15.6 Wingell, Richard J. *Writing about Music: An Introductory Guide*. 3rd ed. Upper
       Saddle River, NJ: Prentice Hall, 2002.
       Another guide intended for undergraduate music students, but useful for gradu-
       ate students who need extra help with writing as well. Wingell covers the major
       challenges in a concise and easily understood manner. Discusses issues associ-
       ated with writing about early music and very new music. Includes clear examples
       in the writing chapters and a student paper (without commentary but with a
       list of questions to consider) at the end. Includes sections on writing program
       notes, concert reports, and seminar presentations in addition to research papers.
       Citation examples are based on Chicago style but include some minor variations.
       The 4th edition is anticipated. First edition reviewed by Glenn L. Glasow in
       Notes 48, no. 2 (Dec. 1991): 534–35.

15.7   Wingell, Richard J., and Silvia Herzog. *Introduction to Research in Music*. Upper
       Saddle River, NJ: Prentice Hall, 2001.
       Intended for graduate students, but Part II, "Writing a Research Paper," includes
       only one chapter on writing and another on format and style. Briefly discusses
       writing annotations and lecture recitals in addition to research papers. Also
       includes a sample article written by Robert P. Morgan that was published in *19th
       Century Music* with commentary. Citation examples are basically the same as
       the previous Wingell entry.

GENERAL WRITING BOOKS

Comprehensive Guides

The two writing textbooks listed next are intended for use in freshman writing classes.
For that reason they both include broad coverage of academic writing; for instance, both

have guides to the three major citation style manuals discussed in Chapter 16 (Chicago, APA, and MLA). Both have companion websites with supplemental materials and exercises. They are helpful for ESL students and for those who need extra help with writing. Because they are well organized and indexed, they are useful as a quick reference guide for any writer.

Many good, comprehensive writing books are available. Others may be suggested by your professor or may already be sitting on your bookshelf. For instance, other helpful titles include: the *Simon & Schuster Handbook for Writers*, 8th ed., by Lynn Q. Troyka and Doug Hesse (Upper Saddle River, NJ: Prentice Hall, 2007); *Prentice Hall Reference Guide*, 6th ed., by Muriel G. Harris (Upper Saddle River, NJ: Prentice Hall, 2006); and *A Writer's Reference*, 6th ed., by Diana Hacker (Boston: Bedford/St. Martin's, 2007). All three titles include special help for ESL writers. Hacker has written other books of potential interest as well. Canadian students should consult her *A Canadian Writer's Reference*, 3rd ed. (Boston: Bedford/St. Martin's, 2004). She also wrote a shorter handbook, similar to *LB Brief* (see entry 15.8), titled *A Pocket Style Manual*, 4th ed. (Boston: Bedford/St. Martin's, 2004).

*15.8 Fowler, H. Ramsey, and Jane E. Aaron. *The Little, Brown Handbook*. 10th ed. New York: Longman, 2007.

Covers developing ideas and writing as well as grammar and usage. The "Cultural Language Guide" notes throughout the book will be a great help to ESL students. Part 9 covers research writing; from planning a research project to finding and evaluating sources. The "Plan of the Book" on the inside front cover makes it easy to find information. More student friendly than *The Writer's Harbrace Handbook*. A shorter and less expensive spiral-bound version, *LB Brief*, by Aaron is also available in a 2nd edtion (New York: Longman, 2005). Sixth edition reviewed in *Reference and Research Book News* 10, no. 3 (June 1995): 46.

15.9 Glenn, Cheryl, and Loretta Gray. *The Writer's Harbrace Handbook*. 3rd ed. Boston: Thomson/Wadsworth, 2007.

Assumes the student has a firm background in grammar and its related language. Talks about the many levels of learning and writing. Good explanations and examples, but not so good to look something up quickly. Use the book outline on the inside cover for finding information. None of the 4 chapters in the "Writing in the Disciplines" section cover music. While informative, not as generally useful as the *Little, Brown Handbook*. Reviewed in *Reference and Research Book News* 18, no. 4 (Nov. 2003): 226.

Compiling Bibliographies

15.10 Harner, James L. *On Compiling an Annotated Bibliography*. 2nd ed. New York: Modern Language Association, 2000.

Short pamphlet covering the compilation of a bibliography, from start to finish, using literature examples. Makes a nice companion to Krummel. See the useful "Annotation Verbs" appendix. Reviewed by Robert Balay in *Choice* 38, no. 7 (Mar. 2001): 1238.

*15.11 Krummel, D. W. *Bibliographies: Their Aims and Methods*. London: Mansell, 1984.

Although Krummel focused his bibliographic work on music, this is a general book on bibliographies. Broader in scope and coverage than Harner. Chapter 4, on annotations, is the most detailed discussion available on the topic. See also Appendix A, "Criteria for Evaluating a Bibliography." Reviewed by Paul A. Winckler in *Library Quarterly* 55, no. 4 (Oct. 1985): 465–66.

Editing

15.12 Cook, Claire K. *Line by Line: How to Improve Your Own Writing*. Boston: Houghton Mifflin, 1985.

Copyrighted by the Modern Language Association, where Cook was a copy editor. Advises writers to "make what you say as good as what you mean." Not intended as a quick help, but gives specific tips on editing, such as cutting unnecessary words. Focus is on writing at the sentence level. An excellent "how-to" book, with examples showing multiple rewrites to fix problems. Includes a glossary and an index. Reviewed by Richard L. Larson in *College Composition and Communication* 37, no. 2 (May 1986): 255.

Grammar, Punctuation, and Spelling

Grammar

15.13 O'Connor, Patricia T. *Woe Is I: The Grammarphobe's Guide to Better English in Plain English*. New York: Riverhead Books, 2003.

Good to look up troublesome words and punctuation quickly. Witty, but does not try too hard to be funny. Chapter titles are meaningful; it is concise; the examples are helpful; and the index is useful. Reviewed by Manya S. Chylinski in *Library Journal* 128, no. 16 (Oct. 1, 2003): 64.

Punctuation

*15.14 Shaw, Harry. *Punctuate It Right!* 2nd ed. New York: HarperPerennial, 1993.

Good resource for answering punctuation questions. Well organized, and includes two glossaries and an index. The chapter titles clearly correspond to their content, for example, "The Comma," and "Period."

15.15 Truss, Lynne. *Eats, Shoots & Leaves: The Zero Tolerance Approach to Punctuation*. New York: Gotham Books, 2003.

This best-selling book on punctuation deserves a second look. Not useful for looking up rules quickly, it is more of a reading book. Uses British terminology. Includes many useful examples of how punctuation can change meaning, but tries too hard to be entertaining. No index. Reviewed by Louis Menand in *New Yorker* 80, no. 17 (June 28, 2004): 102.

Spelling

15.16 Cook, Vivian. *Accomodating Brocolli in the Cemetary, Or, Why Can't Anybody Spell?* New York: Simon and Schuster, 2004.

Another best-selling book with short chapters, quizzes (with answer key), discussions, and examples. British book, but covers American usages as well. Includes pictures of signs as examples. Some of this is simply intended for fun, while other portions are more pragmatic. Includes a short index.

Style and Rhetoric

The first and last books in this section are excellent rhetoric books but are "reading" books, unlike *The Elements of Style*, which is best used as a reference to answer common writing questions quickly.

15.17 Barzun, Jacques. *Simple & Direct: A Rhetoric for Writers*. Rev. ed. New York: Harper and Row, 1985.
Provides useful information broken up into meaningful chapter headings. Students will be able to find sections pertinent to what they need. Good discussion, and examples with answers and explanations as to why the example is good or bad. Includes 12 pages on revision. First edition reviewed by Sarah C. Gross in *Library Journal* 100, no. 19 (Nov. 1, 1975): 2053.

*15.18 Strunk, William, Jr., and E. B. White. *The Elements of Style*. 4th ed. New York: Longman, 2000.
The classic, well-respected, and short guide to good writing. Probably one of the best-selling writing books of all time. Useful as a quick guide to common style problems. Revised edition includes a foreword by Roger Angell. The 1918 edition is available online from the free website *Bartleby.com* at http://www.bartleby.com. See Figure 15-1. Reviewed by John Simon in *Wilson Quarterly* 24, no. 3 (Summer 2000): 125–27.

15.19 Walsh, Bill. *The Elephants of Style: A Trunkload of Tips on the Big Issues and Gray Areas of Contemporary American English*. New York: McGraw-Hill, 2004.
Good information but more entertaining than informative. (Yes, the title is a takeoff on *Elements of Style*.) Uses contemporary examples, which may "stick" and help you remember rules you have read elsewhere. The elephant "out-takes" might be distracting. Reviewed by Tracey N. Wofford in *Technical Communication* 52, no. 1 (Feb. 2005): 74–75.

15.20 Williams, Joseph M., and Gregory G. Colomb. *Style: Toward Clarity and Grace*. Chicago Guides to Writing, Editing, and Publishing. Chicago: University of Chicago Press, 1990.
Useful, but broken up into chapters that are too broad and vague, for example, "Cohesion," "Coherence I," and "Coherence II." Uses good examples with explanations. The final chapter, "Usage," is the most helpful. Reviewed by Craig W. Beard in *Library Journal* 115, no. 20 (Nov. 15, 1990): 77.

Writing Process

*15.21 Zinsser, William. *On Writing Well: The Classic Guide to Writing Nonfiction*. 7th ed. New York: HarperCollins, 2006.

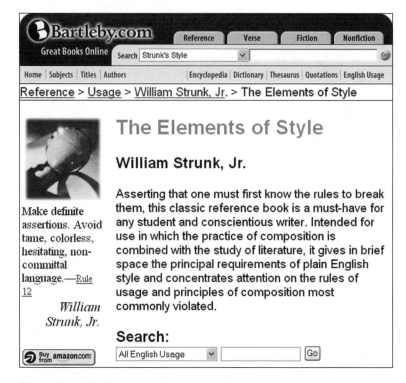

Figure 15-1 *The Elements of Style at Bartleby.com (Courtesy of Bartleby.com)*

Really is a classic; this is the "30th anniversary edition." Not a reference guide, but rather a book to help you understand what constitutes good writing. Zinsser's point of departure is the idea that good writing can be learned and that rewriting is at the heart of the task. Reviewed in *Reference and Research Book News* 21, no. 4 (Nov. 2006): 277.

15.22 Zinsser, William. *Writing to Learn.* New York: Harper and Row, 1988.
Here Zinsser explores the relationship between writing, thinking, and learning. He was inspired by the "writing across the curriculum" movement, which incorporates writing into as many classes as possible. Written in the character of a writer's memoir, including his stint as a critic for the *New York Herald Tribune.* See especially Chapter 12, "Worlds of Music." Here Zinsser explains, "writing about music ... made me a better musician" (p. 213). He also includes writing excerpts from Alec Wilder, Virgil Thomson, and Roger Sessions. Reviewed by Fred M. Hechinger, "Writing Across the Curriculum," *New York Times*, April 13, 1988.

SUGGESTED READINGS

Hess discusses common writing assignments for music history classes. The books listed earlier do not really cover writing book reviews in detail. See the readings by

Fialkoff, Studwell, and Thomson on book reviewing. Schick devotes an entire chapter to recording reviews; see also Frank's article. Krummel and Poultney discuss writing annotations for a bibliography. Botstein considers the influence of analysis on performance. Christgau, a rock critic, examines writing by journalists Anthony DeCurtis and Lester Bangs and professors Sheila Whiteley and Susan McClary. Maus also discusses reviewing concerts and writing program notes. Keller's short article on program notes is helpful. At the beginning of this chapter, the importance of finding models of good writing was mentioned. Chapter 12, "Worlds of Music," of *Writing to Learn* by Zinsser is recommended as a good place to start.

Botstein, Leon. "Analysis and Criticism." *Musical Quarterly* 85, no. 2 (Summer 2001): 225–31.

Christgau, Robert. "Writing about Music Is Writing First." *Popular Music* 24, no. 3 (Oct. 2005): 415–21.

Fialkoff, Francine. "The Art of Reviewing: Mastering the Short Review." *Library Journal* 117 (15 Mar. 1992): 74.

Frank, Mortimer H. "The Record Review Reviewed: Random Thoughts on Standards of Criticism." *Fanfare* 8 (1985): 77–82.

Hess, Carol A. "Score and Word: Writing about Music." In *Teaching Music History*, edited by Mary Natvig, 193–204. Burlington, VT: Ashgate, 2002.

Keller, James M. "Program Notes." *Chamber Music* 17, no. 4 (Aug. 2000): 36–41, 57.

Krummel, D. W. "Annotation," Chap. 4 in *Bibliographies: Their Aims and Methods*. London: Mansell, 1984.

Maus, Fred E. "Learning from 'Occasional' Writing." *Repercussions* 6, no. 2 (Fall 1997): 5–23.

Poultney, David. "Writing about Music," Chap. 7 in *Studying Music History: Learning, Reasoning, and Writing about Music History and Literature*. 2nd ed. Upper Saddle River, NJ: Prentice Hall, 1996. See section titled "Annotated Bibliography," 231–33.

Schick, Robert D. "Reviewing Recordings," Chap. 9 in *Classical Music Criticism*. New York: Garland, 1996.

Studwell, William E. "Book Reviewing in Music: An Art or an Axe?" *Music Reference Services Quarterly* 5, no. 1 (1996): 51–52.

Thomson, Ashley. "How to Review a Book." *Canadian Library Journal* 48 (Dec. 1991): 416–18.

CHAPTER 16

Style Manuals and Citation of Sources

CITING SOURCES AND AVOIDING PLAGIARISM

Providing citations of sources used in your work is a basic scholarly convention. To do so, you will need to adopt a style manual appropriate for your work in music and become familiar with it. Style manuals prescribe conventions for citing sources as well as rules about formatting and usage. Regardless of the style manual adopted, the purpose of citing sources is the same. In addition to demonstrating the scope of your research and providing readers with the bibliographic details necessary to follow up your sources, appropriate citation of sources is essential to demonstrate academic integrity and to avoid charges of **plagiarism**. You must give credit for the words and ideas of others. Many colleges and universities have strict rules regarding plagiarism and have adopted honor codes to encourage students to pledge to do their own work.

Plagiarism can come in many forms, some of which are intentional while others are not. It can range from buying a paper on the Internet to accidentally using another person's ideas without giving proper credit. Making up sources or fabricating information are also examples. Whether intentional or not, however, plagiarism has serious consequences. Every now and then a professional writer or critic or sometimes even a professor is caught plagiarizing. Even for a first offense, a career can be damaged and a reputation tarnished. For students the punishment might include failing the course, being suspended, or even being expelled from college.

Charges of plagiarism are not always easy to investigate. Sometimes a professor might catch a student by using a program such as Turnitin to check research papers. An instructor might be familiar with a particular source and catch a student borrowing from it too heavily without proper citation. Sometimes stolen passages are obvious, and sometimes they are harder to verify.

The following university examples are typical. One student had a paper stolen from her dorm room without her knowledge. Two other students from the same class used the paper. All three were accused of plagiarism, but only the two who stole the paper were punished. Another instance involved a group project. One student in the group used a figure without citation from an unpublished source the professor knew. Although the student said it was an honest mistake, all the students in the group were investigated, were given incompletes for the course, and had their scholarship money held, and letters were sent to all the parents. On the other hand, I once had a student turn in a ten-page paper with over 100 footnotes out of paranoia about being accused of cheating. I will never forget the student who came into the music library with a pile of photocopies in near panic because he had not written down the sources of the photocopies, which he had quoted from in his research paper.

Students who want to plagiarize can do so easily. With so many sources available online it is simple to cut and paste together a paper. It is possible to buy papers, even custom-written ones, online. Professors see reports that plagiarism is rampant and are suspicious as a result. The same technologies that make it easier for students to plagiarize also make it easier for faculty to catch it.

For these reasons it is important that you understand when and how to credit the sources you use in your research. Not only direct quotes but also paraphrases require citation. Use of graphs, charts, musical examples, pictures, and so on are also protected and must be credited. You should also take measures to ensure you are not accidentally using the ideas of others. Your research will borrow heavily from the sources you consult, especially while you are a student. You might honestly become confused about who said what or which ideas are really your own. This is more likely if you are tired or stressed, for example. One professor I know asks his students to wait thirty minutes after reading a source before writing, in order to distance themselves from the ideas of the authors being read.

International students have a special challenge with regard to understanding what is expected in the Western academic system. Repeating the ideas of others is a form of respect and flattery in some cultures. What is a well-known fact in one place may not be in another. Barriers of language can make understanding more challenging. Yet international students are held to the same academic standards with regard to plagiarism.

Examples of Plagiarism

The following section follows Joseph Gibaldi's model in the *MLA Handbook for Writers of Research Papers* of providing examples of unacceptable types of use from specific texts.[1] The following three examples are all from commonly used music titles. The original passage is followed by a use that would be considered plagiarism, followed by a similar example with proper citation.

---

[1]See Joseph Gibaldi, *MLA Handbook for Writers of Research Papers*, 6th ed. (New York: Modern Language Association of America, 2003), 70–73.

Example A: Paraphrasing

The following passage is taken from the *Grove Music Online* article on Beethoven, section 14 "The Symphonic Ideal" by Joseph Kerman, Alan Tyson, and Scott G. Burnham. This passage refers to Beethoven's Symphony No. 3, the "Eroica" Symphony.

Original Source

"Thanks to Nottebohm's monograph on the 'Eroica' sketches, more is generally known about the composition of this work than any other by Beethoven. The sketches show a minimum of false starts and detours. The most radical ideas were present from the start, if in cruder form, and the work seems to have proceeded with great assurance. This is striking indeed, for however carefully one studies Beethoven's evolving style up to 1803, nothing prepares one for the scope, the almost bewildering originality and almost continuous technical certainty manifested in this symphony. In sheer length, Beethoven may well have felt that he had overextended himself, for it was many years before he wrote another instrumental work of like dimensions."

Plagiarism

The stylistic departures in Beethoven's Symphony No. 3 are so radical and bewildering that it is striking that the sketches show that his compositional process was assured and technically certain. Beethoven must have felt that he had overextended himself.

Proper Citation

In their article on Beethoven in *Grove Music Online*, Kerman, Tyson, and Burnham refer to the stylistic departures in the Symphony No. 3 as radical and bewildering and describe Beethoven's compositional process as assured and technically certain, but they wonder if the composer felt he had overextended himself.[2]

Example B: Use of a Distinctive Word or Phrase

This passage is taken from Richard Taruskin's description of Debussy's use of the pentatonic scale in "Voiles" in *The Oxford History of Western Music*.

Original Source

"Since the pentatonic scale, like the diatonic scale, has intervals of two different sizes (whole steps and minor thirds), the harmony seems to come into sharper focus. But harmonic functions nevertheless remain in abeyance, since the pentatonic collection has the crucial element of 'half-steplessness' in common with its whole-tone counterpart: in more formal terminology, both scales are anhemitonic, lacking in semitones."

---

[2]*Grove Music Online*, s.v. "Beethoven, Ludwig van" (by Joseph Kerman, Alan Tyson, and Scott G. Burnham), http://www.oxfordmusiconline.com (accessed July 28, 2007).

Plagiarism

In "Voiles," Debussy's use of pentatonic and whole-tone scales blurs the harmony because of the resulting half-steplessness of the music.

Proper Citation

In "Voiles," Debussy's use of pentatonic and whole-tone scales blurs the harmony, resulting in what Richard Taruskin describes as "half-steplessness" in the music.[3]

Example C: Using Another's Line of Thinking

The passage from *A History of Western Music* that follows proposes Ives's motivations for using American popular song and hymn melodies in his Symphony No. 2.

Original Source

"In his Second Symphony, Ives used themes paraphrased from American popular songs and hymns, borrowed transitional passages from Bach, Brahms, and Wagner, and combined all of these in a symphonic form and idiom modeled on Brahms, Dvořák, and Tchaikovsky. Through this synthesis, Ives proclaimed the unity of his own experience as an American familiar with the vernacular, church, and classical traditions and claimed a place for distinctively American music in the symphonic repertoire. Doing so was a radical act, for although classical audiences accepted folk melodies as sources for concert works, they tended to regard the hymn tunes and popular songs Ives used as beneath notice and entirely out of place in the concert hall."

Plagiarism

When Ives used themes from American popular songs and hymns in his Symphony No. 2 combined with the form and style of the Romantic symphony, it was a bold effort to create a place for this music in the art music tradition.

Proper Citation

Ives's Symphony No. 2 is described in *A History of Western Music* as a synthesis. The authors suggest that by combining themes from American popular songs and hymns with the form and style of the Romantic symphony, Ives made a bold effort to create a place for his native melodies within the art music tradition.[4]

A more detailed discussion of plagiarism can be found in some of the sources listed in the bibliographies and readings that follow. See especially the following. Spatt includes three pertinent chapters (Chapter 3, "Quoting Sources," Chapter 4, "Paraphrasing Sources," and Chapter 10, "Acknowledging Sources"). Lipson's third chapter, "Plagiarism and Academic Honesty," is also recommended. The readings

---

[3]Richard Taruskin, *The Oxford History of Western Music* (New York: Oxford University Press, 2005), 4:75.

[4]J. Peter Burkholder, Donald Jay Grout, and Claude V. Palisca, *A History of Western Music*, 7th ed. (New York: W. W. Norton, 2006), 839.

by Gibaldi and McLemee are useful as well. See the iParadigms website http://www.plagiarism.org for a wealth of information and examples as well. iParadigms is the company that created Turnitin, the earlier-mentioned software for catching plagiarism.

Citation of sources usually requires references within the text as well as a bibliography at the end of a document. The format of the references in the text varies from one style manual to the next. *The Chicago Manual of Style* (Chicago) uses footnotes or endnotes with full bibliographic information, while the style manuals of the American Psychological Association (APA) and Modern Language Association (MLA) use parenthetical citations within the text. The parenthetical citations are abbreviated and refer to the full bibliographic information in the "**Reference List**" (APA) or "**Works Cited**" (MLA). Publications using Chicago, for example, many scholarly journals, may omit the bibliography because all the bibliographic details necessary to find the sources cited are present in the notes.

The bibliography provides the reader with evidence of the scope and nature of your research and a list of works for more detailed or varied reading on the subject. The bibliography should include all works cited in the notes. Additionally, you may be asked to include any sources you consulted (whether cited in notes or not) and/or significant sources that were not available for your use but that may be available to your readers. You should *not* cite general or music reference tools (dictionaries, periodical indexes, bibliographies, etc.).

Footnotes or **endnotes** serve to give credit to another scholar's work, to substantiate a suggestion that might be questioned, and to comment on or explain points made in the text. Notes must be used for quotes from other writings; important information that is not readily known; anything not belonging in the main text but that would be good for the reader to know about; and speculations that are suggested but not proven. Citation of sources is not necessary for widely known facts (e.g., most dates and places of birth and death, unless the information is different from what is generally accepted) or repetition of material already presented in the text. Remember that plagiarism is an actionable offense in most colleges and universities, so, when in doubt, provide a citation. A related concern is the amount of a copyrighted work that may be quoted without receiving permission and possibly paying a use fee.

The following list includes sources useful in compiling citations. The three major style manuals are included, as are those specifically intended for music. A guide to the citation of electronic resources, *The Columbia Guide to Online Style* (*CGOS*), is provided. Next, two citation management software packages, *RefWorks* and *EndNote*, are described, as well as guides for preparing concert and recital programs. Style for concert programs differs from the citations formats provided by the style manuals listed earlier. See Helm and Luper's *Words & Music* and Holoman's *Writing about Music*. Finally, two books that provide a detailed discussion of how to use sources are provided.

The subject headings and call numbers used for the general style manuals vary. Chicago is classed in Z, APA in BF, MLA in PN. The corresponding subject headings vary as well. The best way to search for them in your local library catalog is by title. To find updates and information about new editions, search the style manual website (listed later). The websites for Chicago and Columbia are especially useful. The music-specific style guides are more consistent. They are given the call number ML3797 and often the subject heading "Musical criticism—Authorship—Handbooks, manuals, etc." is assigned.

In addition to the style manuals listed here, refer also to the books in previous chapters that discuss citation styles. Some of the titles in Chapter 1 discuss documentation. Wingell and Herzog (entry 1.7) discuss citation formats briefly, and so do Crabtree, Foster, and Scott (entry 1.12). Two of the writing guides in Chapter 15 also discuss citation. Both the *Little, Brown Handbook* (entry 15.8) and *The Writer's Harbrace Handbook* (entry 15.9) include concise guides to the three major style manuals' citation formats (Chicago, APA, and MLA).

MAJOR STYLE MANUALS

Three major style manuals are listed here: Chicago, APA, and MLA. These are most commonly required by music schools and departments in U.S. colleges and universities. They are most commonly used for music, although there are many others as well. Of the three, Chicago is by far the most widely adopted among journal and book publishers in music. The following core music journals all use Chicago: *Ethnomusicology, Journal of the American Musicological Society, Journal of Music Theory, Music Educators Journal, Music Theory Spectrum, Musical Quarterly, Musical Times,* and *Notes.* The book publishers who follow Chicago include Harvard University Press, Oxford University Press, Routledge, and Yale University Press. APA is used by the *Journal of Music Therapy,* and MLA is used by *Popular Music and Society.* Some journals accept more than one style; the *Journal of Research in Music Education* will accept articles in either Chicago or APA. Some journals develop their own style manuals or use a house style sheet in conjunction with a major style manual.

Although the basic information (author, title, publication details, date, etc.) included in all three styles is identical in most cases, the formats differ. You can keep Appendixes E, F, and G "at your fingertips" to see how these styles handle common music formats.

University of Chicago Press Style (Chicago Style)

16.1 Turabian, Kate L., Wayne C. Booth, Gregory G. Colomb, Joseph M. Williams, and the University of Chicago Press Staff. *A Manual for Writers of Term Papers, Theses, and Dissertations: Chicago Style for Students and Researchers*, 7th ed. Chicago Guides to Writing, Editing, and Publishing. Chicago: University of Chicago Press, 2007.

The "Turabian" is a handy guide to the *Chicago Manual of Style* intended for use by graduate and undergraduate students. This greatly expanded 7th edition includes much more information on research process and style than the earlier editions. Revised by the authors of *The Craft of Research* (entry 1.9). Includes the basics of Chicago citation style. Does not include the information in the larger style manual related to publishing books. J. M. Piper-Burton in *Choice* 45, no. 2 (Oct. 2007): 250.

*16.2 University of Chicago Press. *The Chicago Manual of Style*, 15th ed. Chicago: University of Chicago Press, 2003; *The Chicago Manual of Style Online*, 15th ed. Chicago: University of Chicago Press, 2006–. http://www.chicagomanualofstyle. org.

Probably the most commonly used style manual among music publishers. The only major style manual that is currently available online. Figure 16-1 shows the search screen for the online version. Chicago recommends use of notes (footnotes or endnotes) and bibliographies for the humanities, including music. See its Chapter 17. Citation formats are only one part of Chicago. Other chapters of interest include Chapter 8, on titles (see 8.201–8.205 for musical titles), Chapter 9, on numbers, Chapter 10, on foreign languages, Chapter 11, on quotes, and Chapter 15, on abbreviations (see 15.29 for states and 15.42 for months). Keep in mind that there are differences between the bibliographic and note citation formats. The subscription-based searchable online version is recommended. Also available on CD-ROM. Print reviewed by Lucinda Dyer in *Publishers Weekly* 250, no. 50 (Dec. 15, 2003): 34 and Louis Menand in the *New Yorker* (6 Oct. 2003): 120–26. Online reviewed by Mirela Roncevic in *Library Journal* 131, no. 15 (Sept. 15, 2006): 88.

Figure 16-1 *Chicago Manual of Style Online* Search Screen *(Courtesy of Chicago Manual of Style Online)*

American Psychological Association Style (APA Style)

APA is an author-date system of documentation used by publishers in the areas of music education, music psychology, music therapy, etc. The APA publishes additional guides, including the *Concise Rules of APA Style*, *Mastering APA Style*, and the *APA-Style Helper* software. See the APA Style website at http://www.apastyle.org.

16.3 American Psychological Association. *Publication Manual of the American Psychological Association.* 5th ed. Washington, DC: American Psychological Association, 2001.

APA style uses parenthetical references in the text that include the author and date of the source being cited as well as the page number(s). The full bibliographic information appears in the reference list. Reference lists differ from bibliographies in that they include only the sources cited. APA style includes use of footnotes for explanations and copyright permissions. Chapters 3 and 4 cover citation basics. See the *APA Style* website for updates of electronic citation formats and corrections at http://www.apastyle.org. Reviewed by Barbara A. Simmons in *Technical Communication* 51, no. 1 (Feb. 2004): 113–14.

Modern Language Association Style (MLA Style)

MLA style calls for parenthetical citations in the text, accompanied by a list of works cited. MLA's parenthetical citations minimally include the author's name and page number. The "Works Cited" may include additional sources, but then it is called "Works Consulted." The bibliographic formats are similar to those of Chicago. Footnotes or endnotes are used for explanation or commentary. MLA publishes two versions of its style manual; both (by Joseph Gibaldi) are listed next. Of the big three, MLA is used by the fewest music publishers. Because it is widely enployed by English and writing professors, however, you may have consulted it during your undergraduate years and your music school may have adopted it for theses and dissertations. The MLA website, at http://www.mla.org/style, includes fewer aids than the websites for Chicago, APA, and CGOS; however, there is an FAQ section.

16.4 Gibaldi, Joseph. *MLA Handbook for Writers of Research Papers*, 6th ed. New York: Modern Language Association, 2003.

> This title, written for high school and undergraduate students, includes MLA documentation style as well as information on research and writing. Reviewed by Nicholas Frankovich in *Journal of Scholarly Publishing* 36, no. 3 (Apr. 2005): 179–83.

*16.5 ———. *MLA Style Manual and Guide to Scholarly Publishing*, 2nd ed. New York: Modern Language Association, 1998.

> Intended for graduate students, scholars, and professional writers, the *Style Manual* includes a chapter on theses and dissertations as well as a discussion of publishing. Less up-to-date than the *Handbook*, and a little more cumbersome to use. Reviewed by Paul A. D'Alessandro in *Library Journal* 123, no. 6 (Apr. 1998): 80.

MUSIC-SPECIFIC STYLE MANUALS

*16.6 Cowdery, James R. *How to Write about Music: The RILM Manual of Style*, 2nd ed. New York: RILM, 2006.

> Presents RILM's house style, including the citation style used in its publications. The first edition (2005) includes Chicago documentation examples. Most useful for those writing for RILM, since this style is not likely to become widely adopted. However, benefits from the RILM staff's experience with a broad range of international sources and the inclusion of numerous music examples. Includes chapters on writing abstracts and indexing.

16.7 Helm, E. Eugene, and Albert T. Luper. *Words & Music: Form and Procedure in Theses, Dissertations, Research Papers, Book Reports, Programs, Theses in Composition*, rev. ed. Totowa, NJ: European American Music Corp., 1982.

> Mostly dated; however, Chapter 3, on concert programs is still valid and one of the best available. The program checklist is especially useful.

16.8 Holoman, D. Kern. *Writing about Music: A Style Sheet from the Editors of "19th
      Century Music."* Berkeley: University of California Press, 1988.
      Brief style guide developed for use by the journal in conjunction with Chicago.
      Examples are taken from the journal *19th Century Music*. See the chapters on
      music terminology, musical examples, and concert programs, which are still use-
      ful. The chapter covering citations is dated (concurrent with Chicago 13th ed.).
      A new edition is anticipated. Reviewed by D. W. Krummel in *Notes* 45, no. 3
      (Mar. 1989): 518–20.

CITING ELECTRONIC SOURCES

16.9 Walker, Janice R., and Todd Taylor. *The Columbia Guide to Online Style.* 2nd ed.
      New York: Columbia University Press, 2006.
      Sometimes referred to as CGOS. Includes examples in both humanities (MLA and
      Chicago) and sciences (APA) styles for a wide range of electronic resources, for
      example, blogs, podcasts, and wikis. Full text and full image databases are included
      as well. The humanities chapter focuses on MLA, but Appendix D includes exam-
      ples of Chicago-style endnotes and footnotes. Updates and examples are available
      from the CGOS website at http://www.columbia.edu/cu/cup/cgos2006/basic.html.
      Also includes a discussion of electronic publishing. First edition reviewed by Paul
      A. D'Alessandro in *Library Journal* 123, no. 14 (Sept. 1, 1998): 175.

CITATION MANAGEMENT SOFTWARE

Citation management software can greatly assist you in citing sources, creating bibliographies, and keeping track of useful sources. The two programs listed here work in
conjunction with word processing software (primarily Microsoft Word) to make citation as effortless as possible in a wide variety of styles, including the three major styles
discussed earlier. Citations can be imported directly from many research databases as
well as from websites. These programs are especially useful for big projects, such as
theses and dissertations, or when citation formats need to be changed from one style to
another.

16.10 *EndNote.* Carlsbad, CA: Thomson ResearchSoft, 1994–. http://www.endnote.com.
       EndNote software is sold primarily to individuals, and the database of citations
       is stored by the user. The number of output styles is higher than for *RefWorks*
       (see next), and includes house styles for some music journals. Can only be used
       on computers that have the software loaded on them. Not as user-friendly as
       RefWorks, but does have more advanced functionality. *EndNote* 9 reviewed by
       David Mattison in *Searcher* 13, no. 9 (Oct. 2005): 16–27.

*16.11 *RefWorks: Your Online Research Management, Writing and Collaboration
       Tool.* Bethesda, MD: CSA, 2002–. http://www.refworks.com.
       Unlike *EndNote*, *RefWorks* is licensed primarily to institutions and may be
       available for your use free of charge. *RefWorks* is web-based, and citations are

stored remotely. The advantage to this is that you can work from any computer with Internet access. Easy to use. Figure 16-2 shows the *RefWorks* Advanced Search screen. Includes fewer output style options than *EndNote*, but does include Chicago, APA, and MLA. Reviewed by Ingrid C. Hendrix in *Journal of the Medical Library Association* 92, no. 1 (Jan. 2004): 111–13.

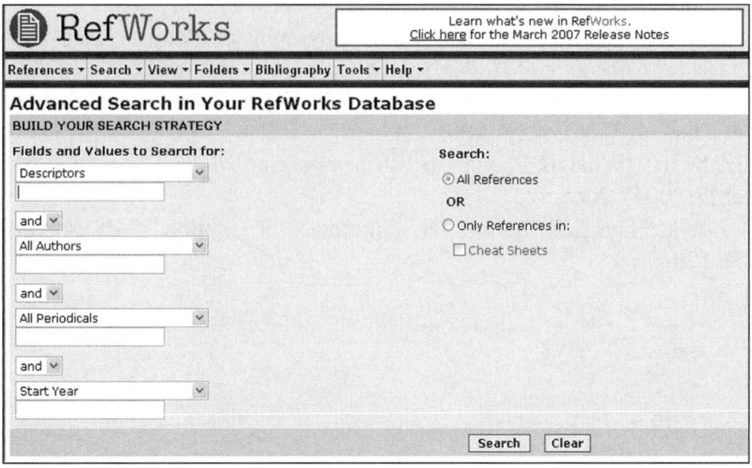

Figure 16-2 *RefWorks* Advanced Search Screen (*Courtesy of RefWorks*)

USING SOURCES

16.12 Lipson, Charles. *Doing Honest Work in College: How to Prepare Citations, Avoid Plagiarism, and Achieve Real Academic Success.* Chicago: University of Chicago Press, 2004.
       See the first three chapters on academic honesty, especially Chapter 3 on plagiarism. The remainder of the book is a guide to citation styles. Reviewed by Erika Dreifus in *Community College Week* 17, no. 15 (Feb. 28, 2005): 16.

*16.13 Spatt, Brenda. *Writing from Sources.* 7th ed. Boston: Bedford/St. Martins, 2007.
       A text for freshman writing courses that includes a detailed discussion of appropriate ways to use sources. See especially Part Two, "Presenting Sources to Others," and Part Three, "Writing from Sources." Includes a chapter on evaluating sources and one with citation examples using MLA and APA. Has a companion website with writing exercises. First edition reviewed by Rick A. Eden in *College Composition and Communication* 37, no. 2 (May 1986): 252–53.

SUGGESTED READINGS

The following readings cover some of the topics related to compiling bibliographies as well as plagiarism. In addition to these Suggested Readings on plagiarism, see the webpage on the topic at the Duke University Libraries website at http://www.lib.duke.edu/libguide/plagiarism.htm. Barzun and Graff offer an overview of documentation.

Barzun, Jacques, and Henry F. Graff. "The Rules of Citing: Footnotes and Bibliography," Chap. 12 in *The Modern Researcher*. 6th ed. Belmont, CA: Wadsworth/Thomson, 2004.

Gibaldi, Joseph. "Plagiarism," Chap. 2 in *MLA Handbook for Writers of Research Papers*. 6th ed. New York: Modern Language Association, 2003.

Howard, Jennifer. "Indiana U. Press Pulls Biography of Pianist Amid Charges of Plagiarism." *Chronicle of Higher Education* 53, no. 31 (Apr. 6, 2007): A24.

Kiernan, Vincent. "Toss Out the Index Cards." *Chronicle of Higher Education* 52, no. 40 (June 9, 2006): A29–A30.

McLemee, Scott. "What Is Plagiarism?" *Chronicle of Higher Education* 51, no. 17 (Dec. 17, 2004): A9.

Menand, Louis. "The End Matter: The Nightmare of Citation." *New Yorker* (6 Oct. 2003): 120–26.

Library of Congress Classification: Class M Outline

For the complete listing, consult *Super LCCS: Class M, Music and Books on Music* (Farmington Hills, MI: Thomson/Gale, 2006).

CALL NUMBERS	SUBJECT
M2	Historical, geographical, and other collections of music
M3	Collected works of individual composers
	Instrumental Music
M6–19	Organ music
M20–39	Piano music
• 22	General collections
• 23	Sonatas
• 32–34	Arrangements and transcriptions
M40–175	Solo instruments without accompaniment
• 40–59	String instruments
• 60–111	Wind instruments
• 115–142	Plucked string instruments
• 145–175	Percussion instruments
M200–298.5	Duets[1]
• 200–212	Piano, four hands
• 217–239	One string instrument with piano
• 240–271	One wind instrument with piano

---

[1]The Library of Congress classification for chamber music includes numbers M180–M999, generally with numbers in the 200s being duets, 300s trios, 400s quartets, and so on.

• 272–283	One plucked string instrument with piano
• 284–298.5	Other combinations
M300–386	Trios
• 310–314	Piano trios
• 349–353	String trios
M400–486	Quartets
• 450–454	String quartets
M500–586	Quintets
• 510–514	Piano and four string instruments
• 550–554	String quintets
• 555–559	Wind quintets
M600–686	Sextets
M700–786	Septets
M800–886	Octets
M900–986	Nonets and larger combinations of chamber music
M1000–1075	Orchestra
• 1001	Symphonies
• 1003	Suites
• 1004	Overtures
• 1010–1011	Piano concertos
• 1012–1019	String concertos
• 1020–1035	Wind concertos
• 1036–1037.4	Plucked string concertos
• 1045–1075	Orchestral pieces
• 1100–1160	String orchestra (including concertos, suites, and overtures for string orchestra)
M1375–1420	Instrumental music for children
• 1378–1380	Piano music for children

Vocal Music

M1500–1518	Operas and musicals
• 1500	Full scores
• 1503	Vocal scores with piano accompaniment
• 1505–1508.2	Excerpts
M1530–1610	Secular choruses
• 1530–1546.5	Choruses with orchestra or other ensemble
• 1547–1600	Choruses, part songs, etc., with keyboard or unaccompanied
M1611–1624.8	Secular songs for one voice
• 1619	General collections
• 1620	Art songs (collections of one composer)
• 1621	Art songs (single songs)
• 1621.4	Song cycles

M1627–1853	National music
• 1627–1630	Folk songs
• 1630.18	Popular songs
M1990–1998	Children's songs
M1999–2199	Sacred vocal music
• 2000–2007	Oratorios
• 2010–2017.6	Masses
• 2020–2036	Cantatas, choruses, etc.
• 2102–2114.8	Sacred songs for one voice
• 2115–2146	Hymnals

Literature on Music

ML1	Periodicals (United States)
ML4–5	Periodicals (Foreign)
ML12–21	Directories
ML47–54.8	Librettos
• 50	Operas (including operettas, musicals, sacred operas, etc.)
ML62–89	Special aspects of music as a whole
• 82	Women and music
• 89	Pictorial works
ML100–109	Dictionaries and encyclopedias
• 100	General
• 102	Special Topics, A–Z
▪ .C5	Church music
▪ .J3	Jazz
▪ .O6	Operas
▪ .P66	Popular music
▪ .T5	Themes and motives
• 105–107	Bio-bibliography
ML113–158	Bibliography
• 113	Guides to historical sets, series, complete works, etc.
• 114–118	By time period
• 128	By topic, A–Z
▪ .C4	Chamber music
▪ .P3	Piano music
▪ .S3	Songs
▪ .V7	Vocal music
▪ .W7	Women in music
• 134	Composers catalogs, thematic catalogs, A–Z
• 136	Library catalogs
• 156	Discography
▪ 156.4	By topic, A–Z
▪ 156.5	By composer, A–Z

▪ 156.7	By performer, A–Z
ML159–3797	History and criticism
• 160	General music history
• 162–197	By time period
• 198–360.5	By region or country
▪ 198–239	Music from the Americas
▪ 240–325	European music
▪ 350–350.5	African music
• 385–429	Biography
▪ 385–400	Collected biography
▪ 410	Composers, A–Z
▪ 416–421	Performers, A–Z
• 549–1092	Instruments
• 1100–1165	Chamber music
• 1200–1270	Orchestral music
• 1400–3275	Vocal music
▪ 1600–2881	Secular vocal music
▪ 2900–3275	Sacred vocal music
• 3469–3543	
▪ 3505.8–3509	Popular music and Jazz

Musical Instruction and Study (scores or books)

MT3	History of music education
MT5.5–7	Music theory
• 6.5	Collections of music for analysis
MT17	Music in special education
MT35	Notation, dictation, ear training, etc.
MT40–67	Composition
• 40	Systems
• 58–64	Forms
• 67	Popular songs
MT90–146	Analytical guides
• 92	Composers
• 95–100	Opera, ballet
• 110–115	Oratorios
• 125–130	Orchestral music
• 140–145	Chamber and solo music
MT170–810	Instrumental techniques
• 180–208	Organ
• 220–255	Piano
• 259–338	String instruments
• 339–538	Wind instruments
• 539–654	Plucked instruments

- 540–557   Harp
- 580–599   Guitar

MT820–949   Voice instruction
• 825–850   Systems and methods
  ▪ 825   American methods
• 855–883   Special techniques
  ▪ 870   Sight-singing methods
• 898–949   Techniques for children

APPENDIX B

Search Tips

The following search tips are helpful in searching online library catalogs, periodical indexes, Internet search engines, full-text databases, and other databases.

BOOLEAN SEARCH TERMS

Sometimes called *Boolean operators*, these terms can be used to narrow, broaden, or refine your search results.

And

"And" is implicit in some databases' keyword or basic search. Using "and" narrows your search by finding only hits that include both search terms. For example, "music and society" will retrieve only records containing both words. In some Internet search engines, "and" must be typed in all capital letters (i.e., "AND"). See Figure B-1 for a Venn diagram illustrating the search "music and society." A variation on "and" in many Internet search engines is using "+" to indicate that a search term must be present.

Or

"Or" broadens your search. Searches with "or" return results that include either term. For example, "flute or recorder" will bring up records that include either. See Figure B-2.

Not

"Not" narrows your search. Some databases use "and not." Use "not" to find hits that exclude a certain term. For example, "African not American" would bring up only

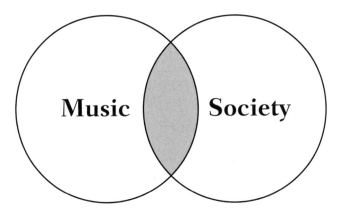

Figure B-1 "Music and Society" Search. Shaded area represents the search results containing both search terms.

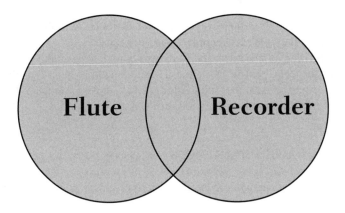

Figure B-2 "Flute or Recorder" Search. Shaded area represents the search results containing either search term.

records with "African" in them and not those with "African-American." See Figure B-3. A variation on "not" in many Internet search engines is to use the "-" to indicate that a search term should not be present.

If you would like to learn more about Boolean search terms, please refer to these websites: Boolean Searching on the Internet. University of Albany Libraries, http://www.internettutorials.net/boolean.html. Venn Diagrams. Colorado State University Libraries, http://lib.colostate.edu/howto/others/venn.html.

NESTING SEARCH TERMS

Search terms can be combined by using parentheses to indicate the groupings. With nesting, your searches work like algebra equations. Remember that parentheses must be

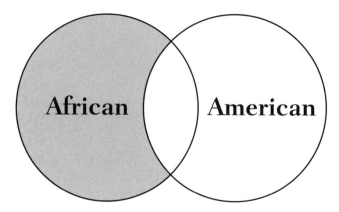

Figure B-3 "African not American" Search. Excludes "African-American" in search results.

used in pairs. For example, "(flute or recorder) and Baroque" will find results including either "flute" and "Baroque" or "recorder" and "Baroque."

The search "(flute or recorder) and Baroque not review" would be the same as just given, but with the term "review" excluded. This is sometimes helpful to eliminate published reviews from your search results. Additional examples include: (flute or recorder) and sonata not trio; (psalmody or hymnody) and (states or America).

TRUNCATION AND WILDCARDS

Symbols for truncation and wildcards vary. Asterisks and question marks are two common symbols.

Truncation is used at the end of words to expand the word forms found by your search. "Sing*" would find "sing," "singer," "singing," and so on. If a database has a limit on the length of search terms, use truncation if your term exceeds the limit. For example, "encycloped*" would find "encyclopedia."

Wildcards are similar to truncation, but they can be used in the middle of search terms. For instance, "fl?te" would find "flute" or "flöte."

PHRASE AND "STRING" SEARCHES

Phrase searches or string searches find the exact phrase indicated. String searches in an Internet search engine are similar to title searches in an online library catalog. The exact phrase is found. They can be helpful in full text databases. These are useful when the individual search terms are common, but the phrase means something very different and/or specific. For example, "first New England school" means something different in music than it does in normal discourse. Phrase searches may be the default in your library's online catalog for keyword searches. Putting words into quotation marks and putting words within parentheses are common ways to indicate a phrase search. Quotation marks must also be used in pairs.

PROXIMITY

Proximity searches specify that search terms appear within a particular number of words in any order. Like phrase searches, they are especially useful in full-text databases because the word **proximity** may correlate with relevancy. These searches can be used to find terms that are adjacent as well. Sometimes databases use "w" for "within" and the number of words in Arabic numerals. Sometimes "n" for "near" is used. For instance, "holiday w2 billie" would find "Billie Holiday" or "Holiday, Billie." The search "music* W3 modern*" would find "modern music," "musical modernism," "modernism in music," etc. These search terms also might be spelled out, and sometimes a slash is added before the number. Some search engines offer other variations as well, such as "not within" so many words.

Remember that variations occur from one database or search engine to the next, so see the help screens available for each one you use.

APPENDIX C

Composers Included as Examples in This Text

Bach, Johann Sebastian (1685–1750)

Beethoven, Ludwig van (1770–1827)

Brahms, Johannes (1833–1897)

Chopin, Frédéric (1810–1849)

Debussy, Claude (1862–1918)

Dufay, Guillaume (1397–1474)

Handel, George Frideric (1685–1759)

Haydn, Franz Joseph (1732–1809)

Ives, Charles (1874–1954)

Josquin des Prez (ca.1450–1521)

Landini, Francesco (ca.1325–1397)

Liszt, Franz (1811–1886)

Machaut, Guillaume de (ca.1300–1377)

Monteverdi, Claudio (1567–1643)

Mozart, Wolfgang Amadeus (1756–1791)

Palestrina, Giovanni Pierluigi da (1525 or 26–1594)

Pérotin (fl.ca.1200)

Schoenberg, Arnold (1874–1951)

Schubert, Franz (1797–1828)

Schumann, Robert (1810–1856)

Stravinsky, Igor (1882–1971)

Verdi, Giuseppe (1813–1901)

Wagner, Richard (1813–1883)

APPENDIX D

International Inventory of Musical Sources (RISM) Publications

The various parts of *RISM* appear in Chapters 8, 10, and 13. This complete listing presents the contents to date of the three main series (A, B, and C) in order. The first volume of *RISM* was published in 1960, and this collaborative international project remains ongoing. *RISM* is also known by its French and German titles, *Répertoire international des sources musicales* and *Internationales Quellenlexikon der Musik*, respectively. *RISM* has been issued by different publishers in various languages. The division of the publications into series, volumes, and parts can make it difficult to understand for first-time users. Finally, the ongoing nature of the project coupled with volumes that were never issued (e.g., A/I/10) create further complications. To date only one section listed here is available online, but additional electronic publication of *RISM* is anticipated. For additional information, see the website of the U.S. RISM Office, http://hcl.harvard.edu/libraries/loebmusic/isham/rism.html, or the Central Editorial Office (Zentralredaktion), http://rism.stub.uni-frankfurt.de/index_e.htm.

SERIES A: SOURCES BY INDIVIDUAL COMPOSERS
(A/I FOR PUBLISHED WORKS AND A/II FOR MANUSCRIPTS)

A/I: Schlager, Karlheinz, and Otto E. Albrecht. *Einzeldrucke vor 1800.* 9 vols. RISM A/I/1–9. Kassel, Ger.: Bärenreiter, 1971–1981. Kindermann, Ilse, Jürgen Kindermann, and Gertraut Haberkamp. *Addenda et Corrigenda.* 4 vols. RISM, A/I/11-14. Kassel, Ger.: Bärenreiter, 1986–1999. *Register der Verleger, Drucker und Stecher und Register der Orte.* 1 vol. RISM, A/I/15. Kassel, Ger.: Bärenreiter, 2003. A/I/10 was never published. A CD-ROM version is anticipated. (entry 10.73)

A/II: *RISM Online: Series A/II, Music Manuscripts after 1600.* RISM, A/II. Baltimore: National Information Services Corp. (NISC), 2002–. http://www.nisc.com. (entry 8.24)

SERIES B: SOURCES BY MULTIPLE COMPOSERS
AND BIBLIOGRAPHIES OF MATERIALS ORGANIZED
BY TOPIC (PUBLISHED BY G. HENLE IN MUNICH)

B/I and B/II: Printed Music in Collections from 1500 to 1799

B/I: Lesure, François. *Recueils imprimés XVIe-XVIIe siècles.* RISM, B/I. Munich: G. Henle, 1960. (entry 10.74)

B/II: ———. *Recueils imprimés XVIIIe siècle.* RISM, B/II. Munich: G. Henle, 1964. (entry 10.75)

B/III: The Theory of Music from the Carolingian Era to about 1500: Descriptive Catalogue of Manuscripts

B/III/1: Smits Van Waesberghe, Joseph. *The Theory of Music from the Carolingian Era up to 1400: Volume I.* RISM, B/III/1. Munich: G. Henle, 1961. Includes Austria, Belgium, Switzerland, Denmark, France, Luxembourg, and the Netherlands. (entry 10.76)

B/III/2: Fischer, Pieter. *The Theory of Music from the Carolingian Era up to 1400: Volume II: Italy.* RISM, B/III/2. Munich: G. Henle, 1968. (entry 10.77)

B/III/3: Huglo, Michel, and Christian Meyer. *The Theory of Music: Volume III: Manuscripts from the Carolingian Era up to c. 1500 in the Federal Republic of Germany (D-brd).* RISM, B/III/3. Munich: G. Henle, 1986. (entry 10.78)

B/III/4: Meyer, Christian, Michel Huglo, and Nancy C. Phillips. *The Theory of Music: Volume IV: Manuscripts from the Carolingian Era up to c. 1500 in Great Britain and in the United States of America.* RISM, B/III/4. Munich: G. Henle, 1992. (entry 10.79)

B/III/5: Meyer, Christian, Elżbieta Witkowska-Zaremba, and Karl-Werner Gümpel. *The Theory of Music: Volume V: Manuscripts from the Carolingian Era up to c. 1500 in the Czech Republic, Poland, Portugal, and Spain.* RISM, B/III/5. Munich: G. Henle, 1997. (entry 10.80)

B/III/6: Meyer, Christian. *The Theory of Music: Volume VI: Manuscripts from the Carolingian Era up to c. 1500, Addenda, Corrigenda.* RISM, B/III/6. Munich: G. Henle, 2003. (entry 10.81)

B/IV: Manuscripts of Polyphonic Music, 11th–16th Centuries

B/IV/1: Reaney, Gilbert. *Manuscripts of Polyphonic Music 11th–Early 14th Century.* RISM, B/IV/1. Munich: G. Henle, 1966. (entry 8.25)

B/IV/2: ———. *Manuscripts of Polyphonic Music c. 1320–1400.* RISM, B/IV/2. Munich: G. Henle, 1969. (entry 8.26)

B/IV/1-2/Suppl. 1: Wathey, Andrew. *Manuscripts of Polyphonic Music: The British Isles, 1100–1400.* RISM, B/IV/1–2 Supplement 1. Munich: G. Henle, 1993. (entry 8.27)

B/IV/3-4: Fischer, Kurt von, and Max Lütolf. *Handschriften mit mehrstimmiger Musik des 14., 15. und 16. Jahrhunderts.* 2 vols. RISM, B/IV/3–4. Munich: G. Henle, 1972. (entry 8.28)

B/IV/5: Bridgman, Nanie. *Manuscrits de musique polyphonique: XVe et XVIe siècles: Italie.* RISM, B/IV/5. Munich: G. Henle, 1991. (entry 8.29)

B/V: Manuscripts of Tropes and Sequences

B/V/1: Husmann, Heinrich. *Tropen- und Sequenzenhandschriften.* RISM, B/V/1. Munich: G. Henle, 1964. (entry 10.82)

B/V/2: Deusen, Nancy van. *Katalog der mittelalterlichen Sequenzen.* RISM, B/V/2. (forthcoming)

B/VI: Printed Writings about Music to 1800

B/VI/1-2: Lesure, François. *Écrits imprimés concernant la musique.* 2 vols. RISM, B/VI/1–2. Munich, G. Henle, 1971. (entry 10.83)

B/VII: Lute and Guitar Tablatures

B/VII: Boetticher, Wolfgang. *Handschriftlich überlieferte Lauten- und Gitarren-tabulaturen des 15. bis 18. Jarhrhunderts.* RISM, B/VII. Munich: G. Henle, 1978. (entry 10.84)

B/VIII: Das deutsche Kirchenlied

B/VIII/1-2: Ameln, Konrad, Markus Jenny, and Walther Lipphardt. *Das deutsche Kirchenlied, DKL: Kritische Gesamtausgabe der Melodien.* 2 vols. RISM, B/VIII/1–2. Kassel, Ger.: Bärenreiter, 1975–80. (entry 10.85)

B/IX: Hebrew Sources of Music and Music Theory

B/IX/1: Adler, Israel. *Hebrew Notated Manuscript Sources up to circa 1840: A Descriptive and Thematic Catalogue with a Checklist of Printed Sources.* 2 vols. RISM, B/IX/1. Munich: G. Henle, 1989. (entry 8.30)

B/IX/2: Adler, Israel. *Hebrew Writings Concerning Music: In Manuscripts and Printed Books from Geonic Times up to 1800.* RISM, B/IX/2. Munich: G. Henle, 1975. (entry 10.86)

B/X: Arabic Sources of Music and Music Theory

B/X: Shiloah, Amnon. *The Theory of Music in Arabic Writings (c. 900–1900): Descriptive Catalogue of Manuscripts in Libraries of Europe and the U.S.A.* RISM, B/X. Munich: G. Henle, 1979. (entry 10.87)

B/X/A: Shiloah, Amnon. *The Theory of Music in Arabic Writings (c. 900–1900): Descriptive Catalogue of Manuscripts in Libraries of Egypt, Israel, Morocco, Russia, Tunisia, Uzbekistan, and Supplement to BX*. RISM, B/X/A. Munich: G. Henle, 2003. (entry 10.88)

B/XI: Ancient Sources of Music and Music Theory

B/XI: Mathiesen, Thomas J. *Ancient Greek Music Theory: A Catalogue Raisonné of Manuscripts*. RISM, B/XI. Munich: G. Henle, 1988. (entry 10.89)

B/XII: Persian Sources of Music and Music Theory

B/XII: Massoudieh, Mohammad Taghi. *Manucrits persans concernant la musique*. RISM, B/XII. Munich: G. Henle, 1996. (entry 8.31)

B/XIII: Sources of Hymnody

B/XIII/1: Hlawiczka, Karol, Jan Kouba, Teresa Krukowski, Marie Skalická, and Leon Witkowski. *Hymnologica Bohemica, Slovaca, Polonica et Sorabica*. RISM, B/XIII/1. (forthcoming)

B/XIV: Les Manuscrits du processionnal

B/XIV/1: Huglo, Michel. *Les Manuscrits du processionnal: Volume I Autriche à Espagne*. RISM, B/XIV/1. Munich: G. Henle, 1999. (entry 10.90)

B/XIV/2: Huglo, Michel. *Les Manuscrits du processionnal: Volume II France à Afrique du sud*. RISM, B/XIV/2. Munich: G. Henle, 2004. (entry 10.91)

B/XV: Sources of Masses in Spain, Portugal, and Ibero-American Countries from 1490 to 1630

B/XV: Urchueguía, Cristina. *Mehrstimmige Messen in Quellen aus Spanien, Portugal und Lateinamerika ca. 1490–1630*. RISM, B/XV. Munich: G. Henle, 2005. (entry 10.92)

SERIES C: DIRECTORY OF MUSIC RESEARCH LIBRARIES (PUBLISHED BY BÄRENREITER IN KASSEL)

C/I: Kahn, Marian, Helmut Kallmann, and Charles Lindahl. *Directory of Music Research Libraries*. Volume 1: *Canada and the United States*. 2nd rev. ed. RISM, C/I. Kassel, Ger.: Bärenreiter, 1983. (entry 13.2)

C/II: Davis, Elizabeth. *Directory of Music Research Libraries*. Volume 2: *Sixteen European Countries: Austria, Belgium, Switzerland, Germany, Denmark, and Spain*. 2nd rev. ed. RISM, C/II. Kassel, Ger.: Bärenreiter, 2001. (entry 13.3)

C/III/1: ————. *Directory of Music Research Libraries.* Volume 3: *Sixteen European Countries: France, Finland, United Kingdom, Ireland, Luxembourg, Norway, Netherlands, Portugal, and Sweden.* 2nd rev. ed. RISM, C/III/1. Kassel, Ger.: Bärenreiter, 2001. (entry 13.4)

C/III/2: *Directory of Music Research Libraries.* Volume 3: *Sixteen European Countries: Italy.* RISM, C/III/2. (forthcoming)

C/IV: Hill, Cecil, Katya Manor, James Siddons, and Dorothy Freed. *Directory of Music Research Libraries.* Volume 4: *Australia, Israel, Japan, and New Zealand.* RISM, C/IV. Kassel, Ger.: Bärenreiter, 1979. (entry 13.5)

C/V: Pruett, Lilian, and James B. Moldovan. *Directory of Music Research Libraries.* Volume 5: *Czechoslovakia, Hungary, Poland, and Yugoslavia.* RISM, C/V. Kassel, Ger.: Bärenreiter, 1985. (entry 13.6)

Sonderband: RISM-Bibliothekssigel Gesamtverzeichnis

RISM Zentralredaktion. *RISM Bibliothekssigel: Gesamtverzeichnis.* Kassel, Ger.: Bärenreiter; Munich: G. Henle, 1999.

Chicago Style at Your Fingertips

The *Chicago Manual of Style* offers two approaches to documentation. The most common calls for a bibliography and either footnotes or endnotes. The less common is an author-date style similar to MLA and APA. The journal *Ethnomusicology* uses the author–date option. The following citations are primarily in the bibliography and notes model. A few examples of the author-date style are included at the end. Please note that in Chicago the bibliographic and note citation formats differ and should not be confused. In Chicago, 15th ed., and Turabian, 7th ed., the bibliographic entry examples are labeled "B" and the note citation examples are labeled "N." See also the "Chicago-Style Citation Quick Guide" at the *Chicago Manual of Style Online* at http://www. chicagomanualofstyle.org/tools_citationguide.html.

BIBLIOGRAPHIC CITATION FORMATS

Books

Book by One Author

Last, First. *Title*: *Subtitle*. Place of publication: Publisher, date.
Kerman, Joseph. *Contemplating Music: Challenges to Musicology*. Cambridge, MA: Harvard University Press, 1985.

Second Book by Same Author (———)

———. *Title*. Place: Publisher, date.
———. *Write All These Down: Essays on Music*. Berkeley: University of California Press, 1994.

Book by Two Authors

Last, First, and First Last. *Title*. Place: Publisher, date.

McKay, David P., and Richard Crawford. *William Billings of Boston: Eighteenth-Century Composer.* Princeton, NJ: Princeton University Press, 1975.

Book with an Editor (ed.), Compiler (comp.), or Translator (trans.)

Last, First, ed. *Title.* Place: Publisher, date.

Crawford, Richard, R. Allen Lott, and Carol J. Oja, eds. *A Celebration of American Music: Words and Music in Honor of H. Wiley Hitchcock.* Ann Arbor: University of Michigan Press, 1990.

Edition Other Than First (no superscript)

Last, First. *Title.* Xth ed. Place: Publisher, date.

Grout, Donald J. *A History of Western Music.* 5th ed. New York: W. W. Norton, 1996.

Book in a Series

Last, First. *Title.* Series Title Series number. Place: Publisher, date.

Schneider, Tina M. *Hymnal Collections of North America.* Studies in Liturgical Musicology 10. Lanham, MD: Scarecrow Press, 2003.

Multivolume Set

Last, First. *Title.* X vols. Place: Publisher, date.

Sanjek, Russell. *American Popular Music and Its Business: The First Four Hundred Years.* 3 vols. New York: Oxford University Press, 1988.

Chapter of a Book (single-authored book)

Last, First. "Chapter Title." Chap. X in *Book Title.* Place: Publisher, date.

Tawa, Nicholas. "A Closer Look at the Jazz Age." Chap. 2 in *Supremely American: Popular Song in the 20th Century, Styles and Singers and What They Said about America.* Lanham, MD: Scarecrow Press, 2005.

Chapter of a Book (multiple authors with an editor)

Last, First. "Chapter Title." In *Book Title*, edited by First Last, pp–pp. Series Title Series number. Place: Publisher, date.

Tick, Judith. "Writing the Music of Ruth Crawford into Mainstream Music History." In *Ruth Crawford Seeger's Worlds: Innovation and Tradition in Twentieth-Century American Music*, edited by Ray Allen and Ellie M. Hisama, 11–32. Eastman Studies in Music 41. Rochester, NY: University of Rochester Press, 2007.

Dissertations and Theses

Dissertation

Last, First. "Title." Document type, University, date.

Langness, Anna P. "A Descriptive Study of Teacher Responses During the Teaching of Singing to Children." PhD diss., University of Colorado, 1992.

Online Dissertation (ETD)

Last, First. "Title." Document type, University, date. URL (accessed date).

Langness, Anna P. "A Descriptive Study of Teacher Responses During the Teaching of Singing to Children." PhD diss., University of Colorado, 1992. http://proquest.umi. com (accessed May 27, 2007).

Journal Articles

Journal Article (print)

Last, First. "Title of Article." *Title of Journal* vol. X, issue X (date): pp–pp.

Rifkin, Joshua. "From Weimar to Leipzig: Concertists and Ripienists in Bach's *Ich hatte viel Bekümmernis.*" *Early Music* 24, no. 4 (Nov. 1996): 583–603.

Journal Article (from an online database)

Last, First. "Title of Article." *Title of Journal* vol. X, issue X (date), URL (accessed date).

Rifkin, Joshua. "From Weimar to Leipzig: Concertists and Ripienists in Bach's *Ich hatte viel Bekümmernis.*" *Early Music* 24, no. 4 (Nov. 1996), http://www.jstor.org (accessed May 27, 2007).

Journal Article (electronic journal)

Last, First. "Title of Article." *Title of Journal* vol. X, issue X (date), URL (accessed date).

Montford, Kimberlyn. "*L'Anno santo* and Female Monastic Churches: The Politics, Business and Music of the Holy Year in Rome (1675)." *Journal of Seventeenth-Century Music* 6, no. 1 (2000), http://sscm-jscm.press.uiuc.edu/v6/no1/montford. html (accessed Apr. 26, 2007).

Encyclopedia Articles

Chicago 15th ed. suggests that encyclopedias be cited primarily in notes.

Encyclopedia Article (print)

Encyclopedia Title, S.v. "Article Title," by First Last.
New Grove Dictionary of Opera, S.v. "Rake's Progress, The," by Richard Taruskin.

Encyclopedia Article (online)

Encyclopedia Title, S.v. "Article Title," by First Last. URL (accessed date).
Grove Music Online, S.v. "Rake's Progress, The," by Richard Taruskin. http://www. grovemusic.com (accessed Apr. 26, 2007).

Scores

Scores

Composer's Last, First. *Title*. Place: Publisher, date.

Brouwer, Leo. *Cuban Landscape with Rain.* Saint-Nicolas, QC: Doberman, 1987.

Liebermann, Lowell. *Sonata for Flute and Piano.* Bryn Mawr, PA: T. Presser, 1988.

Score in a Complete Works Edition

Last, First. *Work Title.* Edited by First Last. Complete Works Edition Title, ser. X, vol. X. Place: Publisher, date.

Verdi, Giuseppe. *Rigoletto (Melodrama in Three Acts).* Libretto by Francesco Maria Piave. Edited by Martin Chusid. The Works of Giuseppe Verdi, ser. 1, Operas, vol. 17. Chicago: University of Chicago Press; Milan: G. Ricordi, 1983.

Excerpt from a Score Anthology

Last, First. "Song Title." In *Anthology Title.* Edited by First Last. Place: Publisher, date.

Caccini, Giulio. "Amarilli, mia bella." In *26 Italian Songs and Arias: An Authoritative Edition Based on Authentic Sources* (for medium high voice). Edited by John Glenn Paton. Van Nuys, CA: Alfred, 1991.

Manuscript Score

Cite the collection in the bibliography and the specific items in the notes.

Collection Name. Library Name. University.

Normand Lockwood Collection. American Music Research Center. University of Colorado at Boulder.

Recordings

Turabian, 7th ed., suggests use of CD instead of compact disc.

Recording (composer emphasis)

Last, First. *Title of Recording.* Performer(s)/Ensemble. Conductor. Label Label number. date. Format.

Bach, Johann Sebastian. *Goldberg Variations, BWV 988.* Glenn Gould. CBS Records MK 37779. 1982. Compact disc.

Beethoven, Ludwig van. *Symphony No. 3 in E-Flat Major, Op. 55, "Eroica."* Cleveland Orchestra. George Szell. CBS Records MYK 37222. 1981. Compact disc. Originally recorded in 1957.

Recording (performer emphasis)

Performer Last, First, instrument/voice type. *Title of Recording.* Performer(s)/Ensemble. Conductor. Label Label number. date. Format.

Fleming, Renée, soprano. *Bel Canto.* Orchestra of St. Luke's. Patrick Summers. Decca 289 467 101-2. 2002. Compact disc.

Ma, Yo Yo (cello), Edgar Meyer (bass), and Mark O'Connor (violin). *Appalachian Journey.* With James Taylor and Alison Krauss. Sony SK 66782. 2000. Compact disc.

Track from a Recording

Last, First. "Title of Track." On *Title of Recording*. Label Label number. date. Format.
Davis, Miles. "So What." On *Kind of Blue*. Columbia CK 64935. 1997. Compact disc.

Liner Notes from a Recording

Author Last, First. Liner notes for *Title of Recording*, by Composer First Last. Label Label number. date. Format.
Hogwood, Christopher. Liner notes for *My Ladye Nevells Booke*, by William Byrd. Editions de L'Oiseau-Lyre 430 484-2. 1993. Three compact discs.

Videos and DVDs

Video/DVD

Last, First. *Title*. Format. Others responsible. Place: Publisher, date.
Hirsh, Lee. *Amandla!: A Revolution in Four-Part Harmony*. DVD. Produced by Sherry Simpson and Lee Hirsh. Santa Monica, CA: Artisan Entertainment, 2003.

Web Content

Website

Last, First/Organization name. "Title." Owner or Title of website. URL (accessed date).
Center for American Music. "Stephen Collins Foster." University of Pittsburgh. http://www.pitt.edu/~amerimus/foster.htm (accessed Apr. 26, 2007).

Weblog Entry or Comment

Name of Blog. URL of blog.
Dial "M" for Musicology. http://musicology.typepad.com.

FOOTNOTE/ENDNOTE CITATION FORMATS

Books

Book by One Author

[1]First Last, *Title* (Place: Publisher, date), page number(s).
[1]Joseph Kerman, *Contemplating Music: Challenges to Musicology* (Cambridge, MA: Harvard University Press, 1985), 10.

Book by Two Authors

[2]First Last and First Last, *Title* (Place: Publisher, date), page number(s).
[2]David P. McKay and Richard Crawford, *William Billings of Boston: Eighteenth-Century Composer* (Princeton, NJ: Princeton University Press, 1975), 465–66.

Book with an Editor (ed.), Compiler (comp.), or Translator (trans.)

[3]First Last, ed., *Title* (Place: Publisher, date), page number(s).

[3]Karl Kroeger, comp., *American Fuging-Tunes, 1770–1820: A Descriptive Catalog* (Westport, CT: Greenwood 1994), 15.

Edition Other than First

[4]First Last, *Title*, Xth ed. (Place: Publisher, date), page number(s).

[4]Donald J. Grout, *A History of Western Music*, 5th ed. (New York: W. W. Norton, 1996), 410.

Book in a Series

[5]First Last, *Title*, Series Title Series number (Place: Publisher, date), page number(s).

[5]Tina M. Schneider, *Hymnal Collections of North America*, Studies in Liturgical Musicology 10 (Lanham, MD: Scarecrow Press, 2003), 50.

Multivolume Set

[6]First Last, *Title* (Place: Publisher, date), volume number: page number(s).

[6]Russell Sanjek, *American Popular Music and Its Business: The First Four Hundred Years* (New York: Oxford University Press, 1988), 2:128.

Chapter of a Book (single-authored book)

[7]First Last. "Chapter Title," in *Book Title* (Place: Publisher, date), pp–pp.

[7]Nicholas Tawa, "A Closer Look at the Jazz Age," in *Supremely American: Popular Song in the 20th Century, Styles and Singers and What They Said about America* (Lanham, MD: Scarecrow Press, 2005), 30–65.

Chapter of a Book (multiple authors with an editor)

[8]First Last, "Chapter Title," in *Book Title*, ed. First Last. Series Title Series number (Place: Publisher, date), pp–pp.

[8]Judith Tick, "Writing the Music of Ruth Crawford into Mainstream Music History," in *Ruth Crawford Seeger's Worlds: Innovation and Tradition in Twentieth-Century American Music*, ed. Ray Allen and Ellie M. Hisama. Eastman Studies in Music 41 (Rochester, NY: University of Rochester Press, 2007), 11–32.

Dissertations and Theses

Dissertation

[9]First Last, "Title of Dissertation" (Document type., University, date), page number(s).

[9]Anna P. Langness, "A Descriptive Study of Teacher Responses During the Teaching of Singing to Children" (PhD diss., University of Colorado, 1992), 220.

Online Dissertation (ETD)

[10]First Last, "Title" (Document type, University, date), URL (accessed date).

[10]Anna P. Langness, "A Descriptive Study of Teacher Responses During the Teaching of Singing to Children" (PhD diss., University of Colorado, 1992), http://proquest.umi.com (accessed May 27, 2007).

Journal Articles

Journal Article (print)

[11]First Last, "Article Title," *Journal Title* vol. X, issue X (Spring 1990): page number(s).

[11]Joshua Rifkin, "From Weimar to Leipzig: Concertists and Ripienists in Bach's *Ich hatte viel Bekümmernis*," *Early Music* 24, no. 4 (Nov. 1996): 585.

Journal Article (from an online database)

[12]First Last, "Article Title," *Journal Title* vol. X, issue X (date), URL (accessed date).

[12]Joshua Rifkin, "From Weimar to Leipzig: Concertists and Ripienists in Bach's *Ich hatte viel Bekümmernis*," *Early Music* 24, no. 4 (Nov. 1996), http://www.jstor.org (accessed May 27, 2007).

Journal Article (electronic journal)

[13]First Last, "Title," *Journal Title* vol. X, issue X (date), URL (date accessed).

[13]Kimberlyn Montford, "*L'anno santo* and Female Monastic Churches: The Politics, Business and Music of the Holy Year in Rome (1675)," *Journal of Seventeenth-Century Music* 6, no. 1 (2000), http://sscm-jscm.press.uiuc.edu/v6/no1/montford.html (accessed Apr. 26, 2007).

Encyclopedia Articles

Encyclopedia Article (print)

[14]*Encyclopedia Title*, s.v. "Article Title," by First Last.

[14]*New Grove Dictionary of Opera*, s.v. "Rake's Progress, The," by Richard Taruskin.

Encyclopedia Article (online)

[15]*Encyclopedia Title*, s.v. "Article Title," (by First Last), URL (accessed date).

[15]*Grove Music Online*, s.v. "Rake's Progress, The," (by Richard Taruskin), http://www.grovemusic.com (accessed Apr. 26, 2007).

Scores

Scores

[16]First Last, *Title*, ed. by First Last (Place: Publisher, date), page number(s).

[16]Leo Brouwer, *Cuban Landscape with Rain* (Saint-Nicolas, QC: Doberman, 1987), 3.

[16]Lowell Liebermann, *Sonata for Flute and Piano* (Bryn Mawr, PA: T. Presser, 1988), 13.

Score in a Complete Works Edition

[17]First Last, *Work Title*, ed. First Last, Complete Works Edition Title, series number (Place: Publisher, date).

[17]Giuseppe Verdi, *Rigoletto (Melodrama in Three Acts)*, libretto by Francesco Maria Piave, ed. Martin Chusid, The Works of Giuseppe Verdi, ser. 1, Operas, vol. 17 (Chicago: University of Chicago Press; Milan: G. Ricordi, 1983).

Excerpt from an Anthology

[18]First Last, "Song Title," in *Anthology Title*, ed. First Last (Place: Publisher, date), page number(s).

[18]Giulio Caccini, "Amarilli, mia bella," in *26 Italian Songs and Arias: An Authoritative Edition Based on Authentic Sources* (for medium high voice), ed. John Glenn Paton (Van Nuys, CA: Alfred, 1991), 9–12.

Manuscript Score

[19]First Last. "Title," score, date, call/box number, Collection name, Library, University.

[19]Normand Lockwood. "Passacaglia ed Inno: Pascail and Hymn," score, Apr. 1994, box 53, Normand Lockwood Collection, American Music Research Center, University of Colorado at Boulder.

Recordings

Recording (composer emphasis)

[20]First Last, *Title of Recording*, Performer(s), Conductor, Label Label number, date, format.

[20]Johann Sebastian Bach, *Goldberg Variations, BWV 988*, Glenn Gould, CBS Records MK37779, 1982, compact disc.

Recording (performer emphasis)

[21]Performer First Last (instrument/voice type), with Ensemble and First Last (conductor), *Title*, Label Label number, date, format.

[21]Renée Fleming (soprano), with Orchestra of St. Luke's and Patrick Summers (conductor), *Bel Canto*, Decca 289 467 101-2, 2002, compact disc.

[21]Yo Yo Ma (cello), Edgar Meyer (bass), and Mark O'Connor (violin), with James Taylor and Alison Krauss, *Appalachian Journey*, Sony SK 66782, 2000, compact disc.

Track from a Recording

[22]First Last, "Title of Track," on *Title of Recording*, Label Label number, date, format.

[22]Miles Davis, "So What," on *Kind of Blue*, Columbia CK 64935, 1997, compact disc.

Liner Notes from a Recording

[23]Author First Last, liner notes for *Title of Recording*, by Composer First Last, Label Label number, date, format.

[23]Christopher Hogwood, liner notes for *My Ladye Nevells Booke*, by William Byrd, Editions de L'Oiseau-Lyre 430 484-2, 1993, three compact discs.

Videos and DVDs

Video/DVD

[24]First Last, *Title*, format, others responsible (Place: Publisher, date).

[24]Lee Hirsh, *Amandla!: A Revolution in Four-Part Harmony*, DVD, produced by Sherry Simpson and Lee Hirsh (Santa Monica, CA: Artisan Entertainment, 2003).

Live Performance

Live Performance (notes citation only; format from Turabian, 7th ed.)

Two format possibilities are shown.

[25]*Title of Work*, by Composer, performers, directed by Director/Conductor, Performance Venue, City, date.

[25]*Interventions*, by Vijay Iyer, performed by American Composers Orchestra and Dennis Russell Davies (conductor), Zankel Hall, New York, March 26, 2007.

[25]Composer or Performer First Last, *Title of Work*, conducted by First Last, Performance Venue, City, date.

[25]Vijay Iyer, *Interventions*, world premiere by American Composers Orchestra with Dennis Russell Davies (conductor), Zankel Hall, New York, March 26, 2007.

Web Content

Website

[26]First Last/Organization name, "Title," Owner or Title of website, URL (accessed date).

[26]Center for American Music, "Stephen Collins Foster," University of Pittsburgh, http://www.pitt.edu/~amerimus/foster.htm (accessed Apr. 26, 2007).

Weblog Entry or Comment

[27]First Last, "Entry Title," Blog title, entry posted Month Day, Year, URL (accessed Month Day, Year).

[27]Jonathan Bellman, "For Whom Bell Plays," Dial "M" for Musicology, entry posted Apr. 12, 2007, http://musicology.typepad.com/dialm/2007/04/for_whom_bell_p.html (accessed Apr. 29, 2007).

Ibid.

Use Ibid. (abbreviation for ibidem) when a note is from the same source as the one preceding it. If the page no. is not the same include the page number.

²⁸Ibid.

²⁸Ibid., 386.

Short Form

Use the short form for a previously cited title when the note does not immediately follow the full citation.

²⁹Kroeger, *American Fuging-Tunes, 1770–1820*, 15.

AUTHOR-DATE SYSTEM

See the *Chicago Manual of Style* for detailed information on the author-date style of citation. In Chicago, 15th ed., and Turabian, 7th ed., the reference-list examples are labeled "R" and the text citation examples are labeled "T." See also the "Chicago-Style Citation Quick Guide" at the *Chicago Manual of Style Online* at http://www.chicagomanualofstyle.org/tools_citationguide.html.

Here are a few examples for the Joseph Kerman book listed earlier.

The reference list entry would look as follows:

Kerman, J. 1985. *Contemplating music: Challenges to musicology.* Cambridge, MA: Harvard University Press.

The in-text references vary, depending the context, whether the author's name has been mentioned, for instance. The following are all possibilities.

(Kerman 1985:10)

(see Kerman 1985:10)

Kerman discusses this point as well (1985).

Kerman discusses this point as well (1985:10).

APPENDIX F

APA Style at Your Fingertips

APA style does not include periods at the ends of citations with URLs or recording citations that end with a parenthetical recording date.

REFERENCE LIST

Books

Book by One Author

Last, Initial(s). (date). *Title*. Place of Publication: Publisher.

Kerman, J. (1985). *Contemplating music: Challenges to musicology*. Cambridge, MA: Harvard University Press.

Second Book by Same Author

Last, Initial(s). (date). *Title*. Place: Publisher.

Kerman, J. (1994). *Write all these down: Essays on music*. Berkeley: University of California Press.

Book by Two Authors

Last, Initial(s)., & Last, Initial(s). (date). *Title*. Place: Publisher.

McKay, D. P., & Crawford, R. (1975). *William Billings of Boston: Eighteenth-century composer*. Princeton, NJ: Princeton University Press.

Book with an Editor (Ed(s).) or Translator (Trans.)

Last, Initial(s). (Ed.). (date). *Title*. Place: Publisher.

Crawford, R., Lott, R. A., & Oja, C. J. (Eds.). (1990). *A celebration of American music: Words and music in honor of H. Wiley Hitchcock*. Ann Arbor: University of Michigan Press.

Edition Other Than First *(no superscript)*

Last, Initial(s). (date). *Title* (no. ed.). Place: Publisher.
Grout, D. J. (1996). *A history of Western music* (5th ed.). New York: Norton.

Book in a Series

Last, Initial(s). (date). *Series title and number. Title of book*. Place: Publisher.
Schneider, T. M. (2003). *Studies in Liturgical Musicology No. 10. Hymnal collections of North America*. Lanham, MD: Scarecrow Press.

Multivolume Set

Last, Initial(s). (date). *Title* (Vols. X–X). Place: Publisher.
Sanjek, R. (1988). *American popular music and its business: The first four hundred years* (Vols. 1–3). New York: Oxford University Press.

Chapter of a Book

Last, Initial(s). (date). Chapter title. In *Book title* (pp. XX–XX). Place: Publisher.
Tawa, N. (2005). A closer look at the jazz age. In *Supremely American: Popular song in the 20th century, styles and singers and what they said about America* (pp. 30–65). Lanham, MD: Scarecrow Press.
Tick, J. (2007). Writing the music of Ruth Crawford into mainstream music history. In R. Allen & E. M. Hisama (Eds.), *Ruth Crawford Seeger's worlds* (pp. 11–32). (Eastman Studies in Music Vol. 41). Rochester, NY: University of Rochester Press.

Dissertations and Theses

Dissertation Obtained from ProQuest Dissertations & Theses

Last, Initial(s). (date). Title. *ProQuest Dissertations & Theses*. (Publication No. AAT XXXXXXX).
Langness, A. P. (1992). A descriptive study of teacher responses during the teaching of singing to children. *ProQuest Dissertations & Theses*. (ProQuest No. 9232704).

Dissertation Abstracted in ProQuest Dissertations and Theses but Obtained from the University

Last, Initial(s). (date). Title (Type of document, Institution, Place). *ProQuest Dissertations & Theses*, AAT XXXXXX.
Langness, A. P. (1992). A descriptive study of teacher responses during the teaching of singing to children. (Doctoral dissertation, University of Colorado at Boulder). ProQuest Digital Dissertations database, AAT 9232704.

Journal Articles

Journal Article *(print)*

Include issue number only if each issue repaginates; see following examples.
Last, Initial(s). (date). Title. *Periodical, Volume* X(Issue X), XX–XX.

666

Grives, S. (2001). Choral performance practice in the eighteenth-century part song: An alternative arrangement of Haydn's *Abendlied zu Gott*. *Choral Journal, 41*(10), 31–36.

Rifkin, J. (1996). From Weimar to Leipzig: Concertists and ripienists in Bach's *Ich hatte viel Bekümmernis*. *Early Music, 24*, 583–603.

Journal Article (electronic journal)

Last, Initial(s). (date). Title. *Periodical, Volume X*(Issue or Article X). Retrieved date, from URL

Montford, K. (2000). L'anno santo and female monastic churches: The politics, business and music of the holy year in Rome (1675). *Journal of Seventeenth-Century Music, 6*(1). Retrieved April 29, 2007, from http://sscm-jscm.press.uiuc.edu/v6/no1/montford.html

Encyclopedia Articles

Encyclopedia Article (signed) Print

Last, Initial(s). (date). Title of article. In Initials(s). Last (Ed.), *Title of encyclopedia* (Vol. X, pp. XX–XX). Place: Publisher.

Taruskin, R. (1992). Rake's Progress, The. In S. Sadie (Ed.), *The new Grove dictionary of opera* (Vol. 3, pp. 1220–1223). London: Macmillan.

Encyclopedia Article (signed) Online

Last, Initial(s). (date). Title of article. *Title of encyclopedia*. Retrieved date, from URL

Taruskin, R. (1992). Rake's Progress, The. *Grove music online*. Retrieved April 29, 2007, from http://www.grovemusic.com

Scores

Scores

Composer Last, Initial(s). (date). *Title*. [Musical score]. Place: Publisher.

Brouwer, L. (1987). *Cuban landscape with rain*. [Musical score]. Saint-Nicolas, QC: Doberman.

Liebermann. L. (1988). *Sonata for flute and piano*. [Musical score]. Bryn Mawr, PA: Presser, 1988.

Score in a Complete Works Edition

Composer Last, Initial(s). (date). *Title*. In Initial(s). Last (Series Ed.) & Initial(s). Last (Vol. Ed.), *Edition title: Series* (Vol. no.). [Musical score]. Place: Publisher.

Verdi, G. (1983). *Rigoletto: Melodrama in three acts*. In P. Gossett (Series Ed.) & M. Chusid (Vol. Ed.), *The works of Giuseppe Verdi: Series. 1, Operas* (Vol. 17) [Musical score]. Chicago: University of Chicago Press.

Excerpt from a Score Anthology

Composer Last, Initial(s). (date). Excerpt title. In Initial(s). Last (Ed.) *Anthology title* [Musical score]. Place: Publisher.

Caccini, G. (1991). Amarilli, mia bella. In J. G. Paton (Ed.), *26 Italian songs and arias: An authoritative edition based on authentic sources (for medium high voice)* [Musical score]. Van Nuys, CA: Alfred.

Manuscript Score *(no examples in APA)*

Composer Last, Initial(s). (date). *Title* [Manuscript musical score]. Collection, Library, Location.

Lockwood, N. (1994). Passacaglia ed inno: Pascail and hymn [Manuscript musical score]. Normand Lockwood Collection (Box 53), American Music Research Center, University of Colorado, Boulder.

Recordings

Recording *(composer emphasis)*

Composer Last, Initial(s). (Date). *Title* [Recorded by Name]. [Format]. Place: Label. (Recording date if different)

Bach, J. S. (1982). *Goldberg Variations, BWV 988* [Recorded by Glenn Gould]. [CD]. New York: CBS Records. (1981)

Beethoven, L. V. (1981). *Symphony No. 3 in E-Flat Major, Op. 55, "Eroica"* [Recorded by the Cleveland Orchestra conducted by G. Szell]. [CD]. New York: CBS Records. (1957)

Recordings *(performer emphasis)*

Performer Last, Initial(s) (Instrument/Voice type). (Publication Date). *Title* [By Composer or with Performer(s)]. [Format]. Place: Label. (Recording date if different)

Fleming, R. (Soprano). (2002). *Bel canto* [With Orchestra of St. Luke's and P. Summers]. [CD]. New York: Decca. (1999)

Ma, Y. Y. (Cello), E. Meyer (Bass), & M. O'Connor (Violin). (2000). *Appalachian Journey* [With J. Taylor & A. Krauss]. [CD]. New York: Sony. (1999)

Track from a Recording

Last, Initial(s). (Publication date). Title of track. On *Title of recording* [Format]. Place: Label. (Recording date if different)

Davis, M. (1997). So what. On *Kind of blue* [CD]. New York: Columbia. (1959)

Liner Notes from a Recording

Author Last, Initial(s). (Date). Title or [Liner notes for] Composer. *Title of recording* [Recorded by Initial(s). Last]. [Format]. Place: Label. (Recording date if different)

Hogwood, C. (1993). [Liner notes for] Byrd, W. *My Ladye Nevells booke* [Recorded by C. Hogwood]. [3-CD set]. London: l'Oiseau-Lyre (1974–75)

Videos and DVDs

Video/DVD

Last, Initial(s) (Contribution). (date). *Title* [Format]. Place: Publisher/Distributor.

Hirsh, L. (Director/Co-Producer), & S. Simpson (Co-Producer). (2003). *Amandla!: A revolution in four-part harmony* [DVD]. Santa Monica, CA: Artisan.

Live Performances

Live Performance (No examples exist in APA manual)

Last, Initial(s). (Date). *Title* [Performed by]. [Live Performance]. Place: Hall.
Iyer, V. (2007, March 26). *Interventions* [Performed by American Composers Orchestra and D. R. Davies]. [Live performance]. New York: Zankel Hall.

Web Content

Website

Last, Initial(s)/Organization name. (date). Title. In *Title*. Retrieved date, from URL
Center for American Music. (2007). Stephen Collins Foster. In *Welcome to the Center for American Music*. Retrieved April 29, 2007, from http://www.pitt.edu/~amerimus/foster.htm

Weblog Entry or Comment

Last, Initial(s). (Date). *Title of blog entry*. Retrieved date, from URL
Bellman, J. (2007, April 12). *For Whom Bell Plays*. Retrieved April 17, 2007, from http://musicology.typepad.com

REFERENCE CITATIONS IN THE TEXT

See the following reference list for the in-text citation examples.

For Multiple Authors (only use page numbers for quotes)

Beethoven's middle period "inspired most of his non-orchestral music" (Kerman and Tyson, 1983, p. 105).

OR

According to Kerman and Tyson, Beethoven's middle period "inspired most of his non-orchestral music" (1983, p. 105).

OR

Kerman and Tyson believe that Beethoven's middle period is the source of much of his non-orchestral music (1983).

For Repetition of Sources in Same Paragraph

Tonal theorists often look no further than the music of Brahms, but "some . . . have been able to extend their activity with considerable power to the music of

Schoenberg, Stravinsky, Bartok, and beyond" (Kerman, 1985, p. 71). However, tonal ideals seem to have "shut them off almost completely from more ancient music" (Kerman).

OR

According to Kerman (1985), tonal theorists often look no further than the music of Brahms, but "some . . . have been able to extend their activity with considerable power to the music of Schoenberg, Stravinsky, Bartok, and beyond" (p. 71). However, tonal ideals seem to have "shut them off almost completely from more ancient music" (Kerman).

More Than One Book by Same Author

Schoenberg's solution to the challenge set by Wagner in *Tristan und Isolde* "was to leave tonality altogether and to organize music in a radically different way" (Kerman, 1994, p. 268). Furthermore, "he was driven to reformulate traditional theory" (Kerman, 1985, p. 91).

Reference List

Kerman, J. (1985). *Contemplating music: Challenges to musicology.* Cambridge, MA: Harvard University Press.

Kerman, J. (1994). *Write all these down: Essays on music.* Berkeley: University of California Press.

Kerman, J., & Tyson, A. (1983). *The new Grove Beethoven.* New York: Norton.

APPENDIX G

MLA Style at Your Fingertips

MLA style allows for either underlining or italicizing titles of books, journals, and so on. Check with your professor about which option to use. Italics are used in these examples. MLA style is explained more fully in the *MLA Handbook for Writers of Research Papers*, 6th ed., and in the *MLA Style Manual*, 2nd ed.; both are by Joseph Gibaldi. Additional examples for web sources are provided at the MLA web site at http://www.mla.org.

LIST OF WORKS CITED

Books

Book by One Author

Last, First. *Italicized Title*. Place of publication: Publisher, date.

Kerman, Joseph. *Contemplating Music: Challenges to Musicology*. Cambridge, MA: Harvard UP, 1985.

Second Book by Same Author

———. *Title*. Place: Publisher, date.

———. *Write All These Down: Essays on Music*. Berkeley: U of California P, 1994.

Book by Two Authors

Last, First, and First Last. *Title*. Place: Publisher, date.

McKay, David P., and Richard Crawford. *William Billings of Boston: Eighteenth-Century Composer*. Princeton: Princeton UP, 1975.

Book with an Editor (ed.), Compiler (comp.), or Translator (trans.)

Last, First, ed. *Title*. Place: Publisher, date.

Crawford, Richard, R. Allen Lott, and Carol J. Oja, eds. *A Celebration of American Music: Words and Music in Honor of H. Wiley Hitchcock*. Ann Arbor: U of Michigan P, 1990.

Edition Other than First (no superscript)
Last, First. *Title*. Xth ed. Place: Publisher, date.
Grout, Donald J. *A History of Western Music*. 5th ed. New York: W. W. Norton, 1996.

Book in a Series
Last, First. *Title*. Series Title in Normal Print Series number. Place: Publisher, date.
Schneider, Tina M. *Hymnal Collections of North America*. Studies in Liturgical Musicology 10. Lanham, MD: Scarecrow, 2003.

Multivolume Set
Last, First. *Title*. X vols. Place: Publisher, date.
Sanjek, Russell. *American Popular Music and Its Business: The First Four Hundred Years*. 3 vols. New York: Oxford UP, 1988.

Chapter of a Book (single-authored book)
Last, First. "Chapter Title." *Book Title*. Place: Publisher, date. pp–pp.
Tawa, Nicholas. "A Closer Look at the Jazz Age." *Supremely American: Popular Song in the 20th Century, Styles and Singers and What They Said about America*. Lanham, MD: Scarecrow, 2005. 30–65.

Chapter of a Book (multiple authors with an editor)
Last, First. "Chapter Title." *Book Title*, Ed. First Last. Series Title Series number. Place: Publisher, date. pp–pp.
Tick, Judith. "Writing the Music of Ruth Crawford into Mainstream Music History." *Ruth Crawford Seeger's Worlds: Innovation and Tradition in Twentieth-Century American Music*. Ed. Ray Allen and Ellie M. Hisama. Eastman Studies in Music 41. Rochester, NY: U of Rochester P, 2007. 11–32.

Dissertations and Theses
Unpublished Dissertation or Master's Thesis
Last, First. "Title." Document type. University, date.
Wiedenbein, Amy S. "A Study of Cécile Chaminade's Career as Compositrice." MM thesis. U of Colorado, 1998.

Published Dissertation (ProQuest)
Last, First. "Title." Diss. University, date.
Langness, Anna P. "A Descriptive Study of Teacher Responses During the Teaching of Singing to Children." Diss. U of Colorado, 1992. Ann Arbor: ProQuest, 1992. 9232704.

Journal Articles

Journal Article (print)

Include issue number only if each issue is paginated separately. See the following examples.

Last, First. "Title of Article." *Title of Journal* vol. X (year): pp–pp.

Grives, Steven. "Choral Performance Practice in the Eighteenth-Century Part Song: An Alternative Arrangement of Haydn's *Abendlied zu Gott*." *Choral Journal* 41.10 (2001): 31–36.

Rifkin, Joshua. "From Weimar to Leipzig: Concertists and Ripienists in Bach's *Ich hatte viel Bekümmernis*." *Early Music* 24 (1996): 583–603.

Journal Article (from an online database)

Last, First. "Title of Article." *Title of Journal* vol. X.issue X (year): pp–pp. *Title of Service*. Date accessed.

Rifkin, Joshua. "From Weimar to Leipzig: Concertists and Ripienists in Bach's *Ich hatte viel Bekümmernis*." *Early Music* 24.4 (1996): 583–603. *JSTOR*. 27 May 2007 <http://www.jstor.org>.

Journal Article (electronic journal)

Last, First. "Title of Article." *Journal Title* vol. X.issue X (date). accessed date.

Montford, Kimberlyn. "*L'Anno santo* and Female Monastic Churches: The Politics, Business and Music of the Holy Year in Rome (1675)." *Journal of Seventeenth-Century Music* 6.1 (2000). 26 Apr. 2007 <http://sscm-jscm.press.uiuc.edu/v6/no1/montford.html>.

Encyclopedia Articles

Encyclopedia Article (print)

Last, First. "Article Title." *Encyclopedia Title*. Ed. First Last. X vols. Place: Publisher, date.

Taruskin, Richard. "Rake's Progress, The." *New Grove Dictionary of Opera*. Ed. Stanley Sadie. 4 vols. London: Macmillan; New York: Grove's, 1992.

Encyclopedia Article (online)

Last, First. "Article Title." *Encyclopedia Title*. Ed. First Last. Date. Publisher. Date accessed.

Taruskin, Richard. "Rake's Progress, The." *Grove Music Online*. Ed. Laura Macy. 2001. Oxford UP. 26 Apr. 2007 <http://www.grovemusic.com>.

Scores

Scores

Composer Last, First. *Title*. Place: Publisher, date.

Brouwer, Leo. *Cuban Landscape with Rain*. Saint-Nicolas, QC: Doberman, 1987.

Liebermann, Lowell. *Sonata for Flute and Piano*. Bryn Mawr, PA: Presser, 1988.

Score in a Complete Works Edition

Last, First. *Work Title*. Ed. First Last. Complete Works Edition Title, series X, vol. X. Place: Publisher, date.

Verdi, Giuseppe. *Rigoletto (Melodrama in Three Acts)*. Libretto by Francesco Maria Piave. Ed. Martin Chusid. The Works of Giuseppe Verdi, ser. 1, Operas, vol. 17. Chicago: U of Chicago P; Milan: G. Ricordi, 1983.

Excerpt from a Score Anthology

Last, First. "Song Title." *Anthology Title*. Ed. First Last. Place: Publisher, date. pp–pp.

Caccini, Giulio. "Amarilli, mia bella." *26 Italian Songs and Arias: An Authoritative Edition Based on Authentic Sources* (for medium high voice). Ed. John Glenn Paton. Van Nuys, CA: Alfred, 1991. 9–12.

Manuscript Score

Last, First. "Title." Date. Ms. Score. Identification no. Collection. Library, Place.

Lockwood, Normand. "Passacaglia ed Inno: Pascail and Hymn." 1994. Ms. Score. Box 53, Normand Lockwood Collection. American Music Research Center. U of Colorado, Boulder.

Recordings (Include format if not a CD.)

Recording (composer emphasis)

Last, First. *Title*. Perf. Ensemble. Cond. Label, date.

Bach, Johann Sebastian. *Goldberg Variations,* BWV 988. Glenn Gould. CBS Records, 1982.

Beethoven, Ludwig van. Symphony No. 3 in E-Flat Major, Op. 55, "Eroica." Cleveland Orchestra. Cond. George Szell. CBS Records, 1981.

Recording (performer emphasis)

Performer Last, First, instrument/voice type. *Title of Recording in Italics*. By First Last. Orch. Cond. Label, date.

Fleming, Renée, soprano. *Bel Canto*. Orchestra of St. Luke's. Cond. Patrick Summers. Decca, 2002.

Ma, Yo Yo (cello), Edgar Meyer (bass), and Mark O'Connor (violin). *Appalachian Journey*. With James Taylor and Alison Krauss. Sony, 2000.

Track from a Recording

Last, First. "Title of Track." *Title of Recording*. Label, date.

Davis, Miles. "So What." *Kind of Blue*. Columbia, 1997.

Liner Notes from a Recording

Author Last, First. Liner notes. *Title of Recording*. By Composer First Last. Label, date.

Hogwood, Christopher. Liner notes. *My Ladye Nevells Booke.* By William Byrd. Editions de L'Oiseau-Lyre, 1993.

Videos and DVDs

Video/DVD

Title. Dir. First Last. Perf. First Last. Format. Distributor, date.

Amandla!: A Revolution in Four-Part Harmony. Dir. Lee Hirsh. DVD. Artisan Entertainment, 2003.

Live Performance

Live Performance

Title. By First Last. Perf. Orch. Cond. Performance Venue, City. Date.

Interventions. By Vijay Iyer. Amer. Composers Orch. Cond. Dennis Russell Davies. Zankel Hall, New York. 26 Mar. 2007.

Web Content

Website

Last, First. "Title of Portion." *Title of Website.* Ed. First Last. Date. Publisher/Owner. Date accessed.

Center for American Music. "Stephen Collins Foster." *Welcome to the Center for American Music.* 2007. U of Pittsburgh. 26 Apr. 2007 <http://www.pitt.edu/~amerimus/foster.htm>.

Weblog Entry or Comment

Last, First. "Title." Weblog entry/comment. Date. Name of Blog. Accessed date.

Bellman, Jonathan. "For Whom Bell Plays." Weblog entry. 12 Apr. 2007. Dial "M" for Musicology. 29 Apr. 2007 <http://musicology.typepad.com>.

PARENTHETICAL TEXT CITATIONS

See the Works Cited for the following text citation examples.

For Multiple Authors

Beethoven's middle period "inspired most of his nonorchestral music" (Kerman and Tyson 105).

OR

According to Kerman and Tyson, Beethoven's middle period "inspired most of his nonorchestral music" (105).

For Repetition of Sources in Same Paragraph

Tonal theorists often look no further than the music of Brahms, but "some ... have been able to extend their activity with considerable power to the music of Schoenberg, Stravinsky, Bartok, and beyond." However, tonal ideals seem to have "shut them off almost completely from more ancient music." (Kerman 71)

OR

According to Kerman, tonal theorists often look no further than the music of Brahms, but "some ... have been able to extend their activity with considerable power to the music of Schoenberg, Stravinsky, Bartok, and beyond." However, tonal ideals seem to have "shut them off almost completely from more ancient music." (71)

More Than One Book by Same Author

Schoenberg's solution to the challenge set by Wagner in *Tristan und Isolde* "was to leave tonality altogether and to organize music in a radically different way" (Kerman, *Write* 268). Furthermore, "he was driven to reformulate traditional theory" (Kerman, *Contemplating* 91).

OR

As Kerman states in *Write All These Down*, Schoenberg's solution to the challenge set by Wagner in *Tristan und Isolde* "was to leave tonality altogether and to organize music in a radically different way" (268). Furthermore, "he was driven to re-formulate traditional theory" (Kerman, *Contemplating* 91).

Works Cited

Kerman, Joseph. *Contemplating Music: Challenges to Musicology.* Cambridge, MA: Harvard UP, 1985.

Kerman, Joseph. *Write All These Down: Essays on Music.* Berkeley: U of California P, 1994.

Kerman, Joseph, and Alan Tyson. *The New Grove Beethoven.* New York: W. W. Norton, 1983.

Glossary

Glossary terms appear in bold the first time they are discussed in the book.

abstract: summary of a book or article; some indexes include abstracts as well as citations

advertencia (It.): (prefatory) note

anejo (Span.): appendix, supplement

Anhang (Ger.): appendix, supplement

année (Fr.): year

annexe (Fr.): supplement

annotation: similar to an abstract, but also includes critical evaluation as well as summary

annuaire (Fr.): yearbook

año (Span.): year

anthology: collection of works, usually by different authors, generally grouped by a common theme

Archiv (Ger.): record office, archive

archive: collections of primarily unpublished materials, such as records or other historical documents

Auflage (Ger.): edition

Ausgabe (Ger.): edition

author-date style: citation style, such as APA, that uses the author's name and the source's date in parenthetical text references rather than footnotes or endnotes

authority headings: established names, titles, or subjects used in library catalogs

autograph: a signed manuscript

avant-propos (Fr.): preface

avertissement (Fr.): (prefatory) note

Band (Ger.): volume

base call number: main portion of a call number, such as ML410 for composer biographies

Bearbeiter (Ger.): editor or arranger

Beiblatt (Ger.): supplement

Beiheft (Ger.): supplement

Beilage (Ger.): supplement, appendix

bibliographic record: description of an item (book, score, recording, website, etc.) in a catalog or index that includes the names of the creators, titles, publication information, and so on

bibliographic utility: large, cooperative database of bibliographic information representing materials held by many different libraries

bibliography: list of sources used or cited in a written work or on a particular topic; some are annotated; may be comprehensive or selective

bibliothéque (Fr.): library

bio-bibliography: list of sources related to a musician including a brief biography

bio-discography: list of recordings related to a musician including a brief biography

blog: a web log; a web page that is frequently updated and contains chronological entries on a particular subject

Boolean search terms: logical operators, such as AND, OR, and NOT, that can be used to refine searches in a catalog or index

Briefwechsel (Ger.): correspondence; exchange of letters

brochure: pamphlet

cahier (Fr.): issue, number, part; pamphlet

call number: set of letters and/or numbers identifying a work in a library, which also can be used to identify the subject and location; examples include Library of Congress classification numbers and Dewey Decimal call numbers

caption: information included at the top of the first page of a score

carta (Span.): letter or chart

catalog: database of bibliographic records for a single library or group of libraries

catalogue (Fr.; also British spelling): catalog

catalogue raisonné (Fr.): descriptive catalog

CD-ROM: compact disc read-only memory; data on a CD-ROM cannot be edited; some databases and indexes are published in this format

citation: reference to another work, along with the bibliographic information needed to find the original source

codex: book of manuscripts

colección (Span.): collection, series

collected set: works of music by various composers brought together in a single publication, usually representing music history generally or a certain style period or genre specifically

collected works edition: the works of a single composer compiled into a single publication

collective uniform title: generic title used to describe a particular genre of composition, for example, "symphonies"

collocate: to put together the various iterations of a particular work

colophon: a notice found in printed works that gives the name of the printer, place and date of publication, etc.

complete works edition: the works of a single composer compiled into a single publication

compte rendu (Fr.): book review

conference papers: published versions of papers read and presentations given at conferences, sometimes called *proceedings* or *congress reports*

congress reports: See **conference papers**

consortium: association of libraries or other institutions that shares resources

controlled vocabulary: words and phrases used to categorize materials, for example, names, uniform titles, and subject headings

copyright: legal right of authors, composers, performers to control the use of their works for a specified period of time; copyright laws vary in different countries

corrigé(e) (Fr.): corrected

critical commentary: included in scholarly editions to list variants in sources, editorial changes, etc.

critical edition: See **scholarly edition**

cross-reference: pointer in a catalog or index from one search term to another similar or related or controlled vocabulary term or phrase in the same work

cuaderno (Span.): issue, number, part

cuadro (Span.): table or chart

Cutter (call number): the second part of a call number, which denotes the author or subject of a work; in the call number ML102 .O6, the ".O6" is the cutter that indicates that the topic of the encyclopedia is opera

Denkmäler (Ger.): monuments

derecho de autor (Span.): copyright

Dewey Decimal classification: classification system made up only of numbers, frequently used in public and school libraries but sometimes used in academic libraries as well

dictionnaire (Fr.): dictionary

digital audio libraries: collections of digital audio files for streaming or downloading

discography: listing or bibliography of sound recordings

disponible (Fr.): available

Druck (Ger.): print, printing, impression

ebook (also **e-book** and **eBook**): electronic book

editer (Fr.): to publish, to issue

éditeur (Fr.): publisher

Einleitung (Ger.): introduction

endnote: explanatory note or citation at the end of a work as opposed to in-text references; endnotes are used in the Chicago style manual

Ergänzungsband (Ger.): supplementary volume

erscheinen (Ger.): to appear, come out, be published

Erscheinungsdatum (Ger.): publication date

Erstausgabe (Ger.): first edition

esemplare (It.): copy

ETD: electronic thesis or dissertation

facsimile: an exact copy of the original

facsimile edition: reproduction of an older work that is designed to be an exact copy of the original

fair copy: a clean copy of a corrected draft of a work

false drops: search results that meet the criteria of the search but are not what the searcher was looking for, for example, baseball articles retrieved while looking for information on perfect pitch

fascicolo (It.): number, issue

fascículo (Span.): number, issue

Festschrift (Ger.): publication on the occasion of a celebration or in honor of someone

filmography: list or bibliography of video recordings

finding aid: description and listing designed to help people find materials in archival or special collections

Folge (Ger.): series, continuation, issue

footnote: explanatory note or citation at the bottom of the page on which it occurs; used in the Chicago style of documentation

full text database: collection of electronic documents that allows you to locate the entirety of a specific document or to search any or all documents in the collection

Gesamtausgabe (Ger.): complete works

Geschichte (Ger.): history

Gesellschaft (Ger.): society, association

Handexemplar (Ger.): composer's or author's copy

Handschrift (Ger.): manuscript

Heft (Ger.): number, part.

Herausgeber; herausgegeben (Ger.): editor; edited, published

historical edition: collection of music by multiple composers intended to represent music history generally or a specific style period or genre

historical set: See **historical edition**

holograph: manuscript in the hand of the composer or author

iconography: book or study consisting of or based on images

imprint: publication information about a work, found in a bibliographic record or on the title page and verso

incipit: short excerpt of a musical theme, included in thematic catalogs

index: list of words or subjects found in a book, usually with the relevant page numbers indicated

inédit (Fr.): unpublished

inédito (Span.): unpublished

Inhalt (Ger.): table of contents

institutional repository: digital collection of material such as student or faculty writings related to or created by an institution, such as a college or university

integrated library software: computer software packages used by libraries for their online catalogs, to circulate materials, to order new items, and so on

interlibrary loan: borrowing and lending of materials between libraries

ISBN, ISSN: International Standard Book Number, International Standard Serial Number; number assigned to books and serials for identification purposes

ISMN: International Standard Music Number; identification number for musical scores that are not widely assigned

Jahrbuch (Ger.): yearbook

journal: scholarly publication, usually appearing regularly, that includes primarily articles

keyword search: search option that allows the researcher to find words in various parts of a bibliographic record or citation, for example, the title, author, publisher, or abstract

Kritischer Bericht (Ger.): critical report or commentary

lexicography: creation of dictionaries and encyclopedias

lexicon: dictionary

Lexikon (Ger.): dictionary

Library of Congress call numbers: classification system developed for library materials by the U.S. national library

Library of Congress subject headings: controlled vocabulary developed for topics by the U.S. national library

libro (It., Span.): book

limit functions: allow the researcher to narrow search results by format, date, or language, for example

literature review: survey of writings on a given topic

livraison (Fr.): issue

magazine: popular (i.e., nonscholarly) publication, usually appearing regularly, that includes primarily articles

manuscript: a source that is handwritten, rather than printed or published; also used for works that have not yet been published but will be

mensile (It.): monthly

mensual (Span.): monthly

mensuel (Fr.): monthly

metasearch engine: Internet search engine that combines the results of other top search engines

microform: reproductions of print documents on microfilm or microfiche

monograph: writing that stands alone, such as a book

musical monument: edition of works by multiple composers representing the music of a region or country

Musikwissenschaft (Ger.): musicology

national library: a library that holds all the works copyrighted in a particular country

Neuausgabe, Neue Ausgabe (Ger.): new edition

obra (Span.): work

obra complètas (Span.): complete works

oeuvre (Fr.): work

oeuvres complètes (Fr.): complete works

offsite storage facility: separate place for holding library materials that are used infrequently and cannot be housed in the main or branch collections of a library

online catalog: online database including the bibliographic records for a particular library or collection

open-access journal: online journal that is available without a subscription fee

opera (It.): work

opus numbers: work numbers for compositions (often assigned by the composer) that are in chronological order

opúsculo (It.): pamphlet, bulletin

organology: study of musical instruments

palabras preliminaries (Span.): foreword

partition (Fr.): musical score

Partitur (Ger.): musical score

peer-reviewed journal: scholarly journal that sends submissions to other scholars for review and comment before accepting them for publication

performing edition: score edited and published for the purpose of being used by performers

periodical: publications such as journals and magazines that are published regularly with the same title

periodical index: database of citations of articles published in journals and magazines; some include full text and/or abstracts; some also include materials in other formats

périodique (Fr.): periodical

Personenteil (Ger.): biographical part of an encyclopedia, as opposed to the subject or topical part

plagiarism: use of the work of others without crediting the authors and sources

plancha (Span.): plate

plate number: number appearing on each page of a printed score, usually at the bottom

prefacio (Span.): preface, introduction

prefazione (It.): preface, introduction

primary source: materials such as manuscripts, letters, recordings originating from or contemporary with the topic of your study; also defined by some as the sources most integral to your research

proceeding: See conference papers

procés-verbal (Fr.): proceedings

proemio (It.): preface, introduction

proprietá letteraria (It.): copyright

proximity: search option that allows the researcher to specify that search terms be located near each other to be retrieved

pseudonym: fictitious name used by an author, composer, critic, and so on

publier (Fr.): edit, publish

publisher number: number appearing usually once on a printed score, often on the cover or title page

quaderno (It.): part, numbered pamphlet

qualifiers: additions to an authority heading used to make them more specific and to avoid confusion, for example, adding (Musical Group) to the heading for the band Grateful Dead

Quelle (Ger.): source

raccolta (It.): collection

Real Simple Syndication (RSS) feeds: a type of web-feed format used for frequently updated material such as weblogs (blogs) or news sites; by checking the feed, users can see if the content of the webpage was updated since the last time they read it

recopilación (Span.): collection

recueil (Fr.): collection, selection, miscellany

rédacteur (Fr.): editor

redactor (Span.): editor

Redakteur; Redaktion (Ger.): editor, editorial matter, editorial staff

redattore (It.): editor

rédiger (Fr.): to edit (a newspaper), to draft or write (an article, etc.)

refereed periodical: See **peer-reviewed journal**

reference list: term used in APA style for a bibliography of sources

Register (Ger.): index

Reihe (Ger.): series, set, tone row

repertorio (It.): repertoire; index

reprint edition: republication of a book or score without changes to the content

review: published critical evaluation of a book, score, website, recording, or other material

Revisionsbericht (Ger.): critical commentary

revista (Span.): review, periodical

revu(e) (Fr.): revised

revue (Fr.): magazine, periodical

riveduto (It.): revised

rivista (It.): review

RSS: Real Simple Syndication: See **Real Simple Syndication (RSS) feeds**

Sachteil (Ger.): subject or topical part of an encyclopedia, as opposed to the biographical part

Sammlung (Ger.): collection

Sämtliche Werke (Ger.): complete works

scholarly edition: music edition based on current standards of editing, for example, the inclusion of a critical commentary and indications of editorial changes

search engine: a retrieval system used to find information in a computer system, such as an online library catalog, periodical index, or the Internet

secondary source: sources that are based on primary sources, for example musical editions based on a composer's autograph manuscript

see: cross-reference that indicates the researcher should look in another place rather than the search term that was just used

see also: cross reference that indicates the researcher should also check another place in addition to the search just completed

Seite (Ger.): page

serial: publications that are issued at regular or irregular intervals with the same title; journals and magazines are examples of serials

série (Fr.): series

sigla: an abbreviation used for a library; they often appear in encyclopedias, indexes, and bibliographies

solfège syllables: syllables used to represent scale degrees (do, re, mi, etc.)

sommaire (Fr.): table of contents

source readings: collection of excerpts from important writings on music, sometimes provided in translation and often with commentary

special collections: collections of rare or valuable materials

stacks: section of a library that includes the materials; stacks may be open or closed to researchers

streaming audio: audio that is continuously delivered to, and available to, the user while it is being delivered by the provider, different from audio that must be entirely downloaded before it can be used

subject headings: topical or genre terms or phrases used to indicate the nature of a resource included in a catalog, index, database, etc.

Tabelle (Ger.): table

table: index, table

table des matiéres (Fr.): table of contents

Tafel (Ger.): plate

Teil (Ger.): part or volume

tertiary source: sources based on secondary sources, for example, directories and chronologies

thematic catalog: catalog of a particular repertory of music that includes a musical incipit to aid with identification of the pieces included

thematic locators: reference tools that help the researcher find a musical work when only the melody is known

title page: page at the beginning of a book or score that includes the title, author, and publisher information

tome (Fr.): volume; division of a book

traduction (Fr.): translation

traduzione (It.): translation

triangulation: using keyword searches to identify the subject headings for a particular topic

trimestral(mente) (Span.): quarterly

trimestrale (It.): quarterly

trimestriel (Fr.): quarterly

truncation: search technique that allows you to enter part of a search term (often with a symbol) to find variants; for example, "symphon*" would find symphony, symphonic, symphonie, etc.

Ubersetzung, Ubertragung (Ger.): translation

uncontrolled vocabulary: keywords

uniform title: authority heading for titles assigned by catalogers for all versions of the work regardless of the title appearing on the score, sound recording, etc.

union catalog: combined library catalog including the holdings of a group or consortium of libraries

Urtext (Ger.): original text

Urtext edition: performing edition intended to be as close to the composer's original as possible without editorial changes or additions

Verein (Ger.): association, society

Verlag (Ger.): publishing house

verso: back of the title page, which often includes the publication date of a published work

Verzeichnis (Ger.): catalog

volume: part of a lengthy or ongoing published work; encyclopedias, collected works editions, journals, etc. are examples of works typically published in volumes

web log: See **blog**

Werk (Ger.): work

works cited: term used in MLA style for a bibliography of sources

Zeitschrift (Ger.): periodical

Zeitung (Ger.): newspaper

Index

This index includes authors, titles, and subjects. Page numbers in bold after titles indicate the page where the numbered entry appears. Page numbers in italic are for figures. Footnotes are indicated with an "n" after the number. The "Suggested Readings" are indexed as "readings" at the end of the appropriate index entries.